Contemporary Conflict Theory: The Journey of a Psychoanalyst

Contemporary Conflict Theory: The Journey of a Psychoanalyst

Selected Papers

Sander M. Abend, MD

IPBOOKS.net
International Psychoanalytic Books

International Psychoanalytic Books (IPBooks)
New York • http://www.IPBooks.net

Published by International Psychoanalytic Books (IPBooks)
Queens, New York
Online at: www.IPBooks.net

Book cover design by Kathy Kovacic of Blackthorn Studio

Interior book design by Medlar Publishing Solutions Pvt Ltd., India

www.IPBooks.net

ISBN: 978-1-949093-13-1

Contents

Part III: Therapeutic Action and Change

Part IV: Countertransference

Part V: Comparative Theory

JAY GREENBERG, PH.D.

Sander Abend: A Personal Reflection

Sandy Abend has been a close friend of mine for more than twenty years. For decades longer I have been an admirer of his.

The qualities that make Sandy a good friend and those that make him an important contributor to our psychoanalytic literature—not to mention an outstanding clinician—are, I think, quite similar. He combines qualities that we don't expect to find together: he is at once gentle and firm, respectful of tradition (even a "true-believer") and open-minded, conservative and innovative, convinced and curious.

These characteristics led him to propose a project that has been an important part of our friendship for a long time now. Sandy invited me to be part of a study group he was putting together; the members were senior analysts, all identified with particular points of view in which we were entrenched. But the announced purpose of the group would be, as Sandy put it, "to read things that we wouldn't ordinarily read." In the balkanized psychoanalytic world of the time (and still although to a lesser extent today) this wasn't the kind of thing that one would imagine could engage the interest of analysts who were deeply committed to ideas and institutions that had shaped their long and successful professional careers. But it worked. Or, I should say, it is working, because the group continues to meet and continues to be a highlight of the professional lives of all of us who participate in it.

The spirit that moved Sandy to create our study group pervades and shapes his writing. More than many of today's thinkers he is committed to a particular theoretical perspective; he is certainly not a pluralist nor (to say the least) is he the sort of analyst who seeks out and embraces the latest trend. Sandy coined the term "modern conflict theory" and he remains loyal to the theory's ideas and to its seminal thinkers. The loyalty is neither simply personal nor abstractly conceptual; he understands and deeply appreciates the enduring clinical value of the contributions of earlier generations of psychoanalysts.

But in virtually everything he has written Sandy quietly but decisively moves the theory into new territory. To mention a few examples: If the patient's fantasies decisively shape his or her experience, he wonders, what about the analyst's? If the austerity of the classical analytic stance creates iatrogenic resistances in our more egalitarian time, can something be gained by offering a "softer" kind of engagement without turning our backs on the access to psychic depths made possible by traditional restraint? If countertransference is both ubiquitous and largely unconscious, how can we fully understand our technical choices, even those choices that seem to follow the dictates of received theory?

All this is to say that Sandy thinks and writes as he does because he respects tradition while maintaining an integrity that demands that he not be limited by it. Perhaps paradoxically, his challenges to received wisdom are as strong and as innovative as they are because they are anchored in his deep appreciation of the contributions of earlier generations. Too many theorists in today's psychoanalytic world believe that change requires the radical rejection and overthrow of what has come before; Sandy knows that for over a hundred years many talented and committed people have been engaged in the difficult and fragile project of exploring the depths of human experience, and that we abandon their insights at our peril. We need to interrogate ourselves and our traditions, not to reactively start opposing schools that discard what has come before.

Because of this commitment Sandy's writing is always subtle; it can even seem quiet. But the reader shouldn't be lulled into complacency; reading Sandy's work carefully we discover, sometimes to our surprise, that familiar ideas have given birth to new and unexpected visions. This volume of collected papers conveys both his careful scholarship and the innovative use that Sandy makes of it.

The theorist I admire shares many characteristics with the man whose friendship I value so greatly. Sandy is at once engaged, inquisitive, and carefully respectful of personal space and privacy. He never intrudes, but he is always available. He pays attention to everything, but doesn't impose what he has noticed unless invited. I have been with Sandy through difficult times in both my life and his, and am consistently impressed by his strength, his courage, and his gentle wisdom. What he offers is invariably generous, supportive and—as with his writing—often surprising. He has played important roles in both my personal and my professional life, and I thank him for it.

MICHAEL S. PORDER, M.D.

Sander Abend: An Introduction

Dr. Sander Abend and I have been professional colleagues and intimate friends for almost 60 years. We were in the same psychiatric residency at Albert Einstein College of Medicine, where our spouses and children intermingled with each other while we continued our professional duties. After obligatory military service we resumed our professional and personal relationship at The New York Psychoanalytic Institute. Following graduation from the institute, in addition to Kris study groups, Drs. Abend, Jacobs, Sax, Willick and I formed a study group where we discussed cases with one another for 10 years. We got to know each other's clinical work intimately. Subsequently, we joined Dr. Charles Brenner's Kris study group, which resulted in Drs. Abend, Willick and I collaborating on the book *Borderline Patients: Psychoanalytic Perspectives*. I should mention that Dr. Abend happened to share an office with Dr. Charles Brenner which led to a mentorship for Sandy and many of us. Sandy went on to form another group with many of our colleagues including Drs. Brenner and McDevitt.

For the moment I will leave the psychoanalytic trail and talk about Sandy the person. Raised in the Bronx, Sandy is a passionate sports fan, with the New York Yankees as his first love. His father Harry Louis Abend was a close name to Henry Louis Gehrig, "The Pride of the Yankees". This coincidence cemented Sandy's love for the team. Sandy's approach to sports is just as scholarly as his approach to psychoanalysis. He researches the players and examines the way the game is played. These include baseball, basketball, football and tennis. He coached basketball in the Navy and taught me tennis as we vacationed together over the years. I actually improved under his tutelage. We also shared many sporting events together.

Returning to his work, these essays and articles plus his recent book demonstrate the breadth of his scholarship and knowledge. He has many teaching skills and is an extraordinary clinician. His clinical work is clearly demonstrated in his early papers, the later ones focus more on clinical theory and the place of compromise formation in our clinical thinking. These papers and essays should be a pleasure and treasure for all of their readers. His work is truly impressive and reading it will be a worthwhile and enjoyable task.

ARTHUR A. LYNCH, PH.D.

Broadening the View of Contemporary Conflict Theory: An Introduction

There are few analysts today who could undertake the task of revising and integrating the foundation of contemporary conflict theory to the broader psychoanalytic corpus. In each of the 26 papers in this volume, Sander M. Abend works to accomplish this. His basic method for each paper is to identify and define the paper's purpose; review the relevant literature; draw support from clinical case material; and use the new findings to redefine the older terms. His intention is two-fold: (1) to demonstrate the coexistence and interrelationship between three major psychoanalytic concepts: unconscious instinctual conflict, compromise formation and unconscious fantasy, and; (2) to evaluate, revise, and integrate older anachronistic concepts (e.g., identity, therapeutic alliance) and to link these revisions into the broader theory. In this approach to theory, Abend's work becomes a "total composite psychoanalytic theory" (Rangell, 1988, 2007).

But there is more that can be written about the importance of Abend's contributions. He addresses ideas that no longer fit clinical evidence, including aspects of countertransference, reality testing, the psychoanalytic process, and theories that do not account for the evolution of identity or borderline pathology. Still, no singular professional identifier captures the complexity of Abend's curiosity and attention. He is interested in the nature of therapeutic action, what influences analytic change, and how the patient's acceptance can represent a negation of the analyst's entire efforts with a simple "yes, but."

Abend takes his time with this work. In his own words, he "turns an idea over and over again in [his] mind, until the evidence begins to make sense" (personal communication).

Once Abend arrives at his findings, he retains and integrates what is valid into theory, discarding completely or conditionally the rest. Following the rules of science, he proposes explanations which are more valid and integrated.

This volume attests to his legacy of establishing the foundations, along with Charles Brenner and Jacob Arlow, of contemporary conflict theory. Abend considers a broad range of subjects not thoroughly explored by Brenner and Arlow. The chapters are organized as five main topics: the psychoanalytic process, unconscious fantasy, therapeutic action and change, transference phenomena and comparative theories.

Part I—The Psychoanalytic Process

In the first section, seven chapters examine problematic psychoanalytic process concepts. Chapter 1 addresses the "problems of identity." This concept was important in the 1950s with Erickson (1956) and Jacobson (1954) offering different theoretical emphases. Conceptual problems, from their efforts, produced too much ambiguity in definition of normal and pathological outcomes, which increased the number of clinical problems related to identity disturbance.

Abend redefines and reformulates the concept of identity, providing a major upgrade. His changes are intended to integrate and locate important terms within structural theory and delineate the interrelationships between identity, self, and sexual identity. The important technical corollary is that "the disturbances of identity and of the sense of identity are to be understood as symptoms which must be subjected to analysis to uncover their significance in the mental life of patients" (Abend, 1974, p. 636).

In Chapter 2, Abend offers observations on reality testing. He highlights how inaccurate or anachronistic definitions hamper clinical understanding, judgement, and efficacy. He advances the idea that reality testing is not a global mental function, as proposed since Freud; rather, it is best understood as a complex psychic activity which leads to highly variable outcomes on a spectrum of possible responses.

In Chapter 3, he addresses a neglected classic, Ernst Kris's "On Some Vicissitudes of Insight." Redirecting us from the popular interest in Kris's illustrations of "psychoanalysis as process" and "the good hour," Abend guides us to the essence of Kris's intent, including the mental functions necessary to achieve insight and the difficulties that may stand in the way. His contribution has been largely unnoticed, even though it offers an important gain in clinical theory.

In Chapter 4, Abend reconsiders "the psychoanalytic process." He begins by addressing a series of questions important to the nature of psychoanalysis: What are the recognizable qualities of the psychoanalytic process and what are it's features? What facilitates this process and what hinders it? He offers two motives for seeking this clarification: one to help distinguish psychoanalysis from other therapies, and another to clarify the steps, operations, and changes that characterize a genuine psychoanalytic process. He discusses in detail six criteria for the process and provides us with a comprehensive understanding of what constitutes psychoanalysis. Refining the necessary conditions for each criterion over time answers questions that help us strengthen our practice and teaching. This refinement provides the essence of psychoanalytic growth and helps us to understand "what psychoanalysis is," "how it is best carried out, of what it brings about in the patient and how it does so, and of what a successful analysis looks like" (Abend, 1990, p. 548).

Chapter 5 highlights the therapeutic alliance. Abend approaches the issue historically beginning with Freud's assessment of the patients' progress. This is determined by the analysands' ability to free-associate, his engagement in treatment, and the presence of the unobjectionable conscious component of the transference; the "vehicle of [treatment] success" (Freud, 1912a, p. 105), Abend continues with Sterba's proposal (1934) that some aspects of the ego are directed toward reality, while others ego aspects move toward the instinctual energies. Abend notes that it is the opposition between these two mindsets that has been in discussions ever since. Friedman (1969) pointed out that this changed the Freudian view. Now the patient works with the analyst because they share the "same purpose" (Friedman, 1969 and Abend, 1996, p. 217). Furthermore, Sterba's therapeutic alliance consists of behaviors that facilitate analytic success; the therapeutic alliance now becomes the consequence of the psychoanalytic process. Abend agrees with Friedman that the patient has no investment in creating a therapeutic alliance. It doesn't gratify the patient's needs but merely offers him or her an adaptive solution in accommodating the necessarily difficult working demands of the analyst (i.e., for the analyst to feel the work is possible and rewarding).

Chapter 6 considers some technical differences at the turn of the 21st Century. Abend describes three periods in which fundamental differences in technique are evident and considers the contributions of Ferenczi, Poland, Hausner, Paul Gray and Jack and Kerry Novick. In the first period, there were disagreements about the nature of insight, as initiated by Jung and Adler. Following this motif to the year 2000, Abend introduces the work of Poland and the experience of being witnessed. This new concept may have a direct and positive impact upon the mind of the analysand by promoting certain aspects of the relationship: e.g., a "concerned, attentive, and comprehending listener" (Abend, 2000, p. 11).

Psychoanalysts have long been divided over the impact of the "analytic relationship" on the course and outcome of the treatment, an idea accorded to Ferenczi but traversing the history of psychoanalysis. Abend offers that there are still those who believe that a realistic relationship provides the basis for therapeutic contact, which can be functionally distinguished from the transference. He points out that these behaviors depend on specific unconscious fantasies unique to each patient for their effect. Some analysts add flexibility to analytic neutrality by invoking the transference-countertransference matrix. Finally, Abend refers to Paul Gray, who stresses refraining from interpretations beyond observable defense activities (1994). Gray also maintains that interpretive attention must remain inside the analytic situation or risk falling into the service of resistance.

Chapter 7 examines "expanding psychological possibilities" and concludes that the essential goal of psychoanalysis is "greater freedom of choice." Abend recognizes that people come to analysis to obtain relief or gain fulfilment. Psychoanalysis is an attempt to treat the rigid cognitive and emotional patterns that are the pathogenic consequences fuelled by unconscious instinctual childhood conflicts. Here, "choice" operates consciously and unconsciously. The patient's diminished state of choice is replaced by the expansion of other psychological possibilities and more flexibility, hence a greater range of choice and new solutions. The essential goal of psychoanalysis is "greater freedom of choice," a result of the patient becoming aware of the unconscious mental conflict that interferes with pleasure.

Part II—Unconscious Fantasy

Part II introduces Abend's contributions to "unconscious fantasy." Abend begins by following the seminal ideas of Nunberg (1926) and Schmideberg (1938), highlighting the potential importance of the patient's theory of cure (Chapter 8). Personal beliefs can influence the patient's behavior in treatment and resonate with the presence of unconscious fantasies. Analysis of these fantasies clarifies the meaning of behaviors and transference wishes in the treatment, and provides material necessary for the reconstruction of the early childhood wishes as the source of the patient's theory of cure. The patient's unconscious fantasies impact theories of therapeutic action—how treatment works. This dynamic affects the clinical practitioner's formation of the theory and recommendations, as well as the criteria for the modification of psychoanalytic technique.

Chapter 9 concentrates on love and object choice. Abend reminds us that the impact of siblings on mental life was an early psychoanalytic discovery, but remained tied to overaggressive rivalries. He explores in two cases of siblings the impact of enduring libidinal bonds in mental life. The persistence of unconscious bonds to older siblings had a lasting effect in their preferences for love partners. These internalized bonds go far beyond the earlier reported defensive functions against incestuous wishes.

In Chapter 10, Abend proposed that unconscious fantasies are "intermediate links in the logical sequences by means of which we seek to clarify the origin and meaning of patients' ways of thinking and behaving." There is evidence that the patients' unconscious fantasies are causal links that produce symptoms. Abend describes how he makes clinical use of fantasies; how he determines their presence and their content. His emphasis is on the traditional psychoanalytic viewpoint that unconscious infantile instinctual conflicts are the core elements of the mind. Unconscious fantasies are constructed from these core elements plus developmental and adaptive experiences, all of which form a personal contextualized narrative for one's current apperception. In both Chapters 10 and 11, Abend emphasizes the importance of uncovering the essential components of the unconscious fantasies and determining the purposes they serve in the clinical situation. The interpretive focus draws upon the analyst's entire understanding of the patient.

Chapter 11 appears 29 years after Abend's first article on the subject of unconscious fantasies, and traces the development of the concept from Freud's earliest thinking to its prominent status in contemporary conflict theory. Abend presents two forms of thinking about technique when he established the formation that gives shape to the clinical material. First he considers versions of what he imagines the patient might have thought as a small child. Then he becomes concerned with activity in the present (e.g., transference fantasies).

Chapter 12—"A Variant of Joking in Dreams" concludes the section. The chapter was stimulated by Mahon's paper, "A Joke in a Dream: A Note on the Complex Aesthetics of Disguise" (2002). The dream shows how an unconscious fantasy can be transformed into something new and wonderful: the Pygmalion story.

Part III—Therapeutic Action and Change

This section addresses therapeutic action and dynamics of change in six chapters. Beginning with an exploration of various factors that influence change for patients in psychoanalytic treatment, Abend then turns to the analysis of intrapsychic conflicts, proposing the use of compromise formation as an organizing principle. Next, he refines the notion of therapeutic action as it is presented in contemporary conflict theory and proposes an analogue of negation. The section closes with a broad discussion on psychic conflict and the concept of defense.

In Chapter 13, Abend explores which factors influence patients to change. He begins his survey by considering the analysand's desire for relief from painful symptoms and life's dissatisfactions. The analysand's personal theory of change comes from the hoped-for expectations of significant others, public expectations, and unconscious fantasies based on infantile wishes and fears. Analytic clinicians also carry personal ideas and beliefs about how treatment will influence patient change. Abend discusses how change was viewed by Freud, Ferenczi, and Rank; Alexander and French; James Strachey; D.W. Winnicott; and H. Kohut. Some have proposed theories of pathogenesis that require modifications in technique.

Abend offers themes that define an understanding of the factors that influence change. One view of pathogenesis includes cogniscience of primitive mental states. There is an effort to change technique away from Freud's technique. This trend has several aims: to call attention to specific transference experiences; to influence developmental struggles; to engage forms of pathology that demand an awareness of the analyst's role in stimulating transference reactions; and to shift from a biological to a meaning perspective. There are obvious technical consequences to these alterations. Interpersonal, relational, and intersubjective perspectives focus on the here-and-now interactional dimensions of the process; Lacanian and narrative theorists emphasize semiotics or constructed narrative histories.

Change is influenced by the patient's view of the analyst's authority, motivation and methods. The patient's past relationships impact the transference experiences, often significantly, yet stress the influential role that conscious and unconscious fantasies about analysis can play in change and in influencing change. Case material is provided to clarify these dynamics.

Chapter 14—"Analyzing Intrapsychic Conflict: Compromise Formation as an Organizing Principle." The most effective way to formulate the patient's problem is through the recognition of intrapsychic conflict and compromise formation. Interactions between intrapsychic conflict, unconscious fantasy, and compromise formation always operate in the psychoanalytic process. Compromise formation as an organizing principle provides a clear description of the conflict's design. It is blueprint that shapes the analyst's understanding.

In Chapter 15 ("Therapeutic Action in Modern Conflict Theory") Abend begins by discussing the difficulty in arriving at a theory of therapeutic action; no psychoanalytic school of thought has successfully done so. He considers the contributions of Freud and his contemporaries, including Anna Freud, O. Fenichel, E. Glover, H. Nunberg, E. Bibring, H. Hartmann, R. Sterba, J. Strachey and others who contributed to the development of ego psychology.

Theoretical variability (pluralism) emerged in the 1960s. There were three important influences: reconceptualization of countertransference; an increased interest in pre-Oedipal development and its effect on pathogenesis and character formation; and the exploration of the complexities in the psychoanalytic situation by Greenson, Modell, Stone, and Zetzel. Loewald (1960) promoted countertransference as a means to better understand the patient. Post-modern subjectivists such as Sandler (1976), Jacobs (1991), and Boesky (1990) concentrated an assault on the concept of positivism and established meaning solely as a co-construction between the analyst and analysand. Following this historical review and overview of recent developments in the theory of therapeutic action, Abend points out that Arlow and Brenner (1964, 1990) were less enthusiastic about the ameliorative effects of the relationship in treatment. Arlow (1969 a,b) emphasized crucial unconscious fantasies. Brenner (1982, 2006) emphasized compromise formations. This is in contrast to those who are convinced that relational distortions resulting from early, preverbal developmental difficulties can be correctively influenced by the new relationship that forms between patient and analyst.

Abend concludes the chapter by considering the "close process monitoring" of Paul Gray (1994) who focuses almost exclusively on defense analysis.

In Chapter 16—"Freud, Transference, and Therapeutic Action" Abend offers a detailed outline for understanding transference in the psychoanalytic process. After 1910, Freud maintained that the analysis of transference was the main factor in therapeutic action; although late in his career, he wrote about the effectiveness of reconstruction, as well. Abend maintains that the analysis of the transference is indispensable to analytic technique, but it is only one mediator of therapeutic action.

In Chapter 17, Abend offers an "analogue of negation." This is a defensive structure that corresponds to negation as an unconscious reply to the unwanted thought or interpretation. Often this is initiated with the overture of an agreeable response to an interpretation from the analyst. The patient appears cooperative and involved. With a sleight of hand and the use of a special conjunction "but" is added to the thought creating a separation between the first and second part of the communication (e.g., descriptors, clauses, or sentences). This takes on the dynamic form of Freud's concept of negation (1905, 1925, 1937). "But" offers a more refined form of resistance in that it affords the patient the deception of cooperation with the comfort of contradiction.

Chapter 18 concerns "psychic conflict and the concept of defense." He reviews the theory of defense in the works of Sigmund (1926) and Anna Freud (1936), four panels on the subject (1954, 1967a, 1967b, 1970), and the contributions of Charles Brenner (1974, 1975, 1979).

Beginning with Freud's (1926) shift in the concept of anxiety as the fearful response to early childhood dangers, and not the result of repression. Anxiety now acts as the signal to initiate defense before the experience becomes too overwhelming. Anna Freud's book elaborates on these earlier findings emphasizing the role of mental agency and defense in psychic conflict. Technically, she emphasized her father's shift in therapeutic action: from "making unconscious conscious," to "where id was, there ego shall be." To achieve this, one needs to focus on the analysis of defense as these were the unconscious mechanisms that blocked access psychic conflict. This new configuration initiates the model of Ego Psychology, which recognizes that "from the standpoint of the mind, the external world interacts with the mental apparatus, of which drive organization, ego functions, and superego tendencies are continuously operating components, and that all behavior is inescapably influenced by the unconscious fantasies which are variously derived from these interactions" (i.e., compromise formation) (Abend, 1981, p. 70). Anna Freud did not go all the way with this new model, in part because she was committed to her father's view of the danger of instincts, a point of (Fenichel, 1938).

Contributions from the four panels include: Brenner's opposition to a mechanistic description of defenses and his proposal that defense could also serve adaptation (i.e., functional relevance) as well as all normal and pathological phenomena. Arlow, Mahler and Valenstien also supported this view. Brenner clarified that defense is not a discrete item because any mental function can be activated to manage unpleasure. The response may be simple or complex but shares a common pathway and opposes unconscious childhood wishes and fears, threat or punishment by superego—one or all of the above. To this more complex model of mind, Arlow emphasizes the central role of unconscious fantasy, Zetzel suggests that defences operate against both anxiety and depression (e.g., fear and narcissistic injury), Greenson notes that any psychic function can serve the role of defense and Brenner adds that conflict may result in either pathological or normal functioning. This was supported by the clinical cases of Tartakoff along with the interesting findings that defenses cannot be assumed to develop hierarchically and cannot be correlated with severity of pathology. Brenner contributed separately from the panels as well, noting his agreement that depressive affect and anxiety are both unpleasurable affect that initiate defense but views depressive affect as on par with anxiety and emerging from the same childhood calamities as anxiety does and not from narcissistic injury, alone.

Abend concludes that the basic discovery of psychoanalysis is the role of defense and unconscious content, "the very ground from which it has sprung" (Abend, 1981, p. 75).

Part IV—Countertransference

Part IV includes six chapters on aspects of transference in psychoanalysis. In Chapter 19, Abend addresses the impact of serious illness in the analyst as it relates to the countertransference, recounting a period of several weeks when he had to interrupt his practice due to an illness. He defines transference, countertransference, and the reality relationship, and discusses Dewald's (1982) recommendation to alter the technique to meet the needs of his patient. The crucial clinical issue: how much information should be offered? Abend's view is that the analyst is less likely than at any time before to be objective and reliable because of the power of the countertransference.

In Chapter 20, Abend explores the impact of life stresses on the analyst's fantasy. He emphasizes countertransference, empathy, and the constraints of an analytic ideal. In Chapter 21, he considers the role of countertransference in psychoanalytic technique. Countertransference was originally defined as unconscious interference with the analyst's therapeutic ability. Since that time, it has grown to include all of the analyst's affective reactions to the patient. Abend guides us through some of the major factors that led to this change, as well as it's potential and disadvantages. In Chapter 22, Abend attempts to answer the question, "What is the fate of the transference in psychoanalysis?" The focus is on two issues within the transference-countertransference spectrum: (1) treatment of the sicker patient (Chapter 23) and (2) the impact of termination (Chapter 24).

In Chapter 23 Abend reviews the psychoanalytic perspective on the treatment of patients in the borderline spectrum. He provides a solid history of clinical work beginning with Freud up to the contributors of the late 1970s. All the major groups of analysts were working on this issue (e.g., Ego psychology, Kleinian and the British school of object relations—Winnicott, Fairbairn, Bion; and the Interpersonal and the French and Lacanian schools).

Freud maintained that there were two broad classes of mental illness: neuroses and psychoses. For Freud, these were differentiated by the patient's ability or failure to maintain a relationship with reality. Freud noted that constitutional factors play a significant role in the pathogenesis determining who gets which illness, yet he also maintains that the different patterns of illness are based on trauma at different stages of development with the more severe forms of mental illness resulting from trauma in the earliest developmental phases, and the less severe forms of illness occurring from trauma in later childhood.[1] With the advent of Ego Psychology Freud's diagnostic assumptions were replaced by the growing complexity of the role of the entire spectrum of ego functioning (i.e., primary and secondary autonomous ego functions engaging adaptive and defensive functions), and the complex volatility it brought to the clinical observation made the earlier simple conjectures less plausible. During the 1930s a new diagnostic group emerged of patients who were more disturbed then the typical neurotic and yet did not decompensate into the realms of acute psychosis. The period stretching from the early 1940s to the 1990s saw a plethora of publications dedicated to the clinical work with this group. During the latter part of this same period work on forms and structure of pathological narcissism also emerged with Kohut and practitioners identified with Self-Psychology making the original contributions. In both areas of pathology, preoedipal determinants were proposed with some theorists identifying failures in particular phases and sub-phases of developmental as critical.

Abend, Porter, and Willick, both jointly and separately, propose another perhaps more cautious view. They propose that persons with severe pathology have "... probably suffered more severe environmental trauma all through their development, and that this psychological damage has more than certain stage specific effects" (Abend, 1991). He goes on to state that these patients' emotional difficulties cannot be treated without a careful assessment of the infantile sexual and aggressive conflicts and their consequence's. Abend and his colleagues use the same basic approach to symptom assessment and treatment of borderline and/or pathological narcissism, relying on compromise formation as the "organizing principle," as he has demonstrated throughout the volume.

---

[1] This fundamental assumption has been challenged by a small group of Contemporary Conflict Theorists.

Part V—Comparative Theory

The last section consists of two chapters that compare contemporary conflict theory and relational theories. In Chapter 25, Abend notes that the issue of the intrapsychic versus the interpersonal is a false dichotomy. Since Freud, most psychoanalytic theorists consider factors that affect the growth of people throughout development from biological, psychological, and sociocultural points of view. People are affected by historical, political, and social influences.

In the final chapter of the volume (Chapter 26), Abend considers "relational" influences on contemporary conflict theory. In this last piece, he highlights that contemporary conflict theorists believe that compromise formations include, within their structure, the relational and the intrapsychic, the pre-Oedipal, the Oedipal, and the post-Oedipal as essential to development. The Oedipal period organizes life's experience from the earlier phases and has a profound effect on the person's mental organization and view of the world. Therefore, understanding the Oedipal period and its ramifications throughout development remains centrally important.

Conclusion

Like Kris, Arlow, and Brenner before him, Abend has been a bold but generous advocate in examining the current theoretical challenges to contemporary conflict theory. He has provided a synthesis to follow the first generation's efforts to reorganize Freud's essential work. This synthesis is original, creating new concepts (e.g., the patient's personal theories of cure, sibling love, and object choice, an analogue of negation, the analyst's own serious illness), as well as a new dynamic understanding of the processes of the mind (e.g., the synchronicity between three major psychoanalytic constructs: unconscious instinctual conflict, compromise formation, and unconscious fantasy). Throughout his work, Abend continuously clarifies these relationships and suggests clinical guidelines in the process.

He also challenges psychoanalytic concepts that no longer fit the clinical evidence. In his articles on countertransference, he has reframed the popular use of the term to reflect troublesome aspects of intensified disturbances from the analyst's unconscious instinctual conflicts, evident in his/her affect or observable participation in the treatment. Abend advances the theories of both Arlow (1979) and Brenner (1985). Like Arlow (1979), he limits the communicative aspects of the analysis to other mental functions like introspection, empathy, and intuition. This allows him to maintain an interactive perspective yet retain countertransference as a singular phenomenon. Viewing countertransference through the lens of compromise formation helps to evaluate it from the point of view of conflict (Brenner, 1985). We need to further evaluate whether this is informative or disruptive in every specific treatment situation.

Finally, Abend has met the challenges to contemporary conflict theory and offered his own insights. We may be left with more questions than answers, but that is the nature of good science. Abend's insights have helped patients who suffer from borderline pathology and pathological narcissism. He is always clear and consistent and relates what he offers in the present to the wisdom of the past. He is always modest and understated as he tries "to conserve what is valid while rendering it ever more complete and useful" (Abend, 1988a, p. 227). This is a book to learn from and to be enjoyed!

References

Abend, S. (1974). Problems of Identity—Theoretical and Clinical Applications. *Psychoanalytic Quarterly* 43:606–637.

——— (1979). Unconscious fantasies and theories of cure. *Journal of the American Psychoanalytic Association* 27:579–596.

——— (1981). Psychic Conflict and the Concept of Defense. *Psychoanalytic Quarterly* 50:67–76.

——— (1982). Some observations on reality testing as a clinical concept. *Psychoanalytic Quarterly* 51:218–237.

——— (1986). Some problems in the evaluation of the psychoanalytic process. In: *Psychoanalysis: The Science of Mental Conflict. Essays in Honor of Charles Brenner*, ed. A.D. Richards and M.S. Willick Hillsdale, NJ: Analytic Press, pp. 209–228.

——— (1988a). Neglected classics: Ernst Kris's "On some vicissitudes of insight in psychoanalysis." *Psychoanalytic Quarterly* 57:224–228.

——— (1988b). Unconscious fantasies and issues of termination. In: *Fantasy, Myth and Reality: Essays in Honor of Jacob A. Arlow, M.D.*, ed. H. Blum, Y. Kramer, A.D. Richards, and A.K. Richards. Madison, CT: International Universities Press, pp. 149–165.

——— (1990). The psychoanalytic process: motives and obstacles in the search for clarification. *Psychoanalytic Quarterly* 59:532–549.

——— (1996). The Problem of Therapeutic Alliance. *Journal of Clinical Psychoanalysis* 5:213–226.

——— (2000). Analytic technique today. (2000). *Journal of the American Psychoanalytic Association* 48(1):9–16.

——— (2016). *A Brief Introduction to Sigmund Freud's Psychoanalysis and His Enduring Legacy*. New York, NY: International Psychoanalytic Books.

———, Porder, M., and Willick, M. (1983). *Borderline Patients: Psychoanalytic Perspectives*. New York, NY: International Universities Press.

Alexander, F. (1950). Analysis of the therapeutic factors in psychoanalytic treatment. *Psychoanalytic Quarterly* 19:482–500.

——— (1954). Some quantitative aspects of psychoanalytic technique. *Journal of the American Psychoanalytic Association* 2:685–701.

——— with French, T.M. (1946). The principle of corrective emotional experience. In: *Psychoanalytic Therapy: Principles and Application*. New York, NY: Ronald Press, pp. 67–70.

Arlow, J. A. (1969a). Fantasy, memory, and reality testing. *Psychoanalytic Quarterly* 38:28–51.

——— (1969b). Unconscious fantasy and disturbances of conscious experience. *Psychoanalytic Quarterly* 38(1):1–27.

——— (1979). The genesis of interpretation. *Journal of the American Psychoanalytic Association* 27:193–206.

——— and Brenner, C. (1964). *Psychoanalytic Concepts and the Structural Theory.* New York, NY: International University Press.

——— ——— (1990). The psychoanalytic process. *Psychoanalytic Quarterly* 59:678–692.

Boesky, D., (1988). Criteria of evidence for an unconscious fantasy. In: *Fantasy, Myth and Reality: Essays in Honor of Jacob Arlow, M.D.*, ed. H. Blum, Y. Kramer, A.D. Richards and A.K. Richards. Madison, CT: International Universities Press, pp. 111–131.

Boesky, D. (1990). The psychoanalytic process and its components. *Psychoanalytic Quarterly* 54:550–584.

Brenner, C. (1974). On the nature and development of affects: a unified theory. *Psychoanalytic Quarterly* 43:532–556.

——— (1975). Affects and psychic conflict. *Psychoanalytic Quarterly* 44:5–28.

———(1976). *Psychoanalytic Technique and Psychic Conflict.* New York, NY: International Universities Press.

——— (1979). Depressive affect, anxiety, and psychic conflict in the phallicoedipal phase. *Psychoanalytic Quarterly* 48:177–197.

——— 1982. *The Mind in Conflict.* New York, NY: International Universities Press.

——— 1985 Countertransference as compromise formation *Psychoanalytic Quarterly* 54:155–163.

——— (2006). Psychoanalysis or mind and meaning. New York, NY: *Psychoanalytic Quarterly* monograph.

Dewald, P. (1982). Serious illness in the analyst: transference, countertransference, and reality responses. *Journal of the American Psychoanalytic Association* 30:347–363.

Erikson, E.H. (1956). The problem of ego identity. *Journal of the American Psychoanalytic Association* 4:56–121.

Fenichel, O. (1938). Review of *The Ego and the Mechanisms of Defence* by Anna Freud. Inter*national Journal of Psychoanalysis* 19:116–136.

Freud, A. (1936). *The Ego and the Mechanisms of Defence.* New York: International University Press, 1946.

Freud, S. (1905). Three Essays on The Theory of Sexuality. *Standard Edition* 7:125–245.

——— (1912). The dynamics of transference. *Standard Edition* 12.

——— (1923). The ego and the id. *Standard Edition* 19:1–66.

——— (1925). Negation. *Standard Edition* 19.

——— (1926). Inhibitions, symptoms and anxieties. *Standard Edition* 20:87–176.

——— (1937). Constructions in analysis. *Standard Edition* 23.

Friedman, L. (1969). The therapeutic alliance. *International Journal of Psycho-Analysis* 50:139–153.

Gray, P. (1994). *The Ego and Analysis of Defense*. Northvale, NJ: Jason Aronson.

Jacobs, T. (1991). *The Use of the Self*. Madison, CT: International Universities Press.

Jacobson, E. (1954). The self and the object world—vicissitudes of their infantile cathexes and their influence on ideational and affective development. *Psychoanalytic Study of the Child* 9:75–127.

Kris, E. (1956). On some vicissitudes of insight in psychoanalysis. In: *Selected Papers of Ernst Kris* (1975). New Haven, CT: Yale University Press, pp. 252–271.

Loewald, H. (1960). On the therapeutic action of psychoanalysis. *International Journal of Psycho-Analysis* 41:16–33.

Mahon, E. (2002). A joke in a dream: a note on the complex aesthetics of disguise. *Psychoanalytic Study of the Child* 57:452–457.

Nunberg, H. (1926). The will to recovery. In: *Practice and Theory of Psychoanalysis Vol. I* (1948). New York, NY: International Universities Press, pp. 75–88.

Panel, (1954). Defense mechanisms and psychoanalytic technique. E.R. Zetzel, reporter. *Journal of the American Psychoanalytic Association* 2:318–326.

Panel, (1967a) Development and metapsychology of the defense organization of the ego R. S. Wallerstein, reporter. *Journal of the American Psychoanalytic Association* 15:130–149.

Panel, (1967b). Defense organization of the ego and psychoanalytic technique. E. Pumpian-Mindlin, reporter *Journal of the American Psychoanalytic Association* 15:150–165.

Panel, (1970). The fate of the defenses in the psychoanalytic process. J. Krent, reporter *Journal of the American Psychoanalytic Association* 18:177–194.

Rangell, L. (1988). Roots and derivatives of unconscious fantasy. In: *Fantasy, Myth and Reality: Essays in Honor of Jacob Arlow, M.D.*, ed. H. Blum, Y. Kramer, A.D. Richards and A.K. Richards. Madison, CT: International Universities Press, pp. 61–78.

_____ (2007). *The Road to Unity in Psychoanalytic Theory*. New York, NY: Aronson.

Sandler, J. (1976). Countertransference and role-responsiveness. *International Review of Psycho-Analysis* 3:43–48.

Schmideberg, M. (1938). After the analysis. *Psychoanalytic Quarterly* 7:122–142.

Sterba, R. (1934), The fate of the ego in analytic therapy. *International Journal of Psycho-Analysis* 15:117–126.

Part I:

The Psychoanalytic Process

CHAPTER 1

Problems of Identity—Theoretical and Clinical Applications[1]

[Abend, S.M. (1974). *Psychoanalytic Quarterly* 43:606–637]

Introduction

Despite a spate of papers that appeared during the 1950s on the topic, the concept of identity continues to be an elusive one used by different workers to mean different things, invoked in connection with a very diffuse group of clinical conditions, and no author has as yet offered a precise, clear definition that has succeeded in winning general acceptance.

Nevertheless, Erikson's (1956) term for specific postadolescent upheavals, "identity crisis," has caught the fancy of the educated laity and crept into popular usage to refer to a variety of adult disturbances involving major or minor alterations or uncertainty in regard to conscious self-definition, ideals, and/or life goals. Perhaps in part for this reason, Kohut (1971) recently wrote that identity, like personality,

---

[1] The ideas presented in this paper were stimulated by the work of the Kris Study Group on the topic of Identity, under the leadership of Dr. Kenneth Calder. Although the point of view expressed is my own and not shared by the group as a whole, its development reflects the contributions of our mutual efforts. In addition, Drs. Leo Spiegel, Martin Willick, Michael Porder, and, in particular, Charles Brenner, made many valuable suggestions.

"Although often serviceable in a general sense . . . is not indigenous to psychoanalytic psychology; it belongs to a different theoretical framework which is more in harmony with the observation of social behavior and the description of the (pre)conscious experience of oneself in the interaction with others than with the observations of depth psychology" (p. xiv).

The very idea of identity seems to contain some intrinsic ambiguity, as can be seen even in its standard English definitions. This quality is reflected in the efforts of most psychoanalytic writers to give it a specific technical meaning. Erikson (1956), for example, appears intentionally to maintain a certain elusiveness in the following passage: "At one time, it will appear to refer to a conscious *sense of individual identity*; at another to an unconscious striving for a *continuity of personal character*; at a third, as a criterion for the silent doings of *ego synthesis*; and, finally, as a maintenance of an inner *solidarity* with a group's ideals and identity" (p. 57). A number of writers, however, do not accept Erikson's views and prefer to use the term "identity" to refer to an individual's unique personal identity, a mental entity that comes into existence as one consequence of the separation-individuation phase of early psychic life.

Naturally, this confusion has led to an increase in the number of clinical problems that different authors present as revealing disturbances of identity. Thus, in addition to the particular symptom complex of young adults described by Erikson, we find various psychotic and borderline syndromes of children and adults, patients with severe narcissistic difficulties, depersonalization, fugue states, and amnesias, the problems of twins, artists, and impostors, and a variety of overt sexual deviations included in this clinical grab bag. In short, the spectrum is now so broad that it appears to defy efforts to isolate common factors that might be of help in constructing a meaningful, inclusive definition. Moreover, the recent upsurge of interest in problems of the self has resulted in still further overlap and confusion in terminology and in clinical theory, making the need for clarification and uniformity even more pressing than before. I propose in this paper to pursue a redefinition of terms, which I hope will make possible clearer delimitations and thereby enhance communication about our case material and our ideas.

I think it will prove useful to reserve the concept of identity and its problems for certain varieties of disturbance involving the characteristic consolidations of young adults, as suggested by Erikson. However, I think it is necessary that we be more precise about what we understand identity to mean, and to clarify the relationship of the concept to the general psychoanalytic theory of the mental apparatus. The difficulties some workers have connected with developmental problems of early life could better be collected under the rubric of problems of the self, although this, too, is a concept which requires greater precision of definition. Finally, I think a third category, problems of sexual identity, can meaningfully be separated from the others. These proposed distinctions are certainly somewhat arbitrary, but I believe them to be logical in themselves and not contradictory to the accepted tenets of psychoanalytic theory. In matters of definition, arbitrariness alone is not objectionable. The important question is whether the divisions are clear and are useful in their application to clinical material.

Historical Review

Webster's New Collegiate Dictionary (1959) illustrates the inherent ambiguity of the term identity in the several definitions given. The word is derived from the Latin *idem*, meaning the same, as in the "sameness of essential character; sameness in all that constitutes the objective reality of a thing; selfsameness; oneness." Further definitions include: "unity and persistence of personality; individuality" and "the condition of being the same with something described or asserted." Thus, as in mathematics, identity has come to stand for something that is the same as something else, leading to its common usage to highlight a quality (or qualities) of the individual that links him to other individuals or groups, as in, for instance, Freud's "Jewish identity." Yet the term also has an inner aspect, meaning precisely those special qualities whose "sameness" over time permits the individual to establish his own unique and consistent sense of himself—a particular individual identity. By extension, it also means those specific features that distinguish one individual from all others; thus, one speaks of identity cards and identifying data or characteristics.

Erikson (1956) expressed this polarity most succinctly: "The term identity . . . connotes both a persistent sameness within oneself . . . and a persistent sharing of some kind of essential character with others" (p. 57). Although he recognizes the beginnings of the establishment of these qualities in early development, in his view a final identity is not fixed until the close of adolescence. It "includes all significant identifications, but it also alters them in order to make a unique and a reasonably clear whole of them" (p. 68). He considers identity "an *evolving configuration* . . . gradually integrating *constitutional givens, idiosyncratic libidinal needs, favored capacities, significant identifications, effective defenses, successful sublimations, and consistent roles*" (p. 71).

Though not limiting his conception to social roles, values, and ideals, Erikson places considerable emphasis upon them. He also includes an extrapsychic dimension in the form of those reciprocating responses from the surrounding society to the individual (such as recognition, expectations, and similar feedback), which he believes contribute importantly to self-definition and hence to the process of identity formation. He looks on the turmoil that often accompanies this postadolescent growth stage as a "normative crisis." In his view, pathology lies only in an exaggeration of this upheaval to which some individuals are subject, a syndrome he calls "identity diffusion." Through composite case histories, he has outlined a rather severe, prolonged regressive and disorganized period, typically marked by a sense of isolation, disintegration of the sense of inner continuity, extreme shame, inability to derive pleasure from activities or relationships, disturbance in time perspective, passivity, anger, and mistrust of others. Probably because his formulations rest so heavily on their social-descriptive aspects, because he has nowhere offered in clear metapsychological terms a statement of his view of identity formation, and because he centers his attention upon processes of late adolescence and early adulthood, others have found his ideas insufficiently explanatory and have preferred to approach the question of identity formation as an aspect of early childhood development.

Greenacre (1958) has also stressed the fact that identity has both an inner and an outer face, but she sees them rather differently from

Erikson: "It means, on the one hand, an individual person or object, whose component parts are sufficiently well integrated in the organization of the whole that the effect is of a genuine oneness, a unit. On the other hand, in some situations identity refers to the unique characteristics of an individual person or object whereby it can be distinguished from other somewhat similar persons or objects. In one instance, the emphasis is on likeness, and in the other on specific differences" (p. 612). She goes on to imply that both inner experiences of oneself and perceptions of the outer aspect of one's body or self contribute to identity formation. By identity she is referring to an inner structure of the mind, whereas she uses the term "sense of identity" to imply an awareness of this structure involving comparison and contrast with others. In a most important passage, she says that an individual's "self-image, based . . . on a fusion of implicit, but generally not clearly focused, awareness of his own form and functioning with his wishes as to how he would like to appear and to function . . . forms the core on which his sense of his own identity is built" (pp. 613–614).

Greenacre specifically emphasizes the central role of body image in this core of identity. Her interest in early tactile and visual perceptual influences on body image formation leads her to speculate on the significance of the perceptions of one's own and others' faces and genitalia in particular, and to postulate that traumata in this area during very early development are important in the pathogenesis of perversions and fetishism. In a summary statement, she says the sense of identity comes into some kind of preliminary working form during the anal phase, but reaches special development with the phallic-oedipal period. By that time the child "himself existing in a world of outer objects, knows he has thoughts and memory, appreciates relative size, but has knowledge of sexual differences, knows the names of his body parts and of himself. He is . . . aware of himself as a unit in a group" (pp. 625–626). Later developments in and beyond adolescence, she recognizes, generally modify this sense of identity.

Mahler (1958), too, in a presentation to a panel on Problems of Identity, indicates her view that the self-feelings resulting from the complex psychic differentiation processes in young children are synonymous with their sense of identity. The children with autistic and symbiotic psychoses studied by Mahler can be described as suffering from identity disturbances.

Jacobson (1964) is in general agreement with Greenacre and Mahler in understanding identity as related to self-feeling or self-awareness, qualities which arise in the young individual as a result of the processes of early differentiation of the self from the non-self. She is in partial agreement with Erikson's concept of identity formation, but does not wish to restrict this psychic process to ego synthesis: "I would prefer to understand by identity formation a process that builds up the ability to preserve the whole psychic organization—despite its growing structuralization, differentiation and complexity—as a highly individualized but coherent entity which has direction and continuity at any stage of human development" (p. 27). She says that from the clinical standpoint, ". . . serious identity problems appear to be limited to neurotics with specific narcissistic conflicts, and to borderline and psychotic patients" (p. 29).

Jacobson does approach a more rigorous metapsychological clarity, defining self-representation as "unconscious, preconscious and conscious endopsychic representations of the bodily and mental self in the system ego" (p. 19). These begin to arise from accumulating memory traces of pleasurable and unpleasurable experiences. Drive investment, of course, is of the self-representations and not of the ego itself. Because of the nature of the primitive mental apparatus, self-representations are highly variable and in tenuous relation to objective reality. This is true of both bodily and mental representations, and of early object representations as well. Advancing development presumably leads to the acquisition of more and more realistic images of the self. In time, Jacobson says, "some concept of their sum total will (simultaneously) develop, *i.e.*, an awareness of the self as a differentiated but organized entity which has continuity and direction . . . " She then concludes that this awareness "will find an emotional expression in the experience of personal identity" (p. 23).

Spiegel (1959) is also interested in persons suffering from identity disturbances, including those with depersonalization and derealization symptoms. While acknowledging the defensive meaning of these feeling-states, he seeks an "ego-psychological" basis for them in the data of perceptual studies. He agrees with the definition of self-representations as mental images of the body and body states, and suggests that "self" is a collective term for the totality of these body images. Developing interesting analogies from gestalt psychology experiments, he suggests that an ever-growing accumulation of experiences, subjected to "pooling," comes in time to form a more or less stable inner frame of reference against which new experiences can be compared and evaluated. He states that this constant frame of reference constitutes an important aspect of the self and is the ground on which a continuing personal identity rests.

None of these writers addresses him- or herself to the distinction between the accumulation of a vast number of self-representations of body parts, feelings, and so forth, which collectively form a self, and ideational representations of the total self. But an interesting paper by Keiser (1958) presents some pertinent clinical material in pursuing a different topic, that of the relation of body image formation to certain disturbances of abstract thinking. Keiser's study suggests that important representations of separate parts of the body, unintegrated into the whole, may be maintained and used for defensive purposes, while at the same time a fully developed sense of the total self—indeed perhaps more than one unified self-concept—is also clinically in evidence. This suggests that it is incorrect to assume that the existence of unintegrated self-images is necessarily to be taken as evidence of developmental arrest or fixation, or explained entirely on economic grounds, as some recent work seems to do.

Eissler (1958), whose paper was also included in the panel on Problems of Identity, based his idea of the sense of identity on "the ego's capacity to experience itself as a continuum." He felt that this is not fully established before genital maturity at puberty. He also proposed that the self be understood as a fourth structural differentiation in the mind, coequal with id, ego, and superego, but his ideas did not win general acceptance at the time of presentation. However, Levin (1969), much interested in Kohut's recent work on narcissism and the analysis of the self, also proposes considering the self as a separate entity, suggesting that it is both the seat of most intractable resistances and that it is equivalent to feeling and/or all subjective emotional experience. He attempts to distinguish this concept of the self from that of the ego, which he seems to see as restricted to thinking and other regulatory functions and the more logical, objective responses to and integration of external perceptions. Kohut (1970), although pleased that others share his interest in studying the self, does not agree with Levin's somewhat unique theoretical proposals.

Lichtenstein (1961), in an intricate and highly idiosyncratic line of thought, proposes that man, unlike all other creatures, has to seek identity as an overarching theme of his entire life. He suggests that in a fashion analogous to "imprinting," mothers, through their expectations and needs, implant an early pattern in their children that becomes elaborated into an "identity theme" that will influence to some degree all subsequent self-other relationships. Partly on philosophic grounds, Lichtenstein places this rather special dyadic view in a superordinate position in regulating human mental activity. His concept, however, has not been found persuasive by most other analysts.

The Kris Study Group, which met in 1961–1963 under the chairmanship of Arlow to consider problems of identity, studied patients with depersonalization, fugue states, and amnesia, as well as impostors, those with perversions, and certain problems of twins, but were able to reach no uniform conclusions. One member of the group, J. Frosch, suggested a classification of problems according to whether subjective or objective (*i.e.*, externally observable) signs of disorder were present. The only other systematic attempt to organize the material was offered by Margolis (1962). He suggested that the term self-image be restricted to denote only self-representations of body anatomy and body feelings, which come eventually to constitute a body image—a physically derived subclass of self-representations. After making the observation that identifications begin as processes of becoming like an object but, through their assimilation and contribution to ego growth, end in further differentiations of self and object, Margolis turned to the terms which most interest us. He suggested that self, sense of self, and identity are used synonymously and interchangeably to depict the awareness of individuality, uniqueness, differentiation from others, and the integrity of the physical and mental self as a unit. He agreed with this usage and proposed to distinguish from this the sense of identity, which he saw as a broader concept including the idea of likeness to others and hence the aspect of identity problems that has a social dimension and a relation to external reality.

In brief then, different authors use the same term to mean different things; different terms to describe essentially the same thing; or designate as synonymous terms which may imply quite different concepts to other people. When these linguistic complications are grafted onto a conceptual problem that has such inherent ambiguity to begin with, the results are altogether confusing and uneconomical; this is what has emboldened me to propose some revisions.

Redefinitions and Reformulations

In re-examining the terms in common use in writings on identity and their relationship to one another, the terms seem to fall naturally into two groups: the first consists of self-representation, self, self-image, and sense of self; the second is composed of ego identity, personal identity, identity, sense of identity, and sexual identity. Among them, *identity* and *self* are the constructs most in need of clear theoretical definitions, although I believe that *sense of identity* and *sense of self* are as useful clinically and that *sexual identity* occupies a special place all its own.

Self-representation, Self, Self-image, and Sense of Self

Self-representations are ideas about oneself, or part of oneself. They may refer to anatomical or other physical qualities, feeling-states, or functions, and may range over a complete spectrum from objectively realistic to totally unrealistic ideas. They are originally derived, no doubt, from perceptual experiences of the inner and outer world, which become memory traces, and from analogous wishful mental phenomena. Though the integration of perception, memory, and thinking is considered to be in the province of the ego (so that the processing of self-representations is a task of that structure), the content of individual ideas can and, in fact, must inevitably reflect both drive and regulatory features, which we assign to the other great structural entities as well. It is also easily demonstrated that self-representations can be either conscious, preconscious, or unconscious.

Self is a mental construct composed of self-representations. It has been suggested that the self be defined as the sum of all self-representations, but I feel that there is some advantage in being able to understand certain self-representations as excluded from the concept of the self, as this is in accord with clinical experience. Therefore I think that *self* should instead be taken to mean all of those self-representations that refer to the individual as a whole, including those that seem to focus primarily on a particular part or function, but do so in such a way as to maintain an awareness of its place as a portion of the entire individual.

As Greenacre (1958) has pointed out, ideas about the self are based on fusions of realistic and wishful versions of the individual's form and functioning, and remain so to a greater or lesser degree throughout life. When one considers, in addition, that projective and introjective mechanisms introduce distortions into the distinctions between self-representations and object representations—even in well-integrated persons—it becomes easy to understand why the self remains an agglutination of ideas of ever-shifting and inconstant aggregate outline, despite its quality of continuity and sameness. One may consider the "shape" of the self as analogous to that of a tidal beach, whose finite details are continuously changing from moment to moment, yet which gives on the whole an impression of changelessness.

Some writers, like Levin (1969), refer to the self in the sense of the experiencing portion of the mind. This usage seems so well established that it obliges us to attempt to bring it into alignment with the conceptualization under consideration. To experience something means simply to register in consciousness inner and/or outer perceptions, and this function, as previously noted, is assigned to the ego in our structural theory. The fact that it is the self which is undergoing a given experience is available upon conscious introspection (except under pathological circumstances), but unless there are particular reasons for its inclusion in consciousness at any given moment it remains part of the preconscious background. It would invariably be of interest clinically to understand *why* an awareness of self is part of a given experience, just as the reciprocal exclusion would be a phenomenon important to investigate, but for our immediate purpose these are tangential questions. We need to be able to explain *how* it is that one can readily, if necessary, arrive at this judgment. It seems logical to suggest that some system of scanning and comparison with previous experiences must provide the necessary information. We can therefore make use of Spiegel's (1959) formulation that the self is composed of pooled self-representations (former perceptual experiences that become memory traces, more or less consolidated and available for purposes of comparison), which serve to provide a frame of reference for inner experiences.

Another source of confusion about the self is our tendency to use the same word to refer to the entire person, or the entire mind of an individual. When used in the sense of the mind as a whole, the self may be understood to describe the totality of id, ego, and superego, as reflected in their interaction. Some analysts do prefer to use the term in this way, while in general usage the self will often refer to the individual as a whole. Despite these consequences of the limitations of our language, one should in scientific discussion attempt to maintain conceptual clarity by indicating precisely how one means the term to be used. I suggest that the self be understood as a mental construct, an idea (or a set of ideas), or as Kohut (1971) has called it, a "content of the mind" (p. xv).

The self comes into existence as a result of the separation-individuation processes of early life and the maturation of the mental apparatus. It reaches a degree of stability, as Greenacre has said, when a child can conceptualize himself as existing in a world of objects, knows he has a mental life, appreciates relative size and sexual differences, and is aware of his individual specifiers. While this process begins earlier, it reaches special development in the phallic-oedipal phase.

In summary, then, the *self* is a mental construct consisting of a set of ideas known as self-representations—a fusion of what were originally inner and outer perceptual experiences of varied degrees of objective reality with later, more abstract ideas about the individual's physical and mental qualities. These have in common that they depict the whole individual as an entity, separate and distinct from others and continuous in time. The self's boundaries are inconstant because of the capacity of wishful self-representations and projective-introjective mechanisms to distort its realistic qualities, and because certain partial representations may or may not be included in the total self at any given moment.

Self-image is a diffuse term used by analysts and nonanalysts alike to allude to ways in which individuals envision themselves. "Image" implies a close link to actual percepts, particularly visual ones. This term is related to body image, which is generally understood to refer to more or less concrete anatomical self-representations. Margolis (1962) has suggested that we restrict its use to mean exclusively those self-representations that compose the body image. I believe this would be a worthwhile emendation, but I am afraid that self-image is so firmly ensconced in its looser, nontechnical usage as to preclude reclamation and might best be left in the realm of descriptive language.

As here defined, the self is a theoretical abstraction, useful to us in organizing data and in communicating with one another. However, as with other abstractions in our field, it is altogether misleading and incorrect to treat it as if it had an actual psychic existence and to speak as though people can be in touch with or directly aware of any such entity within themselves. That there are self-feelings of many kinds is of course evident, but as Spiegel (1959) specifically cautions, "The relation of self-feeling to the self is not immediately given but is a subject for investigation . . ." (p. 88). He states that self-feeling does not imply a direct connection with the self as defined.

How then are we to refer to the variety of self-feelings which we hear about from patients in the course of our clinical work? Although other terms have been used, *Sense of Self*, recommended by Spiegel and so used by others as well, seems best suited for this purpose. It implies subjective awareness, which is what we wish to emphasize in this context. The suggestion that self-feelings be investigated should alert us to the danger of permitting our theoretical beliefs about the formation, the integrity, or the functions of the self to lead us to assumptions regarding the meaning of self-feelings as reported by patients. Instead, these should be subjected to analytic scrutiny through free association in exactly the same careful fashion with which symptoms, dreams, and all other analytic data are (or should be) treated. Sense of self, then, refers to raw analytic data; that is to say, what patients tell us they experience or believe about themselves as whole, discrete, unique, continuous beings, or to some disturbance thereof.

Ego Identity, Personal Identity, Identity, Sense of Identity, and Sexual Identity

Ego identity was the term introduced by Erikson (1956), probably to reflect the crucial role played by what he called "ego syntheses" in the consolidations of late adolescence and young adulthood which contribute to the final, stable formation of an identity as he sees it. Others feel that this term may imply a too restrictive understanding of complex processes (although this is manifestly not Erikson's intention), and it is relatively little used.

Personal identity is not actually a technical psychoanalytic term at all, although Jacobson (1964) used it to refer to the subjective feeling related to the formation of a more or less unified idea of the self. Yet it does convey the idea of a combination of those unique features that identify one as oneself and none other to oneself and to the outside world. As such, it becomes a part of the self-awareness of the child that results from the developmental processes of early life, as emphasized by Mahler (1958), Greenacre (1958), and Jacobson (1964). Naturally, as development continues, the manifold aspects of a personal identity will increase in number and in complexity and serve to specify particular aspects of the growing person's interactions with his surroundings.

Erikson (1956) and Blos (1962), (1972) hold that, with the closure of adolescence, these unique identifying features take on a new permanence and stability and are accompanied by the making of life choices recognized by the individual and his society to be of lasting and generally irreversible significance. Just as most analysts feel that the identification processes of the Oedipal period play a crucial role in character formation and eventually in neurosogenesis, so Erikson and Blos feel that the stage-specific formations of postadolescence are to be assigned an analogous primacy in identity formation.

This point of view leads to a psychoanalytic definition of *Identity* more restricted than what has heretofore often been understood by that term. It would be used to describe a loosely organized set of conscious and preconscious self-representations that serve to define the individual in a variety of social contexts. Included in its composition we would expect to find ideas regarding specific professional, social, and sexual roles and preferences, aspects of the person's political and religious ideology and other unique values, and his more important personal interests and avocations. These self-representations are formed at a relatively high level of psychic development and are therefore complex products of instinctual drives, defenses, identifications, and sublimations, as well as reflecting the influence on these of constitutional givens and of the special contributions made by the particular individual's life experiences and opportunities. In favorable circumstances, we expect to find a reasonably stable synthesis of these ideas and the qualities they represent taking place during young adulthood, but as with the self, we need not expect what we call *identity* to be either sharply outlined or rigidly maintained. These self-representations, too, will have a certain proportion of wishful as well as realistic influences. Of equal importance, circumstances generally dictate that attention will be paid now to one aspect of identity, now to another, which contributes to the sense of indistinct margins, despite the fact that by definition we include only features available to consciousness. It is also true, of course, that some degree of change over time, under the influence of maturational and other forces, is to be expected in the various parameters of identity in most, if not all, persons. Ideas at this level of abstraction may contain some notion of the future as part of their intrinsic content, which could contribute to a sense of continuity.

This construct, like the self, is a theoretical abstraction and has no "real" existence in the mind, even though the self-representations that constitute one's identity are individually available to introspection. Patients do, of course, report subjective feelings and thoughts about their "identities" as well as about those specific aspects of mental life which we would include in its province. Once again, a separate term is required to indicate this experiential data; logic and symmetry suggest that *Sense of Identity* should be used for this purpose. It is hard to imagine significant alterations or other disruptions of the class of self-representations that compose identity's not disturbing the person consciously and leading to subjective manifestations of some sort, yet it should be noted that the reverse is not invariably true. Analytic investigation of reported feelings and thoughts about identity or its components aims at clarifying what they mean in the mental life of the patient. Automatic assumption that they necessarily reflect changes in what our theory describes as identity may lead to error. In either case, a proper understanding of the complaints is achieved only by deciphering the unconscious infantile conflictual sources from which they ultimately stem.

There remains to be considered a special class of conscious and unconscious self-representations dealing with the *Sexual Identity* of the individual. These begin with early perceptions of anatomical differences and are very much increased by ideas stemming from the sexual theories of childhood and the wishful fantasies, identifications, and fears of the Oedipal period. The result is a complex group of self-representations, more or less confused and contradictory, and of varying degrees of reality consonance, about the individual's body, genitalia, sexual role, behavior, and functioning. Once formed, this particular set of ideas plays a vital part in the further mental development of the person, especially in determining pathology, either in the form of symptoms or of character traits and their consequences. Analysts will continue to need a way to refer to these ideas as distinguished from the other kinds of self-representations, precisely because of their unique importance in our clinical and theoretical discussions. To speak of *sexual identity* as a way of referring collectively to this group of self-representations seems unambiguous and unlikely to cause further confusion. This group of ideas may be considered a special, indeed central, aspect of the self as defined in this paper. Some of its conscious components also form a part of what we have proposed to call identity.

From this it follows that the *self* is the largest, most inclusive term of those defined above, while *identity* is a more limited concept, referring in fact to a specific part of the self and not to be thought of as separate from it or as supplanting it in any way. *Sexual identity* is another important differentiation within the self, of maximum clinical significance, and it constitutes a portion of the individual's identity as well.

These redefinitions and reformulations have been undertaken in the hope that they would provide a convenient pathway by which to approach the clinical study of problems of identity. With that in mind, I would next like to consider the application of these ideas to case material.[2]

Clinical Applications

What is proposed here is a set of distinctions based upon phenomenology. The term "identity problem" ought to be reserved for those adult patients who display disturbances in the assumption of comfortable and stable social, sexual, and professional roles, and/or in the crystallization of important conscious ideals, values, beliefs, and special interests. In a more general way this could also be described as a problem in self-definition in relation to external reality. It implies having trouble in finding or feeling qualities of similarity in oneself to various groupings of different orders of concreteness in society (*e.g.*, a specific religious sect, a profession, those who share an avocational preference, political philosophy, *etc.*).

---

[2] I am grateful to Drs. Milton Horowitz, Norman Margolis, and Herbert Wyman, who have kindly permitted me to use their clinical material for some of the following illustrations.

Disturbances may appear in several forms, of which frank or implied falsification of personal characteristics (as in varying degrees of imposture) is the most obvious.

Disorganization, delay, and inhibition in selecting the qualities that underlie choices is another common form of disturbance, as in Erikson's cases. Less easily recognizable at first is the variation marked by seemingly intense involvement in groups, causes, or roles, which abruptly drops away, only to be replaced by a succession of other equally intense but fundamentally superficial immersions. There are also certain individuals who seem to be securely ensconced in their social milieu until the loss of a significant personal relationship uncovers the lack of substance beneath their apparent adjustment (the so-called "as if" characters might be included in this group).

If individuals suffer primarily from a disturbance in the sphere of manifest sexual behavior (homosexuality, bisexuality, fetishism, etc.) without important accompanying difficulties in the other areas subsumed under identity, as described above, then they belong in the category that I have suggested we call problems of *sexual identity*. Finally, those whose pathology encompasses more diffuse, and often, though perhaps not invariably, more profound disruptions in the integrity and reliability of self-awareness and self-perceptions—such as in delusion formation and other manifestations of psychosis, severe depersonalization, amnesias, fugue states, grandiosity, and related narcissistic phenomena at all levels of severity—should be distinguished from the foregoing groups and considered instead as demonstrating problems of the *self*.

It must be emphasized that in any of these cases, the analytic task remains the same. The phenomenology is, as always, merely the starting point of our investigations, and it is evident that, whether originally observed by us or first reported by the patient, its significance must be unraveled by the analytic method. Whether we are considering imposture, difficulty in making a career choice, homosexuality, or severe depersonalization, we are confronted with the necessity of tracing the meaning and the origins of the problem to their genetic and dynamic sources by way of the intricate network of derivatives we inevitably encounter. As with other symptoms, the familiar unconscious libidinal and aggressive conflicts arise from the interaction of the wishes, fears, and defenses of infantile mental life for their basic structure and need to be resolved to afford therapeutic relief.

At this point, the question may be raised as to why we should bother with the clinical distinctions proposed herein, or with the concepts of identity and self at all, if the analytic work is not thereby altered and the underlying conflicts with which we are already accustomed to dealing remain, as usual, at the core of the therapeutic task. The most reasonable answer I can offer is that the ever-present problem of choice of neurosis, as it were, continues to exert its fascination on us all. Not all patients complain of or reveal the disturbances with which we are concerned in this paper, and the challenge of attempting to understand why some do and others do not remains before us. Our technique can tell us only how it came about that one particular patient developed his or her special problems. I believe we are still quite some distance from formulating an insightful hypothesis that might lead to the illumination of these larger questions. It is the much more modest aim of this contribution to offer what I feel is necessary preparatory work: to clear away some of the confusion regarding clinical criteria, terminology, and the relation of certain of these ideas to fundamental theory, which makes the greater problems all but unapproachable.

It is beyond the scope of this paper to attempt to demonstrate the complexities of the problems in all three categories of disturbance. My interest arose out of a study group devoted to problems of identity, and I will content myself with attempting to illustrate some of the points raised about those cases I feel should be included in this group. It remains to be said that we should not be surprised to find some patients with identity problems demonstrating difficulties in the area of the self as well, since identity as here defined is but a limited aspect of that larger conceptual entity. Ironbound distinctions are not intended; rather, judgment as to major prominence and relative importance should be exercised in questionable instances to make the classificatory decision.

Case I

A man in his thirties with manifest sexual disturbance, hypochondriasis, and depersonalization also had impostor-like tendencies, although it was his paralyzing anxiety and work inhibitions that led him to seek analysis. He took advantage of actual educational experiences on the Continent to alter his personal mannerisms and behavior so as to mislead others into believing he was from an upper-class, wealthy, and cultured European family. This falsified "identity" served to master and deny all strong emotions, to maintain a defensive identification with a phallic mother, and to both incorporate and deny his family's earlier conversion from Judaism, which he associated with the tragic and painful death of his mother when he was still very young. The analysis ultimately revealed that the central significance of the disturbance in identity was to defensively deny powerful and threatening unconscious castrated and degraded self-representations.

Case II

A twenty-year-old woman entered analysis in a state of extreme confusion, agitation, and near despair. At the time, she was a kindergarten teacher and a college student with some aspirations to be an actress. Soon after beginning treatment, she gave up her work and schooling to concentrate on an acting career, into which she threw herself with enormous enthusiasm. Despite some initial success, she soon revealed difficulty in keeping herself from projecting her own conflicts into the parts she played. Her interest waned and she developed the idea of becoming a psychiatrist, a plan she attempted to put into execution with great seriousness in spite of considerable analytic work on the irrational sources of her motivation. A highly emotional erotic transference quickly developed from the very outset of her treatment. This helped to bring out her confused, intensely overstimulating upbringing at the hands of an openly seductive, psychotic mother and a father who was nearly as disturbed and seductive in his own way. The analysis, still in progress, has so far indicated that a major source of her confusion rests in unusually severe, conflicting, and conflicted identifications with each of these unsatisfactory parents.

Case III

An interesting variant was presented by a woman in her thirties, the daughter of a prominent person, who made an interracial marriage and was the mother of two children. She entered analysis because of agoraphobia, sexual inhibition, and anxiety attacks accompanied by depersonalization. She could not feel "fully herself" as a wife and mother, but needed to cling to a particular reassuring idea of herself represented by the formula, "I am Mr. X's daughter." A special adolescent trauma was the death of an older brother, following which she tried to reshape her life to be his psychological heir (as she was his legal heir). Severe sexual conflicts erupted; their origins were much clarified by the analysis which uncovered significant childhood traumata. She also recalled a period of *pseudologia fantastica* in adolescence. In this case, the identity disturbance is revealed by the psychological rejection of certain choices and roles which she had in fact made, and the clinging to an identifying connection to her past reality. Again the core importance of the symptom was an attempted defense against unacceptable unconscious castrated and devalued self-representations.

As indicated earlier, it is possible for subjective problems in the sense of identity to be present in the absence of any signs of the descriptive criteria of identity problems proper; analysis may reveal that the complaint has a meaning unrelated to identity *per se*.

Case IV

A woman in her twenties who was in analysis for multiple travel phobias and obsessional rituals complained from time to time of feeling unsure of herself—who she really was and where she was going in life. These statements came to be understood as attempts to deny states of intense sadomasochistic sexual excitement of a dangerous incestuous origin. There was never any reflection of true identity disturbance. She was a student with clear, consistent preferences, had a love affair which progressed to marriage, and maintained the same interests and activities throughout the course of a relatively short analysis. She had made a peculiarly unsuitable marriage in her teens to a man of totally different background from her own, which ended in divorce. She also had a fantasy, dating from early adolescence, of having come from another planet at age twelve to occupy her present body. Despite these earlier symptoms, her conscious self-representations, goals, interests, social ties, and roles were remarkably stable.

To conclude this section on clinical applications of this way of defining problems of identity and of the sense of identity, I would like to describe one case in greater detail. From all of my own clinical material, this young man most resembles those composite case histories proffered by Erikson, and his lengthy analysis has provided the opportunity to trace many of the factors that underlay his difficulty in choosing a career. It is interesting to note that although he represents a common variety of identity problem and was all too aware of his difficulty in making important life choices, when he periodically complained of feeling "uncentered," of a "lack of identity," or of "unsureness about myself, my person," as in Case IV, this proved to be not primarily related to his actual problem with identity as we define it. Rather, the analysis of these subjective complaints revealed that they were derivatives of specific feelings and ideas about himself, which were not acceptable to consciousness. The very real problems of choices and of performance, which were central to his identity disturbance, rested essentially on various aspects of his Oedipal conflicts, although it will be evident that he was struggling with enormous narcissistic difficulties as well.

Case V

R was a good-looking, athletic young man with a distracted manner, who began treatment shortly after dropping out of college just before his twenty-first birthday. He complained that he was unable to be productive and described how he spent so many hours in depressive rumination that he could not study effectively. He was a habitual procrastinator, and furthermore, he had felt no interest in any course, nor did he have any goals he considered meaningful. He was preoccupied with feelings of inadequacy and failure. Although he met young women easily, he soon managed to alienate all of them, to his intense disappointment and frustration. He was mistrustful and guarded in all relationships, took pleasure in nothing, and felt estranged from his family.

The patient's father was a successful and respected physician, a man of high moral standards who had been an outstanding student and was inclined to see achievement as a simple function of effort. This made him intensely critical of his son's difficulties. He was a genuinely loving and fair-minded man, though impatient, but his relationship with R was complicated by blatant competitiveness. This seemed clearly enough to be in reaction to the obvious flirtatious admiration the mother bestowed upon the young man. She was a creative and talented individual, quite childlike and self-centered in many ways, and she demanded reciprocal attention from her adored offspring.

R was the middle of three children and the only male. He had been very attached to his older sister, who had died in her twenties of complications of her first pregnancy. His younger sister, who was now away at college, had been barely tolerated. R had always had learning problems of one sort or another, especially complicated by reading difficulty grossly disproportionate to his evident intellectual gifts. He was something of a social misfit, often assuming the role of clown and never fully accepted by his peers.

When treatment began, he was working with disadvantaged children and living with his parents. He took no interest in his job and was quite unreliable, largely because of his utter disregard for the realities of time, scheduling, or the needs and feelings of others. In the early months of treatment this attitude emerged as but one manifestation of his highly narcissistic, self-centered orientation and behavior. During analytic sessions, as elsewhere, he paid very little attention to what was said to him. His own stream of speech was rambling and appeared candid enough at first, but it soon became evident that he was attempting to conceal a highly guarded stance in which he consciously diverted his thoughts from anything that threatened to be too upsetting. He spent considerable amounts of time in grandiose daydreaming, which drove away the feelings of inadequacy. An early dream, in which a zeppelin was shot down by a plane, he interpreted as expressing his fear that the analysis would take away this protection and bring him down to earth to face his actual, painful feelings of failure.

R gradually revealed his extreme sexual inhibition; adolescent masturbation had not begun until age nineteen after his sister's marriage. His erotic interest in her became evident and he told of peeking at her and at his mother as well from prepuberty on, almost surely with their unconscious connivance. Two important early memories emerged, both of which returned over and over for further work throughout the course of analysis. The first was a memory involving his being displaced by the birth of his younger sister. The second memory was of a terrible automobile accident that took place when he was five in which several members of the family, including himself, were injured and required hospitalization.

Toward the end of his first year of treatment, R attempted to move into an apartment of his own. The analysis had begun to expose the intensity of his incestuous attachment to his dead sister, and the actuality of her tragic death made it extraordinarily difficult for him to talk about her. He had failed to grieve appropriately, primarily because to have done so would have been to acknowledge a love about which he felt guilty and ashamed. Nevertheless, it gradually became clear that she had been fully aware of his interest and had returned it in kind. The relation of her death to the pregnancy fixed the idea in his mind that sex had been responsible for her death. His recognition of this in turn ushered in the first real exploration of the highly sadistic and guilt-ridden nature of his sexual feelings and fantasies.

His behavior remained immature and self-centered. His penchant for frequent traffic violations and parking tickets was symptomatic of his disregard for limits and rules to which he felt himself an exception. He was invariably angry at being caught and penalized, and could not see that his behavior gratified a profound unconscious need for punishment and humiliation.

Despite considerable apprehension, he managed to obtain admission to a local university and resumed classes toward the end of his second year of treatment, dropping his unfulfilling job. He decided to study history for no rationally apparent reason. It soon became evident that the choice was largely determined by resistance, since it soon was obvious that he preferred the academic study of history to examining his personal history in analysis. At this juncture he was quite willing to talk about current concerns, but very reluctant to look closely at his past. As soon as he attempted to study, however, the extreme eroticization of his visual functioning was manifest. This of course clarified an important aspect of his trouble in learning. He would go to the library to work and within minutes he would be flooded by sexual excitement and start looking at girls instead of his books.

Primal scene derivatives entered the analysis, and in particular bodily curiosity was worked with extensively. It emerged that the sight of the female genital produced a specific reaction consisting of disorganization, confusion, and pseudo-stupidity. This also took place whenever, in studying or reading, he attempted to get to the essential core of any matter, thus rendering comprehension and orderly learning nearly impossible.

Until this time, the only career aspirations to come up were briefly considered ideas of becoming a professional athlete or musician. He had considerable talent in both spheres, but his previous efforts had been hampered by his grandiose expectation that he would perform at star level without instruction or practice. When he was unable to live up to this impossible goal, he became frustrated and discouraged, and consequently could not sustain effort or interest for very long. Then he began to express the wish to become an engineer like his admired and envied brother-in-law, with whom he became quite friendly. This ambition was in no way connected with a realistic appraisal of his own abilities, nor was it based on an assessment of what such a career would actually be like. As his grief for his dead sister began to emerge, the competitive and defensive aspects of his attachment to his brother-in-law soon became evident as well. With their clarification, his interest in becoming an engineer suddenly faded. Shortly thereafter he managed to win a young woman away from an older suitor and had his first affair, accompanied by much conscious anxiety and guilt. This brief relationship served to bring out much more sexual material, chiefly of a sadomasochistic nature, and in particular linked the act of penetration to his memories and fantasies of the violent, terrifying automobile accident and its sequelae.

Rather suddenly R started to talk about going into medicine and impulsively registered to take several difficult science courses over the summer. The attempt to explore his motivation for this step was experienced by him as if the analyst were actually trying to prevent him from advancing; thus his wish to compete with the analyst and his physician father emerged. Later there emerged a fantasy that he would in time discover a cure for the illness that had claimed his sister and thus magically undo her death. As his desire to acquire the envied equipment, knowledge, and power of his admired rivals appeared in dreams, fantasies, and multiple displacements, R became very provocative toward his father and nearly precipitated the untimely interruption of his treatment. He did manage to get a severe finger infection which he persuaded his father to "operate" on, thus satisfying by way of masochistic submission some of his unconscious need to suffer at the hands of his father.

In the fourth year of the analysis, many anal attitudes and concerns came into focus. besides various indicators of his anal erotic interests, the stubborn defiance that underlay his unproductiveness, disorganization, and procrastination began to become apparent to him. He gradually gained conviction that his failures were an unconsciously gratifying means by which he was able to frustrate and disappoint his parents. He became much more aware of his deep resentment toward both of them. With the admission of his anger, fears of bodily mutilation entered consciousness. For the first time he brought up—and re-experienced on the couch—sensations in his chest which in adolescence had given rise to the fear that he was growing breasts like a woman.

There were alternating states of bodily feeling equivalent to phallic expansiveness and pride on the one hand, and of dirty, worthless feelings of degradation and castration accompanied by intense shame on the other hand. Childhood memories of bodily and sexual curiosity brought back into awareness the fact that his father had had a medical office on the first floor of the house in which the family resided in R's earliest childhood. He recalled his wonderment and wish to peek at the "secret" activities of his father, memories that still served to screen primal scene fantasies of a confusing and exciting nature. For the first time, intense feelings of fear and hatred of his mother emerged, connected with impressions of her as powerful, intrusive, controlling, and domineering.

He began to express his fearful belief that success in any endeavor would merely result in his mother's taking it away or destroying it, an idea that led to the uncovering of vagina dentata fantasies and was connected to a transient claustrophobia as well. Subsequently he was able to resume more serious efforts to meet women, and more sexual material emerged. It became clear that he had been tremendously overstimulated in childhood by his mother's and sister's exhibitionism and seductive attention to him. He began to better comprehend his ever-present fear that he could not control his own impulses. A particular feature of his defective response to reality considerations was now understandable as an expression of his belief that despite being able to reach valid judgments of what is right, wise, or safe, he could not act in accordance with these judgments, because his impulses overpowered his rational capacities and controls.

In the fifth year of treatment he started to think about becoming a teacher. The idea was rooted in wishes to undo the embarrassing and frustrating failures of his own

childhood by teaching others, as well as to master the forbidden and secret knowledge possessed by adults, which had seemed so elusive when he was small. Thus, this ambition, too, was invested with magical wishes to supplant and replace each parent. Typically, he proceeded by precipitously changing his program without seeking advice or investigating the requirements, a continuation of his wish to be an exception to the rules and of his need to sow the seeds of potential failure.

He entered a prolonged period of regression, marked by apparent confusion, lack of progress, depression, and discouragement. Intense anger at his mother, reflected in a predominantly hostile maternal transference, was most in evidence. Oral and anal material overshadowed everything else, and his often-repeated conscious desire was to break away and free himself from the engulfing, penetrating, crippling influence of his mother and the analyst. Despite the troublesome feelings, he passed his courses and continued to date a series of women, though without much joy. Only very gradually did he come to the painful realization that the angry surface of his rebellious feelings served to conceal and deny his own powerful positive attachment to his mother, which could be expressed at this point only in pregenital terms, which seemed at once highly dangerous and deeply shameful to him. This was unmistakably expressed when a transient sleep disturbance arose, appearing in the analytic situation in the form of several sessions of acutely restless "overstimulation" on the couch, leading to the recall of similar states that had occurred while he had lain next to his mother on her bed as a small boy. The recollection and understanding of the genesis and meaning of these excited states were followed by dramatic relief and relaxation.

As he began to anticipate graduation and become anxious, the defensive aspect of the regressive material could be better understood. He seemed sure of his wish to become a teacher. Some erratic changeability, however, was still reflected in his shifting ideas of a subject specialty before he settled on one that offered realistic employment opportunities and represented his most consistent and relatively unconflicted performance.

Around the time of his graduation, aggressive and competitive wishes toward men he viewed as superior began to come out clearly in the analysis and directly in the transference. Beating fantasies, fears of loss of control, and a true recognition of his own violence and destructive wishes reached expression. This gave rise to periods of retreat, under the influence of guilt of a depressive character, during which he was filled with ideas of hopeless inferiority, feelings of worthlessness, and fears of retaliation. Nevertheless, he was intermittently able to be freely competitive in sports, to take pride in his strength, and to perform at a high academic level. Alternately he felt weak, frightened, afraid of injury, and of becoming effeminate.

For a time, he became seriously involved with an attractive young woman who proved to be highly neurotic and had severe conflicts which dovetailed with his own unconsciously sadomasochistic view of sexual relations. He became acutely conscious of triangular relationships with obvious Oedipal coloration and suddenly developed an interest in reading Freud in competition with and emulation of the analyst.

By now well into his sixth year of treatment, he suffered severe anxiety when he began some part-time substitute teaching. As he had done on many previous occasions, he spoke of feeling "uncentered," "not sure of who I am," of having "no identity," and similar expressions of subjective discomfort in the area of self-feelings. Such feelings had inevitably arisen either at times of crisis when he was facing a new and threatening situation, or following a defeat or disappointment that particularly damaged his self-esteem. The complaints could be understood as a manifestation of castration anxiety and narcissistic injury, and in time came to be seen as expressing the latent thoughts, "I feel like an impotent little boy again" or "I am afraid I am changing into a woman." They also served as defensive reassurances to himself and to others that he was too weak to be able to damage anyone else.

A persistent preoccupation with stealing arose, appeared in dreams and fantasies, and in time brought out his envy of the analyst and his father, expressed in terms of money and what it symbolized. In the course of the resolution of this issue, he assumed partial responsibility for his fee for the first time and was able to acknowledge how much he had hated to admit his need for help, since to him that was tantamount to admitting a humiliating inferiority. These conflicts had also played a great part in his trouble with both learning and teaching anything.

The analysis of the Oedipal competition with increased understanding now included more direct recall of his early attachment to his mother, of his fear of, as well as his love for, his father, and of his impatient ambition to be grown up and powerful. It led to significant advances in self-confidence, diminution of anxiety, damping of the regressive swings, increased independence, and easier, more comfortable relations with his parents. He broke off the unhappy affair with his difficult woman friend and began to seek more gratifying companionship. For the first time he could think of the possibility of success in reaching the realistic goals of his analysis and his life. With the increased stability of self-esteem, reality testing, and social and professional functioning, the discussion of termination, and the analysis of what it represented, commenced.

Summary

The concept of identity and an understanding of the clinical problems involved remains an area of confusion in the psychoanalytic literature. This is the result in part of inherent ambiguity in the term, in part of theoretical differences among various authors, and also in large measure of inconsistent use of terminology which reflects a lack of general agreement as to definition and meaning. A number of proposed redefinitions and reformulations are offered which are intended: 1, to bring our understanding of the important terms in line with the dictates of modern structural theory; and 2, to establish a clear but more delimited meaning for the concept of identity as a subgroup of the larger entity, the self, and to specify the relations between them. The clinical and theoretical importance of sexual identity requires that its place in these formulations be independently clarified, along with its interrelationship to the self and to identity.

Clinical use of the proposed redefinition of identity is illustrated with case presentations. A more logical grouping of case material is thus facilitated. The primary implication for technique that arises from these ideas is the re-emphasis of a principle which is familiar but nevertheless stands in need of continued rediscovery and repetition: that the disturbances of identity and of the sense of identity are to be understood as symptoms which must be subjected to analysis to uncover their significance in the mental life of patients. A priori assumptions regarding the meaning of such problems, which arise from developmental or other theoretical hypotheses, can be misleading and can hinder optimal therapeutic application.

References

Blos, P. (1962). *On Adolescence. A Psychoanalytic Interpretation.* New York: The Free Press of Glencoe, Inc.

——— (1972). The Epigenesis of the Adult Neurosis. *The Psychoanalytic Study of the Child* 27:106–135.

Eissler, K.R. (1958). Panel on Problems of Identity. *Journal of the American Psychoanalytic Association* 6:131–142.

Erikson, E.H. (1956). The Problem of Ego Identity. *Journal of the American Psychoanalytic Association* 4:56–121.

Greenacre, P. (1958). Early Physical Determinants in the Development of the Sense of Identity. *Journal of the American Psychoanalytic Association* 6:612–627.

Jacobson, E. (1964). *The Self and the Object World.* New York: International Universities Press, Inc.

Keiser, S. (1958). Disturbances in Abstract Thinking and Body-Image Formation. *Journal of the American Psychoanalytic Association* 6:628–652.

Kohut, H. (1970). Discussion of The Self: A Contribution to Its Place in Theory and Technique by Douglas C. Levin. *International Journal of Psychoanalysis* 51:176–181.

——— (1971). The Analysis of the Self. A Systematic Approach to the Psychoanalytic Treatment of Narcissistic Personality Disorders. Monograph Series of *The Psychoanalytic Study of the Child*, No. 4. New York: International Universities Press, Inc.

Levin, D.C. (1969). The Self: A Contribution to Its Place in Theory and Technique. *International Journal of Psycho-Analysis* 50:41–51.

Lichtenstein, H. (1961). Identity and Sexuality. A Study of Their Interrelationship in Man. *Journal of the American Psychoanalytic Association* 9:179–260.

Mahler, M. (1958). Panel on Problems of Identity. *Journal of the American Psychoanalytic Association* 6:131–142.

Margolis, N. (1962). Unpublished. Included in the Records of the Kris Study Group, Library of the New York Psychoanalytic Institute.

Spiegel, L.A. (1959). The Self, the Sense of Self, and Perception. *The Psychoanalytic Study of the Child* 24:81–109.

Webster's New Collegiate Dictionary. Springfield, MA: G. & C. Merriam Co. (1959).

CHAPTER 2

Some Observations on Reality Testing as a Clinical Concept

[Abend, S.M. (1982). *Psychoanalytic Quarterly* 51:218–237]

ABSTRACT

This paper asserts that reality testing is a complex ego activity which cannot be characterized globally as either intact or defective. In normals, neurotics, and "borderlines" it is actually a highly variable function. Some problems of nomenclature are addressed. Among many analysts, there is an implicit tendency to concretize the means by which reality testing is performed. This may lead to certain conceptual problems and clinical inaccuracies. The relationship of reality testing to unconscious conflicts from all phases of development is emphasized and illustrated. Issues in the technical handling in analysis of manifestations of disturbed reality testing are discussed.

Several years ago, while I was participating in a Kris Study Group on "borderline cases" in psychoanalytic treatment,[1] my attention was drawn to certain problems in the clinical evaluation of patients'

[1] The Kris Study Group of the New York Psychoanalytic Institute, under the chairmanship of Dr. Charles Brenner, met from 1973 to 1977. A preliminary summary of its findings was presented to the New York Psychoanalytic Society on April 25, 1978. A

capacities to test reality. In the course of discussions, colleagues tended to speak of reality testing as though it could be characterized globally as either intact or defective, and as if the criteria for reaching that judgment in respect to any given patient are well established and generally understood by all analysts. In fact, the term was applied to different kinds of data. Sometimes it referred to what the analyst thought of how the patient acted in various life situations as described in analytic sessions; at other times, it was applied to behavior in the sessions themselves. At still other times, it reflected an evaluation of their patients' reported thoughts, judgments, perceptions, and/or interpretations of themselves, their analysts, or other people and situations they had encountered. It also became apparent, as examples accumulated, that the extent and degree of failure or defect in reality testing was quite variable, as was its tendency to persist or recur.

The literature on the topic is extensive but rather confusing. A review of a number of essential contributions, in conjunction with an examination of the clinical material brought forward in the Study Group, suggests that some clarifications and simplifications concerning reality testing are warranted. I believe that insofar as analytic data shed light on the problem, the aberrations of reality testing which afflicted the sicker patients we studied are not demonstrably different in nature from those milder fluctuations inherent in all neurotic symptomatology or, for that matter, from those evident in so-called normal mental functioning, when it is subject to very close scrutiny as well. They are, to be sure, far more blatant and disruptive, both in the analytic situation and in the lives of those more disturbed patients. However, the assumption that their increased severity is attributable to a unique underlying defect of some kind, or to essentially different mental mechanisms, has not been convincingly documented, in my view, while similarities to lesser degrees of difficulty are, on the other hand, clinically verifiable.

Our collaborative work on "borderlines" led me to become interested in certain implications of reality testing as a clinical concept which

---

monograph based on this material is currently in press (Abend, Porder, and Willick, 1982).

apply to all patients, not just to the sickest ones. To my knowledge, the literature does not contain a generally comprehensive formulation of the problem along lines which are supported by the clinical findings of psychoanalysis. Detailed illustrations of the data in respect to reality testing in "borderline cases" can be found in the Kris Study Group monograph (Abend, Porder, and Willick, 1982). For the purposes of this presentation I will confine myself to the following: (1) summarizing certain key contributions to the sizable literature on reality testing; (2) underlining the disadvantageous tendency to concretize the means of testing reality; (3) highlighting the potential confusion inherent in certain aspects of nomenclature; (4) formulating, in a general way, what can be said about all degrees of disturbance of reality testing from the standpoint of metapsychology; (5) raising questions about the kinds of conflicts which contribute to these problems; (6) offering a suggestion that subjective disturbances in the feeling of reality are more accurately regarded as independent symptoms, unrelated to those other disturbances of perception, thought, judgment, and behavior subsumed under the heading of faulty reality testing; and, finally, (7) calling attention to certain problems of technique in respect to the analysis of these disturbances, in the milder as well as the more blatant forms in which they are regularly encountered in the analytic situation.

Although the essence of Freud's ideas about reality testing was already implicit in Chapter VII of *The Interpretation of Dreams* (1900), he actually introduced the term in his 1911 paper, *Formulations on the Two Principles of Mental Functioning*. His interest was in formulating the development of the mental apparatus, especially in respect to the evolution of the secondary process. In a key passage he stated, "A new principle of mental functioning was thus introduced; what was presented in the mind was no longer what was agreeable, but what was real, even if it happened to be disagreeable" (p. 219). The operation of the reality principle, which only partly supplanted the (newly renamed) pleasure principle, assumed, among other things, acquisition of the means to distinguish what is real from what is merely imagined. Freud's description of the factors involved in this developing capacity was, in essence, a preliminary formulation of the ego functions which facilitate reality testing, although, as Hartmann (1956) pointed out, this paper antedated the beginnings of ego psychology by a dozen years. Freud (1911) included heightened importance of the sense organs and of *consciousness* and *attention; memory* and *objective judgment* were added to complete the picture. These are contrasted in operation to *repression*, which Freud said merely follows the dictates of the pleasure-unpleasure principle. Reality testing, unlike repression, may lead to decisions about the truth or falsity of ideas.

In *A Metapsychological Supplement to the Theory of Dreams* Freud (1917) addressed the problem of how hallucinatory images are sometimes able to overpower reality testing. He began with an idea, first expressed in *Instincts and Their Vicissitudes* (1915), that perceptions of external events can be distinguished from perceptions from inside the organism according to whether or not they can be made to disappear by muscular action. He then reasoned that the system *Cs (pcpt)*" must have at its disposal a motor innervation which determines whether the perception can be made to disappear or whether it proves resistant. Reality-testing need be nothing more than this contrivance" (1917, p. 233). He went on to suggest that unacceptable reality might, by influencing the withdrawal of cathexis from the system *Cs (pcpt)*, abolish the possibility of reality testing, thus already clearly stating the case for a defensive interference with reality testing. The essential point was to emphasize the distinguishing of perceptions from ideas, or, in other words, the crucial decision was whether a given mental stimulus originated inside or outside the mind.

Freud restated his ideas in the paper "Negation" (1925), with additional refinements. The question became "whether something which is in the ego as a presentation can be rediscovered in perception (reality) as well. It is, we see, once more a question of *external* and *internal*. What is unreal, merely a presentation and subjective, is only internal; what is real is also there *outside*" (p. 237). He added that presentations of perceptions are not always faithful; they "may be modified by omissions, or changed by the merging of various elements. In that case, reality-testing has to ascertain how far such distortions go" (p. 238). Once again he had emphasized that perceptions are vulnerable to defensive alteration, and he laid the burden of assessing that possibility upon reality testing.

Although these contributions unmistakably reveal the stamp of clinical experience, they are expressed in the form of theoretical expositions of mental development, to which Freud was devoted throughout his career. A recent extensive review article by Hurvich (1970) indicated that much of the subsequent literature on the subject follows this model, addressing itself to presumptive explanations of the psychological factors involved in gaining and exercising a knowledge and understanding of reality in mental life. Clinical studies of the circumstances under which reality testing fails are fewer in number. Ferenczi's classic "Stages in the Development of the Sense of Reality" (1913) is a case in point. Its sole clinical base is the observation that obsessional patients believe in the omnipotence of their thoughts, feelings, and wishes. His description of the antecedent stages of magical thinking, which has become so widely accepted, is a hypothetical construct of compelling intuition. The theoretical and developmental speculations of other writers have given rise to some less convincing theories.

For instance, in Federn's (1952) work, an explanatory model different from Freud's was utilized. He suggested that what he called the "sense of reality" becomes the means of distinguishing internal from external stimuli. This qualitative experiential distinction is a function of the "boundaries of the ego" acting analogously to organs of perception. He applied his theory to clinical problems, explaining symptoms of estrangement (Federn, 1927) by means of a postulated mechanism of variability in the energic investment of the ego boundaries. Although Federn's ideas no longer appear to command much attention from contemporary analysts, they do illustrate very well several problems which have continued to complicate the clinical study of reality testing in subsequent years.

The first of these is the problem of nomenclature. E. Weiss (1952), in his introduction to Federn's *Ego Psychology and the Psychoses*, indicated that *reality testing* is a term to be applied only to the process of obtaining knowledge of reality, while *sense of reality* refers to the more important discrimination of what is real and what is unreal.

Modell (1968) pointed out the efforts of analytic observers to break down the reality testing concept into separate parts, noting the lack of uniformity which resulted. Unfortunately, he then inadvertently illustrated the problem when, after stating his agreement with Frosch's (1964) attempt to distinguish the *relationship with reality* from *reality testing*, he went on (pp. 90–91) to use both terms somewhat differently from the way Frosch did.

Frosch (1964) actually proposed differentiating three areas, the *relationship with reality*, the *feeling of reality*, and the capacity to *test reality*, although he acknowledged that they are functionally interwoven (p. 84). He said that the relationship with reality "involves a person's capacity to perceive the external and internal world and the appropriateness of his relationship with them" (p. 84). Feelings of reality refer to subjective sensations of the reality (or alteration of it) of what is perceived, while testing of reality means the capacity to "evaluate appropriately the reality of phenomena going on around and within . . . " (p. 86). On the other hand, Modell (1968) apparently thought of the relationship to reality as referring to the degree of psychological interest an individual is able to maintain in external reality, while all evaluative functions were subsumed under the heading of reality testing, in his interpretation.

Still further confusion may attend the distinction between *reality principle* and *reality testing*. While it is clear that Freud meant the reality principle as an abstract conception, its ramifications in respect to describable mental functioning include aspects attributed by others to reality testing. In "Notes on the Reality Principle" Hartmann (1956) pointed out that the reality principle is used in two different ways: (1) the idea of taking into account, from the standpoint of adaptation, the "real" features (*i.e.*, according to the observer) of an object or situation, and (2) the tendency to shift activities away from immediate needs for discharge. Difficulties in the first area clearly manifest themselves as misreadings or misjudgments of features of reality, while problems in the second area may appear as impulsivity or, generally speaking, as difficulties in control of libidinal and/or aggressive tensions. The behavior which expresses these latter tendencies is often described as unrealistic or inappropriate by clinicians. Careful examination of the mental content of analysands who have control problems of this sort may indeed reveal that they are able to assess reality quite well, including the possible consequences of their activities, but disregard such assessments in favor of immediate gratification of certain of their instinctual urges. Hartmann (1956) also stated that "the reality principle includes both knowledge of reality and acting in regard to it" (p. 252). It seems to me, however, that analysts, in evaluating reality testing problems, do not seem especially concerned with distinguishing such patients from others who appear actually to misperceive or misjudge features of reality.

In point of fact, all these niceties of nomenclature seem to be ignored in actual practice. The analysts in the Study Group and those in clinical conferences, discussion groups, and seminars I have attended by and large disregard these attempted distinctions which have entered the literature and speak only of patients' reality testing when they discuss clinical material. In the broadest sense, *they use the term defective reality testing to express a clinical judgment that certain of a patient's views of the world, that is to say, of people and situations, are, or appear to be, quite unrealistic.* Those who are dedicated to greater precision of thought and definition may disagree with or criticize such usage, but I believe it is the rule and not the exception among contemporary analysts.

A second problem that persists in complicating the understanding of reality testing, sometimes in subtle ways, stems from an implicit concretization of the means by which reality is assessed. Freud himself was fond of mechanical analogies, and Federn's (1952) notion of the ego boundaries as a sort of organ of perception, although expressed impressionistically, is also a mechanistic model. It is as though reality testing is a function performed by a piece of psychic apparatus—a complicated measuring and recording device of sorts. Its components, to be sure, are sense organs, consciousness, attention, memory, and judgment, as Freud said in 1911, all arranged in some contraption like a scientific instrument, as it were. This "instrument," then, may be imagined to be working properly or not as an entity; or perhaps instead it may be regarded as having a certain inherent degree of accuracy, less in sicker patients, greater in those who are healthier.

The implication of this concrete model of how reality testing is performed is that individuals have some sort of baseline capacity in this regard, albeit one which can be altered by special circumstances, such as psychotic decompensation or drug intoxication, to choose obvious examples. Furthermore, this baseline reading, whatever it may be, affords a fundamental measurement of the severity of the pathology which afflicts a given patient. Thus, "intact reality testing," included in a clinical assessment, may be offered as a reassurance of analyzability while, conversely, "defective reality testing" immediately suggests more grave pathology and reservations about analyzability.

Perhaps a more sophisticated version of this theoretical assumption is that the variations in reality testing observed in healthier patients are attributable to the impact of neurotic conflicts, but that other, sicker patients' psychic apparatuses include some more global "weakness" or "defect" in the sphere of reality testing. This latter condition may be presumed to be derived from constitutional sources or from early traumatization, or both, but whether the origin is specified or not, it is regarded as comprising a sort of deficiency state, *i.e.*, "defective reality testing," with implications for pathology and analyzability as noted.

Modell (1968), who explicitly disagrees with the notion that reality testing works in an all-or-nothing way, nevertheless suggests a more complex, but fundamentally analogous, explanation of how it works, based upon "two organs for the structuring of reality." One is represented by genetically determined autonomous ego structures, which are impaired only if there has been an absence of the maternal environment in the course of development. The second is a structure formed by each individual that requires "good enough mothering" for healthy development. Even in psychotics, he believes, the autonomous structures can provide accurate data of reality, although it is likely to be masked by the effect of the pathological functioning of the second organization. According to Modell, the central theme of this second structure is related to the capacity for acceptance of (painful) separateness of objects.

All such schemata suffer from the disadvantage that they tend to favor categorical distinctions, which may interfere with accurate observations of the specific and highly individual variability of reality testing. They also seem to favor the belief that reality testing is a capacity which, from a developmental standpoint, is primarily derived from and influenced by the earliest interactions with the environment.

Hartmann's (1956) contribution to the subject was a complex and sophisticated analysis of the issues involved, and it defies ready synopsis. He elaborated on Freud's point that the reality principle is a modification of the pleasure principle, showing that ego development leads to a reassessment of pleasure values. While the id does not change, the interactions of the systems can and do become modified. What are altered, then, are not the characteristics of pleasure-unpleasure, but the conditions which determine each of them. For instance, for a child, instinctual renunciation may be compensated for, and thus facilitated by, the anticipation of parental approval as a substitute kind of pleasure. Instinctual renunciation, originally merely unpleasurable, can actually become pleasurable as the ego develops.

Hartmann also noted that there is not a simple correlation between the degree of objective insight and the degree of adaptiveness of the corresponding action that follows upon it. He observed that what may be adaptive in one respect may well interfere with adaptation in another.

He moved to the heart of the question of reality testing when he showed that even knowledge of reality is subject to inevitable distortion. As a consequence of the child's great dependence on objects, these relationships influence his or her mind in respect to such fundamentals as concept formation, language, habits of thought and emotion, and even perception. The pleasures to be gained from conforming often lead to "the acceptance by the child of erroneous and biased views which the parents hold of reality" (p. 256). In short, tensions will develop between a knowledge of, in Hartmann's language, "objective" or "scientific" reality and a knowledge of *social* reality. The concept of objective reality as used by Freud, Hartmann said, is opposed both by what we refer to as magical thinking and also by a view of reality "in which not validation but intersubjective acceptance is used as a criterion . . ." (p. 259).

Certainly our studies of "borderline" patients (Abend, Porder, and Willick, 1982) have confirmed the correctness and importance of Hartmann's observations on social versus scientific reality. Moreover, the influence that parental reality pathology has on a child's development is neither confined to the earliest months of life nor limited to the mother's relationship with the child. One patient, for example, had totally internalized her father's propensity for frightening and bizarre catastrophic hypochondriacal beliefs and preoccupations. Another had taken in and taken over her mother's pathological denials of, and distortions regarding, the circumstances surrounding her father's repeated abandonments of them, which began during the latter part of the second year of her life and recurred until his final departure when she was twelve. To these we may add that when one or both parents are very sick themselves, children not infrequently develop powerful needs to deny the painful reality they observe—*i.e.*, the manifestations of the illness of their parent(s)—and also to deny what they themselves really wish in respect to that reality.

Another major contribution to the understanding of reality testing was Arlow's (1969a) paper, "Fantasy, Memory, and Reality Testing." His essential point was that there is a continuous and inescapable interaction between what he called "fantasy thinking" and the perceptual input registering aspects of external reality. He referred to a striking visual analogy of two motion picture projectors' simultaneously flashing images on opposite sides of a translucent screen. Continuous ego activity must go on, evaluating and attempting to integrate these different factors in reaching judgments about what is real. However, fantasy thinking is largely unconscious and is inevitably centered around the crucial instinctual concerns of childhood mental life and their associated conflicts and derivatives. It is therefore likely to be a source of wishful and defensive distortions in the amalgamated final products of the ego's perpetual integrative activities, which can never be completely discounted. Although Arlow stopped short of saying so categorically in this paper, we can see that Freud's concept that reality testing must discriminate between inner and outer sources of stimuli describes a task that is impossible to accomplish in any absolute sense.

No individual is without an unconscious fantasy life, and no individual completely and permanently abolishes the influence of instinctual conflicts on it, even with the aid of analysis. Even with optimal results, one cannot maintain continuous conscious awareness of all these conflictual elements. Therefore, no individual can always take into account their impact on the perception and evaluation of external stimuli. Thus, it follows that reality testing is always potentially subject to some limitations. It is not so much a question of defective reality testing as opposed to intact reality testing, but of assaying the nature and degree of the defect, a far more relative and variable distinction. The clinical issue becomes one of evaluating how significant its effect is and of ascertaining the circumstances in which the extent and impact of deficiencies in reality testing are most likely to be evident. Implicit in this task is the assessment of the role of various factors, such as unconscious fantasies and the effect of social forces, both familial and cultural, to which Arlow and Hartmann have called attention. The possible impact of special features, such as physical limitations and handicaps and their psychological elaborations, may also be added to the list of influences to be considered.

Viewing the problem from another perspective, *all degrees of disturbance of reality testing may be understood as manifestations of the impingement of unconscious conflict and its consequences on the capacity to perceive, remember, think, and judge with "realistic" objectivity.* This constitutes the "final common pathway" in which biological, psychological, and social forces become confluent and achieve their pattern of expression. It follows from this restatement that conflicts from *all* stages of development, not just the very earliest ones, may bring about such disturbances, and this can be readily confirmed by clinical observation. On the other hand, tempting as the search for broadly and uniformly applicable explanations for the so-called more serious degrees of disturbed reality testing may be, analytic data do not support across-the-board distinctions and explanations very well at all. What the Kris Study Group observed was that material from *many* conflicts at *all* levels seemed involved in the reality testing deficiencies of "borderlines."

Hartmann (1956) pointed out that highly charged areas, such as sexuality, are particularly vulnerable to subjective deformation, and the material considered by the Kris Study Group confirmed that many manifestations of problems with reality testing appeared in the context of the complications of sexual wishes and their attendant conflicts and fantasies. This is hardly a new observation; Freud, Ferenczi, and others have noted that special conditions in respect to reality apply to sexual wishes in the mental life of humans. In present-day psychoanalysis, we place emphasis on the role of anxiety, which is invariably associated with the child's observations of the anatomical differences between the sexes and of the primal scene, and which also accompanies infantile theories of sex and childbirth and the wishes connected with them. In the clinical setting of analytic therapy, it is precisely these anxiety-laden wishes, fantasies, thoughts, and experiences that frequently appear to be associated with perceptual distortions, persistent irrational beliefs, and alterations of memory. In fact, late in his life, when Freud departed from his schematic dichotomy regarding patients' relation to reality and described the split in the ego in respect to reality (1927, 1940), it was clinical material of precisely this nature that he cited as evidence for his revised postulate. Modell (1968) has, quite correctly in my opinion, related these later observations of Freud's to the theoretical problem of reality testing.

Arlow (1969a), with reference to an observation made by Lewin (1948), noted and described patients who, because they unconsciously equate reality with the female genital, treat it in a manner analogous to the way fetishists treat the genital itself: "They refuse to face it. They cannot take a really good look at anything. This tendency influences them in the direction of impracticality and propels them into unrealistic behavior in many areas of their lives" (Arlow, 1969a, p. 44).

The small group of patients studied most thoroughly by the Kris Study Group on "borderlines" demonstrated without exception that sexual conflicts interfered with reality testing, sometimes in dramatic fashion. Other conflicts, of course, also did so. For example, murderous rivalry with a sibling, completely concealed from consciousness by strong reaction formations, so pervaded the mental life of one patient that she regularly misinterpreted social and professional situations and was convinced that others, who represented sibling substitutes, were hostile toward her. She selectively exaggerated minor incidents and ascribed motivation to others' behavior in accordance with her projected aggression and guilt. *What was clear in the clinical material we studied was that any and all conflicts, not just early ones, could bring about unconscious interference with reality testing.* Furthermore, even with these very ill patients, whose reality distortions were more blatant and more persistent than those we usually encounter with neurotic analysands, analytic progress was regularly accompanied by notable improvement in their reality testing. This served to support the impression that the amelioration of sexual and aggressive unconscious conflicts from all levels of development leads to improved ego functioning in those areas which subserve reality testing.

I should now like to take up a third problem, already in evidence in Federn's work, that even today continues to complicate the study of reality testing: the assumption that alterations in subjective feelings about reality, such as the sense of estrangement or derealization, as we usually call it, are inherently linked to the other manifestations of faulty reality testing we have been considering. Since Federn's explanation of this symptom was essentially an economic one, derived from the model of a sense organ of reality perception whose functioning was affected by changes in cathexis, this kinship seemed an entirely plausible one. Frosch treated them as correlated, as do, I believe, most contemporary analysts. Yet, unless one subscribes to the notion that an organ of reality perception exists and that alterations in its mode of functioning are perceived as subjective variations in the feeling of reality, why should a structural correlation be assumed?

In fact, explanations of derealization which are independent of content, *i.e.*, of its unconscious meaning, are derived from theoretical assumptions about the functioning of the mental apparatus which necessitate subscribing to a belief in endopsychic perception. A quite different approach is advocated by Arlow (1966, 1969b), who suggests instead that the report of such subjective experiences should be treated the same as any other analytic data—subjected to scrutiny, with the aid of free association, to determine its exact meaning in the mental life of the patient. My own preference is for the latter course. An analogous critique concerning subjective reports of identity disturbances was put forth by Spiegel (1959) and elaborated on by Abend (1974).

In the small study population of "borderline" patients to which I have referred, symptoms of estrangement and the like were, in fact, not a notable feature of *any* of the cases, contrary to expectation. In contrast, a recent clinical instance which occurred in a patient whom I did not consider to be severely ill serves to illustrate the relation of derealization to conflict, and so-called "higher-level," phallic-oedipal conflict at that. This young woman had been struggling in her analysis against acceptance of the importance in her mental life of unconscious fantasies of having been castrated. She was knowledgeable about analysis and psychodynamics and recognized and understood the implications of her own associations very well, but an important transference manifestation of her wish for phallic equality was expressed through her stubborn, argumentative, although generally good-humored resistance to my interpretive efforts. In one session, which centered on memories of a serious childhood injury, its interconnection with the theme of castration was unmistakable, but she continued to make fun of these connections and of my "Freudian orthodoxy" to the end of the hour. The next day she reported that on leaving the office she had been overcome by a powerful and distressing feeling that everything around her had changed and felt strange and unreal. She was so upset that she had to sit down on the steps which lead to my office suite for quite some time before she had felt able to go home. She had wept uncontrollably, not knowing quite why. The feelings of derealization persisted all that night and were still present on this, the following day, although to a milder degree. So distressed was she, and distracted by these uncomfortable feelings, that she could not recall what we had been talking about in the session before she became upset.

Other material reintroduced the theme of sexual differences, which reminded her of the content of the previous hour. Her subsequent associations focused on this material until she spontaneously brought up the recollection that in her childhood one of the ways she had of distinguishing between males and females was that the latter have to sit down to urinate! Suddenly the connection to her need to sit down the previous day was clear.

Her weeping (Greenacre, 1945), the accompanying feeling of sadness, and the need to think that what she saw and felt were strange and unreal (referring to perceptions of her own and others' anatomy and to fantasies of damage to her genitalia) became progressively clarified as well. Confirmatory material continued to "pour out," so to speak, and toward the end of the hour she observed that the feelings of unreality were gone.

The proposition that a greater propensity to experience symptoms of derealization is derived from problems at the very earliest stages of development is difficult to document with analytic data, as are analogous theories about the vulnerability of reality testing. An uncritical adherence to this theoretical position may, as in the Federn example, reduce the analyst's interest in seeking out the specific unconscious content connected with these symptoms. Certainly, such an assumption might have handicapped the analysis of the incident just recounted. To concentrate both on disturbances of reality testing and on alterations of feelings of reality (even if, as I believe, the two are unrelated) as symptoms, rather than as manifestations of deficiency states or developmental defects, can facilitate our understanding of them in yet another way. To so identify them—that is, as symptoms—calls attention to the fact that they are the product of compromise formation. Accordingly, the role of the superego in their genesis is more likely to be appreciated than it would be otherwise. This point was elaborated and convincingly documented by Stein (1966) in his paper, "Self Observation, Reality, and the Superego." One of the patients in the Kris Group "borderline" study was so agitated by guilt following her first gratifying coital experience that she would not answer her telephone afterward, convinced that her parents were calling to berate her.

Stein (1966) also addressed the important question of how analysis attempts to deal with patients' faulty reality testing in the following passage:

> Our approach differs from other psychotherapies in that we explicitly *avoid* reality testing—at least in the usual sense.

> We need not tell our patients that they have misjudged a life situation, nor do we as a rule give in to the temptation to correct a misapprehension of some analytic event. Instead, we attempt to correct, by analysis, those distortions of self observation which become evident in the analytic situation. By attaining a clearer vision of his own mental processes, by unsparing honesty with himself, we hope that our patients' distortions of perception of the outer world will be reduced to a minimum (p. 276).

This theoretically sound technical prescription is one which is frequently ignored, to judge from clinical discussions. Two chief rationales for explicit educative or confrontational comments are often presented. One is simply that "sicker" patients require such help as part of an adequate therapeutic program to enable them to manage their lives. This appears to be based on an assumption that their problems with reality testing derive from, or at any rate constitute, a deficiency state rather than represent a potentially reversible symptom. The latter view is a more accurate assessment, and it yields a more fruitful analytic benefit, as I have tried to indicate.

The second justification for correcting patients' misinterpretations and misjudgments is that this step facilitates analytic scrutiny of the sources of the distortion. Here, an adequate discussion would necessitate the detailed examination of a number of specific clinical instances, but this would be beyond the scope of this presentation. Obviously, the range of possible technical approaches is broad. For instance: supplying correct information; indicating directly that a misperception or misinterpretation exists; implying that is the case by virtue of questioning the patient's basis for a statement or a judgment, calling attention to the manner in which such material has been presented, or offering interpretive commentary as to the source and nature of the distortion without any of the above intervening steps—all these constitute a variety of technical maneuvers which may be applied in different situations.

On the whole, analysts are probably more alert to the advantages of the stance advocated by Stein (1966) when distortions arise in respect to the analyst, since the possibility that correction may serve to blunt or discourage the expression of transference fantasies and their accompanying affects is widely recognized and generally regarded as undesirable. The handling of situations in which events and relationships outside of the analysis are being described is less uniformly agreed upon, according to my observations. These pose interesting questions for discussion, among which is the sometimes overlooked one of the possible unconscious dynamic significance of the patient's *presenting* such distortions to the analyst. What transference fantasy or fantasies may be expressed in such behavior on the part of the analysand?

To illustrate the point, the following brief clinical example, commonplace rather than unusual, will serve. A married woman, in analysis for a number of years, from time to time reported incidents in which she experienced her husband as contemptuous, critical, and belittling, if not outright abusive. Although throughout the analysis her accounts of his behavior had consistently given the impression of a rigid, angry, and perfectionistic man, the incidents in question appeared to the analyst to be distorted, exaggerated, and misinterpreted. Furthermore, at other times the patient had given indication of an awareness that she tended toward a selective skewing of the picture in her describing of her husband. Attention to the disturbance in reality testing had been focused for a long time on establishing its exact nature and then elucidating the unconscious sadomasochistic fantasies which contributed to its genesis. This conventional approach perhaps delayed an appreciation that the patient was subtly issuing an appeal to the analyst to intervene and rescue her, which corresponded to some aspects of important family romance fantasies. However, the distortions of reality testing had still another, more specific meaning. They proclaimed that the patient was merely a small, frightened, confused, and innocent child, who wished from the analyst only a parent's sympathy and protection, not the response of a romantic hero. In this defensive transference fantasy she also repeated the wish for her mother's aid and comfort against an older brother, who was at times haughty and ridiculing.

In sum, it seems fair to say that the technical handling of faulty reality testing is not a simple matter, but that it poses many problems.

Implicit theoretical assumptions about the origin of the difficulty are likely to exert an influence on analysts' technique. A more explicit consideration of the basis for one's approaches to the varied spectrum of manifestations of faulty reality testing may prove illuminating and useful in clinical practice.

Summary

In clinical discussions, reality testing is spoken of as though it can be characterized globally as either intact or defective; it is, in fact, invoked in respect to different kinds of clinical data and is both varied and variable in its manifestations.

Freud's ideas on the subject are summarized. He emphasized the distinction between internal and external sources of mental stimuli and noted the potential for defensive and wishful alterations of perception.

The problem of inconsistent and confusing nomenclature is addressed. Attempts to define different aspects of reality testing have not produced uniformity of usage and seem to be ignored in actual practice by most analysts. Analysts apparently use the idea of defective reality testing to express their clinical judgment that certain of a patient's views of the world, that is to say, of people and situations, are or appear to be quite unrealistic. An implicit concretization of the means by which reality testing is assessed seems rather widespread. This concretization leads to certain incorrect assumptions tending to favor categorical distinctions which may interfere with accurate observation of the specific and highly individual variability of reality testing.

All degrees of disturbance of reality testing may be understood as manifestations of the impingement of unconscious conflict and its consequences on the capacity to perceive, remember, think, and judge with realistic objectivity. Conflicts from all stages of development, not just the very earliest ones, may bring about such disturbances. The assumption that alterations of subjective feelings of reality, such as derealization, are closely linked to the other manifestations of faulty reality testing is questioned. Although unrelated, both kinds of disturbance are most usefully regarded as symptoms, that is, as products of compromise formation, and the superego, like the other components of instinctual conflict, plays a role in their genesis.

Analysis of the important conflicts that interfere with reality testing, comprising ego functions, regularly leads to improvement in its manifestations, even in "borderline" patients. Certain problems in the technical handling of manifestations of disturbed reality testing are noted.

References

Abend, S.M. (1974). Problems of identity. Theoretical and clinical applications. *Psychoanalytic Quarterly* 43:606–637.

——— Porder, M.S. and Willick, M.S. (1982). *Borderline Patients: Psychoanalytic Perspectives.* New York: International University Press.

Arlow, J.A. (1966). Depersonalization and derealization. In: *Psychoanalysis—A General Psychology: Essays in Honor of Heinz Hartmann*, ed. R.M. Loewenstein, et al. New York: International University Press, pp. 456–478.

——— (1969a). Fantasy, memory, and reality testing. *Psychoanalytic Quarterly* 38:28–51.

——— (1969b). Unconscious fantasy and disturbances of conscious experience. *Psychoanalytic Quarterly* 38:1–27.

Federn, P. (1927). Narcissism in the structure of the ego. In: *Ego Psychology and the Psychoses*, ed. E. Weiss. New York: Basic Books, 1952, pp. 38–59.

——— (1952). *Ego Psychology and the Psychoses*, ed. E. Weiss. New York: Basic Books.

Ferenczi, S. (1913). Stages in the development of the sense of reality. In: *Sex in Psychoanalysis.* New York: Basic Books, 1950 pp. 213–239.

Freud, S. (1900). The interpretation of dreams. *Standard Edition* 4/5.

——— (1911). Formulations on the two principles of mental functioning. *Standard Edition* 12.

——— (1915). Instincts and their vicissitudes. *Standard Edition* 14.

——— (1917). A metapsychological supplement to the theory of dreams. *Standard Edition* 14.

——— (1925). Negation. *Standard Edition* 19.

——— (1927). Fetishism. *Standard Edition* 21.

——— (1940). Splitting of the ego in the process of defence. *Standard Edition* 23.

Frosch, J. (1964). The psychotic character: clinical psychiatric considerations. *Psychiatry Quarterly* 38:81–96.

——— (1970). Psychoanalytic considerations of the psychotic character *Journal of the American Psychoanalytic Association* 18:24–50.

Greenacre, P. (1945). Pathological weeping. *Psychoanalytic Quarterly* 14:62–75.

Hartmann, H. (1956). Notes on the reality principle. In: *Essays on Ego Psychology: Selected Problems in Psychoanalytic Theory*. New York: International University Press, 1964, pp. 241–267.

Hurvich, M. (1970). On the concept of reality testing. *International Journal of Psycho-Analysis* 51:299–312.

Lewin, B.D. (1948). The nature of reality, the meaning of nothing, with an addendum on concentration In *Selected Writings of Bertram D. Lewin* ed. J.A. Arlow. New York: The Psychoanalytic Quarterly Inc., 1973, pp. 320–322.

Modell, A.H. (1968). Object Love and Reality. *An Introduction to a Psychoanalytic Theory of Object Relations*. New York: International University Press.

Spiegel, L.A. (1959). The self, the sense of self, and perception. *Psychoanalytic Study of the Child* 14:81–109.

Stein, M.H. (1966). Self observation, reality, and the superego In *Psychoanalysis—A General Psychology: Essays in Honor of Heinz Hartmann*, ed. R.M. Loewenstein, et al. New York: International University Press, pp. 275–297.

Weiss, E. (1952). *Introduction to Ego Psychology and the Psychoses by P. Federn*. New York: Basic Books.

CHAPTER 3

Neglected Classics: Ernst Kris's "On Some Vicissitudes of Insight in Psychoanalysis"[1]

[Abend, S. (1988). *Psychoanalytic Quarterly* 57:224–228]

At first glance it may seem surprising that I suggest regarding Ernst Kris's extraordinary paper, "On Some Vicissitudes of Insight in Psychoanalysis," as a neglected classic, since it is cited in the literature with considerable frequency. In my experience, the majority of references to it are for reasons that are quite peripheral to its central thesis. Authors often note a passage to be found in the introductory paragraphs in which Kris characterizes psychoanalysis as a process, although he meant by that no more than that psychoanalysis has a quality "of progressive development over time in a definite direction" (p. 253). Another reason analysts have for referring to the paper is that they recall that Kris describes in it what he calls "the good analytic hour," one in which many strands of the material seem to come together in an especially comprehensible and meaningful way. In fact, both of these ideas are presented by Kris merely as preparatory to the exploration of

[1] I wish to express my appreciation to Drs. Manuel Furer and Charles Brenner, whose commentaries increased my understanding of Kris's work, and to my colleagues of the C.O.P.E. Study Group on the Psychoanalytic Educational Process, whose deliberations gave me the idea of writing this paper.

the problems that really interest him. These have to do with the nature of insight in psychoanalysis, the quality of the ego functions involved in acquiring insight, and some subtle difficulties that can affect the experience of obtaining insight in certain patients. His conclusions are by and large overlooked, even though they are derived from admirably astute and sophisticated clinical observations, and though they represented a significant advance in clinical theory at the time the paper was first published. In my opinion, his exposition of the issues that drew his attention is still valuable and deserves more notice than it receives; that constitutes my justification for designating this paper a truly neglected classic.

Kris compares the uniquely elaborate configuration of connections that he says marks the so-called "good analytic hour" with the far more usual "oscillating character of other analytic sessions." He goes on to describe the familiar pattern of typical analytic work, during which analyst and patient are struggling to make sense out of dimly perceived, fragmentary patterns of unconscious mentation. He says of it, "Over a stretch of time the analyst can piece together some of the slight elevations in the patient's productions, as they reveal outlines of a larger submerged formation" (p. 256). One purpose of the paper is to expand our awareness of the operation of ego functions, particularly the silent, integrative ones, and he suggests that the so-called "good analytic hour" is evidence that such integration has been going on in the patient, below the surface of conscious awareness, as the analysis proceeds.

Kris's careful attention to the qualities of good analytic hours leads him to conclude that these have an "infantile prototype," by which he means that the patient's way of experiencing such hours is influenced by some prominent unconscious attitude or fantasy drawn from infantile mental life. He adds, "It seems also relevant to stress that this prototype determines the state of the transference. It is not so that positive transference determines the successful work of the ego" (p. 257). Without fanfare, he has thus profoundly altered Freud's formulations, as set forth in the papers on technique (1912, 1915) and the *Introductory*

Lectures (1916–1917), about patients' motivation for pursuing the difficulties essential to productive analytic achievement.

Kris has barely warmed to his task, for he concludes that the experience of insight itself also has an infantile prototype. He records observations of various activities that superficially resemble insight, but in which, in actuality, aims such as compliance in the service of concealed transference gratifications, or activity unconsciously designed to achieve or maintain a competitive independence from the analyst, may predominate. Another type of pseudo-insight is the tendency of certain patients to artificially synthesize everything in their lives into the same model, perhaps one derived from a single childhood catastrophe.

He attributes these miscarriages of insight to incomplete neutralization of the energy involved in the integrative function of the ego. Kris is clearly trying to reconcile the then relatively new concepts of autonomy of ego functions and neutralization of energy with the facts of clinical observation. He reaches the sort of conclusion that characterizes the work of the best analytic thinkers: "It is as if in every case the function of insight was differently determined, and its impact differently embedded in the balance of the personality" (p. 263). Kris has grasped that the very activities that are integral to the analytic enterprise have important unconscious meanings that are unique to each patient, and that these must receive analytic scrutiny, since the total autonomy of these vital ego functions is no more than an heuristic fiction.

The radical nature of this approach to analyzing may be less than obvious to our current awareness, since the principles involved have been thoroughly absorbed into modern theory and practice. Nevertheless, trying to impart these ideas to candidates reminds one that this is far from self-evident material; perhaps even experienced practitioners may lose sight of some ramifications of these issues from time to time.

Kris goes on to illustrate aspects of his conclusions by means of a detailed examination of some subfunctions of the ego, so to say, that subserve insight and the patient's ability to participate in the analytic process. He mentions first the control of temporary and partial regression, such as is necessary for optimal free association. Less satisfactorily autonomous variants of this capability are encountered in those difficult patients who may drift into isolation and soliloquy, thus losing effective contact with the analyst, and in the ones who are unable to relinquish control sufficiently to permit the requisite access to "all levels of inner sources." The essential ability to exercise reasonably objective self-observation is likewise subject to excessive investment in instinctual meaning that may serve to limit its utility. Kris mentions patients who are prone to compulsive self-criticism that masquerades as self-awareness, and others whose self-observation shades into "narcissistic introspection." Clinical experience with patients who display prominent versions of one or another of these powerful resistances must have been familiar to many analysts before Kris recorded his observations, but his thoughtful and convincing identification of what these patterns signify is a valuable contribution to clinical theory.

Kris concludes the paper with some observations about changes in other aspects of ego functioning that may be noticed only as analysis progresses, including the diminution of the tendency toward certain kinds of actions and the modulation of the affective accompaniments to the periodic reappearances of critical conflictual material. These, too, seem hardly revolutionary to our current sensibility. Perhaps the greatest tribute to the nature of Kris's thought is precisely the degree to which these ideas seem familiar, even elementary, to experienced analysts of today. A rereading of this paper with its historical context in mind cannot fail to stir renewed appreciation for the gifts of the man who wrote it. Clear, accurate, clinical observations and descriptions are coupled with a thorough, subtle, and even profound pursuit of their implications for theory and practice. Courageous revision of established ideas is presented in a modest, careful, and understated fashion that seeks to conserve what is valid, while rendering it ever more complete, correct, and useful. The paper exemplifies a standard of work to which we might all aspire, to our own benefit and to that of the profession.

References

Freud, S. (1912). The Dynamics of Transference. *Standard Edition* 12.

——— (1915). Observations on Transference-Love. (Further recommendations on the technique of psycho-analysis, III.) *Standard Edition* 12.

———(1916–1917). Introductory Lectures on Psycho-analysis. *Standard Edition* 16.

Kris, E. (1956). On some vicissitudes of insight in psychoanalysis. In: *Selected Papers of Ernst Kris.* New Haven: Yale University Press, 1975, pp. 252–271.

CHAPTER 4

The Psychoanalytic Process: Motives and Obstacles in the Search for Clarification

[Abend, S. (1990). *Psychoanalytic Quarterly* 59:532–549]

ABSTRACT

One motive for regarding psychoanalysis as a "process," and for attempting to define its exact nature, is to enable analysts to clarify their criteria for distinguishing authentic psychoanalysis from other therapies that resemble it or are derived from it. In the present climate of theoretical pluralism, any list of defining qualities that could win wide acceptance would of necessity be cast in terms of such general quality as to limit its utility as a precise template. Another motive for holding on to the "process" concept arises from the unpredictable nature of analytic progress in even the most satisfactory cases.

The direct stimulus for seeking a clarification of the nature of the psychoanalytic process is a pragmatic one. A more precise delineation of the steps, operations, and changes that characterize a true psychoanalytic process would be of considerable help to analysts who are charged with evaluating the clinical work of others, and it would also enhance our ability to assess the utility of theoretical and technical innovations. Sharpening our criteria could also be of great benefit to us in the conduct of our own work with analytic patients and in our efforts to teach others proper technique. There is a less immediately apparent stimulus for the search: we hope to learn something more about those aspects of the psychoanalytic experience that still lie outside of the region covered by our accepted explanatory concepts.

To judge from the frequency with which the term psychoanalytic process is employed, there is a widely held assumption among analysts that there *is* such a thing as a specifiable psychoanalytic process, even though its exact nature has not been defined. For that matter, neither have its characteristic steps been satisfactorily described. In 1984, at the beginning of the collaborative exploration of the subject, of which this and several other papers in this collection are the product, I presented an outline of some problems frequently encountered in attempts to evaluate the psychoanalytic process (Abend, 1986). Analysts, both singly and in groups, formally and informally, regularly judge reports of treatments as succeeding in demonstrating a psychoanalytic process, or as failing to do so. Underlying this practice is an implicit conviction that real psychoanalysis can be distinguished from mere psychoanalytic therapy, and that true psychoanalysis can also be distinguished from certain treatment procedures which the practitioner and his or her patient call psychoanalysis, but which are in fact something else. These distinctions are especially common whenever significant differences in theoretical orientation enter the picture, but they are also often found among colleagues who share the same theoretical position.

By examining problems that lie at the margins of consensus, like the treatment of atypical cases and severe pathology, or the efforts to validate new theoretical stances and technical modifications, I tried to show that our widely accepted propositions are so general in nature that their application is, of necessity, a highly subjective undertaking. It usually rests on refinements and interpretations of the general propositions which are personal and idiosyncratic, or which are shared by subgroups of varying sizes, but which often lead to controversy rather than resolving it. In making that assessment, I did not mean to be nihilistic. I did not believe at that time, any more than I do now, that any treatment that chooses to call itself psychoanalysis is thereby entitled to the name, nor do I believe for a moment that we cannot distinguish good psychoanalysis from bad.

Following a suggestion that arose in our study group, I will try to look for those qualities that often seem to enable large numbers of analysts to recognize the work of others as authentically psychoanalytic in nature. I am by no means certain that this central core of features constitutes a process, but it does provide a description of what psychoanalysis looks like, albeit one that is still cast in rather broad general terms. The six features to be outlined are not intended to constitute even a limited definition of psychoanalysis. However, it may be said of all of them with justification that unless this, and this, and also this are present, the treatment in question is not a true psychoanalysis, irrespective of how helpful it may be as a therapy. Such a list may permit us to redraw the lines at the periphery of what is agreed upon so that we can address the problems that still trouble and divide us in a more productive manner. Later on I shall also consider some implications of our preference for thinking of psychoanalysis as a process in the face of our longstanding difficulty in reaching agreement about its fundamental nature.

The first characteristic to be described has to do with unconscious mentation and its relationship to consciousness. Psychoanalysis has always distinguished itself from other psychologies and other therapies by virtue of its emphasis on unconscious mental contents. Its therapeutic effectiveness has been attributed in large measure to the bringing of previously inaccessible unconscious contents into a meaningful relationship with conscious mental life. Analysts are convinced that wishes, impulses, memories, fantasies, defensive operations of the ego, and superego influences that exist outside of conscious awareness exert a continuous influence on people's normal and pathological mental activities, and consequently on their behavior. The accumulation of clinical experience and the consequent refinement of theory over the years has led to a better understanding of the nature of the unconscious, and a progressively more sophisticated grasp of how the mental apparatus functions to maintain the barriers between unconscious material and consciousness. Analysts of different schools would be likely to identify different aspects of the unconscious as significant, and would also formulate what they identify in varying conceptual languages, but no one whose claim to be a psychoanalyst is taken at all seriously by others dismisses the unconscious as irrelevant, or reduces it to an insignificant role in his or her clinical theory. All analysts would probably agree that in the course of a productive analysis patients may be expected to gain an increasing tolerance for the conscious awareness of formerly sequestered, unacceptable unconscious contents.

A second dimension of the analytic process follows directly from the first. Psychoanalysts since Freud have been interested in identifying and altering those qualities or forces in the mind that function to resist the recognition, revelation, and comprehension of the nature and significance of the unconscious. These aspects of mind, at least partially unconscious themselves, are subsumed under the rubric of resistance or defense. The term "resistance" is less frequently employed today than in the past because it carries the connotation of opposing the goals of analysis or the activities of the analyst, while defense is generally thought of as a more objective and more flexible concept. Defenses are those activities of the mind aimed at warding off other mental contents, including thoughts, perceptions, wishes, memories, fantasies, and/or affects, the full conscious awareness of which would be experienced as unpleasurable. Our current understanding of defensive functioning is far more complex than in the past; we now realize that any mental activity can be used to serve defensive ends; thus, for example, one affective trend or form of instinctual expression may at times be used to defend against another.

It would not be quite accurate to suppose that the concept of resistance has disappeared from the scene. Weinshel (1984) for one, perhaps because he wants to hew closely to Freud's original use of the process concept, speaks of patterns of resistance, and their sequential reduction by interpretation, as constituting the essence of the psychoanalytic process. Certainly he means to emphasize the complexity of defensive alignments, and the repetitive work required to moderate their effectiveness. Whether one shares Weinshel's preference for such a narrow focus in speaking of the psychoanalytic process or not, all analysts would be likely to agree that much patient and repetitious analytic work is necessary in order to make analysands aware of their defensive (or resistance) patterns, as well as of how and under what circumstances they are employed. Successful analysis can be seen to demonstrate changes in the nature and/or intensity of the patient's typical defensive patterns, as well as in their effectiveness. Some defensive patterns seem to change without much explicit interpretive attention being paid to them, presumably as a result of other dimensions of the analytic work. Much remains to be learned in this area.

A third quality that characterizes all treatments that purport to be psychoanalysis is the recognition of the continuing influence of the childhood past upon the present. Putting aside for the moment the different emphases that the various theoretical schools of psychoanalysis place on just which aspects of the patient's past are considered to be important, and on how these should be approached technically, all have in common a realization that childhood mental life strongly influences the present in people of all ages. Both an individual's particular life experiences and the nature of that person's childhood mental functioning contribute to the formation of specific patterns of mental activity that persist into adulthood. These influence the outcome of the infantile instinctual conflicts and the quality of the individual's significant interactions with others. The analytic experience, notably but not exclusively by means of the transference, must demonstrate to analysands just how influential their past experiences have been in determining their current emotional lives. The respective roles of actual events, perceptions, memories and repression, fantasies of various kinds, and the entire range of ego functions and superego influences, as well as the impact of biological givens, whatever these may be, vary from individual to individual. As one of our study group put it, each of us seems to "package" his or her past in a unique and characteristic way, and the analytic process should serve to make that individual aware of its outline and importance in his or her life.

This leads us to a consideration of the fourth factor in the analytic process, the transference. For our immediate purposes we need not be concerned with the theoretical debates about the sources and nature of the transference, nor about how it is to be utilized in the course of doing analysis. No treatment that would justifiably be called a psychoanalysis would fail to place the interpretation of the transference at the center of its technique. Transference is also both recognized and interpreted in psychotherapies derived from psychoanalysis; therefore attention to the transference does not constitute a unique aspect of psychoanalysis, merely an essential one. Analysts have long understood that the transference becomes a vehicle by means of which analysands pursue important childhood wishes and their later derivatives. At the same time, the transference serves as a resistance to the recognition of aspects of the unconscious, and as a stage upon which one sees enacted the repeated patterns of interpersonal relationships and of instinctual expression from the past. It also reflects a new dimension of interpersonal experience in that the analyst interacts differently with the patient in response to his or her transference than have any other people in the analysand's past or present life. Specifically, the nonjudgmental acceptance of the patient's transference expressions and their analysis by means of interpretation in place of other kinds of response are quintessential features of the psychoanalytic process. This favors, among other things, analysands' ability to recognize the irrational historical determinants of their transference.

Change deserves to be considered independently as an essential component of the psychoanalytic process, in spite of the fact that change has either been mentioned explicitly, or else is an implicit aspect of each of the four features of the process that have been described already. The very notion of a process implies changes over a period of time; the analytic process has a direction (E. Kris, 1956), it is going somewhere, which means that some things must be seen to be changing. The term structural change is often used, presumably to refer to alterations in the psychic makeup which are more stable and permanent than other unspecified varieties of change might be. In my view, the term is unsatisfactory because it is seductively vague; it is employed as an article of faith in the superiority of analysis. Just which structures are involved in structural change are not self-evident, nor are they always spelled out by analysts when they make use of the term in writing or discussion. Neither are there clear explanations of what the metapsychology of other, presumably non-structural types of change might be. It should be remembered that identifications and responses to suggestion, or other forms of transference influence, are accompanied by changes in psychic structure, and not necessarily ones of a transient nature at that. The changes that result from psychoanalytic progress can be described as changes in the functioning of the analysand's mental apparatus, changes in the compromise formations that express his or her instinctual life, changes in the quality of his or her relations with others, changes in manifest behavior and/or in a variety of other ways. In any case, it is inconceivable to me that a genuine analytic process can be said to take place without the accompaniment of some significant, demonstrable changes in the analysand.

The sixth and final aspect of the analytic process is of a different order than the foregoing ones. Perhaps it is to be regarded less as an actual part of the process than as the framework that encompasses and facilitates it. I refer to the analytic situation, which comprises a set of conditions. I think that more substantial disagreement about the specifics of the analytic situation will be encountered, even among analysts who share the same theoretical orientation, than would be true of any of the other aspects of the analytic process. The great majority of analysts are in accord that frequent sessions of consistent duration are essential, but much more is meant by the analytic situation than simply the agreed-upon set of practical arrangements for the work. An implicit contract exists, in which the actions and attitudes of both participants are to some extent prescribed. Analyst and patient begin with a conscious accord about the purpose for which they are to meet, and about the behaviors expected of each in order to bring about the desired result. Departures from these expectations on the part of the patient express aspects of the analysand's problems; they therefore are regarded and treated by the analyst as constituting an integral part of the analytic work. Analysts' departures from the ideal are as inevitable; these are technical errors, often, but not always, the result of countertransference. Tension invariably exists between the patient's conscious, realistic goals in meeting with the analyst and his or her unconscious, irrational ones. The analysis of these tensions is part of the analysis of the transference, and hence of the analytic process itself.

I believe that optimum analytic technique demands that the analyst attempt, insofar as possible, to limit his or her activities to observing and analyzing patients' mental functioning. No other mode of intentionally influencing the patient, except through the medium of neutral interpretation, is to be thought of as analytic, although patients are surely always influenced by other aspects of their experiences with, and relationships to, their analysts. My emphasis here is on how the analyst consciously conceives of the analytic task. This limiting prescription may be the most controversial one in the entire domain of technique, and it has been the subject of at-times fierce debate since the early days of psychoanalysis. Nevertheless, the model of a relatively restricted and neutral way of dealing with patients is one to which the majority of analysts have always subscribed.

Our list of characteristics of the psychoanalytic process can be summarized as follows: (1) acknowledging the importance of the dynamic unconscious, (2) attention to and alteration of the patterns of defenses, (3) clarifying the influence of childhood experience on current mental functioning, (4) concentration on the transference, (5) achievement of presumably stable changes in the nature of the analysand's mental activities, and (6) utilization of a framework for treatment, called the analytic situation, that firmly restricts the means by which the analyst seeks to influence the patient.

Taken together, this combination of features distinguishes psychoanalytic treatment from many other kinds of therapy. However, it does not differentiate good psychoanalysis from not-so-good psychoanalysis, nor perhaps even from those treatments that would more properly be described as psychoanalytic psychotherapy. I have elected to word my descriptions of these essential aspects of psychoanalysis in language that is sufficiently general so that analysts of different theoretical persuasions could probably agree with all of them more or less as written. At the same time, no analyst, regardless of his or her theoretical stance, would regard this list as comprising a satisfactorily complete description of psychoanalytic treatment. The specific refinements and addenda that each one would want to add to this core description of the psychoanalytic process would raise precisely those controversial questions that so often lead to debate, disagreement, and even at times acrimony in our administrative, educational, and scientific activities. In short, in respect to the pragmatic motives that stimulated this investigation of the nature of the psychoanalytic process, I do not believe that the descriptions of its features as I have given them help us very much. On the other hand, if I were to offer a more complete and precise description of what *I* believe constitutes a valid psychoanalytic process, the number of analysts who would agree with it would undoubtedly shrink notably, even within the sizable subset of analysts to which I belong, who think of ourselves as mainstream adherents to the traditional Freudian emphasis on instinctual conflict and structural theory. Given the increasingly pluralistic nature of psychoanalysis, both here at home and in the international arena, no easy resolution of our dilemma seems likely.

The problem of trying to define exactly what constitutes true psychoanalysis in an atmosphere of competing theories is by no means a new one. I believe it is precisely this long-familiar problem that helps explain our tendency to employ the term "process" even while we continue to search for a better delineation of it. The term holds out the promise of an attainable certitude that is very appealing. One of the definitions of process that I came across is "A particular method of doing something, generally involving a number of steps or operations."[1] This suggests that we can view psychoanalytic "process" as something akin to a manufacturing process, that is, a series of specific, and therefore specifiable, operations that should lead to a given result. It goes beyond the idea that a psychoanalytic treatment has a direction, that it proceeds toward an end point. It conveys the sense that there are certain measures that the practitioner must take, and that these produce or encourage certain responses from the patient, and that the whole

---

[1] *Webster's Deluxe Unabridged Dictionary*. Second Edition. New York: Dorset & Baber, p. 1434.

can be described as a kind of linear sequence, a recognizable set of progressive changes marking progress to a conclusion.

Despite, or perhaps because of, the repetitious, circular, indirect, and often confusing nature of the day-to-day work of analysis, and the difficulty in judging when a satisfactory end point has been reached, most analysts, myself included, hold to a conviction that only certain methods are the correct ones that will promote a psychoanalytic process, just as only certain kinds of patients' responses are indicative that a genuine psychoanalytic process is in place. Other steps and responses characterizing other therapies may more or less closely resemble psychoanalysis, but these are actually other processes, not true psychoanalytic processes at all, no matter what their practitioners may think. The impetus for this conviction is precisely the challenge that is posed by the introduction of competing theories and therapies that claim to be psychoanalytic.

Although Freud introduced the term *process* in 1913, and controversies about the nature of psychoanalysis have been with us in one form or another even longer, the term process appears to have gained currency mainly since the introduction of the many forms of therapy collectively designated as psychoanalytic psychotherapy. As psychiatric and clinical psychological education became increasingly influenced by teachers who had been psychoanalytically trained, methods of exploratory or dynamic therapy based on the theories and techniques of psychoanalysis proliferated. Controversy about the theoretical shifts that were introduced as alternative or evolutionary forms of psychoanalysis promoted the tendency of analytic traditionalists to relegate these trends to the class of psychotherapies, while reserving the term *psychoanalysis* exclusively for their own version of Freud's methodology. Many proponents of emerging theories clung just as vehemently and tenaciously to the term psychoanalysis for their methods, even including some who wanted to set Freud aside as hopelessly outmoded.

Accounts in the literature of the struggle with proponents of Alexander's "corrective emotional experience" and with the various interpersonal schools are early examples of this tendency. Interest in defining the psychoanalytic process and in differentiating it from psychotherapy emerged at that time, and has persisted to the present day. Putting aside the intensity of feeling that always seems to accompany the competition among emerging theories in psychoanalysis, and among their proponents, it is nevertheless evident that our educational and organizational activities, as well as our scientific growth, would be enhanced by a clarification of just which steps, methods, or operations analysts should employ in their treatment procedures, and which should be avoided. By the same token, more accurate distinction of those responses on the part of the patient, signaling that a genuinely psychoanalytic treatment is in progress, from those that indicate that other varieties of change are taking place, would also be of great benefit to clinicians, educators, and administrators alike. The latter task has been made more imperative, as well as more difficult, by our efforts to apply psychoanalytic understanding and technique to an ever-wider spectrum of psychopathological disorders.

The theme of the most recent International Congress in Rome was the common ground of psychoanalysis. Both official and unofficial discussions underlined the difficulty in ascertaining which are the common elements of psychoanalysis among the vast range of schools and practitioners of markedly different theoretical persuasions, intellectual and cultural backgrounds, and personal loyalties and experiences that exist in the analytic world of today. Wallerstein's featured address (1989) stressed the importance of the unified core at the heart of an increasingly pluralistic theoretical superstructure. In support of his view, he referred to the definition of the essence of psychoanalysis offered by Freud (1914) in "On the History of the Psycho-Analytic Movement":

> It may thus be said that the theory of psycho-analysis is an attempt to account for two striking and unexpected facts of observation which emerge whenever an attempt is made to trace the symptoms of a neurotic back to their sources in his past life: the facts of transference and of resistance. Any line of investigation which recognizes these two facts and takes them as the starting-point

> of its work has a right to call itself psycho-analysis, even though it arrives at results other than my own (p. 16).

However, the designated discussants (Lussier, 1989); (Schafer, 1989) did not agree with Wallerstein's broad and inclusive emphasis. Nor can we by any means be certain that Freud would have done so, either. After all, at other times Freud gave different, more distinctive and limiting definitions of the essence of psychoanalysis than the one Wallerstein cited.

> The assumption that there are unconscious mental processes, the recognition of the theory of resistance and repression, the appreciation of the importance of sexuality and of the Oedipus complex—these constitute the principal subject-matter of psycho-analysis and the foundations of its theory. No one who cannot accept them all should count himself a psycho-analyst (Freud, 1923, p. 247).

And, in a well-known footnote added to the *Three Essays on the Theory of Sexuality* (1905) in the edition of 1920, he wrote:

> It has justly been said that the Oedipus complex is the nuclear complex of the neuroses, and constitutes the essential part of their content. It represents the peak of infantile sexuality, which, through its after-effects, exercises a decisive influence on the sexuality of adults. . . . With the progress of psycho-analytic studies the importance of the Oedipus complex has become more and more clearly evident; its recognition has become the shibboleth that distinguishes the adherents of psycho-analysis from its opponents (p. 226).

Are infantile sexuality and the conflicts associated with it still to be regarded as the foundation upon which the psychoanalytic edifice rests, or not? A glance at the six prepublished introductory statements about the theme of the Rome Congress (Abrams, et al., 1989), written by a distinguished group of intellectual leaders of psychoanalysis from around the world, yields an interesting answer to that question. Adherence to the idea of the centrality of infantile sexuality is no longer universal. Two of the six statements fail to so much as mention the subject, two others make a passing reference to it as having secondary significance, while only two of the six authors indicate a continuing insistence on the predominant importance of what Freud once called "the shibboleth that distinguishes the adherents of psycho-analysis from its opponents."

When I earlier mentioned the dilemma we face in constructing an inclusive and acceptable list of features of the psychoanalytic process, I might well have chosen this issue as an exemplar. The descriptions of the six aspects of the psychoanalytic process presented above make no explicit reference to infantile sexuality or to the Oedipus complex, although I am one of the legion of analysts who regard that omission as an irredeemable flaw. Personally, I cannot consider any description of the psychoanalytic process as satisfactory or complete if it fails to emphasize the vicissitudes of infantile sexuality. Yet to insist on its inclusion would, as we have seen, be likely to cause any number of our analytic colleagues around the world to object, or to proffer qualifications or other specifications that many of us would find equally problematic.

Psychoanalysis today is faced with a profusion of theories and therapeutic emphases. Subjective convictions stemming from different kinds of analytic training, varying theoretical beliefs, and the expectable range of individual sensitivities lead analysts to understand and formulate what their analysands tell them in significantly different ways. These differences are inevitably reflected in the nature of analysts' interventions, and thus in their patients' subsequent responses. The analytic processes that result, insofar as that term is meant to describe treatments as a characteristic series of steps, stages, or operations and responses, are distinctively different from one another. The question of whether we have one psychoanalysis or many, of whether these are variations on a common ground or a disparate family with little in common but its ancestor, has never been more important, or more troublesome, than at the present time. That very pressure motivates our search for a definitive outline of the psychoanalytic process, while the conditions that prevail seem to assure that any description that is broad enough to embrace our diversity will fail to satisfy our desire for greater scientific and administrative clarity.

I believe that there is another, perhaps not unrelated source of analysts' wishes to hang on to the process concept in the face of the trouble we have in specifying its nature. To examine it we must turn back to Freud's introduction of the term in 1913.

> The analyst . . . cannot determine beforehand exactly what results he will effect. He sets in motion a process, that of the resolving of the existing repressions. He can supervise this process, further it, remove obstacles in its way, and he can undoubtedly vitiate much of it. But on the whole, once begun, it goes its own way and does not allow either the direction it takes or the order in which it picks up its points to be prescribed for it (p. 130).

His model of a process laid less emphasis on a description of the interwoven fabric of the analyst's operations and the patient's responses, and more on the idea that the conditions under which analysis takes place and the nature of the analyst's activities serve to facilitate a somewhat independent and unpredictable process within the patient. In that respect, Freud's view of the analytic process may be likened more to other biological processes, such as digestion or reproduction (the latter an analogy employed by Freud), than to a manufacturing process. Another of the definitions of process that I found in *Webster's*, "A continuing development involving many changes," applies better to this usage.

Freud's formulation was more than a reflection of the grounding in biology and medicine that characterized his thinking and theoretical models. It also stemmed from an accurate clinical observation that is as cogent today as it was in 1913. We must still admit that no matter how confident the analyst may be in his or her understanding of the patient, and in the application of his or her technique, much of what transpires in analysis is beyond the analyst's ability to predict, influence, or explain. The rate and direction of change in the patient's mental functioning, and its ultimate extent, are unknown at the start of treatment, and remain so to a significant degree throughout its course. To be sure, with clinical experience an analyst may develop the ability to form reasonable estimates of these variables, at least with some patients, as their analyses proceed. Few if any analysts are able to say how they arrive at such judgments in a very clear way, and none would be very startled if their predictions had to be modified as the analyses they conduct unfold.

More important, our grasp of what it is within our patients that ultimately determines the rate, direction, and extent of intrapsychic change remains fragmentary and unsatisfactory. Time and again, we fall back on impressionistic quantitative formulations that are difficult to document and impossible to prove. Such ideas as the amount and extent of trauma, the age and delicacy of the organism at which it occurs, the effects of inherent or congenital factors, the strength of one drive or the other, the stickiness of the libido, postulated ego deformations, defects, or deficits, prestructural damage, and the like all represent theoretical efforts to account for this uncertainty. Those unknown or unidentified qualities that determine the nature of resistances, and the tenacity or flexibility of analysands' patterns of all classes of mental activity, continue to engage our best theoretical minds today, as they did Freud and his contemporaries. I think it is just exactly the mysterious, elusive nature of what we do not yet understand about how our patient's minds work in the therapeutic encounter that lends support to our resonance with Freud's invocation of the concept of a process set in motion by analysis.

This is not to suggest that we are in accord with his earliest formulation, which might be taken to imply that what goes on within the patient, once set in motion by the impact of analysis, thereafter proceeds independently of the analyst's further interventions. I doubt very much that Freud meant his conception of the process to be taken that way, but in any case, today we would all probably agree that the analyst's attitudes, thinking, and activities all continuously affect the patient throughout the duration of analysis. Furthermore, what I have referred to for convenience as the patient's responses, by which I mean his or her repertoire of attitudes, thinking, and activities, also exert a continuous influence on the analyst. These mutual influences contribute to the formation of an extraordinarily intricate network of constantly shifting interactions, of which only a certain portion are ever fully identified and understood, even in the most successful analyses. It is pointless to argue, as some have done, over whether the analytic process is to be thought of as what takes place between two participants, or as what goes on within the analysand under the sway of the analytic situation. These are arbitrary distinctions that do not describe different processes, but are merely different ways of talking about what transpires in analysis.

Whether psychoanalysis is one process or many, and how it, or they, can be distinguished from analytic psychotherapy, inflames parochialism, leading to invoking the process concept in the service of debate, rather than of discovery. In training, we learned to call our detailed records of session-to-session work "process notes." In that sense, process means simply a careful, sequential description of the data of observation, nothing more. Conscientious observation and recording of data is fundamental to any scientific enterprise, and I do not see that any special benefit is obtained by attributing to the term process more weight than it can conveniently carry.

In short, it is my opinion that there is not much to be gained by speaking of psychoanalysis as a process; what we are really interested in doing is refining our understanding of what psychoanalysis is, of how it is best carried out, of what it brings about in the patient and how it does so, and of what a successful analysis looks like. The better we can answer those questions, the better we can both practice psychoanalysis and teach others how to do it.

References

Abend, S.M. (1986). Some problems in the evaluation of the psychoanalytic process. In: *Psychoanalysis—The Science of Mental Conflict:*

Essays in Honor of Charles Brenner, ed. A.D. Richards and M.S. Willick. Hillsdale, NJ: Analytic Press, pp. 209–228.

Abrams, S., et al. (1989). Pre-published statements for the 36th International Psychoanalytical Congress in Rome, 30th July to 4th August 1989. *International Journal of Psycho-Analysis* 70:3–28.

Freud, S. (1905). Three Essays on the Theory of Sexuality. *Standard Edition* 7.

——— (1913). On Beginning the Treatment. (Further recommendations on the technique of psycho-analysis I.) *Standard Edition* 12.

——— (1914). On the History of the Psycho-Analytic Movement. *Standard Edition* 14.

——— (1923). Two Encyclopaedia Articles. *Standard Edition* 18.

Kris, E. (1956). On some vicissitudes of insight in psycho-analysis. *International Journal of Psycho-Analysis* 37:445–455.

Lussier, A. (1989). Discussion of R.S. Wallerstein, presented at the 36th International Psychoanalytic Association Congress, August, Rome.

Schafer, R. (1989). The Search for Common Ground, Discussion presented at the 36th International Psychoanalytical Association Congress, August, Rome.

Wallerstein, R.S. (1989). Psychoanalysis: The Common Ground, presented at the 36th International Psychoanalytical Association Congress, August, Rome.

Weinshel, E.M. (1984). Some observations on the psychoanalytic process. *Psychoanalytic Quarterly* 53:63–92.

CHAPTER 5

The Problem of Therapeutic Alliance

[Abend, S.M. (1996). *Journal of Clinical Psychoanalysis* 5(2):213–226]

I will treat the concept of the alliance as a problematic aspect of the larger and far more elusive question of what makes analytic treatment move forward. It seems to me unarguable that whatever factors enable the treatment to move ahead constitute essential contributors to a fruitful outcome, and therefore they deserve the most careful study. The issue is not simply a theoretical conundrum, but also has technical consequences of considerable practical significance.

Freud laid the cornerstone of the concept of a therapeutic alliance, although he did not speak of it in those terms, in his 1912 paper on "The Dynamics of Transference," as a feature of his exposition of how he conceptualized neurosogenesis and the analytic method of treatment at that time. Friedman (1969), in an incisive and convincing study of the subject, observes that Freud did so in a not entirely successful effort to resolve a theoretical paradox concerning the patient's motivation, and Friedman goes on to expose the persistence of that paradox in the work of subsequent theorists.

You will recall that Freud had already discerned that the transference, as the vehicle for the expression of the patient's unconscious desires, supplies the underlying emotional force which binds the patient to the doctor, and hence commits him or her to the treatment process He also saw that it simultaneously powers the patient's resistance to the doctor's influence, and, by extension, to the requirements of the treatment situation. Freud's extraordinary theoretical and technical imagination enabled him to construct a revolutionary proposition for the analytic treatment of neurosis out of this apparent contradiction, but in order to do so he had to postulate a division of the elements of transference that has left us a troublesome legacy.

His solution was to identify and split off a helpful, conscious, unobjectionable positive component of the transference which, he says, serves the goals of the treatment. Meanwhile, a combination of the negative aspects of transference, and its unconscious erotic component, contributes to the patient's unwillingness or inability to cooperate in the treatment program; that is to say, it accounts for the resistance.

Freud did not believe that some emotionally unencumbered, mature, drive-free aspect of the patient's personality provides enough strength to overcome entrenched neurotic dispositions. Rather, he says that the analyst makes use of the unobjectionable positive transference attachment in order to influence the patient to do the unwelcome tasks of analysis. He called this influence a form of suggestion, by which he meant suggesting that the patient cooperate within the treatment situation by altering resistant behavior in favor of remembering, and then expressing in words, the repressed keys to his or her neurotic difficulties. The unobjectionable positive element of the transference that Freud identified as the motor of treatment progress is the direct ancestor of today's therapeutic alliance.

Freud also noted that "all emotional relations of sympathy, friendship, trust and the like are genetically linked with sexuality and have developed from purely sexual desires" (1912, p. 105).The unobjectionable positive transference is not an exception to this dictum, so his isolation of it from those elements of transference involved in symptom formation and resistance is purely pragmatic, a case of theory's being bent to support a technical necessity. Freud needed to account for his clinical discovery that no matter how much the patient is suffering, and no matter how strong his or her conscious wish to change may appear to be, there are always also powerful motives, operating largely, if not entirely, outside of conscious awareness, that oppose any change, that lead the patient to cling tenaciously to long-established adaptations, modes of gratification, self-deceiving rationalizations, and defenses. Some lever other than common sense, or exhortation, or education had to be found, by means of which the analyst could hope to induce motion in the entrenched emotional substructure of the patient's illness, along with the sufferer's cooperation, and despite his or her dedicated opposition. The unobjectionable positive transference was the lever he devised.

When Freud first set down his theory of treatment in his papers on technique, he wrote as if the distinction between what makes treatment move forward and its ultimate effectiveness did not require much attention. Later in his career, he knew better, but even in his famous study of the factors that limit analytic success, "Analysis Terminable and Interminable" (1937), he said in passing, and without elaboration, that of course when analysis works, we know how and why it does so (p. 221) Today, nearly sixty-odd years later, most of us are less comfortable about that assertion, but for Freud, his original conviction that, in suitable cases, successful method equals successful outcome, did not have to be modified or explained.

When we speak, for example, of the patient's becoming engaged in a psychoanalytic process, our basis for doing so rests mainly on observations of how the patient behaves in the treatment situation. For Freud, this meant primarily the patient's ability to observe the fundamental rules. A relatively unreserved flow of free associations was a sign of a cooperative attitude toward the analyst and the treatment. Of course, this cooperation must in addition include the patient's developing a satisfactory mode of response to the analyst's interventions. Since resistance is inevitable (in fact its analysis is an essential aspect of the treatment), the analyst's interpretations of its nature and purpose are supposed to be given thoughtful consideration by the patient. A disposition to be convinced by the analyst's interpretations and reconstructions, and to please the analyst by making the effort to overcome the impulses to continue resisting, in favor of resuming the production of associations, are further indications that treatment is moving along, that a collaboration is in place. I have shifted to the present tense in this description because, while I was describing Freud's theory of seventy years ago, similar fundamental principles still characterize the assessment of the therapeutic alliance today.

In ascertaining the status of the therapeutic alliance, the analyst in practice is most likely to be thinking about the patient's ability to cooperate with him or her in the treatment setting Is the patient candid and forthcoming? Is he or she willing and able to reflect upon what is going on in treatment spontaneously, or at least in response to the analyst's invitations to do so? Is the patient likely to consider seriously what the analyst has to say, as well as what he or she says and feels? Is the patient capable of sustaining a commitment to expression in verbal form rather than in behavior, or especially, misbehavior? Is there a conscious acknowledgment of partnership in the enterprise of therapy? I believe these are the sort of questions analysts ask themselves when deciding about the presence of a therapeutic alliance.

If, in addition to these factors, the patient is generally optimistic about the outcome of treatment, and if his or her life seems to be improving along with the increased level of self-understanding that is attained, it is reasonable for the analyst to think that the therapeutic alliance has been instrumental in moving treatment forward in a satisfactory fashion, and toward a successful outcome. It is only when the characteristic signs of a collaborative attitude appear and the treatment process seems to progress, but without much accompanying change in the patient's difficulties, that we begin to wonder Or else, of all things, the signs of therapeutic collaboration are not so readily apparent, but the patient, perhaps without even the slightest hint of appreciation, seems to be getting better anyway, we also begin to wonder about the so-called alliance. Or, and these days this problem is probably more common than ever, we may encounter patients with whom there is very great difficulty in establishing anything resembling a conventional therapeutic alliance With them, our energies and efforts have to be directed first to the task of establishing and strengthening a proper collaborative atmosphere. In light of such varieties of clinical experience, what may have seemed unquestionable about the links between therapeutic alliance, good treatment progress, and satisfactory outcome no longer constitute quite so assured and comfortable a set of assumptions.

In order to address the complexities that lie just beneath the surface of the concept of the therapeutic alliance, it will be helpful to have a grasp of how it has evolved from its origins in early Freudian theory. I cannot do full justice to the history of these ideas at this time, because to do so would require an extensive study dedicated solely to that purpose. Instead, I will present brief highlights to mark the sometimes bumpy path the idea of the alliance has followed in the decades since 1912.[1]

Sterba (1934) was the first to take advantage of Freud's introduction of the structural theory, suggesting that some elements in the ego are focused on reality, while other aspects of it are more closely linked with instinctual energy. The opposition of these different tendencies constitutes a theme that has been incorporated into work on the alliance concept ever since. The question of what motivates the reality-focused dimensions of the ego is left unaddressed, even when Sterba adds the now familiar notion that identification with the analyst supports the reality-directed tendencies, and is therefore to be fostered by the analyst. The radical new assumption was to postulate the presence of autonomous areas of ego functioning, the precise origins of which are not specified, with which the analyst can make an alliance. Freud seemingly echoed this suggestion in "Analysis Terminable and Interminable" (1937) by referring to "an alliance with the ego of the patient to subdue certain parts of the id" (p. 233), but without surrendering his opinion that the positive transference continues to motivate the patient's working in analysis. In Friedman's assessment, Freud's reservations aside, Sterba laid the groundwork for a viewpoint eagerly taken up by many theorists since then that "The ego ally works with the analyst not because of the personal relationship between patient and physician, but because at least as regards that fragment patient and physician share the same purposes" (1969,

---

[1] In doing so I am especially indebted to Friedman's (1969) scholarly article on the therapeutic alliance in which he addresses the complications which made their appearance up to the time his work was published, in a fresh and fascinating way. His provocative assessments seem undeservedly overlooked by contemporary theorists.

p. 143). Friedman goes on to express his reservations about the assumption, and he concludes that Sterba's therapeutic alliance actually consists of behavior within the analysis that "shows the success of the analysis" (p 144). In other words, it is less a tool of the analytic process than a consequence of it.

Other trends in psychoanalysis that were to have a bearing on the problem of therapeutic alliance were emerging as well. For example, the interpersonal school was casting doubt on instinctual drives as the explanatory bedrock of human motivation, both within and without the treatment situation. In a related trend, doubt was being expressed about the then prevalent technical injunction to minimize the patient's opportunities for transference gratifications, in order to make his or her crucial wishes more readily available for analytic scrutiny. Also, increasing attention was being paid to preoedipal determinants of character structure and psychopathology. This expressed itself in the recognition of maternal transference elements that do not involve fantasies of sexual congress, reproduction, and their attendant rivalries and consequences. The enlargement of the horizons of transference also got increased impetus from the efforts of analysts to apply psychoanalytic treatment methods to more severely disturbed patients.

As a result of these developments, many analysts began experimenting with modifications of the standard technique of analytic treatment. One such effort laid stress on treating certain aspects of the relationship between patient and analyst as realistic, that is to say, as aside from or independent of the transference proper. Another trend expanded the spectrum of the kinds of motivations thought to energize the patient's behavior, subdividing the range of detectable and analyzable transference into many more components than those which had composed Freud's original theoretical universe. Accompanying these changes was a new attention, at times rather hotly contested, to what kinds of gratification within the relationship with the analyst should be considered permissible, or even advantageous, to promoting the analytic process, rather than regarded as subversions of the necessity to analyze transference wishes in an atmosphere of acceptable and accepted frustration.

Among traditional analysts there gradually crystallized a widely, although far from universally accepted, supposition that fundamental early childhood needs are actually fulfilled by the analytic experience. It was suggested that the matrix of the analytic relationship is to be conceived of as maternal, and as lending necessary support to the patient's participation in analysis, and his or her growth as an individual as a result of that experience. Stone's (1961) thoughtful formulations give the most explicit and elaborate summary of this position by postulating that the analysand seeks not only the primal mother, who signifies the satisfaction of bodily needs, but also the secondary mother, the figure who fosters growth through separation and the acquisition of understanding and control. The therapeutic alliance therefore is said to include several components: the driving force of the primordial wishes, the mature transference derived from the model of the secondary, growth-promoting mother, the acceptable tender erotic transference, identification with the analyst, and, finally, rational appraisal of the analyst and confidence in his or her ability to provide genuine help. Stone also advises the analyst not to impose unnecessary frustration upon the patient. This latter technical recommendation is also emphasized by Zetzel (1956, 1966) and by Greenson (1965), both of whom think that too much frustration of not unreasonable wishes may lead to inhibition or prevention of the patient's cooperative participation in the analysis. Guidelines for determining what is permissible and what is excessive frustration are not laid down; it is implicit in these recommendations that the competent analyst can rely upon his or her clinical judgment to make the determination of what each patient needs and can tolerate.

Countervailing opinions on all aspects of these proposals have come from many quarters. It is not my intention to review these debates in detail, but I shall mention some of the important reservations which continue, in one form or another, to help frame the ongoing discussions of theory and technique in these controversial areas. Anna Freud (1968), for one, was at times rather skeptical about the practical value for clinical analytic work of the intensified interest in the influence of the early, preverbal stages of infant development. I need hardly add that different views on this subject still prevail among analysts who work only with adults, as well as among the child analysts, including those who have devoted research attention to infant and child development. Arlow and Brenner (1966) long ago challenged the assumption that a basic maternal transference is at the core of all analytic attachments, citing as evidence clinical material that does not fit such a formula. Long-standing controversies about how to regard and utilize countertransference in clinical work, and about the analytic treatment of borderline and other varieties of more disturbed patients, are still very much with us, and these latter problems have directly or indirectly had an influence on our notions of therapeutic alliance.

Brenner (1979) differed with Zetzel's and Greenson's ideas about therapeutic alliance by demonstrating that in their illustrations, full and accurate analytic understanding might have been more productive than the changes in the analysts' personal behaviors they recommended. In a related vein, M Stein wrote about the "unobjectionable transference" (1981), showing that in certain kinds of patients, what passes for a benign, positive, and productive transference attitude, rather than functioning to help overcome resistance, as Freud had believed, actually serves as a crucial resistance against the emergence of important analytic material.

Some years ago I tried to show that in charged situations personal countertransference considerations may render suspect the analyst's objective best clinical judgment about patients' needs. It is generally acknowledged that more difficult analytic patients frequently stimulate heightened countertransference potential in their analysts, so it may well follow that our best clinical judgment about changes in technique thought to be necessary to facilitate a therapeutic alliance in such cases could be less reliable than is often thought.

Friedman's conclusions about the therapeutic alliance go even further in questioning its rational basis. Here is Friedman on the subject:

> In his life the patient wants freedom from the pain of symptoms and realization of his wishes and fantasies. In the consulting room these are adjusted to the person and procedure of the

> psychoanalyst. Any idea that *apart from these desires* the patient wishes to, or should wish to, engage in a process *per se* is supported by neither analytic theory nor common sense, but solely by the analyst's natural desire for cooperation, since the analyst *does* wish to engage in a certain process *per se* for which reason he has chosen it as an occupation (1969, p 152).

Friedman wants to remind us that the patient has no primary motivation to form a therapeutic alliance; he or she is motivated by other things, and what we are used to calling the therapeutic alliance merely reflects the patient's ability to adapt to the conditions under which the analyst is willing to work toward the patient's ends. The analyst, on the other hand, does need to feel some sense of alliance to sustain his or her conviction that the difficult task of treatment is worth pursuing with a given patient, in the face of all the obstacles normally encountered in the course of doing the work.

None of this is meant to imply that the analytic patient is a schemer who consciously intends to placate or fool the analyst into giving him or her what is desired. In fact, the patient's ability to adapt to the conditions of treatment is determined to a great extent by character structure and psychopathology, and mostly by the unconscious dimensions of both. Nor is it to suggest that what the analyst wants in the way of an alliance is at all unreasonable, excessive, or merely self-serving. Far from it. The kind of treatment we have to offer does place certain demands on the analyst, as well as on the patient. There are conditions that promote its effectiveness, as well as those that make a good outcome less likely, and it makes good sense to study and clarify them as best we can.

Up to now, I have talked about what the analyst observes, measures, requires, encourages by way of a therapeutic alliance What about the patient's need for a sense of alliance? Certainly he or she wants to believe that the analyst is both competent and interested in trying to help. There is more, however; to a greater or lesser degree, the patient wants to feel understood and accepted. The patient is also likely to want to feel affirmed, both in regard to his or her views of reality, and for the sake of vital self-esteem. It is probably essential for the analysand to feel that the analyst is reliable, an assessment which he or she surely reaches about the analyst's own personal character, as well as about the consistency of the analyst's working habits. Some, but not all, patients and analysts would add that it is also important for the analysand to have a sense that the analyst is a real person, and not simply a magisterial therapeutic authority And some analysts and patients would therefore also emphasize that it is important that the way treatment is conducted supports the patient's sense of being equal to the analyst as a person, rather than to inadvertently damage or diminish that sense of equality.

As I have moved down this potential list of what may be involved in the patient's experience of alliance, or its absence, it becomes readily apparent that all these qualities are far from uncomplicated. Not all of them matter to the same degree or in the same fashion to each patient. In point of fact, the opposite is surely true; reliability, equality, affirmation, and the like will mean something different to each patient, something quite unique, in fact. For every one of these qualities in every single patient, a combination of conscious and unconscious factors will determine whether he or she feels adequately understood, accepted, and cared for, and so forth. What is more, such feelings will not be the same at all times, since even the most tactful and sensitive analyst sometimes does or says things that disappoint the patient's desires, either through necessity, or by mistakes in judgment. In addition, there are spontaneous fluctuations in the patient's internal, unconscious dispositions that contribute to disruptions in the sense of alliance with the analyst, regardless of the analyst's technical handling of the case. Just as the patient's unconsciously determined attitudes, perceptions, expectations, and reactions shape his or her ability to participate in what the analyst would subsume under the therapeutic alliance, they invariably also affect the patient's experience of the analyst as a genuine ally.[2]

---

[2] Some emerging schools of psychoanalytic thought, such as self psychology, interpersonal or intersubjective psychoanalysis, and at least certain varieties of developmental

Freud started by calling his alliance a part of the transference, and most analysts writing about therapeutic alliance since then seem to follow him in that regard. However, some analysts definitely prefer to think that they can differentiate aspects of the patient's reaction to the analyst, which they call the transference, from other aspects, which they consider to be part of the real relationship. Others would argue that some reactions of the patient to his or her analyst are a consequence of how the analyst behaves in the here-and-now, and that these are distinguishable from those reactions which have inner sources, rooted in the patient's past. I believe that the central issue is whether such attempts at differentiation have any reliable functional significance, that is to say, can these antitheses truly be treated as separable from one another in practical terms? Some analysts would unhesitatingly say yes to that question, and their technique would be guided by that viewpoint. Others, myself among them, are more skeptical about the usefulness of such distinctions, and the individual analyst's technical posture will reflect that caution.

I would draw the contrast in viewpoint this way: one stance treats the different aspects of patients' responses to their analysts as if they were stratified, with the more rational, mature, and reality-determined levels resting on top of the more primitive, irrational substructure.

Such a hypothetical topography has common-sense appeal, in that it seems to follow the time sequence of development, and the familiar sketch of consciousness, or ego, riding atop the buried id, or unconscious structure. It is acknowledged that "deeper" strata have an influence on those closer to the surface, but the working assumption of

---

and object relations theories, lay stress in their formulations on an expanded spectrum of primary motivations in human beings, or on a widened horizon of analyzable transference types. It follows that the analysts who advocate one or another of the approaches I have mentioned might well have views on the problem of therapeutic alliance that reflect the special qualities of their preferred clinical theories. I am not in a position to trace out such potential differences, a task I shall have to leave to colleagues who have devoted themselves to the elaboration of each of those theories. My own commentary on the problem of therapeutic alliance should be taken to be confined to issues that lie within the parameters of mainstream or traditional psychoanalytic thought.

this theoretical preference is that these levels can be treated as divisible from one another. Consequently, there are times when the analyst can and should speak to the patient as though he or she addresses only the uppermost, rational, mature person.

The other conceptualization regards the patient's responses in the analytic situation as more of an amalgam; that is to say, while the more and the less irrational qualities can be described separately, in practice they always constitute an admixture which affects the patient's perception, judgment, memory, and behavior. From this technical vantage point, the analyst will be on theoretically shaky ground if he or she ever disregards the irrational side, and speaks to the patient as if in some instances only the rational surface matters.

I do not mean to exaggerate the importance of these differences, nor to suggest a false degree of polarization. I believe that most mainstream analysts attend to the unconscious meanings of interactions with their patients, whether or not they apologize for their minor mistakes, sometimes giving patients a bit of information about their personal circumstances, expressing sympathy, congratulations, or the like on noteworthy occasions, or from time to time either confirming or challenging a patient's opinion about something that transpires between them. By the same token, those analysts who tend to restrict such behaviors do not necessarily behave like the unresponsive, rigidly distant caricature of orthodoxy that some advocates of a more naturalistic style of interaction with patients are prone to depict. I doubt that in most instances it is crucial to the outcome of treatment whether one style or the other prevails, unless the tilt is an extreme one. What is more, if it becomes clear that to a particular patient it seems to matter a great deal whether, for example, the analyst makes an occasional personal revelation or not, I would expect most analysts of either persuasion to pay attention to that need, and to try to learn more about that patient's sensitivity; in short, to bring it into focus as an analytic issue.

Nevertheless, there are more categorical advocates of building a therapeutic alliance who would argue that patients cannot be expected to understand and accept the degree to which the analytic situation is not like other social situations. They assume that patients do not readily realize that, let us say, when the analyst does not answer questions or accede to requests for information, these are merely technical devices employed for the benefit of the treatment, and not a form of mistreatment. I submit that analysts who feel very strongly about the necessity to attend to the "reality" of the interaction between analyst and patient may be less consistently inclined to seek out and clarify the unconscious meaning to the patient of the analytic atmosphere, situation, and relationship. To hold firmly that all aspects of the patient's relationship with the analyst are manifestations of transference is to commit the analyst to the endeavor to analyze the transference in all its complexity. To have the idea in mind that nothing which transpires between patient and analyst is to be treated as an exception to this principle, that nothing is to be regarded as outside the analysis, makes it less likely that something important in the patient's unconscious dispositions will be overlooked. In some cases, this may make all the difference in the world to the outcome, and the analyst can never tell in advance which cases these will be.

That said, we must also remember just what we mean by the phrase "analyzing the transference." In every theory of therapeutic action, analyzing the transference means helping the patient learn that past relationships and situations, and how they were integrated into his or her emotional makeup, continue to decisively influence present relationships and situations. The shadow of the past distorts the patient's ability to evaluate the present, and learning to recognize, understand, and evaluate these distortions is a major task of analytic treatment. For this to happen, the patient must have some capability to accomplish a transformation of staggering theoretical complexity; he or she has to gain an understanding of the influence of the irrational components of his or her mind on its rational functioning, using that same irrationally encumbered mind for the purpose. To go back to my earlier shorthand designations, the mind I have compared to an amalgam has somehow to be able to examine itself and identify its component strata! No wonder analysts are so interested in the concept of a therapeutic alliance. It seems impossible to conceptualize the treatment process without it. In sum, the therapeutic alliance concept rests on the dubious assumption that the patient is motivated to be rational about his or her irrationality (see Friedman [1969], for a full discussion of the question of the patient's motivation in the treatment situation). But since our theories of how treatment works all depend on the patient's ability to be rational about his or her irrationality, it is easy to understand why the alliance concept is so appealing to many analysts.

To return to the question of technique, rather than theory, we would probably all agree that the more difficult the patient, the more likely we are to be concerned about the therapeutic alliance and how to foster and strengthen it. When the analyst seeks to establish a therapeutic alliance by altering the conditions of the treatment situation, the task of gaining an analytic understanding of why the patient has such problems in accepting and adapting to the special requirements of the treatment will be more difficult to accomplish. As analysts work with borderline and other difficult patients in increasing numbers, the ramifications of this technical problem take on ever more importance, as anyone who is familiar with the literature can attest.

The temptation to address the patient at times as if his or her reasonable adult side is available for an intellectual and emotional contact that is free of the influence of the unconscious is almost irresistible, and often takes subtle forms. Let us not forget that analysts must acknowledge the ubiquitous power of the unconscious in their own mental functioning, while at the same time remaining appropriately confident of their rational judgment and clinical skills. It is a peculiar mental balancing act, and the patient's stance in treatment has a comparable ambiguity. Especially when things do not appear to be going so well in treatment, we want to call the patient to our side, to enlist his or her better nature and reasonableness to help in the struggle against the powerful forces arrayed against treatment progress. Unfortunately, the analyst is more likely to go wrong by taking the patient's reasonableness at face value, than by keeping the unconscious at the center of his or her attention. This is the oldest lesson on the history of psychoanalytic thought, but one whose importance, for better or for worse, cannot be nullified, even by mutual agreement between patient and analyst.

References

Abend, S.M. (1982). Serious illness in the analyst: Countertransference considerations. *Journal of the American Psychoanalytic Association* 30:365–379.

——— Brenner, C. (1966). The psychoanalytic situation In: *Psychoanalysis in the Americas*, ed. R.E. Litman. New York: International Universities Press.

Brenner, C. (1979). Working alliance, therapeutic alliance and transference. *Journal of the American Psychoanalytic Association* 27 (Suppl.): 137–157.

Freud, A. (1968). Difficulties in the path of psychoanalysis: A confrontation of past with present viewpoints. In: *The Writings*, Vol. 7. New York: International Universities Press, 1971, pp. 124–156.

Freud, S. (1912). The Dynamics of Transference. *Standard Edition* 12:97–108.

——— (1937). Analysis Terminable and Interminable. *Standard Edition* 23:209–253.

Friedman, L. (1969). The therapeutic alliance. *International Journal of Psycho-Analysis* 50:139–153.

Greenson, R. (1965). The working alliance and the transference neurosis. In: *Explorations in Psychoanalysis.* New York: International Universities Press, 1978, pp. 199–224.

Stein, M. (1981). The unobjectionable part of the transference. *Journal of the American Psychoanalytic Association* 29:869–892.

Sterba, R. (1934). The fate of the ego in analytic therapy. *International Journal of Psycho-Analysis* 15:117–126.

Stone, L. (1961). *The Psychoanalytic Situation.* New York: International Universities Press.

Zetzel, E. (1956). Current concepts of transference. *International Journal of Psycho-Analysis* 37:369–378.

——— (1966). The analytic situation. In: *Psychoanalysis in the Americas*, ed. R.E. Litman. New York: International Universities Press.

CHAPTER 6

Analytic Technique Today

[Abend, S. (2000). *Journal of the American Psychoanalytic Association* 48(1):9–16]

When Freud first devised psychoanalysis, it was as a specialized medical technique for the treatment of certain kinds of neuro-psychological ailments, the neuroses. Although he never abandoned his convictions regarding the biological substrate of those conditions, experience soon led him to drop the effort to conceptualize either the illnesses or the treatment method in any terms other than purely psychological ones. He also came to appreciate that an individual need not be trained as a physician in order to understand the problems analysis was intended to relieve, or to practice the method successfully. As time went on, he and his followers applied his invention to a broader range of emotional problems, including what later generations of analysts would regard as conditions resulting from deviations in normal development, as well as some psychoses and borderline states.

Not only did Freud change his ideas about psychoanalysis as he went along, but, as is well known, fundamental differences of opinion about the technique soon arose among his former students. First to appear were arguments about content, that is to say, about the exact nature of the insight into the workings of their minds that analysands should be helped to acquire. Adler and Jung were merely the first in a long line of analysts whose views on that subject departed sharply from those of Freud, and today's pluralism is certainly marked by a multiplicity of views on what sorts of insight, if any, are crucial to the curative effect of psychoanalysis. It is probably safe to say that one thing analysts today all agree on, regardless of theoretical allegiance, is the importance of unconscious mental life. However, the varying emphases they place on the attainment of insight into that life (as against other dimensions of the analytic experience) and, even more important, their differing opinions about what the vital content of such new self-knowledge should be, pose another question altogether.

The second nexus of controversy to make its appearance, for which initial credit is nowadays accorded to Ferenczi, concerns the influence of the relationship between analyst and patient on the course and outcome of the analysis. Freud's views on the matter are well known. An emotional attachment to the analyst had to be formed before interpretations could have any beneficial influence, and, in fact, this "unobjectionable positive transference" was the only lever the analyst could use to get the patient to face the difficult aspects of the treatment. The neurotic segments of the transference were at once the expression of the patient's problematic desires, the primary manifestation of resistance, and the stage on which the treatment's power came alive. Countertransference consisted simply of the persistence of analysts' blind spots *vis-à-vis* segments of their analysands' unconscious minds. The neurotic relationship existed as an inclusion body in the matrix of the reality relationship between the analytic pair. Certain familiar prescriptions for how the analyst should behave in order to maximize the effectiveness of the analysis of transference were distilled from Freud's early experience and codified for his students.

From the time of Ferenczi's radical challenge, ideas about the role of the relationship between analyst and analysand have proliferated. How to conceptualize various aspects of its complexity, and to understand the possible beneficial (or detrimental) impact of the relationship on the treatment process, has occupied the imagination of analysts to this day. In consequence of one or another formulation of the various possibilities, significantly different recommendations for how the analyst ought to think about the analytic interaction, and how he or she ought to behave in the clinical situation, have been presented over the years. The resulting controversies have at times led to acrimonious debates about the limits of what is to be thought of as true psychoanalysis. If anything, the uneasy ecumenism of today's psychoanalytic scene has highlighted the major differences that currently exist in regard to prescriptions for managing the analytic relationship.

In more recent times, a third dimension of the attempt to redefine technique has become evident. Interest in the mind and its role in the human condition has hardly been confined to physicians and psychologists, after all, and the emergence of psychoanalysis in the past century soon enough attracted the attention of philosophers and other academics. Proposals to alter the traditional notion of psychoanalysis as a form of treatment, medical or otherwise, of neuropsychological ailments have attempted to shift fundamental assumptions about the psychoanalytic enterprise, its goals, its parameters, and its techniques.

In fact, philosophy, linguistics, and the like have fascinated and influenced many analysts whose training and orientation are based on the conceptual model Freud established, or on one of its close variants.

As our profession moves into its second century, we find ourselves in an unprecedented intellectual environment. With new data from the neurosciences just now on the verge of being integrated into psychoanalytic thinking, we are about to enter an exciting era of theoretical modification, or so it appears. Interestingly enough, our current theoretical base, from which such changes will have to be developed, is already in a state of flux never before seen in our history. Not only have we a wider range of viewpoints than ever before, but the current *zeitgeist* facilitates an unprecedented degree of dialogue among analysts of different persuasions. Attesting to this state of affairs, our journals and scientific meetings display a diversity of opinion of extraordinary magnitude, at least when compared with what most of us were accustomed to seeing for so many years.

This issue of *JAPA* is fairly representative of the breadth of current theoretical diversity. While it would be something of an exaggeration to suggest that all major points of view are given voice, the reader will find in the articles herein references to nearly every recognized psychoanalytic position. Certainly a number of cutting-edge issues are explicitly addressed, and from sharply different postures. I will not attempt to mention, even in cursory fashion, all of the authors included here, and all of the ideas to be encountered in their papers. To do so in this brief introduction could succeed only in doing injustice to the thoughtful complexities you will encounter in these pages. Instead I will highlight a few problems that appear throughout these papers, in one guise or another. Though I may cite specific instances, my goal is not to summarize or evaluate these contributions. I wish merely to call the reader's attention to some of the points of theoretical controversy that engage our leading thinkers as we enter the new century.

Warren Poland's plenary address, "The Analyst's Witnessing and Otherness," and the several commentaries on it, offer an ideal place to begin. Poland calls attention to an aspect of the relationship between patient and analyst that he believes contributes to the effectiveness of analysis, though heretofore it has gone unnamed. What he calls "witnessing" is the idea that that something important happens in the mind of the analysand in consequence of the experience of having had a concerned, attentive, and comprehending listener as he or she has struggled to express what self-reflection has unearthed. In Poland's opinion, this phenomenon is different from containment or holding, concepts derivative of early mother-child interactions. Poland does, however, locate its initial prototype in another aspect of early development, the acquisition of the psychological distinction between self and other. In that sense, he seems to see its significance in a universal dimension of human psychology, though one that has an individual history in each of us, which changes as we pass through other developmental stages, including aging and the anticipation of death. It is interesting that Poland, despite his grounding in the psychology of instinctual conflict, does not suggest that the analyst try to understand the meaning of the experience of being witnessed as uniquely derived from the peculiarities of each patient's personal fantasy life. Instead, he treats the experience as a general feature of human psychology, a special version of which occurs in psychoanalysis. It is not surprising, then, that he proceeds to connect his observations and theorizing with the concerns of certain philosophers engaged with aspects of human mental life and experience related to the topic of "otherness." Perhaps it is because of Poland's interest in the contributions of philosophy to psychoanalysis that he does not address the usual analytic question of just what an experience—here, that of being witnessed—means to a particular patient, and why it has that meaning and no other. It is striking that none of the discussants—of whom more in a moment—found this feature of Poland's presentation remarkable. Poland also expresses himself eloquently on the current debate about intersubjectivity. Insisting on the validity of both one-person and two-person psychologies, he treats these as defined by perspective, rather than as constituting a categorical contradiction.

It is a fascinating commentary on our current state of theoretical discourse that each of the half-dozen discussants of Poland's paper finds something quite different in it, to which each responds, in agreement, disagreement, or both, from his or her angle of interest. It is notable that among them only one, Andre Green, sees fit to remind us that Freud's psychoanalysis was centered on the vicissitudes of sexuality. Green wonders, not for the first time, what has happened to psychoanalysis if we no longer think that way these days? Poland responds that he, for one, takes the significance of sexuality as a given, even though his current paper address other concerns. It is not at all clear that the other discussants would echo Poland on that score, any more than they exactly mirror his views on how to conceive of, or conduct, the psychoanalytic encounter. Further, there is certainly disagreement with Poland's remarks on the advent of intersubjectivity into psychoanalytic theory, especially in regard to the theory of technique.

Other questions about the nature of the relationship between analyst and patient, and its role in technique, also make their appearance in these pages. The assumption that there exists a functionally distinguishable realistic relationship, which provides the basis for therapeutic contact and thereby facilitates the conduct of the analysis of the transference relationship, survives here after literally decades of debate. Psychoanalytic camps have long been divided between those who see the irrational transference relationship as only one dimension of the complex emotional connection between analyst and patient, coexistent with a more rational, perhaps essential alliance between them, and those who think that such operational distinctions are deceptive, appealing to the analyst's needs, rather than reflecting psychological truth. Both positions are given voice in this collection of papers.

Robert Hausner reconsiders the arguments of some in the latter group, and dismisses them in favor of the concepts of the therapeutic and working alliances. As is often true of analysts who prefer the alliance concepts in any form, he believes that certain modifications of the analyst's behavior promote the alliance to the benefit of the treatment. He appears to think that the meanings given by the patient to aspects of the analyst's behavior that are aimed at supporting the alliance are derived simply from the early developmental prototype of the alliance. He appears not to consider that these behaviors depend for their effect on their stimulation of specific fantasies unique to each patient, as those holding the contrary view would surely contend. In this we may detect an echo of the question, noted earlier, about the significance of witnessing, though here it is raised in quite a different context, one with whose assumptions Poland would not likely agree.

Jack and Kerry Kelly Novick, following a line of thought they have been developing for some time, arrive by a different route at the idea of a realistic relationship between patient and analyst. They see such a relationship as reflecting the presence of less pathological capacities for relating, and thus more as a product of successful analysis than a consequence of the analyst's supportive behavior. Henry Smith, in a candid and logically rigorous presentation, takes a quite different position. He argues not only that the analysand's behavior cannot be fractionated into rational and irrational components, but that the same disquieting assessment must be applied also to the psychology and behavior of the analyst. In Smith's view, this is not a discouragement to analytic technique, but a more precise and accurate way of understanding its complexities, for better and for worse.

Changing views of the role of the relationship in analytic technique present a number of different questions, and options, in today's pluralistic theoretical spectrum. It might be said of Smith's assessment of the analyst's psychological position that it is consonant with the underlying basis of current intersubjectivist views of the analyst as participant in the analytic encounter, though he adopts none of the intersubjectivist prescriptions for modifying the analyst's behavior from the traditional stance of Freudian neutrality. Another attempt to adapt the historical image of analytic neutrality to the increased sophistication of our present appreciation of the intricacies of the transference-countertransference matrix is offered by Ronald Baker. He, like Smith and others in these pages, regards himself as a traditional ego psychologist, rather than as a proponent of intersubjective or relational models, but he sees room in his interpretation of the neutral position for considerable flexibility. A clear line of demarcation can be drawn between theories of technique, from Ferenczi to the present, that advocate deliberate, consciously intended shifts from the traditional Freudian specifications regarding the analyst's behavior and those that reject such modifications. Theories addressing variations in analytic behavior that are unconsciously determined are less easy to classify, with the papers of Baker, the Novicks, and Smith each posing quite different formulations, not at all compatible, of these thorny issues.

Just as the questions regarding the role of the relationship in analysis and technique have become increasingly complex and sophisticated, so also are the issues currently raised regarding the content dimension of psychoanalytic insight. I have in mind the lively controversies concerning what the analyst's attention should be focused on, and also certain suggested limitations with respect to the optimal content of interpretive activity. An unusual case in point is provided by Paul Gray. Following a theoretical direction for which he has been known for many years, he repeats his advocacy of restricting the analyst's interpretive activity to the observable defense activities of the patient, as they appear in analytic productions. He contends that for suitable patients this technique will give access to instinctual derivatives, which he conceives of very much in traditional Freudian terms. He also maintains, as he has previously, that interpretive attention to anything in the patient's material that deals with life outside the analytic situation, whether with reference to the past or to current life events, is inadvertently in the service of the patient's resistance. Paradoxically enough, this aspect of Gray's position corresponds with the views of certain contemporary relational theorists. They too recommend confining analytic attention to the so-called here and now of the analytic situation, though their ideas are based on an entirely different rationale, one with which Gray would hardly agree, and which would lead to insight with an entirely different kind of content.

Fred Busch, acknowledging his debt to Gray, further pursues his interest in determining the optimal level of interpretive attention. He too sees as inadvisable interpretations that offer the analyst's view of unconscious structures or contents that are at a remove from the patient's conscious comprehension. Another version of his cautionary advice is implicit in Josephs' concern about variants of superego analysis. It is worth noting that Busch's criteria for effectiveness rests on the familiar principle of the patient's affective responsivity, expressed in the phrase "emotionally meaningful." I imagine that few analysts of any theoretical stripe would question the shibboleth of affective or emotional meaningfulness as a test of interpretive accuracy and timeliness. However, it is not so easy to specify how affective meaningfulness is determined or measured. Our contemporary understanding of affect in mental life, as vividly demonstrated by the range of material presented at the recent Santiago Congress of the International Psychoanalytical Association, hardly serves to clarify that familiar precept of analytic technique. It is surely not just a matter of affective display in response to interpretations, as all experienced analysts know that some varieties of affective response to the analyst's activity can signify something other than therapeutic impact. Busch, Josephs, and others would certainly be likely to agree with this observation. I believe they would agree also that we all have much more to learn about technique and its assessment as we enter the new century. On that, pluralism offers us no grounds for disagreement.

CHAPTER 7

Expanding Psychological Possibilities

[Abend, S.M. (2001). *Psychoanalytic Quarterly* 70(1):3–14]

Introduction

In my opinion, the essential goal of psychoanalysis can be summed up in a simple phrase: "greater freedom of choice," given the understanding that "choice" means something more than its common-sense implication of making conscious decisions. What is actually implied by the word *choice*, and what analysis hopes to help the patient achieve, is an expanded universe of psychological possibilities, in place of the restricted set he or she was constrained to live with before treatment. In this short essay, I shall strive to explain why I prefer this definition of goals, and I will illustrate how I understand its application with short clinical examples. For the sake of clarity, I shall also mention very briefly the time-honored distinction between analytic goals and life goals, and cast a passing glance at the analyst's goals, as he or she engages in the work of analysis.

I first encountered the conception that analysis seeks to expand the analysand's freedom of choice during my analytic training, and I continue to embrace it, even though I have since come to appreciate that the term *choice* does not refer simply to the realm of conscious, cognitive activities. Greater freedom of choice is meant instead to designate an increased flexibility, a widened spectrum of possible responses to inner and outer stimuli, including, although not limited to, much that transpires outside of deliberate conscious control. I believe that my adherence to this formulation follows logically from my view of what lies at the core of the varieties of human psychological distress that analysis hopes to alleviate. According to my theoretical beliefs, psychoanalysis attempts to treat the pathogenic consequences of unconscious instinctual conflicts, originating in childhood, and persisting in the form of rigid patterns of emotional and cognitive reactivity that function to restrict a person's affective and behavioral choices and responses.

I fully agree with those who point out that there are crucial shaping and limiting influences attributable to inherent and acquired biological factors, and also to the effects of environmental experience on human development and behavior. However, in my view, these are not the primary foci of concern in psychoanalytic treatment, even though they may have to be taken into account. I agree instead with Kris's (1947) idea that the subject matter of psychoanalysis is "human behavior viewed as conflict" (p. 6). Since I adhere to the traditional Freudian ego-psychological understanding of conflict, I conceptualize the outcome of conflict in the theoretical language of unconscious compromise formations. This means that, beginning in childhood, our libidinal and aggressive desires are modulated by a variety of ego functions, operating largely out of conscious awareness, to defend against unpleasure, whether realistic or fantastic in nature. These ego functions also simultaneously serve to make possible as much instinctual gratification as circumstances appear to allow.

Rational and irrational moral constraints, both anticipatory and consequential either to real actions or fantasies, also play a vital role in determining the dynamically complex arrangements we call compromise formations. A more or less stable matrix of compromise formations, in which the aforementioned biological and experiential components are structurally embedded, constitutes each person's psychological makeup. It is inherent in its nature that this network of compromise formations channels the child's, and later the adult's, strivings and reactions into an individually characteristic, limited preferential set of emotional-cognitive-behavioral patterns. Since the determinative developmental history and underlying structural composition of these patterns lie, for the most part, outside the person's conscious understanding, they are significantly, although not totally, resistant to change by life experience and/or by the exercise of conscious will alone. This is largely true of the maladaptive and uncomfortable dysphorias we classify as symptoms, and perhaps even more so of the complex, relatively stable defensive and adaptive arrangements we refer to as character traits.

Freud's Formulation of Psychoanalytic Goals

Given this set of operative background assumptions, it seems reasonable to hold to an only slightly modified version of Freud's original formulation of psychoanalytic goals. By expanding the analysand's comprehension of the pertinent historical and structural influences that were previously inaccessible to his or her consciousness, analysis seeks to equip the individual to beneficially alter the repertoire of possible choices (whether automatic or deliberately intended) of response, reaction, plan, and/or behavior that are available to deal with inner and outer circumstances. Freud first thought of this as enabling mature, conscious, more or less rational judgment to determine certain actions and reactions, in place of continuing to permit archaic, irrational patterns, originally fixed in place in an immature mental apparatus, to limit the options of the troubled adult.

Experience has taught us that Freud's (1933) aphorism, "where id was, there shall ego be" (p. 80), is both inaccurate and inadequate to describe this goal. I prefer to say instead that analysis enables the formation and use of new compromise formations, which permit the individual to achieve a greater degree of satisfaction in life and a commensurate reduction in unnecessary suffering. We have also come to appreciate that mere intellectual insight into what was previously unknown is often insufficient to produce the desired changes. No analyst today would suggest that the acquisition of insight is all that transpires in a successful analysis, or even that it identifies the sole therapeutic influence of the analytic experience. Nevertheless, increased self-understanding is still regarded as the keystone to the analysand's achievement of greater freedom and flexibility in psychological life.

Understanding the Unconscious

My assignment in this paper is not to describe the complexities of therapeutic action, nor even the full dimension of the impact of analysis. Instead, I am to concentrate on the question of goals, by whatever means these are to be reached. Thus, I place emphasis on understanding just how the persistent influence of unconscious mental functioning acts as a limiting, restrictive determinant of human emotional life, thought, and behavior. Psychoanalysis, therefore, seeks to expand the analysand's grasp of his or her unconscious mind and its role in mental reactions and decisions. One consequence will be the person's increased ability to recognize the archaic, less satisfactory patterns, and how they affect his or her life. Even more important, it is hoped that through analysis, better choices will become available, or, stated in terms of my preferred theoretical language, that new compromise formations will emerge, ones that address old dilemmas in a more satisfactory way than was possible before. Thus, the fundamental desires that motivate people psychologically can be dealt with more productively than before, with less unpleasant affect, restriction, self-defeat, or self-punishment, and correspondingly more satisfaction and success, along with their attendant pleasure.

Clinical Examples

Simple, familiar clinical illustrations may help to clarify these ideas. Ms. A, a successful woman in her early thirties, developed a paralyzing fear of flying that threatened her career. This was the symptomatic precipitant that brought her to treatment, although, not surprisingly, she also had other dissatisfactions, chiefly concerning the quality of her romantic attachments. Successful treatment uncovered several layers of the unconscious determinants of her phobia, with progressive relief of her anxiety and the gradual disappearance of this debilitating restriction on her life. It was also helpful in other aspects of her psychological functioning as well. While it can be argued that other kinds of treatment interventions might have relieved her phobic inhibition, in point of fact this woman was profoundly mistrustful of being influenced in any way, and previous behavioral approaches had consequently not proven helpful in her case. The advantage of the analytic approach was that the sources and nature of her suspicions were also illuminated, and this work aided her in being able to respond more positively to treatment. Not incidentally, her analytic treatment also illuminated other aspects of her conflicts about her career, and clearly helped her to fulfill her considerable ambitions in other ways besides the relief of her fear of flying. She was enabled to pursue her personal goals with less accompanying distress and a much greater degree of conscious satisfaction.

In another situation, Mr. B sought treatment because he was unable to find a satisfactory love relationship with a suitable woman. His analysis revealed that, far from his conscious understanding, many aspects of his character structure contributed to his pattern of making problematic object choices, of which one recurrent feature was their tendency to mercurial mood swings and lack of sustained devotion to him. A lengthy and ultimately successful treatment provided a sufficient increase in his understanding of the determinants of this pattern to eventually increase his flexibility to the point that he could permit himself to find and marry a suitable woman, with whom he built a stable, satisfying marriage. To be sure, his happier choice also reflected the unconscious components of new compromise formations, in addition to his better conscious judgment. Moreover, his increased insight helped him to recognize and break away from his previous proclivities, and materially aided him in the construction of the new solutions to his fundamental conflicts.

In a third, not unusual case, a young man, Mr. C, came to analysis because of recurrent depressions and difficulty in school. His analysis gradually uncovered a powerful set of unconscious submissive, dependent, and essentially masochistic ties to an apparently severely disturbed parent. Over time, this patient was able to achieve a level of independence and self-reliance previously undreamed of by him, along the way choosing a new career path and also gaining considerable relief from his depressive tendencies. Even though one might plausibly posit that other treatment approaches might also have helped with Mr. C's depressive symptoms, it is difficult to imagine that the satisfaction he gained from his growing sense of independence, and the increase in self-esteem that accompanied it, would have been achieved as easily without the hard-won insight into the nature of his antecedent psychological enslavement provided by the analysis.

In citing these brief examples, I have deliberately refrained from attempting to illustrate specific alterations in the relevant compromise formations. To do so would have required far more detailed clinical descriptions, and in any case, would not have achieved my primary aim. I am aware that there are other useful theoretical dialects besides that of compromise formations that could also be employed to describe the kinds of analytic outcomes I have mentioned. For my present purpose, I wish to place emphasis on the crucial role of unconscious patterning in determining these patients' difficulties, and the analytic focus on effective enlightenment about these patterns, as a means of enabling these patients to construct less restrictive ways to deal with their affects, their desires, and their choices of activities and relationships.

Psychoanalytic Goals and Life Goals

This seems to be the appropriate point to bring up the distinction between psychoanalytic goals and life goals. As important as it was to Ms. A to satisfy her professional ambitions, and for Mr. B to find a wife and have a family, I consider those specific aspirations to lie in the realm of life goals, not analytic ones. Unanticipated, unpredictable internal factors, as well as a host of external variables, including the vagaries of fortune, can affect whether specific, concrete life goals are achieved, or prove instead to be unattainable. This observation is long familiar to psychoanalysts, and the distinction between the two categories has been discussed in the past (Ticho, 1972). I think one might say that analytic goals are centered on helping the analysand to acquire better psychological tools and skills with which to pursue his or her life goals. Whether these new capabilities are employed successfully or not in each case is a question whose answer must include a consideration of the operation of many forces and factors, some of which lie outside the purview of psychoanalytic therapy.

It seems to me that the distinction between the class of concrete, specific life goals, on the one hand, and that of internal psychological capacities that individuals may alter and expand as a result of analytic treatment, on the other hand, is rather easily detailed and understood. However, I believe that an intermediate type of goal also exists, one that may pose a more difficult problem of classification. Consider, for example, the paralyzing anxiety that tormented Ms. A when she was forced to contemplate an airplane trip, or the depressive cast that so troubled Mr. C over a period of several years. These are familiar instances of what analysts, following medical tradition, are accustomed to regard as part of the symptom picture that leads patients to seek relief through therapy in the first place. For Freud, who built on the model provided by his training as a neurologist, there was no question that his psychoanalytic technique was an empirically derived method of treatment of the underlying illnesses, of which neurotic symptoms were only the surface manifestations. Subsequent evolution of the field of psychoanalysis has raised complicated conceptual issues in place of his early certitude.

What Psychoanalysis Can Achieve

It would take us much further afield than I wish to go in this essay to address the many intellectual and political influences that have contributed to the blurring of once simple, clear-cut notions of psychoanalytic cure. Suffice it to say that in many psychoanalytic circles today, the very idea of conceiving of psychoanalytic goals in terms of the cure of symptoms is specifically negated. Furthermore, from relatively early on in the history of psychoanalysis, the fact that the underlying unconscious underpinnings of even manifestly painful symptoms often provides important hidden gratification to the individuals who complain of them came to be appreciated as one explanation of patients' resistance to change. Then, too, clinical experience has dictated a deep respect for the often intractable effects of biology, and of traumatic life experiences, on the psychological makeup of many analytic patients. Their troubles may prove to be more or less immutable, despite their own best efforts and those of their analysts. Later in the course of psychoanalytic history, the proposed philosophical shift away from the historical model of disease, treatment, and cure added a further dimension to the vexing problem of defining the goals of analysis.

As far as I am concerned, if an analysis that I conduct does not succeed to any significant degree in relieving the painful distress about which my patient complains when we first agree to work together, I cannot easily reassure myself that a satisfactory analytic outcome has been achieved. Of course, a full assessment of results is often far from simple, since other, unarticulated goals frequently enough emerge as analysis unfolds, and subtle and complex combinations of achievement and disregard, of redefinition and reorganization, of satisfaction and acceptance of limitation, characterize all analytic experiences. That said, I nevertheless always try to keep in mind what patients tell me they suffer from at the start, as well as what other miseries come to light as we work together. The self-comforting reminder that limitations exist which are beyond the power of even the best analysis to overcome is always ready to hand, sometimes even properly so. Nevertheless, this realization rarely succeeds in assuaging my personal sense of disquiet, if my efforts do not help the patient to attain some relief from the troubles that brought him or her to my office in the first place.

The balancing of this view of what I hope my analytic skills can help my patients to achieve with the recognition that both analysis in general, and this analyst in particular, are far from perfect and far from omnipotent, is one of the burdens of our profession. I suspect that other colleagues struggle to deal with it in much the same fashion that I do.

This inner tension also plays an important technical role, expressed in the necessity to monitor my countertransference, while working with my patients on their own evaluations of their satisfactions and disappointments with the results of our combined endeavors.

Before I pursue further this natural segue into the issue of the analyst's goals, I would like to briefly restate my own view of the aims of the analytic enterprise. I regard psychoanalysis as a form of treatment for various kinds of psychological distress. As such, it is focused on the miseries of which the patient complains, this being understood to include certain kinds of problems uncovered and identified during the course of analysis, which the patient may have been unable to articulate at the outset of therapy. The means by which relief is to be achieved center on an investigation and elaboration of crucial unconscious elements in the patient's makeup that play a role in his or her distress. The procedure, it is hoped, will thereby facilitate the patient's attainment of a new level of flexibility and conscious and unconscious choice in dealing with psychological conflicts. The result, in successful cases, is a reduction in certain dimensions of the patient's emotional suffering, and a consequent increase in the amount of pleasure and satisfaction that can be attained in life, always commensurate with the possibilities realistically open to him or her.

The Psychoanalyst's Goals

As to the psychoanalyst's goals, I would emphasize the effort he or she makes to attain and maintain an analytic attitude toward whatever the patient may present. This deceptively simple formula requires some elaboration. The idea that the analyst can function in keeping with Bion's (1967) celebrated advice, "[free from the influence of] memory and desire" (p. 19)—solely as an otherwise unmotivated, sensitive recipient of the patient's immediate conscious and unconscious communications—is, in my opinion, a romantic fiction. So, too, the idea that the analyst is merely interested in understanding and interpreting the unconscious of his or her patients is an anachronistic oversimplification of the task of analysis.

In a similar vein, it has by now been widely acknowledged that a once-popular opinion—the belief that analytic training, good character, and personal analysis are enough to make of the analyst a uniformly objective, scientific observer of (and thus a neutral interpreter of) the patient's psychology—is naively optimistic. Our current emphasis on the intersubjective nature of the analytic encounter unmistakably illuminates what were long quietly recognized, if at times minimized, sectors of professional disquiet about how analysts, as human beings, actually function.

I do not, however, join those analysts who have seized upon this modern elaboration of the role of the analyst's personality and limitations on his or her work to construct a new prescription for liberalizing former constraints on the analyst's technical stance and practice. It is my opinion that the analytic attitude which I advocate requires of the analyst his or her best possible devotion to the task of reacting to the patient's behavior and communications in a particular fashion. I take this to mean that the analyst attempts, at all times, to understand what is going on in the patient, in him- or herself, and between them, and to translate this understanding, in the analyst's own mind, into the conceptual terminology of our profession. In my case, this terminology is that of conflict and compromise formation, but even if the analyst prefers another theoretical dialect, I hold that the adoption of an analytic attitude entails the same essential elements.

It is by now firmly established that a scrutiny of one's own inner responses, impulses, and behavior is an essential part of the analyst's effort to understand. The acquired understanding is then communicated to each analytic patient in as timely, sensitive, diplomatic, and honest a fashion as the analyst can manage to achieve. Other modes of deliberately attempting to influence the patient besides the transmitting of the kind of understanding I have described, to which the shorthand appellations "interpretation" and "insight" are usually applied, are not part of the ideal analytic attitude.

That the ideal attitude is impossible for the analyst to achieve or sustain, and that in consequence, subtle, or sometimes not so subtle, means of trying to impact the patient also take place in analysis, is beyond question. Thus, my view of things is not that the analyst must accomplish the impossible, nor delude him- or herself that it *is* possible. Rather, the analyst's task is to strive to have and sustain an analytic attitude toward patients, and to maintain as much self-awareness about his or her variations from this model—temptations to add something more or to take something away from it—as possible. More cannot be expected, as we have come to realize. Neither, in my opinion at least, should anything less than one's best efforts to approach that standard of excellence be enshrined in analytic technique. I do not agree at all with those who suggest that attempting to adhere to this formula turns the analyst into an uncaring, unempathic surgeon of the psyche, indifferent to outcome or suffering, or unengaged with the patient's life. On the contrary, I think it holds the promise of maximizing the patient's prospects for defining and finding his or her own best potential. This, to be sure, is no insignificant goal, and obviously one well worth the challenge it imposes on analyst and analysand alike.

Conclusion

In summary, then, one can restate the goals of psychoanalysis in the following way: Patients seek relief from certain miseries and dissatisfaction, as well as the successful pursuit of greater fulfillment in life. Analysis hopes to help them in these aims by illuminating the nature of those unconscious mental activities that contribute to their troubles and interfere with their satisfactions. It is hoped that sufficient new understanding of the history and nature of those unconscious dimensions of their psychological functioning will enable analysands to achieve an increased level of flexibility and a greater range of choice, deliberate or otherwise, of thought, emotions, and behavior. This expansion of psychological possibilities, in turn, can help them to attain their more proximate goals of decreasing unnecessary pain and of finding greater pleasure. The analyst, in exercising his or her skills in the service of the patient's quest, tries to aid in the gradual expansion of the patient's useful self-knowledge. He or she does so, insofar as possible, without otherwise attempting to dictate or to persuade the patient to live life according to any precepts other than those valued independently by the patient.

References

Bion, W. (1967). Notes on memory and desire. In: *Melanie Klein Today: Developments in Theory and Practice, Vol. 2: Mainly Practice*, ed. E.B. Spillius. London: Routledge, 1988, pp. 17–21.

Freud, S. (1933). New Introductory Lectures on Psycho-Analysis. *Standard Edition* 22.

Kris, E. (1947). The nature of psychoanalytic propositions and their validation. In: *Selected Papers of Ernst Kris*. New Haven: Yale University Press, 1975, pp. 3–23.

Ticho, E. (1972). Termination of psychoanalysis: treatment goals, life goals. *Psychoanalytic Quarterly* 41:318–333.

Part II:

Unconscious Fantasy

CHAPTER 8

Unconscious Fantasy and Theories of Cure

[Abend, S.M. (1979). *Journal of the American Psychoanalytic Association* 27:579–596.]

Some patients display a market interest in how analysis effects its "cures"; they even evolve theories of their own to account for its results. Two such individuals I have analyzed revealed the presence of these ideas gradually during the course of their treatment; their beliefs had the important practical consequence of influencing the way they behaved in the analytic situation. The uncovering and analysis of these fantasies helped to clarify the meaning of their behavior, as well as the transference wishes incorporated therein, and eventually led to the reconstruction of the unconscious fantasies of childhood origin from which their theories were derived. These findings, which I shall illustrate, are related to observations of others regarding the unconscious significance of the wish to be "cured" or "fully analyzed" and its psychic elaborations.

I also believe that the influence of such unconscious fantasies can be detected in the theories of cure put forth by some analysts as well as other therapists, and that they may contribute to the degree of acceptance that these theories receive from other colleagues. Finally, I shall try to indicate how the same phenomena may affect clinical decisions to modify treatment technique even in the absence of explicit formulations regarding the theory of cure.

That the conscious, more or less realistic thoughts about analysis and its outcome which are held by patients are invariably connected to unconscious fantasies derived from childhood mental life is by no means a recent observation. Nunberg (1926) noted that individuals gain unconscious gratification from talking about themselves to the analyst, and that the "cure" they wish for also has an unconscious significance. He was well aware that this affected the patient's behavior in the analytic situation, since the infantile instinctual aims emerged seeking satisfaction in the form of transference wishes. He gave a number of examples from his own experience.

Schmideberg (1938) observed that patients have unconscious fantasies about what it means to be "fully analyzed," which are "replicas of the child s ideas of what it is like to be grown up" (p. 123). She emphasized that these were likely to be unrealistically grandiose, perfectionistic, and omnipotent, to make up for the humiliation associated with childhood helplessness and inferiority; these latter feelings are often associated as well with the neurotic illness and its symptoms. She agreed with Nunberg that the cure is conceived of unconsciously in terms of libidinal gratification. She made the point that there are also neurotically determined urges to remain ill; the so-called negative therapeutic reaction is an outstanding example of their expression in behavior. About it she said, "The unconscious guilt which prevents the patient from getting well is largely due to the nature of the unconscious infantile fantasies which underlie the rational wish to get well" (p. 124).

She summed up her main point of view thus: "In my experience, analysis of the patient's fantastic expectations and idealization of analysis is of the greatest therapeutic importance because these ideas often constitute the core of his transference neurosis, are closely bound up with the negative therapeutic reaction, and present a subtle but most effective resistance towards accepting reality" (p. 131). She also emphasized that unconscious attitudes and fantasies of an analogous nature in the analyst can become important sources of countertransference difficulty by affecting, among other things, supposedly rational standards and expectations regarding the results of analysis.

During the post-World War II period substantial refinement of the concept of transference and its place in the theory of cure, as well as increased interest in and knowledge of the earlier stages of child development, were reflected in newly emerging ideas about the nature of patients' responses to the analytic situation. Malcapine (1950), for example, contended that psychoanalytic technique creates, through a multiplicity of factors, such as curtailment of the object world, constancy of environment, establishment of a fixed routine, and so on, enough reminders of the infantile situation to engender a regressive adaptation on the part of the analysand. Waelder (1956) agreed that the analysand who comes seeking help, who unilaterally exposes himself or herself, and who obtains reassurance against anxiety is of necessity in the position of a child *vis-à-vis* the adult analyst. Spitz (1956) believed that the analytic situation created a parallel to the infant-mother situation, likening the couch to the crib, and free association to the unselective, uninhibited productions of the small child. It seemed natural that analysts like Winnicott (1956), Nacht (1962), and Gitelson (1962) would propose that the therapeutic effectiveness of the analyst is analogous to the beneficial influence of an appropriately responsive mother on the development of the infant. One gains the impression from the literature of this period that it was to be assumed that patients invariably respond unconsciously to the analytic situation in terms of the earliest mother-infant interactions in clinically significant ways.

Arlow and Brenner (1966) were moved to express their disagreement with the implication that the analytic situation must inevitably evoke the same type of unconscious fantasy in all analysands. Such an automatic assumption on the part of the analyst was potentially misleading, they contended, and they illustrated their thesis with case material demonstrating, for instance, that a given patient's positive image of the analyst as helpful, empathic, and understanding could be derived from experiences with the father, rather than the mother, and that reactions to terminations of analyses do not always center around object loss and mourning, as had been suggested, but may have other predominant characteristics instead. In any event, it was by then quite clear to all analysts that various aspects of the analytic situation do always evoke some unconscious fantasies or other in all analytic patients, even though not invariably the same ones, and that these fantasies are reflected in their behavior in sessions.

More recently, Applebaum (1972) called attention to still another important interface between supposedly rational ideas about treatment and the unconscious fantasies from which they are in part derived. She pointed out the shortcomings of using what she regards as an inadequate view of "motivation for change" as a valid predictive factor in assessing a prospective patient's likelihood to benefit from analysis. The studies that she criticized, in her opinion, gave too much weight to consciously available material presented at the time of the initial evaluation. She also noted the role played by unconscious wishes to defeat, undermine, and ridicule the would-be helper in some patients' responses to analysis. She further stated that "The transference fantasies can convert the real gratifications of the analytic situation into ends in themselves, and so promote the wish to continue the treatment while blocking further progress towards development of a wish to change" (p. 55).

My own interest in still another variation of this class of observations was first aroused in the course of working with a young man who displayed an unusual degree of curiosity about how analysis worked. In time I was able to learn from him that he had evolved his own rather well-developed theory to explain its results, and it was possible to trace this conscious hypothesis back to its unconscious childhood antecedents. It was of particular interest that his behavior in the analytic situation could be satisfactorily comprehended and modified only when the complete structure and childhood origins of his fantasies had emerged. This was true despite the fact that some relevant elements of the transference had been understood and interpreted to the patient earlier in the treatment. The persistence of his behavior, despite the attention that had been paid to clarifying its meaning, is certainly indicative of the importance of these transference wishes and fantasies. I also think it possible that some essential quality of conviction in regard to the transference interpretations was supplied only when these specific fantasies, into which the transference wishes had been elaborated, were fully worked out and understood. In this instance, the wishes had to do with the patient's desire for sexual enlightenment at the hands of a substitute parent figure who would be more gratifying than his own parents had been.

The patient was a 27-year-old unmarried man who sought analysis for depression and extreme social and professional inhibitions. He had managed to complete college, although not without several interruptions for substantial periods. He had not been able to hold a job since, and at the time his analysis began he was so immobilized that he was ignoring the efforts of friends and relatives to help him find employment. He had had but one brief passionate love affair several years earlier, when he was far from his family in a milieu entirely strange to him and them. He had subsequently permitted his parents' opposition to dissuade him from his intention to marry the young woman; since the end of this liaison he had dated only infrequently, with great self-consciousness and tension, and had not been able to bring himself to make sexual overtures to any of the women he did see socially.

He was the oldest child of a well-to-do prominent family. His father had retired from the family enterprise at an early age because of what the patient knew only as "a weak heart." As a boy of five, the patient had had to be very quiet about the house in order not to disturb his father's ritual afternoon nap. His mother, a forceful, brusque, opinionated woman, controlled the household. The children were raised almost entirely by nannies, in conformance with rigid and demanding standards of proper behavior as ordained by the mother.

The patient appeared to be unusually *unknowledgeable* about psychoanalysis, considering he had been educated at one of the nation's leading universities, but he approached the task with manifest diligence and a conscientiousness consonant with his obsessional character structure. He soon displayed a high degree of interest in and curiosity about the way psychoanalysis was supposed to work. He did not ask me questions, but revealed his preoccupation through his associations; he frequently recounted his observations and speculations about the way we were working together, and how he imagined it might be affecting him. As connections between his current behavior, both in and out of the transference, and its childhood determinants were interpreted to him, he reacted with apparent amazement and wonder as well as interest. The persistence of this unsophisticated fascination seemed excessive, and I began to call it to his attention.

His associations soon confirmed that his naïveté was unwittingly exaggerated and represented the childhood "innocence" that implied the wish for sexual enlightenment from knowledgeable adults, as well as a denial of his competitive wishes. His intellectualism, which contributed to his curiosity about theoretical matters, in part gave expression to an entirely unconscious desire to compete with the analyst by learning all that the latter must know about "how to do it," and in part was defensive against affects, especially those associated with his competitiveness. Much of this material was subsumed in the fantasy of being an apprentice or, as it had appeared in a conscious version during the patient's adolescence, a medieval squire devotedly serving a knight as preparation for eventually assuming his own manly role. These were later elaborations of an unconscious fantasy from childhood of learning to be a man via homosexual submission to an admired father figure. In that construction, he simultaneously was able to deny his fearful and guilt-arousing hostile competition and substitute for it a gratifying love relationship with the father, plus a reassuring promise of future permission to function in a masculine way without incurring danger or punishment. In fact, his father's older brother had played just such a symbolic role in the young man's life after the father's decline; as self-appointed mentor, he had welcomed confidences, accepted the boy's admiration, and taken much time and trouble to counsel and advise him.

The clarification of this material did not affect the patient's behavior in analysis very much, although he did gradually become somewhat freer to express himself, less cautious, constricted, and "good," both in sessions and in his life outside. He continued to exhibit his curiosity about how analysis worked and eventually was able to reveal his own idea of the process of cure. His image of a cold, stern, moralistic, demanding mother had come to be connected in his mind with a puritanical Christianity which was antithetical to sexuality. Psychoanalysis and his analyst represented to him Jewish ethical standards, which he associated with the Old Testament, and which he thought of as "warm and earthy," *i.e.*, tolerant of sexuality. Thus, he was coming to me as a student, convert, or acolyte, to learn a new doctrine to replace the old one; this new religion was to include and therefore make permissible the sexual feelings and wishes proscribed in childhood.

The infantile sources of this fantasy were childhood perceptions and fantasies concerning the difference between his mother and a particular nanny who had had full charge of him from the time of his birth until he went off to school. The latter, a white Christian with an Old Testament given name of Esther, was of course of a different ethnic background and social class from his mother; in his mind she was "warm and earthy." It was his use of those words in describing her which gave the first indication that she was the actual figure behind his characterization of the Old Testament and Jewish morality. While these qualities may indeed have been accurate assessments of her personality as compared with his mother's, this could not be determined with absolute assurance. They were certainly derived in large measure from the fact that it was Esther who cared for his physical needs in early childhood, and he in consequence had far more access, visual and tactile, to her body than he did to his mother's. When he was a little older he sometimes wondered whether he was not actually her child, rather than his mother's. Thus, the fantasy of cure was a rationalized version of the idea that if he had only *really* had this other, different mother, she would have truly loved him and instructed him sexually at first hand, so that he would know how to make love to women and compete successfully with other men.

When this man progressed enough to fall in love with a suitable and responsive woman, he chose a Jewish woman—and subsequently reacted to me as if I were identified with the cold, forbidding, possessive, and controlling gentile mother who disapproved of his love affair.

Another patient with quite different pathology from the one just described also persisted for some time in unusual behavior in the analytic situation. In his case the emphasis was on anal fantasies. He had a sexual disturbance involving a preoccupation with a perverse sadomasochistic masturbatory fantasy. On occasion he felt compelled to enact a diluted and disguised version of his fantasy with a sexual partner; this behavior, consciously quite repugnant to him, he rationalized as "getting it out of my system."

In analysis, despite his high conscious motivation, he edited and controlled his utterances and spoke so softly—sometimes for hours at a time—that it was all but impossible to understand what he could bring himself to say. Even after some months he spoke despairingly of his feeling of inability to alter this behavior with his analyst, although he realized it was severely handicapping the prospect of progress; he hoped eventually to overcome this problem, but for the present, he said one day, it was "just something I have to get out of my system." This turn of phrase provided a useful clue which initiated a more productive exploration of the meaning of his behavior. Only the fact that there was some specific connection between how he acted on the couch and his sexual behavior was clear; its exact nature was still obscure. The masochistic and sadistic transference wishes and their associated conflicts slowly unfolded as the analysis progressed, while the patient's behavior changed only very gradually.

Long after the patient was able to talk more freely and much more understandably, he continued intermittently to display aspects of his early behavior in the analysis. Long periods of constricted, semi-intelligible verbalization, accompanied by depressive affect, unconsciously represented a protective armor against imagined sadistic assaults from the analyst, and, simultaneously, both an implacable torture of the analyst-victim and a mournful conviction of permanent loneliness as punishment for his evil wishes. Still later, when he could acknowledge his rage more openly, he indulged himself in days of abusive, accusatory behavior when he felt he had an acceptable excuse to express criticism of his analyst.

Considerable work on the homosexual side of the transference clarified much of the complex relationships he had with his father and his older brother, both of whom had appeared physically overpowering to the patient in childhood. His mother had always been depicted as maddeningly controlling and belittling to all men. Now his helpless rage and fury at her emerged in a new and more convincing form; he believed that she had somehow accepted his father's and brother's masculinity, which he himself had so admired and envied, to a much greater extent than she had his own; he was supposed to have been a girl, an image of herself. There was substantial evidence that his view of her attitude was not entirely imaginary, although it may have been exaggerated.

His mother had worked in the family business from the time my patient was a toddler, and he came to believe she cared much more about money that she did about him. Her withholding temperament contributed to his fantasy that she had deliberately refused to give him an attractive manly body and phallus as well as the love and admiration he imagined these would have helped him to win. He was chronically resentful and melancholy, but felt compelled to try to placate her and unable, consciously at least, to express defiance or rebelliousness. Angry submission characterized many of his relationships with other women, particularly those older than himself. His anal fantasies were subsequently reinforced by his knowledge that his father suffered from bleeding hemorrhoids. He even confused this condition with the severe blood dyscrasia which eventually claimed his father's life. His confusion of the anus with the female genital, and his vivid conviction of the possibility of violent castration were also reinforced by his views of his father's illnesses, as was the related regressive condensation of phallus and feces. His belief was that his masculinity in general and his penis in particular were disgusting and unacceptable to his mother, and he had fantasies in childhood of submissively accepting torture, *i.e.*, castration, to win her love; these ideas both humiliated and terrified him. His sadism toward women was both vindictive and defensive, and its role in the transference became clearer as the foregoing material emerged. His tremendous sexual guilt and belief in his unlovability were also now more comprehensible.

At this point in the treatment, the patient acknowledged that he permitted himself to behave toward his analyst in ways that would never be acceptable in any other situation, because he believed it was somehow good for him to do so. He thought of himself as expressing his rage and frustration at his mother by treating me as he would have liked to treat her. He imagined that he controlled me, made me "take all his crap," as it were, although he simultaneously often feared and sometimes wished that I would retaliate by hurting and humiliating him, and/or sending him away for good. He regarded his sadistic thoughts, feelings, fantasies, and impulses as noxious substances inside his body; to keep them in caused him pain and misery and made him "sick," *i.e.*, unlovable, but to release them had always seemed still more dangerous, destructive, and disgusting. Thus, he felt gratified and relieved, either when he could stubbornly withhold what he imagined I wanted him to produce for me, or discharge it in a display of gleeful incontinence; either seemed to him a more or less safe way to get his hatred "out of his system." He was, of course, although unaware of it for a long time, enacting his regressively distorted versions of infantile sexual interaction at the same time he expressed these angry wishes and feelings. The fact that he continued to be accepted without the retribution he expected, and even requested, meant that, despite his own deep-seated convictions to the contrary, he might not be so dirty, shameful, worthless, and unlovable after all, especially if he could succeed in getting what he unconsciously regarded as the source of his self-hate "out of his system" for good.

Once it is clear that the pseudorational goals of analysis, that is to say the wish to be "cured," "fully analyzed," or the like, are derivatives of unconscious wishes for the fulfillment of childhood libidinal desires, it is not surprising to discover that the ideas patients have about how analysis will help them achieve these goals correspond to the typical sexual theories and fantasies originally constructed by children in connection with these same libidinal wishes. Such invasion of supposedly mature conceptual thinking by the irrational mental substructure is not by any means exceptional, nor is it limited to the obviously neurotic individual. In fact, the interplay of unconscious mental life and the more or less rational, objective thought processes of everyday life is continuous and unavoidable; this means that no scientific theory—including those of the humanistic and physical sciences—can ever be said to be completely free of influence from the irrational wishes, theories, and fantasies of early childhood. Investigators in all branches of inquiry have been known to misconstrue data, disregard facts, and concoct improbable formulations for what we can only assume are powerful psychological reasons of their own. Unconscious motives and concerns are liable to inspire brilliant accurate insight on occasion, just as they can at other times lead to outlandish fallacy; the correctness of a given scientific theory or hypothesis has only to do with its consonance with the data it seeks to explain, not at all with its relation to the unconscious mind of its author. However, one may feel safe in guessing that whenever egregious error is in evidence, the omnipresent unconscious has played a significant role.

The foregoing generalizations should suffice as justification, if one is needed, and introduction, to an inquiry into the possible influence on the scientific thinking of analysts and other therapists of unconscious factors similar to those which lead analysands to develop their theories of cure. For the sake of clarity, I shall concentrate on parallels to the two varieties of fantasy about how analysis works that emerged from my case material, although one would expect there to be others as well, in both patients and analysts, corresponding to the entire range of possible sources in childhood mental life. I think one can readily detect the outlines of these unconscious fantasies in some theories of cure, and I would also conclude that the degree of acceptance of a given theory among individual practitioners is likely to be connected, among other things, to the residual attraction of its unconscious appeal. I would like to re-emphasize that these linkages, even if present, do not of necessity invalidate the theories or the clinical judgments derived from them. They are, as with unconscious factors in general, potentially able to interfere with objectivity and, therefore, with that optimal evaluation of clinical data upon which such judgments should ideally be based.

Let us consider, for example, the early theory of analytic effectiveness, which rested on the concept of strangulated affects whose release and discharge were believed to be essential to bring about recovery. It is often referred to, suggestively enough, as the cathartic method and bears a more than passing resemblance to the ideas my second patient drew from his anal fantasies and preoccupations. The theory of anxiety with which Freud replaced his earliest formulations was not, in this respect at least, much more satisfactory than its predecessor. The idea that libido denied normal discharge became somehow converted into a toxic force or substance whose manifestation was anxiety has a general similarity to my patient's fantasies. The reformulation of anxiety theory published in 1926 was, of course, a radical departure, although even so, as we know, the original theory lived on in the concept of actual neurosis for another analytic generation.

Bibring (1937) clearly stated the conceptual fallacy: "In the theory of defensive mechanisms and of resistance there is no longer a place for the theory of catharsis, although the latter seems to be continued in concepts such as damming-up and letting out, or discharge" (p. 178). Even now, 40 years later, though the term abreaction is rarely heard, a belief in the beneficial effect of emotional discharge appears to linger.

If one pays attention to the language of the popular psychologies one can hardly escape the conclusion that in the minds of many people the mere act of expression, particularly of strong feelings, continues to be assigned a therapeutic value in its own right. Such assumptions are probably supported by the experiences of some of these individuals in therapies more or less descended from analysis. Certainly, those of us who are trained in and practice classical analysis are less likely to make the same methodological error; we no longer simplistically believe that discharge is a desirable end in itself. Yet I think even many of us are prone at times to shift momentarily backward in our conceptual thinking and regard some particularly affect-laden, difficult revelation made by a patient as intrinsically useful, that is, as somehow able to further his or her analytic progress, rather than to see it for what it really is, the result of analytic progress which has already taken place.

The theory evolved by my other patient explains infantile libidinal frustration, not as the result of some imagined deficiency of the child that was, but on the basis of parental failure or inadequacy. If only the parent (or parents) had been different, the outcome that pains the patient would also have been different in its thesis. However, even where the patient's perception of the parents' problems is an accurate and meaningful one, this retrospective fantasy always serves to both communicate and disguise the patient's desires for other gratifications of a totally unrealistic nature. In other words, while the parents stand accused, perhaps justly, of having failed to meet the legitimate needs of the child for certain instinctual satisfactions, concealed behind this lies the reproach that they have frustrated the patient's infantile wishes in other ways as well; the latter ones, central to the analytic work as a rule, are invariably outside of the patient's conscious awareness at the outset of treatment.

I believe one can detect the influence of fantasies similar to that of my patient who wanted to see me as a "teacher" who would fulfill his unconscious wish for a different kind of mother and father in the objections some of our colleagues have about the way classical analysts work with patients. To emphasize the fact, as they seem to do, that the therapist must be a warm, human, concerned, interacting "real" person suggests that what they most disapprove of in the behavior of the analyst-stereotype they decry is our unwillingness to gratify patients' libidinal wishes. Here, too, the less rational and realistic desires seem to be undetected as they ride along below the surface, attached to the consciously acceptable, readily understandable, appealing, "legitimate" needs of the suffering patient.

Nor are analysts themselves immune to the attraction of this type of fantasy. The suggestion that specific pathogenic aspects of parent-child interactions create specific problems for certain patients and require that the analyst's behavior must specifically counteract these harmful experiences to be beneficial appears again and again in the literature. Winnicott (1956) believed, particularly with sicker patients who suffered from a not-good-enough early (*i.e.*, maternal) environment, that the analytic setting and the analyst, more than interpretation, by being "good enough in the matter of adaptation to need," provide an opportunity for the patient to trust in a deeply-regressed state in such a way as to bring about a developmental shift: ". . . for the first time in the patient's life an opportunity for the development of an ego, for its integration from ego nuclei, for its establishment as a body ego . . ." and so forth. Only after this development, he felt, "There can at last follow an ordinary analysis of the ego's defenses against anxiety" (p. 387). Nacht (1962) emphasized that the benevolent attitude of the analyst, sensed correctly by the patient, was necessary for analytic work to progress; too much neutrality would repeat the frustrations of childhood and would lead to sadomasochistic development. ". . . it is of more value, from the curative point of view, to have a mediocre interpretation supported by a good transference than the reverse" (p. 208). Gitelson's (1962) more sophisticated view was that curative factors reside in the inherent developmental potential of the child-patient, provided the environment in the person of the mother or the analyst allows adequate opportunity for their emergence. The healing intention of the analyst, along with sensitivity, are sufficient, but he makes it clear that the analyst's instructive, advisory, and persuasive activities are not to be necessarily regarded as suggestion, but as fostering influences of the kind that emanate from the effective mother during the child's early development.

Alexander was perhaps the most outright advocate of the analyst's adoption of corrective postures. In 1925, his conception of the analytic process was that the analyst actually takes over the functions of the superego, *i.e.*, that his role was literally parental: "During treatment the analyst has thought and interpreted instead of the patient, indeed, by reconstructing the past he has done some remembering in his stead. From now on all this must be the patient's own concern" (p. 31). Much later (1950, 1954), when his theories had been elaborated into technical precepts whose controversial nature is familiar to all of us, he stated his rationale thus: ". . . every neurosis is an attempt at adaptation to an early family situation. This is the meaning of Freud's early statement that somewhere and somehow the neurotic is right—in other words, that the seemingly irrational symptoms and the underlying emotional reactions at some time in the past were sensible . . . the neurotic solution was an attempt at adaptation to the parental behavior; in the transference repetition the parental response is replaced by the analyst's objective attitude and by a different interpersonal climate" (1954, p. 695).

Such viewpoints cannot be dismissed as historical curiosities, like the cathartic method, because it is regularly suggested even now that certain adult patients with deviant development require that the analyst add an educative function to his ordinary interpretive tasks. Not all such recommendations emphasize the developmental view of analytic therapy, nor encourage parental activity on the part of the analyst, but the idea of undoing or correcting specific damage caused by parental failings, as distinct from analyzing conflicts within the patient, recurs and recurs.

Perhaps even more important to consider is that most, if not all, analysts at times make the judgment that one or another patient's special problems render it advisable to modify the technical approach we believe proper in the usual analytic situation. Whenever we do so we run some risk of instituting a kind of "corrective emotional experience," of, in other words, substituting our own subtle version of the fantasy of an alternative, better, parent as a theory of how best to ameliorate a patient's distress, instead of confining ourselves to the consistent interpretation of unconscious conflicts. Since the potential for unwittingly entertaining such theories of analytic cure, derived from ubiquitous unconscious fantasies, is always bound to be present to some degree, it behooves the analyst to be aware of the danger. This recognition can perhaps aid, as does the scrutiny of countertransference feelings, in understanding the clinical situation, and in carefully weighing the available data as objectively as possible before deciding in favor of the modification of technique under consideration.

Summary

It has long been known that patients' wishes for cure by analysis give expression to unconscious wishes for instinctual gratification which originate in childhood mental life. Patients sometimes develop theories about how they believe analysis attains its ends; these are likely to affect the way they behave in the analytic situation, and analysis of them may therefore constitute an important contribution to progress in the analysis. Two illustrative cases are presented; in both, the unconscious determinants of the patients' theories turn out to be infantile sexual fantasies connected with their unconscious wishes for instinctual satisfaction. It is further suggested that analogous unconscious fantasies also influence the theories of analysts and other therapists about how analysis works. In some instances these factors, while not affecting theory formation explicitly, may, without being recognized as doing so, contribute to decisions regarding the modification of analytic technique. Awareness of that possibility may aid analysts in assessing the indications for such proposed modifications.

References

Alexander, F. (1925). A metapsychological description of the process of cure. *International Journal of Psycho-Analysis* 6:13–34.

——— (1950). Analysis of the therapeutic factors in psychoanalytic treatment. *Psychoanalytic Quarterly* 19:482–500.

——— (1954). Some quantitative aspects of psychoanalytic technique. *Journal of the American Psychoanalytic Association* 2:685–701.

Applebaum, A. (1972). A critical re-examination of the concept "motivation for change" in psychoanalytic treatment. *International Journal of Psycho-Analysis* 53:51–59.

Arlow, J. and Brenner, C. (1966). The Psychoanalytic Situation. In: *Psychoanalysis in the Americas*, ed. R.E. Litman. New York: International Universities Press, pp. 23–43.

Bibring, E. (1937). Symposium on the theory of the therapeutic results of psychoanalysis. *International Journal of Psycho-Analysis* 18:170–189.

Freud, S. (1926). Inhibitions, Symptoms and Anxiety. *Standard Edition* 20:77–174.

Gitelson, M. (1962). On the curative factors in the first phase of analysis. In: *Psychoanalysis: Science and Profession*. New York: International Universities Press, 1973, pp. 311–341.

Macalpine, I. (1950). The development of the transference. *Psychoanalytic Quarterly* 19:501–539.

Nacht, S. (1962). Curative factors in psychoanalysis. *International Journal of Psycho-Analysis* 43:206–211.

Nunberg, H. (1926). The Will to Recovery. In: *Practice and Theory of Psychoanalysis*, Vol. I. New York: International Universities Press, 1948, pp. 75–88.

Schmideberg, M. (1938). "After the analysis . . ." *Psychoanalytic Quarterly* 7:122–142.

Spitz, R. (1956). Transference: The Analytic Setting and its Prototype. *International Journal of Psycho-Analysis* 37:380–385.

Waelder, R. (1956). Introduction to the discussion on problems of transference. In: *Psychoanalysis: Observation, Theory, Application*, ed. S. Guttman. New York: International Universities Press, 1976, pp. 240–243.

Winnicott, D. (1956). On transference. *International Journal of Psycho-Analysis* 37:386–388.

CHAPTER 9

Sibling Love and Object Choice

[Abend, S.M. (1984). *Psychoanalytic Quarterly* 53:425–430]

The importance of sibling rivalry and its consequences in mental life was one of the earliest discoveries of psychoanalysis. In contrast, the love ties which exist between siblings have commanded far less interest, no doubt because it was readily observed that the appearance of such material in patients' associations primarily served defensive functions. There are circumstances, however, in which the libidinal bonds between siblings come to assume a powerful and lasting significance in the development of certain individuals. I have analyzed two patients whose preferences in love partners in adult life were profoundly influenced by persistent unconscious attachments to older siblings.

The responses of colleagues during the several years which have elapsed since I first described these cases[1] confirms that individuals of this type are not so infrequently encountered as might be imagined, although no one analyst is likely to see enough such cases to permit him to undertake a study in depth of the conditions which determine this unusual course of libidinal development. Perhaps this explains why no clinically based reports of this observation appear in the analytic literature, so far as I can determine, although it is true that actual brother-sister incest, occurring in much more disturbed individuals, has been

---

[1] Presented at the Rudolph M. Loewenstein Memorial Meeting of the New York Psychoanalytic Society and Institute, New York, November 12, 1977.

described (Reich, 1932). I have consequently decided to present this material as a brief communication. I hope that other descriptions of examples of this variant form of development will be forthcoming and eventually permit a better understanding of its genesis.

The theme of powerful sibling love, whether or not consummated, is, of course, extremely common in history, legend, and literature. Analysts have by and large regarded it, when it emerges in analytic work, as merely a preliminary layer; a less threatening derivative of the incestuous wishes and fantasies which involve the parents. The artists responsible for the myths and stories which utilize the sibling love motif presumably share our analysands' demonstrable need to defensively displace libidinal wishes from parents onto siblings. Therefore, they weave into their creative endeavors this more accessible and more acceptable version of forbidden love. The apparently prevailing view that these fantasies are only secondary formations which produce no impact distinguishable from the effects of the nuclear oedipal fantasies is, on the whole, correct. There are, however, as I have indicated, some exceptions in which the sibling love, while unquestionably used to defend against even more disturbing ideas, has all the same left an ineradicable stamp on the pattern of object choice in later life. I will present only those features of my patients that illustrate this aspect of their development.

The first, a man of twenty, came to analysis because he had dropped out of college as a consequence of severe work inhibition. He was quite depressed and, it turned out, almost totally preoccupied with his inability to pursue relationships with women to the point of emotional or physical intimacy. He was glib and nervy, as well as physically attractive, and had no difficulty in meeting women, but something always went awry, and in each case he was soon rebuffed.

He was the middle child of three, with a sister three years older and another one two years younger. His mother was apparently an immature person, who behaved toward her son in a seductively flirtatious and possessive manner which was at the same time hostile and belittling. His father was quite critical and openly competitive with him, but also loving and generous. The patient's conscious attitudes toward his mother at the commencement of his analysis were those of fear, revulsion, and hatred. It took more than five years of painstaking analytic work before he could tolerate any awareness of his intense unconscious loving attachment to her.

His older sister was regarded by friends and family as unusually warm, loving, sensitive, and genuine in her feelings for others. The patient idolized her, and she was also much more than usually devoted to him. From the time he was very young, he recalled, he and his sister were in the habit of exchanging private glances which conveyed special warmth and tenderness. During his adolescence they would frequently visit one another's rooms, sometimes in nightclothes, to have long talks, at times accompanied by affectionate caresses or massages which missed becoming frankly erotic play by the narrowest of margins. At the same time, he was very inhibited in his sexual development, avoiding both masturbation and exploratory petting with the girls he met at school, although he did go out on many dates.

His sister became engaged to be married when the patient was about seventeen years old. He became very upset at the new distance she suddenly put between them, but it was only after she married and left home that he was able to commence masturbating and could permit himself to become sexually active with the girls he met.

As his analysis began to help him overcome both his childish, narcissistic thoughtlessness, which often alienated others, and the extreme inhibition and tendency toward self-defeat which sprang from his conflicts about competing with other men, he enjoyed more success in his social life. From this first affair, through a long series of casual relationships, and even when he at last became seriously involved with a woman toward the end of the treatment, it was possible to observe a distinct repetitive pattern in his choice of love partners. These women were all three to five years older than he, usually had taken some seductive initiative toward him, and generally permitted him to act in a rather irresponsible and dependent fashion (*e.g.*, in regard to money, appointments, *etc.*); in short, like a "kid brother." His initial sense of attraction to these women was determined by his being able to establish an intimate, warm kind of eye contact, which he unconsciously associated with the glances he used to exchange with his sister. Whatever the woman's physical appearance might be, the analytic material invariably included comparisons to his sister, indicating the continuing importance of her as a standard against which other women were to be measured. The special features of personality he sought in women were those of liveliness and charm, which were reminiscent to him of his sister; and of a preparedness to openly express their admiration of his physical attractiveness, just as his sister had so often done.

It should be noted that conscious awareness of the erotic nature of his attachment to his sister and of her seductive behavior toward him was not easy for him to accept, even when the pattern of his current life preferences revealed such a marked tendency to find women similar to her that its significance could no longer be denied.

The second case is that of a young woman whose father became stricken with a chronic, slowly progressive, ultimately fatal neuromuscular ailment during her childhood. As a consequence of his illness he became confined to home, and he grew gradually more self-centered and regressed in personality as his invalidism increased. The patient was unable to continue to admire and idealize him, though her image of him from early life remained that of a man of great tenderness and kindness. She had a brother, four years older, with whom there had been a good deal of stimulating physical play throughout her childhood. He was apparently rather exhibitionistic and sexually precocious. The patient thought of him as extraordinarily attractive and felt proud on those occasions during her adolescence when he treated her as if she were his date. As was also true of the other patient I have described, she suffered from conscious jealousy when her sibling married.

Her analysis revealed that she tended to be interested in two different kinds of men. She imagined falling in love with an older man, stable, kind, and understanding, who would gently initiate her into sexuality, and whom she would eventually marry. Clearly this figure of fantasy was derived from her childhood image of her father. However, the men who actually attracted and stimulated her sexually were, by contrast, generally youthful, physically handsome and athletic, and, as a rule, somewhat impulsive, self-centered, and immature individuals who very much resembled her brother, both in personality and in body type. The man with whom she had her first serious love affair was, in fact, the son of a man who had been professionally associated with her mother, and as the analytic material unfolded, it became unmistakably evident that he unconsciously represented her own brother. Her dreams, various manifestations of her transference attitudes, as well as later examples of her positive responses to men she met, all further confirmed this division in her emotional life, modeled on the different images of her brother and her father.

It seems unlikely that the clinical phenomenon of sibling love relationships which produce a lasting effect on the preferred characteristics of the love objects chosen in adulthood is so rare and unusual as its failure to be noted in the literature of psychoanalysis might suggest to be the case. Indeed, as I have indicated, informal discussions with a number of colleagues have appeared to confirm the supposition that we do encounter individuals of this type with some regularity, although in insufficient numbers to facilitate the identification of those factors critical to the determination of this particular developmental outcome.

My own clinical examples shared the following characteristics: (1) each patient was a younger sibling, attracted to an opposite-sex older sibling who was at the height of the oedipal stage at the time of birth of my patients-to-be; (2) in each case, descriptions of the character of the older sibling obtained from my analysands indicated that they were, in both cases, exhibitionistic, seductive, and unusually interested in their respective younger siblings throughout the latters' childhood and adolescence; and (3) there appeared to have been some aspect of the parent of the opposite sex of each patient which rendered them more than usually difficult and dangerous for the younger child to love and admire in the conventional way.

These observations, in so small a sample, seem to me as yet insufficient to convince us that they constitute the crucial factors which account for the result in question. It would be of interest to see whether other similar cases that come to light also share these characteristics. At the very least, attention to this variant course of libidinal development may prove of interest to analytic practitioners; perhaps in time a more satisfactory explanation of how it comes into existence will be forthcoming.

Reference

Reich, A. (1932). Analysis of a case of brother-sister incest. In: *Annie Reich: Psychoanalytic Contributions*. New York: International Universities Press, 1973, pp. 1–22.

CHAPTER 10

Unconscious Fantasies, Structural Theory, and Compromise Formation

[Abend, S.M. (1990). *Journal of the American Psychoanalytic Association* 38:61–73]

Although the existence of unconscious fantasies is an empirical assumption, in the clinical situation unconscious fantasies are treated as if they have a concrete existence. Unconscious fantasies form intermediate links in causal chains of which clinical observations constitute one end, and the components of unconscious conflicts the other. Like all clinical material, fantasies may be affected by actual experiences; they may also be revised, layered, and can function to alter and disguise other fantasies, as well as to provide gratification. From a technical standpoint, it is most important to analyze their constituents and to adduce their primary purposes in the clinical situation of the moment.

The nature of the evidence that identifies the presence of particular unconscious fantasies is discussed. Although a single analytic session is presented by way of illustration, I am convinced that the analyst's entire understanding of the patient inevitably channels his or her interpretive focus on the associational material of each analytic hour.

The existence of unconscious fantasies is an explanatory assumption that is closely derived from clinical observation. It goes back almost to the very beginning of Freud's work. At first he attributed the etiology of hysteria solely to sequestered traumatic memories, but it was not long before Freud came to recognize that the traumatic stimuli could be fantasies rather than always simply unadorned memories. The locus to which he assigned their sequestered state was an unconscious stratum of the mind; emphasis on the study of the unconscious became the feature that most clearly distinguished psychoanalysis from other psychotherapeutic approaches. Though analysts' understanding of the phenomena they encounter has continued to evolve in succeeding decades, the value of the concept of unconscious fantasies for clinical theory has never been challenged. No analyst has contributed more to our understanding of the significance of unconscious fantasies in the clinical practice of psychoanalysis than has Arlow (1961, 1963, 1966, 1969a, 1969b, 1972, 1981), whose work illuminates many aspects of the subject.

Unconscious fantasies constitute a useful conceptual tool in our formulation of the causal chains we construct to account for patients' symptoms and character traits. At the same time, we regard them as more than abstractions; we think of them as actual entities in patients' minds. To utilize Freud's archeological analogy, we treat them as akin to recoverable artifacts of the individual's past. Since we assign them a real existence, we need to say something about the way we detect their presence and ascertain their content. While there are many intriguing questions about the origin and nature of unconscious fantasies, I shall concentrate on how I make use of the concept in my clinical formulations, and on the nature of the clinical evidence that indicates that specific unconscious fantasies are active in patients' emotional lives. Since I utilize structural theory, and the central formative influences of childhood instinctual conflicts that it addresses so well, as the cornerstone of my approach to clinical material, my discussion will illustrate how unconscious fantasies are viewed from that conceptual vantage point. I also hope to show that psychoanalytic evidence does not easily speak for itself; not only does the analyst's theoretical stance affect his view of evidence, but his entire accumulated experience with his patient inevitably colors and shapes his way of understanding the specific material that supports his selection of an interpretive focus.

Rangell, in his discussion (1986, unpublished) of a paper I presented on unconscious fantasies and their relation to issues of termination of analysis (Abend, 1988), referred to unconscious fantasies as a "way station," and went on to point out that analysts are interested both in what came before the fantasy and in what comes afterward. Unconscious fantasies are intermediate links in the logical sequences by means of which we seek to clarify the origin and meaning of patients' ways of thinking and behaving. In analysis, we usually trace these metaphoric pathways backwards; that is to say, we begin with the observables, the symptoms and character traits, complex defenses, passionate interests and adaptations that come to our attention in patients' presentation of themselves to us. The analytic method enables us, under favorable circumstances, to see how these are given shape by underlying unconscious fantasies. While all analysts would probably agree that both actual experiences and the intrinsic qualities and characteristics of the mental apparatus together contribute to the formation of unconscious fantasies, the way analysts prefer to describe those antecedents reflects their particular theoretical emphases and differences. As indicated, I lay stress on the current version of the traditional view that unconscious infantile instinctual conflicts are the core elements that constitute the stuff of which unconscious fantasies are composed, and in my clinical thinking I am likely to treat unconscious fantasies as more or less elaborate embodiments of the essential elements of critical instinctual conflicts. In other words, unconscious fantasies are one variety of compromise formation (Brenner, 1979, 1982) and present an especially useful way of understanding the nature and composition of the underlying conflicts that give rise to them.

To put it somewhat differently, I believe that libidinal and aggressive drive derivatives, that is to say wishes, together with their accompanying affects, and some modulations produced by defensive ego attributes and superego influences, are combined in the form of certain of the varieties of thought of which I imagine small children to be capable. These incorporate real and/or distorted perceptions, interpretations of experience, and memories into abbreviated scenarios that may be, or may become, unacceptable to consciousness, and are therefore relegated to the domain of the unconscious.

I cannot say for certain that these unconscious fantasies have all actually been conscious at one time, or even that my patients literally thought them, in the forms I reconstruct, at some point in their lives. However, I do formulate, for myself and my patients, the unconscious fantasies of which I detect evidence, as if these were literally thoughts they once had as small children. I am liable to use language that reflects that assumption in communicating my conjectures about their unconscious fantasies to patients in analysis. Sentences like, "You might once have thought, or believed, or imagined, or wished," followed by the specific content of the fantasy I think I have recognized, would be typical.

I take it for granted that we all agree that complex layering affects the form that clinical material takes in analytic work with adults, or even adolescents and older children, for that matter. Thus a particular fantasy may be a revision of earlier ones—a revision that reflects later experiences and influences. Fantasies formed in adult life may also appear as if unconscious, although one must bear in mind Kris's (1956) contribution to the metapsychology of preconscious synthesis as pertinent to an accurate understanding of these phenomena. I assume that when lines of thought, that is to say fantasies whose content indicates they were formed in adulthood, are unconscious, it is because they are thematically related to childhood equivalents of which they may be regarded as current derivatives. It is their relation to the infantile conflicts that renders them unconscious, and that accounts for the technical difficulties in recovering them, and subsequently helping patients to become and remain aware of their outlines and sources. Transference fantasies may well be the most frequently encountered variety of such current unconscious fantasies, but equivalent responses to other contemporary figures and situations also reflect how compromise formation, taking the form of unconscious fantasies, continues to affect patients' behavior and reactions, and influences the analytic material.

By and large, it is less important precisely to dissect the layering process that progressive development may impose than to address its most essential components. A commonplace example would be the analysis of networks of contemporary and past compensatory fantasies designed to defensively alter or replace other experiences or fantasies of painful loss, injury, inferiority, or humiliation. From the standpoint of advancing the analytic work, which came when, or what material was made use of at what point in development, though interesting, is usually less important than a correct elucidation of the defensive aim of the compensatory fantasies. For comparable reasons, I am less interested in the potential distinctions between preconscious and unconscious formations, and between current derivatives and their infantile antecedents, than I am in coming to understand the compromise formations that gave rise to them, and the conflictual elements of which these compromise formations are composed.

Kris (1956), in "On Some Vicissitudes of Insight in Analysis," uses his observation of how hidden shapes in the patterning of mental activity gradually come to light during analysis as part of the evidence he adduces for the operation of preconscious synthetic ego functioning. For my purposes though, his account seems most useful as a description of one way in which unconscious fantasies are uncovered in the course of analytic work. As a contrast to the unusual clarity of the so-called "good analytic hour," he describes

> "... the oscillating character of other analytic sessions in which the battle of forces becomes first dimly perceivable, and then traceable, when over a stretch of time the analyst can piece together some of the slight elevations in the patient's productions, as they reveal outlines of a larger submerged formation" (p. 256).

So it often seems, as we struggle to make sense of clinical material. Less often, there are sessions wherein a particular unconscious fantasy seems to spring up spontaneously, like a bubble rising to the surface of a simmering liquid. As did Kris, I have used a metaphor suited to the concrete representation of the interface between the unconscious and consciousness. I strongly suspect that the latter type, the apparently spontaneous achievements, are to some extent deceptive; they are in all likelihood just as much the product of gradual and cumulative analytic effort as other varieties of reconstruction. By way of illustration, I shall recount a single hour from the fifth year of analysis of a young woman. This session followed the death of her mother two days earlier.

Mrs. A., the product of a privileged, but emotionally sterile New England puritan background, has a predominantly obsessional character structure. Her problems reflect the influence of masochistic solutions to her central conflicts around the expression and control of both aggressive and libidinal impulses. Mrs. A.'s mother died of a lingering illness whose inevitable outcome had been evident for many months. During this period of anticipating her mother's death, the patient had recapitulated in the analysis much of the history of her ambivalent relationship to her mother, including her considerable understanding of her conflicts about wishing for her death, as well as her fears of the loss of the relationship.

The session began with Mrs. A. saying that she still did not feel any different—no tears. She had said repeatedly that she had been unable to cry during the terrible last days of her mother's illness, and had hoped for an experience of emotional release and relief when the anticipated and dreaded end finally came. Mrs. A. went on to say she had felt shaky for some hours after receiving the news by telephone. The following day she had been occupied with the funeral arrangements. She made no mention of having called me to cancel her session. She repeated that she looked forward to a release, to tears perhaps, at the service scheduled for the next day. I said she appeared to feel she had stored up sadness and tears, and would feel relieved when she could finally let them out. My unspoken thoughts included some idea about anal fantasies of constipation and relief, but I wondered how and when that might be included in any interpretive work. Mrs. A. responded, "I don't really expect to—but it would make me feel better. I don't think I'll have an explosive outburst."

She went on to talk about the events and her reactions of the previous day, including shedding a few tears at the awareness that mother was really gone for good, alongside a mild feeling of disbelief and a sense of being unable to decide anything. In accordance with her mother's wishes, it had been planned to have two services, one locally to accommodate some of the immediate family and friends who could not or would not travel, and another at the subsequent interment at the family plot located in another state. Although Mrs. A. expected to make the journey, she could not make up her mind whether to take her infant child along. Her husband had been out of town at a business meeting when the death occurred, and Mrs. A. had found herself unable to ask him to cut short his trip and return immediately; he was scheduled to arrive at about the time of our session. She complained about his selfishness in not offering to come back to be with her without being asked. Her associations shifted to her father, whom she had consistently described as self-centered and demanding, much like her husband. The patient had acted as his chief helper in making all the funeral arrangements, thereby outshining her brother, much as she had always done. She returned to the subject of her indecision about the funeral trip. I asked about her concerns about separating from her child. She confirmed that that prospect troubled her, and went on to express regret that her mother has to wait around to be buried. She, her father, and her brother would all go with her mother on the train, she added. I said, "You talk of her as if she were still alive." She replied, "We all do, we don't refer to the remains, or her corpse or body." She then recounted some irritating debates about the proposed nature of the service to be held locally: "I'm complaining," she said, "because other people won't let me get to the point of being emotional because of their own weird needs. I feel I have to be matter-of-fact. When someone read the obituary notice others burst into tears, but I didn't." My patient continued to talk of her inability to let emotions out. I finally said, "You speak as if emotions were like some substance actually inside you that's unable to come out, constipated, as it were, like feces that can't be let out, and you think you'll feel better when the blockage finally breaks up and lets go." She answered, "I think that's right; I feel that people are blocking me from letting go." Then she told me how she had spent hours calling friends on the telephone to tell them about it, how she had needed the release of talking about it to others.

I thought then of the transference, of talking in analytic sessions. The idea that talking, especially talking in analysis, represents a kind of relieving discharge had long since been connected to anal symptoms and fantasies. This previously gained understanding certainly contributed to my way of looking at her feeling of emotional blockage. Mrs. A. went on to compare herself to her brother, who only talks about himself, and how he feels, while she speaks instead about her mother. She mentioned how glad she was that many people who cared for her mother were around her at the end. I was certain she had some thoughts about not having been there herself, but instead of inquiring about that, I said merely, "You are glad she wasn't alone." "Yes," she replied, "I feel so sorry for her, but not really sad, but shaky instead. I know it's silly to feel sorry for mother, she's dead, but I think I am feeling it for myself as well, I don't know, I can't explain it." I commented, "I think you are right, but you're puzzled because you feel anxiety instead of sadness. That's because dying is something you imagine in terms of being left alone, abandoned, and you feel it for mother because she is the one who is now alone, but also for yourself since you can imagine how it feels by putting yourself in her place; being all alone always meant to you feeling scared and upset." I did not add that this often had appeared in the form of a fantasy of being punished for being bad, though we had seen that many times in the analysis.

"It's true I think of her as lonely now, but that is silly, she can't feel anything. I'm feeling a little guilty that I wasn't with her, too, when she died, though I know I couldn't leave my baby all alone." I said, "It sounds as if you might feel you left your mother all alone." Mrs. A. replied, "She had other people there." I continued, "But you weren't one of them, so I think you accuse yourself of not loving her enough." After the briefest of pauses, Mrs. A. said, "I know I wished her dead, but I still loved her, too; I didn't want her to be alone." She then spoke of going along to the funeral with her father and brother, and at this point, with just a few minutes left of the session, mentioned what had been obvious all along, that she would also have to miss the next two sessions because of the funeral trip. I asked whether she had any thoughts about being separated from me at this difficult time. She said she had been undecided about coming even today; she had wanted to wait for her husband to arrive home since that would put him on an equal footing with me, her analyst. Before I could even think of trying to clarify that rather cryptic remark, she added that she had been afraid she would have an outpouring of emotion here, at the session, and that would make her feel ashamed of herself. As the hour ended, she was comparing herself to her brother, taking pride in being better controlled than he in her behavior.

In this example of analytic material I thought there was sufficient evidence of the influence of unconscious fantasies about anal discharge and loss of control, and about aspects of separation and loneliness, to warrant interpretations along those lines. The anal fantasies in question are actually an interrelated group of ideas, some of which contradict, or counteract, others. The fantasy equating her emotions with feces helps account for her conviction that a discharge of emotion would afford feelings of relief and pleasure. On the other hand, it also helps to explain her taking her ability to control anal and emotional discharge as a source of pride, since it represents a developmental achievement of significance to a child. Both these fantasies were, at least in part, influenced by her reactions to her younger sibling—envy of the baby's imagined freedom to gratify its impulses to discharge at will, and of the physical care and attention that followed, on the one hand, and feelings of superiority at being able to control her sphincter, and thereby gain parental approval, in contrast to the incontinent baby, on the other. Other fantasies derived from the feces-emotions equation included: (1) her fear that free discharge of words or feelings is a nasty, disagreeable activity unwelcome to the recipient, perhaps even destructive to the relationship; (2) the persistent conviction that she was being pressured to produce thoughts, words, and feelings by the analyst, much as her strict nanny had demanded compliance in anal, as in all other matters; and (3) interrelated ideas that she could gain love by complying, and the resentful conviction that by withholding she expressed silent anger and independence, could each be recognized at times. Her attitudes toward control and release were also influenced by her connection of the fecal mass with the phallus;

retention and discharge thus became involved in fantasies about genital integrity, damage, loss, restitution, and their attendant affects of pride and shame. These, too, reflected her rivalry with her brother, and aspects of her different relationships, real and imaginary, with both her father and her mother.

In the session reported, only the longing for relief associated with the unconscious fantasy that emotional blockage is like painful constipation was actually interpreted to her. I could not determine whether she also longed for me to actively intervene to produce the discharge, though I wondered about that to myself. However, I thought there was also clear evidence in the material of her pride in her self-control compared to her younger sibling, of her envy of his self-indulgent releases, and of her wish to avoid humiliation by not having an emotional discharge in my presence, none of which I commented upon in this session.

It seems almost unnecessary to acknowledge that analysts who rely on a different theoretical emphasis would approach the material in this analytic hour differently, and work with what the patient presented very differently, as well. Even a colleague who shares my theoretical stance might well be inclined to understand this segment of illustrative material quite differently from the way I did. I do not believe that any single session can possibly provide convincing proof of the accuracy of the formulations that guide the analyst's work with that patient in that hour. Even the long familiar empirical principles of evidence derived from Freud's observations of free association in the analytic setting have to be applied with care.

Consider Mrs. A.'s response to my comparing her attitude toward her emotional blockage to physical constipation. First she said, "I think you are right. . . ." but we know from Freud (1937) that such consciously stated agreement has no evidentiary value. She added, "I feel that people are blocking me from letting go." Here, even though she used the very words of my interpretation, which might suggest an unconscious confirmation, she used them in a different way, not one that necessarily agrees with the substance of my remark. However, she then went on to describe spending hours talking to various people about what had happened, and how that provided a sense of release for her. That indeed sounds confirmatory—an unconsciously determined elaboration of the essence of what I had interpreted. At the time, during the session, my thoughts went to the transference. Since she had turned to others for relief, was she suggesting that I had not helped her to express her feelings sufficiently, or had even interfered with her doing so? I recalled much previous work on the unconscious ramifications of speech in general, and of speaking in sessions in particular. Controlling her utterances to keep from exploding, or from injuring others or embarrassing herself; using her sessions as a safe depository for unpleasant or potentially damaging thoughts and feelings; carrying on an imaginary battle with me for the right to say or withhold what was inside her; forcing me to sit back and take all the emotional "crap" she wanted to dump on me had come up repeatedly.

What the patient said in that brief segment of the hour, through lines of association evoked in me, that I assume are paralleled by something in her, seems to fit in a particular way into the ongoing work of the analysis. I have no doubt that my formulation of the fantasies was shaped as much by what had gone before, in over four years of analysis, as by the words and nonverbal communications of this session. My sense of the correctness of the interpretations is a reflection of my previously gained knowledge of this patient, along with, or as a background to, what came forth in response to my comments. The same considerations apply to my way of working with the separation material, but I shall limit myself to the one small sample of material, since the same principles and caveats apply in both instances.

A complete accounting of every manifestation of material touching on or elaborating her fantasies about anal discharge, withholding, control or its absence, their interconnections with object relations, autonomy, gender issues and identifications, their relation to symptoms, character traits, and the transference, and their developmental history, would fill a book. Yet that matrix of material, that cumulative experience with the patient, is essential evidence for the aptness of this particular interpretive emphasis. To be sure, each hour is a new laboratory experiment, so to say, and new findings, new directions, addenda, corrections, and clarifications emerge, just as do confirmations and elaborations of previously won understanding. In a discussion of evidence, I am convinced that a single session can do no more than provide an illustration. Just as many alternate lines of interpretation and inquiry could have suggested themselves to other analysts, so did other pathways occur to me during the session, not to mention in retrospect. Puzzling transitions and unanswered questions abound.

It is my view that an understanding of this woman's conflicts, their organization into networks of unconscious fantasies, and the way these affect her thinking, her emotional reactions, her symptoms and other behavior, including the transference, has been built up gradually over the course of the analysis. Only the analyst's prolonged immersion in the emotional life of the analysand provides the requisite sense of conviction about how best to understand the material as it is presented. Given the omnipresent pressure of resistances to understanding the unconscious, in ourselves as well as in patients, maintaining that sense of conviction, without shutting off receptivity to new meanings is central to the proper performance of our analytic endeavors.

References

Abend, S.M. (1988). Unconscious fantasies and their relationship to issues of termination of Analysis. In: *Fantasy, Myth and Reality: Essays in Honor of Jacob A. Arlow*, ed. H.P. Blum, Y. Kramer, A.K. Richards, and A.D. Richards. Madison, Conn.: International Universities Press, pp. 144–165.

Arlow, J.A. (1961). Ego Psychology and the study of mythology. *Journal of the American Psychoanalytic Association* 9:371–393.

——— (1963). Conflict, repression and symptom formation. *International Journal of Psycho-Analysis* 44:12–22.

——— (1966). Depersonalization and Derealization. In: *Psychoanalysis—A General Psychology: Essays in Honor of Heinz Hartmann*, ed. R.M. Loewenstein, L.M. Newman, M. Schur, and A.J. Solnit. New York: International Universities Press, pp. 456–478.

——— (1969a). Fantasy, memory and reality testing. *Psychoanalytic Quarterly* 38:28–51.

——— (1969b). Unconscious fantasies and disturbances of conscious experience. *Psychoanalytic Quarterly* 38:1–27.

——— (1972). Some dilemmas in psychoanalytic education. *Journal of the American Psychoanalytic Association* 20:556–566.

——— (1981). Theories of pathogenesis. *Psychoanalytic Quarterly* 50:488–514.

Brenner, C. (1979). The components of psychic conflict and its consequences in mental life. *Psychoanalytic Quarterly* 48:547–567.

——— (1982). *The Mind in Conflict.* New York: International Universities Press.

Freud, S. (1937). Constructions in Analysis. *Standard Edition* 23.

Kris, E. (1956). On some vicissitudes of insight in analysis. In: *Selected Papers of Ernst Kris.* New Haven: Yale University Press, 1975, pp. 252–271.

CHAPTER 11

Unconscious Fantasy and Modern Conflict Theory

[Abend, S.M. (2008). *Psychoanalytic Inquiry* 28(2):117–130]

This article traces the evolution of the concept of unconscious fantasy from its origins in Freud's early clinical writings to its place in the theory and practice of modern conflict theory. The central role played by Arlow's clarification of the ubiquitous influence of unconscious fantasy life on aspects of normal mental functioning such as perception, memory, thinking, and reality testing is highlighted. Some contemporary clinical applications of our understanding of unconscious fantasies are added to the long familiar awareness of its role in symptom formation.

In preparing this review of the role of the concept of unconscious fantasy in modern conflict theory, I reaffirmed my previous conviction that it remains an essential foundation stone of our theoretical edifice, and that it continues to occupy a central position in the technique of analyzing intrapsychic conflict. Given the cumulative magnitude of the evolutionary changes that have marked the development of mainstream Freudian psychoanalysis during the latter decades of the 20th century, not to mention the diversity and complexity introduced into the field by the flourishing of other theoretical points of view, it is somewhat surprising that this key element of psychoanalytic thought has persisted with only rather minor refinements for so many years. Speaking as one who is comfortable wearing the label of

Freudian traditionalism, I find it reassuring that I can even now revisit what Freud and such respected teachers as Kris, Arlow, Rangell, and Brenner have said about unconscious fantasy (not to mention what I myself have written on the subject) and still feel as convinced of the validity and utility of the ideas expressed in those papers as when I first encountered them.

Since the death of Freud, no analyst in the mainstream tradition has contributed more to our understanding of the part played by unconscious fantasy in normal and pathological mental life than has Jacob Arlow. However, it is noteworthy that Arlow strongly emphasized the important place that the concept of unconscious fantasy occupied in Freud's ideas from the time of his earliest clinical studies to the very end of his career. In 1894, in his paper on *The Neuropsychoses of Defense*, Freud mentioned that not only experiences and feelings, but also ideas that a person finds incompatible with his or her ego, could be rejected from conscious awareness and become the seeds of later neurotic afflictions. He mentioned, as an example, certain conscious erotic thoughts involving another person, about which the subject might be quite distressed. Although an idealizing contemporary scholar could plausibly regard this statement of Freud's as a meaningful hint of what would much later evolve into an appreciation of the importance of unconscious fantasies as a causative factor in neurotic symptom formation, it is clear in Freud's writings of that period that he was rather far from emphasizing any such formulation. His interest was centered, instead, on his growing appreciation of the role of sexuality in neurosogenesis, on the etiological importance of childhood experiences, and on the sequestration of such memories out of conscious awareness.

By the time of Freud's publication of the Dora case (1905a), however, he spoke with assurance on the subject of unconscious fantasy: "A symptom signifies the representation—the realization—of a phantasy with a sexual content, that is to say, it signifies a sexual situation. It would be better to say that at least *one* of the meanings of a symptom is the representation of a sexual phantasy" (p. 47). He went on to describe the analysis of Dora's cough as derived from imagining oral sexual activities between her father and Frau K.

The careful reader will have observed that at this stage of his thinking the fantasies that Freud believed to be important were, in all likelihood, at first conscious ones that had been pushed out of consciousness by defense measures, and which had to be recovered by psychoanalysis. However, it should be noted that his conceptualization of the unconscious mind was then still very much in a formative state; it was considered to be an inchoate entity whose contents were subject to the primary process, and quite different from organized, coherent verbal forms of thought. It is interesting that, over half a century later, Arlow (1969b) was to be concerned about clarifying the relationship between daydreaming, or conscious fantasy, and unconscious fantasy, but we shall address that problem in good time; for now, I will ask you to return to 1905, when Freud published *Three Essays on the Theory of Sexuality* (1905b).

His elaboration of infantile sexuality sets forth in detail the normal range of childhood fantasies about the sexual act, pregnancy and childbirth, and the anatomical differences between the sexes. He considered these ideas to be a universal aspect of childhood mental life and he saw them as inevitably subject to repression. Thus, these products of childhood imagination turn into unconscious fantasies that are of crucial significance in psychological development. We need not here concern ourselves with Freud's efforts to understand the circumstances in which the fate of these fantasies would be to favor one or another version of normal sexual development, or instead predispose to later neurosis or perversion. It is sufficient for our present purpose to recognize that Freud, by this time, had established unconscious fantasy life in an essential position in his theory of both normal and pathological development, as well as having assigned it an important place in the technique of psychoanalytic treatment of the pathological conditions.

In Freud's subsequent monumental shift from the earlier topographic model of the mind to its successor, the structural one, he continued to assign a central role to the part played by certain fantasies of childhood. The reasoning that eventually drove him to change his theoretical schema of the mental apparatus is set out in a series of papers, of which *The Ego and the Id* (1923) and *Inhibitions, Symptoms and Anxiety* (1926) are the significant cornerstones. However, his description of the crucial developmental importance of fantasies concerning castration, and their role in bringing an end to the Oedipus complex and in the formation of the superego, are laid out in explicit detail in his short 1924 paper, *The Dissolution of the Oedipus Complex*. The difficulty analysts have, even today, in helping patients gain access to these fantasies, not to mention the degree of controversy they have aroused in subsequent debates about Freudian theory, offer evidence in support of Freud's contention that these fantasies are subject to repression early in childhood. He was convinced, and, based on years of accumulated clinical experience, Freudian analysts ever since have remained equally certain, that these fantasies persist in an unconscious form, exerting their determinative influence on normal and pathological development.

Before we leave the subject of Freud's utilization of the concept of unconscious fantasy in his body of work, it is worthwhile to mention a late-career emendation to Freud's theory of technique that, it seems to me, has implications for the potential importance of unconscious fantasies as factors in pathogenesis. In his 1937 paper *Constructions in Analysis*, Freud made the point that successful analytic work need not invariably result in the conscious recapturing of repressed memories of past experiences. Instead, he observed, "Quite often we do not succeed in bringing the patient to recollect what has been repressed. Instead of that, if the analysis is carried out correctly, we produce in him an assured conviction of the truth of the . . . [analyst's] . . . construction which achieves the same therapeutic result as a recaptured memory" (p. 265–266). This made a place in technique for the therapeutic value of the analyst's inferring the presence of, then reconstructing and interpreting, certain repressed unconscious fantasies, without requiring for confirmation that the patient must subsequently recapture the memory of once having consciously entertained the fantasy involved. A sense of conviction on the part of the patient might be achieved by the preponderance of subsequent analytic material that fitted the pattern of the reconstruction. Years later, Kris gave a vivid description of how such reconstructive analytic work might look in *On*

Some Vicissitudes of Insight in Analysis (1956). He talked of segments of analysis "when over a stretch of time the analyst can piece together some of the slight elevations in the patient's productions as they reveal outlines of a larger submerged formation" (p. 256).

Finally, in our evaluation of Freud's contributions to establishing the role of unconscious fantasies in theory and technique, it is helpful to note that he never systematically revised many of the ideas that he formulated during the years when his topographic theory held sway in order to make them more consistent with the implications of his later structural theory. Thus, he never resolved questions about the precise nature of unconscious fantasy life, treating the fantasies primarily as if they were merely distorted versions of instinctual wishes belonging to the system *Ucs*. Freud was aware of certain inconsistencies in his theoretical structure; in fact he acknowledged the theoretical conundrum posed by unconscious fantasies in his 1915 paper *The Unconscious*, in a passage cited by Arlow (1969) when he took up the issue later on. Freud (1915) said:

> Among the derivatives of the unconscious instinctual impulses . . . there are some which unite in themselves characters of an opposite kind. On the one hand they are highly organized, free from self-contradiction, have made use of every acquisition of the system *Cs*., and would hardly be distinguished in our judgment from the formations of that system. On the other hand, they are unconscious and are incapable of becoming conscious. Thus *qualitatively* they belong to the system *Pcs*., but factually to the *Ucs* . . . of such a nature are those fantasies of normal people as well as of neurotics which we have recognized as preliminary stages in the formation both of dreams and of symptoms and which, in spite of their high degree of organization, remain repressed and therefore cannot become conscious [pp. 190–191].

In this 1915 paper, Freud's best effort to distinguish between his conception of the fundamental nature of the system *Ucs*. and of the systems *Pcs.* and *Cs.* came to rest on his proposed differentiation between thing-presentations and word-presentations, and their respective states of cathexis. Freud admitted a few years later, in 1923, that the shift to the structural hypothesis that he outlined in *The Ego and the Id* had been necessitated, in part, by the incontrovertible clinical evidence that there are aspects of mental activity involved in defense, or resistance, that are also fully unconscious, and retrievable only through psychoanalytic effort, just as is true of the instinctual impulses. Even so, although he now placed greater emphasis on the descriptive and dynamic qualities of the unconscious stratum, rather than on the former systemic distinctions, Freud did not pursue the full implications of this important change in order to clarify the status of unconscious fantasy life. Thus, it remained a task for Arlow, whose 1964 collaboration with Brenner, *Psychoanalytic Concepts and the Structural Theory*, took up the precise question of reformulating earlier Freudian concepts in the light of later theorizing, to try to make consistent sense of those problematic aspects of the concept of unconscious fantasy.

Kramer (1988), in his summary of Arlow's contributions to psychoanalysis, concluded that his thinking about how to reconcile the apparent paradox of the confusing metapsychology of unconscious fantasy evolved over a number of years, and finally came to fruition in two important papers published in 1969. In the first of these, *Unconscious Fantasy and Disturbances of Conscious Experience*, Arlow (1969b) stated unequivocally that our "understanding of the role of unconscious fantasy has been hindered greatly by drawing too sharp a distinction between conscious and unconscious" (p. 4). He relied on the idea, expressed some time earlier by his friend and frequent collaborator, Brenner (1955), that different mental contents are fended off from consciousness with a greater or lesser measure of countercathectic force. Arlow went on to say that "ease of accessibility of a particular mental representation to consciousness may vary" (p. 5). Thus, the line of demarcation between daydream and unconscious fantasies, in Arlow's opinion, is less important than had been previously thought. He went on to elaborate a sophisticated view of the ways in which unconscious fantasies influence various aspects of conscious experience.

Arlow made a particular point that conscious and unconscious fantasy activity is a *constant* feature of mental life. He suggested that we should speak of unconscious fantasy *function* (emphasis added), rather than unconscious fantasy, precisely to highlight the ubiquitous, continuous nature of unconscious fantasy activity, and to underline its omnipresent influence on the surface phenomena of mental life.

Consistent with the ideas of Freud, Arlow proposed that unconscious fantasies tend to be clustered around certain basic instinctual wishes, affording a measure of wishful gratification. Different versions of related fantasies can appear at different developmental stages, he thought, but Arlow made clear that the fantasies invariably include defensive components as well as superego elements, along with the important wishes they contain. He demonstrated that unconscious fantasies influence mythology and metaphor, as well as symptom formation and other psychic phenomena.

Perhaps most important, in this paper Arlow began to explicate the idea that unconscious fantasy function always interacts with and influences the data of perception. He summed up this point as follows: "Unconscious daydreaming is a constant feature of mental life. It is an ever-present accompaniment of conscious experience. What is consciously apperceived and experienced is the result of the interaction between the data of experience and unconscious fantasying as mediated by various functions of the ego" (p. 23). He presented a number of clinical examples illustrating this principle in operation in such situations as déjà vu, parapraxes, and disturbances of the sense of self.

Finally, in the closing paragraphs of this paper, Arlow described a visual model of his conclusion about the interaction of unconscious fantasy and perception in a passage that probably stands out more vividly in the minds of students of his work than does anything else he ever wrote or taught:

> The idea for such a model occurred to me several years ago. It was after a Thanksgiving dinner and a friend had brought a

> movie projector to show the children some animated cartoons. Since we did not have a regulation type movie screen, we used a translucent white window shade instead. During the showing of the cartoons, I had occasion to go outdoors. To my amusement I noted that I could watch the animated cartoons through the window on the obverse side of the window shade. It occurred to me that an interesting effect could be obtained if another movie projector were used to flash another set of images from the opposite side of the screen [pp. 23–24].

This concrete representation of the mutual influence of the internal stimulation derived from what he called unconscious fantasy function, and the external stimulation of perceptual data exquisitely depicts the point about mental functioning that Arlow was so interested in clarifying.

In the second paper he published in the same year (1969a), *Fantasy, Memory, and Reality Testing*, Arlow extended his ideas about the influence of unconscious fantasy function to include its impact on reality testing and memory. He suggested that the mind's perceptual apparatus should be conceived of as an active version of the translucent screen in his famous visual model. He proposed that the perceptual apparatus continuously monitors external data (that is to say, what we ordinarily think of as perceptions), and simultaneously is also always receiving internal stimuli, by which he meant not only the long familiar notion of somatic signals, but also the pressure exerted by unconscious fantasies. The task of reality testing thus amounts to the operation of those mental activities involved in distinguishing external "facts" from internal "fantasies." Arlow was quick to point out that defining reality testing in this way was not an original idea of his, citing, among others, Hartmann (1956). Arlow's emphasis was the perhaps underappreciated constant state of impingement on perception from internal sources, thus underlining that the struggle to achieve reliability in reality testing is a perpetual challenge for everybody.

Memory, too, falls into the category of mental functioning subject to shaping by unconscious fantasy. Here Arlow cited Freud's paper on

Screen Memories (1899) as already making this point. Arlow called attention to the unavoidable conclusion that all memory, whether we speak of its form at the time of the original encoding of current experience, or about each subsequent occasion of its recall from the storage capacities of the mind, is affected by unconscious fantasy function, as well as by the objective reality of what has transpired. This helps to explain how memories revisited at various stages of the individual's development, or even at different moments during the course of an analysis, can be construed in quite different ways. Presumably the so-called external facts are always the same, but alterations in the relevant unconscious fantasies that interact with, and thereby modify the way that these data are experienced, accounts for varying emphases, additions, deletions, and changes in interpretation of the contents of the memories in question.

A. Rothstein (personal communication, 2004) helped me to appreciate that Arlow's explication of the role played by individuals' unconscious fantasy life in shaping their perceptions, memory, reality testing, and, for that matter, their thinking, judgment, theory building, and the like, provides a coherent psychoanalytic explanation for the personal variability in people's interpretations of truth and reality, and their convictions about psychoanalytic theory as well. Rothstein has further elaborated the implications of this intersection between the classical tradition, of which Arlow remained a representative, and the emerging intersubjective paradigm in a paper, *Compromise Formation Theory: An Intersubjective Dimension* (2004). It cannot be too strongly emphasized that it was precisely the phenomenon that Arlow explicated that would, not long after his papers on the subject appeared, energize the psychoanalytic subjectivists' epistemological criticism of positivism. What is all the more striking about this observation is the fact that Arlow himself apparently never applied the subjectivists' conclusion about the inevitable limitations on the reliability of the analyst's objectivity to himself, and to his own view of technique, even though he was well aware of the usefulness of attending to the analyst's inner musings, fantasies, and associations in the ongoing effort to understand analysands' productions! It seems likely to me that, at least in part for that reason, Arlow never quite received full recognition for the value of his contribution by the advocates of the subjectivist position.

Arlow was but one among many mainstream analysts who demonstrated the usefulness of applying the concept of unconscious fantasy to the task of deciphering the meaning of a number of clinical phenomena, and to revealing the psychodynamic underpinnings of many issues in applied psychoanalysis, including jokes, mythology, literature, religious beliefs, and certain artistic creations as well. A few analysts (Boesky and myself among them) have tried to outline some criteria for the reliable identification of the presence of particular unconscious fantasies in patients' analytic material. Boesky's case material permitted him to illustrate the familiar evidentiary principles of context and contiguity, and of the convergence of multiple sources of comparable or similar data into comprehensible coherence. I added the observation that the analyst's preferred theoretical orientation always shapes his or her understanding, and that his or her cumulative experience with each analytic patient contributes greatly to the analyst's sensitivity to the unconscious contributions to the surface material, in any given hour or segment of that patient's analysis.

Now I shall try to outline the current status of the concept of unconscious fantasy in the theory and practice of psychoanalysis from the vantage point of modern conflict theory. I shall make no attempt to integrate the rather different views of unconscious fantasy life that have been proposed by Kleinian theorists over the years, nor to enter the debates on the subject that arose between mainstream Freudians and their Kleinian counterparts.

I will begin by referring to Rangell's (1988) emphasis on unconscious fantasy as "an intermediate product" (p. 61). They take the form of compromise formations incorporating drive wishes and their modifications by defensive alterations and superego input. At the other end of the chain in which they appear are the "final psychic outcomes" (Rangell, 1988, p. 61), that is to say the observable surface phenomena of symptoms, character traits, moods, and the like. He called unconscious fantasies "way stations," when seen from either one of two directions. Going forward, "they play a role, either transiently or in a more enduring form, in the dynamic of character development and symptom formation, as well as in external action and behavior" (p. 61). Operationally in the course of analytic practice, they are encountered in what might be considered a retrograde direction, appearing as intermediate links in the successful unraveling of the underlying unconscious conflicts that lie behind the observable surface of analytic material.

In my view, analysts treat unconscious fantasies as more than mere abstract conceptual tools; we tend to regard them as concrete entities in patients' minds whose presence we first infer, then detect, and finally reconstruct. We start from the patient's presentation of analytic material, which we automatically tend to classify as symptoms, character traits, moods, wishes, defenses, interests, predilections, adaptations, and so on, in whatever form they appear. Dreams and daydreams, memories, accounts of contemporary or past events, and associative responses to the analytic situation, including the analyst's comments, are all subject to this scrutiny and classification. When the work proceeds well, we think we can detect underlying formations that we conceive of as the unconscious thoughts or scenarios that we call unconscious fantasies, and which are giving shape to the surface material.

In my clinical work, this technical thinking takes one of two forms. In one type, I regard these unconscious fantasies as versions of what I imagine the patient might have thought as a small child. An example might be something like, "When you were hospitalized for an appendectomy as a boy of four, you probably thought you were being punished for wishing your baby sister got sick and went away . . . or for masturbatory fantasies . . ." or for whatever the analytic material seems to indicate the child's unconscious causal connections to have been. As in Freud's (1937) *Constructions in Analysis*, a reconstruction of that kind, if offered to the patient as an interpretation, might lead to memories that appear to confirm some such thought, or to related memory material that is consistent with it. In other situations, the appearance of subsequent analytic material, even without recaptured memories, could serve to establish a sense of conviction in the correctness of their construction. Needless to add, in the absence of such confirmatory evidence, the analyst must be prepared to reconsider the accuracy of the reconstruction.

A second variety of construction and interpretation of unconscious fantasies involves, not childhood thinking, but contemporary mental activity. Transference fantasies are probably the most commonly encountered versions of this class of unconscious fantasies. Sometimes the analyst detects evidence suggesting some such fantasy; let us say one involving the analyst's encouragement, approval, or disapproval of some plan, wish, or action of the patient's. Transference fantasies of that kind may exist, but not be verbalized. In response to the analyst's interpretation, the patient may admit having consciously withheld such a fantasy to avoid possible discomfort. In other cases, its presence may be confirmed by the patient's subsequent introspective attention, or it is merely reconstructed, even though it remains entirely unavailable to the patient's consciousness. The more difficult it is for the patient to identify and acknowledge these transference fantasies, the more likely I think it is that they resonate with deeply repressed childhood fantasies.

Once again, I do not mean my description of the reconstruction and interpretation of unconscious fantasies to give the impression that I think that I or any other analyst is always correct in our formulations, but I will not repeat a description of the criteria by which the accuracy or inaccuracy of the reconstruction is to be determined. Neither will I elaborate what has been elsewhere fully outlined, that is to say the centrality in modern conflict theory of regarding compromise formation as the organizing principle of mental life. The structure of unconscious fantasies follows this organizing principle, and the constituent elements of which the fantasies are composed can be dissected and identified accordingly by following the usual psychoanalytic method.

It is, on the other hand, worthwhile to restate that clinical material is, as a rule, richly textured and characterized by complex layering. Unconscious fantasies dealing with the same or similar conflicts may appear in altered form in the course of an analysis, reflecting different developmental capabilities, and the influence of varied external circumstances. Also, some fantasies are constructed to modulate, deny, or otherwise defend against other fantasies; wishful fantasies of triumph and success to deal with experiences, or fantasies of loss, defeat, humiliation, and the like, are the most familiar examples of this phenomenon. In my work, I am always interested in trying to understand the apparent psychic purposes that are served by the fantasy in question, as well as seeing the nature of the component wishes, defenses, affects, and moral concerns involved in its structure.

The particular clinical situations whose relevant unconscious fantasies have most captured my attention are those that involve patients' theories of how they imagine analysis is going to cure them, and those concerning the termination of treatment (Abend, 1979, 1988). The interested reader can consult my papers on those subjects; they present my findings in detail, along with illustrative case material. In examining both these groups of unconscious fantasies, and their effects on the analytic process itself, I was struck by the idea that analysts, as well as their patients, are influenced by applicable unconscious fantasies in formulating or adopting their favored theories of cure and termination. Indeed, it follows from Arlow's description of the ubiquitous power of unconscious fantasy function to affect perception, judgment, memory, and thinking, that psychoanalysts and their theoretical constructions and preferences cannot be exceptions to this controlling rule of mental activity.

It is obvious that patients' fantasies about cure and termination can have an influence on how they behave in treatment, and thus the identification and interpretation of those fantasies to the patients would have an important practical effect on how the work proceeds. I also found (1979) that patients' fantasies about how analysis works were invariably derived from childhood unconscious fantasies embodying core conflictual matters in their lives, so their clarification is helpful to a thorough analysis of central issues in their analyses. For example, a fantasy that the analysis is a kind of apprenticeship, whereby the analysand will learn how to be a man, sexually and otherwise, could be a version of an important element of that analysand's childhood Oedipal fantasy life, in which submission to the father was imagined to lead to the acquisition of his powerful phallus. Thus, a patient who displays a submissive, respectful attitude towards his male analyst, coupled with an apparently eager hunger for knowledge from him, may thereby be enacting such a fantasy. It is possible that in a case like that the appearance of great dedication to the work of analyzing on the part of the patient is deceptive: more a matter of display to satisfy the underlying fantasy than true deep immersion in the analysis.

It may be less self-evident, but it is no less true, that the analyst's fantasies about cure and termination can have an effect on how he or she conducts the treatment. The management of the termination phase is particularly subject to variations derived from the analyst's theories (see Buxbaum, 1950, for a case in point). From the standpoint of evaluating theories and technique, the validity of analysts' differing opinions of what is most effective is neither supported nor negated by the fact that personal unconscious fantasies play a role in determining their preferences, because this must be true, to some extent, for all of us. A careful review of clinical experience, and examination of clinical evidence and effectiveness, is the only way reliably to assess our theories and practice. Of course, it is also true that evaluation of the data of experience and outcome is a process that is itself not entirely free of the influence of the evaluator's unconscious fantasy function, as Arlow's formulation makes clear. Perhaps this expression of "irreducible subjectivity," to adapt Renik's (1993, p. 553) celebrated phrase, helps to account for the enormous difficulty that confronts our profession when it comes to comparing competing theories, schools of thought, and technical precepts.

With this cautionary note in mind, I have reflected anew in recent years on the role that my own inner life has played in determining my theoretical and technical choices and preferences. Although considerations of personal discretion restrict me from providing a frank and detailed account of what I know about myself in this regard, it is certainly true that my fascination with Freud's ideas, and my choice to train at the New York Psychoanalytic Institute—then, as now, one of the premier bastions of Freudian teaching—were in part a reflection of personal desires, and were also in part determined by emotionally important relationships with certain teachers and friends. The education that unfolded was very satisfying to my overdetermined fascination with the process of discovering hidden meanings and decoding signs that reveal the true significance of seemingly mysterious surface phenomena and events. It will come as no great surprise to add that my inner preferences and tendencies also contribute to important recreational interests of mine, like my devotion to the literature of espionage and detective stories, to codes and ciphers, and so on. I certainly thought of the model typified by Sherlock Holmes in my pleasurable immersion in the challenge of medical diagnostics during my preparatory education, and this imagery, reinforced to be sure by its childhood antecedents, carried over quite naturally to my early conceptualization of the work of psychoanalysis. Bonds formed with new friends and teachers, along with a deep sense of enlightened conviction, grew from my personal analysis and solidified my posture as an advocate of Freudian conflict theory. Years of practical experience have somewhat (but only somewhat) modified my views, just as decades of accumulated clinical experience have helped the Freudian corpus gradually to evolve, without altering a fundamental belief in its core postulates.

I remain today as convinced as ever that the impact of childhood instinctual conflicts, shaped in part by experiences both of that period of life and of later ones, are of critical importance in influencing normal and pathological development. An analytic search for the compromise formations to which those conflicts give rise, including the network of unconscious fantasies that incorporate and express them, remains the centerpiece of my view of the analytic task. I do not intend by this emphasis to slight the importance that I have learned to attribute to the relationship that develops between the members of each analytic pair, but I feel less certain than some other analysts seem to be that we have a good understanding of how the relationship contributes to the analytic process and outcome. I do include the task of attending as carefully as possible to the task of understanding what the relationship means to each patient, and to track the varied versions of its conscious and unconscious significance as an essential part of the analytic work. I think of my strong wish to be a helper and a healer, which also has childhood antecedents, as playing a role in my professional choice and demeanor, just as much as my curiosity about mysteries does. As important as I think that attitude is, I do not assume that patients automatically understand and respond to me in the way that I like to think of myself, but instead I give primacy to the challenge of detecting and understanding exactly what it is that they feel, wish, fear, and imagine our relationship to be, at every step along the analytic path. Helping analysands to come to understand the unconscious elements in their psychic lives, and the many ways in which those elements affect their current emotions, thoughts, attitudes, and actions, carried out with the most consistently applied analytic temperament of interested, benevolent neutrality that I can maintain, is how I try to do my analytic work. My personal fascination with coming to understand the meanings behind the surface appearance of symptoms, character traits, adaptations, defenses, passions, and other such intrapsychic phenomena has not diminished in the slightest degree as I have struggled to learn how to see more clearly, and to communicate what I see more effectively to my patients. I shall close my remarks by emphasizing a theoretical postulate that is re-evoked in almost every clinical discussion with like-minded colleagues. When we puzzle together about how to make sense of a bit of material, or an aspect of behavior, or any other clinical manifestation, sooner or later one of us is likely to repeat our mantra-like conviction in some such words as these: "It all depends on the fantasies!"

Summary

1. The idea that repressed unconscious fantasies influence symptom formation and normal development dates back to the earliest period of Freud's theory and practice.
2. Because of Freud's view of the nature of the unconscious from his formulation of the topographic model, he was not able to satisfactorily reconcile the organized, secondary-process characteristics of unconscious fantasies with his conceptualization of the inchoate nature of the unconscious stratum of the mind.

3. Mid-century thinkers, of whom Arlow was the most active, suggested that conscious and unconscious fantasy life constitute a continuum of sorts, with varying degrees of difficulty characterizing and determining their access to consciousness.
4. Arlow emphasized the continuous, ubiquitous role that unconscious fantasy function plays in shaping the panoply of conscious experiences.
5. A host of symptoms, moods, character traits, and other clinical manifestations can be analytically clarified by uncovering the relevant unconscious fantasies that affect them, using the psychoanalytic method to do so.
6. At least equally significant is the finding that mental functions like perception, memory, thinking, judgment, and reality testing are all influenced by unconscious fantasy function.
7. This observation applies to the mental activity of analysts, just as it does to that of their analysands, thus helping to explain the unavoidable subjectivity of analytic work and theorizing.
8. Attention to the contributions of unconscious fantasies to both patients' and analysts' theories about how analysis cures, and to their ideas about the termination of analysis, can have great practical importance for the conduct of analysis.

References

Abend, S. (1979). Unconscious fantasies and theories of cure. *Journal of the American Psychoanalytic Association* 27:579–596.

——— (1988). Unconscious fantasies and issues of termination. In: *Fantasy, Myth and Reality: Essays in Honor of Jacob A. Arlow, M.D.*, ed. H. Blum, Y. Kramer, A.D. Richards, and A.K. Richards. Madison, CT: International Universities Press, pp. 149–165.

——— (1990). Unconscious fantasy, structural theory, and compromise formation. *Journal of the American Psychoanalytic Association* 38:61–73.

——— and Brenner, C. (1964). *Psychoanalytic Concepts and the Structural Theory*. New York: International Universities Press.

Arlow, J.A. (1969a). Fantasy, memory and reality testing. *Psychoanalytic Quarterly* 38:28–51.

——— (1969b). Unconscious fantasy and disturbance of conscious experience. *Psychoanalytic Quarterly* 38:61–73.

Boesky, D. (1988). Criteria of evidence for an unconscious fantasy. In: *Fantasy, Myth, and Reality: Essays in Honor of Jacob Arlow, M.D.*, ed. H. Blum, Y. Kramer, A.D. Richards, and A.K. Richards. Madison, CT: International Universities Press, pp. 111–131.

Brenner, C. (1955). *Elementary Textbook of Psychoanalysis*. New York: International Universities Press.

Freud, S. (1894). Neuropsychoses of Defense. *Standard Edition* 3:45–61.

——— (1899). Screen Memories. *Standard Edition* 3: 303–322.

——— (1905a). Fragments of an Analysis of a Case of Hysteria. *Standard Edition* Vol. 7 (pp. 7–122).

——— (1905b). Three Essays on the Theory of Sexuality. *Standard Edition* Vol. 7 (pp. 135–243).

——— (1915). The Unconscious. *Standard Edition* 14:166–204.

——— (1923). The Ego and the Id. *Standard Edition* Vol. 19:12–59.

——— (1924). The Dissolution of the Oedipus Complex. *Standard Edition* 19:173–179.

——— (1926). Inhibitions, Symptoms and Anxiety. *Standard Edition* 20:87–172.

——— (1937). Constructions in Analysis. *Standard Edition* 23:257–269.

Hartmann, H. (1956). Notes on the Reality Principle. In: *Psychoanalytic Study of the Child*, Vol. 2. New York: International Universities Press, pp. 31–53.

Kramer, Y. (1988). In the visions of the night: perspectives on the work of Jacob Arlow. In: *Fantasy Myth and Reality; Essays in Honor of Jacob Arlow, M.D.*, ed. H. Blum, Y. Kramer, A.D. Richards, and A.K. Richards. Madison, CT: International Universities Press, pp. 9–39.

Kris, E. (1956). On some vicissitudes of insight in analysis. *International Journal of Psycho-Analysis* 37:445–455.

Rangell, L. (1988). Roots and derivatives of unconscious fantasy. In: *Fantasy, Myth and Reality: Essays in Honor of Jacob Arlow, M.D.*, ed. H. Blum, Y. Kramer, A.D. Richards, and A.K. Richards. Madison, CT: International Universities Press, pp. 61–78.

Renik, O. (1993). Analytic interaction: conceptualizing technique in light of the analyst's irreducible subjectivity. *Psychoanalytic Quarterly* 62:553–571.

Rothstein, A. (2004). Compromise formation theory: an intersubjective dimension. *Psychoanalytic Dialogues* 15:415–431.

CHAPTER 12

A Variant of Joking in Dreams

[Abend, S.M. (2007). *Psychoanalytic Quarterly* 76(4):1361–1365]

Introduction

Upon reading Eugene Mahon's charming, brief clinical paper, *A Joke in a Dream: A Note on the Complex Aesthetics of Disguise* (2002), I was reminded of some notes I made a number of years ago about a psychoanalytic patient who presented a dream in which a joke was hidden in the manifest content of the dream. Not only was the dreamer himself consciously unaware of the dream joke, but the analyst, too, was taken by surprise in the course of listening to the report of the dream. Though obviously related to Mahon's observation, and to Freud's original comments on absurdity in dreams (1900), the incident I recalled seems to me to represent a variant on those themes not elsewhere described, and is offered herewith as a matter of clinical interest.

Clinical Background

My patient, a man in his late twenties, had come to analysis because of a near-paralytic degree of inhibition in his sexual life and in his ambition to establish a career. He had managed with some difficulty to be graduated from a prestigious university. He had had but one rather serious sexual liaison, which was broken up by his parents, who objected to his girlfriend's ordinary, middle-class background.

He came from a socially elevated, quite wealthy family; he resented his parents' controlling influence and their emotional coldness, and he was quite contemptuous of what he regarded as their hollow and pretentious life style. He was, however, all but totally incapable of expressing his anger and rebellious inclinations toward them directly, except through his failures, which frustrated and disappointed them. At the beginning of his treatment, he was not at all consciously aware of that aspect of his complex needs to defeat himself at every turn.

In analysis, the patient always behaved in an unusually formal manner for someone of his generation. He seemed obsessively conscientious and polite, and expressed great interest in how psychoanalysis works and in what he was expected to do in order to cooperate with the treatment. In his sessions, although he was quite soon able to speak of the anger and contempt he felt toward his parents and siblings, he always treated the analyst with great respect, and never displayed the slightest evidence of resentment or doubt about analysis in his behavior or his verbal productions.

The Dream Session

In a session that took place toward the end of his first year of analysis, the patient reported a dream whose content I shall reconstruct. It should be borne in mind that I was not in the habit of recording sessions or making verbatim notes during sessions; I made some terse notes afterward. The dream, and the analytic work which followed, are therefore reconstructed as faithfully as the analyst's memory permits. The dramatic nature of the joke rendered this material especially vivid.

> I was flying in a two-seater plane with my friend, X, to go up to his family's place in Bar Harbor [Maine] on a beautiful day, when suddenly it was raining heavily on us, even though the surrounding sky was still clear. I looked down and saw that we were actually flying over my uncle's *finca* [estate] in Spain.

Now the reader should be aware of the analyst's mind-set while listening to the account of the dream. All the events, locales, and personae of the dream material were in fact real aspects of the patient's life as I had come to know it. The only sense of dreamlike strangeness was the sudden shift of weather and location. However, at the moment the patient identified the view of his uncle's place in Spain (which, as mentioned, actually exists, and which the patient had frequently visited), the phrase, "The rain in Spain falls mainly on the plane" thrust itself into the analyst's consciousness. Altogether startled, and also a little amused, I blurted those words aloud. The analysand was, if anything, even more startled by my exclamation, and said, "What? You're making fun of me."

Not even with the benefit of hindsight am I able to suggest that I had an analytically coherent rationale for my intervention. It was totally spontaneous and lacking any planned, conscious intent as far as aiding the work of analysis was concerned. I was simply overcome by a burst of pleased surprise at recognizing the familiar, then quite popular phrase as the verbal translation of the dream's imagery, and I said it aloud, doubtless in a tone of voice that indicated my affective state of the moment. This was quite out of character as far as my usual analytic demeanor was concerned. Fortunately, in my opinion, I was able to recover and then to address the patient's unexpected response to my interjection in a more conventionally analytic fashion.

We quickly ascertained that he had no conscious awareness of the joke concealed and expressed in his description of the dream. He had no difficulty in agreeing with my translation of its imagery into words once we discussed it, and he was, of course, thoroughly familiar with the musical comedy *My Fair Lady* and the famous song from which the phrase "the rain in Spain falls mainly on the plain" was taken. We pursued his immediate impression that I was making fun of him, and in short order arrived at an explanation.

Consciously, he was still just as hopeful and enthusiastic about analysis as his usual behavior indicated, but he soon acknowledged being aware at times of an underlying attitude of skepticism, both about the process and about at least some of what I had to say to him. His habitual politesse, and his ingrained restraint about acting in any way that he imagined might displease me, had up to that time prevented him from mentioning any such thoughts. Although we had of late spoken about the intense negativity of his feelings toward his family and their behavior, he had always believed that he harbored no such attitude toward me, or about analysis and its conventions and restrictions. The analytic work on this dream and our subsequent interchange exposed for the first time his unconscious wish to rebel and ridicule. "This dream analysis stuff" (which stood for the entire analytic enterprise) "is just a lot of nonsense" was what he wished to be able to say aloud. His first defensive response was to project the wish to ridicule onto me, but in the course of that single session, he was able to see and acknowledge his own concealed hostility, his fear of expressing it directly, and his anticipation of retaliatory punishment, all neatly encapsulated into the dream and its sequelae.

Discussion

In Mahon's (2002) paper, a sarcastic, joking remark appeared in the manifest content of his patient's dream, though it was attributed to the analyst. The analytic work revealed the underlying conflicted, sadomasochistic wishes expressed and disguised in the dream. Mahon contrasted his emphasis on defensive disguise of forbidden wishes as motivators for the dream joke with Freud's ideas about jokes and dreams.

It is certainly the case that when Freud was writing *The Interpretation of Dreams* (1900) and *Jokes and Their Relation to the Unconscious* (1905), he was mainly interested in clarifying the nature of the primary process in operation, and in demonstrating the nature of the instinctual wishes that dominate unconscious mental life, seeking expression through various outlets. Perhaps the closest he came to the kind of material that captured Mahon's interest, and my own as well, is in his discussion of absurdity in dreams (1900, pp. 431–435). He said:

> A dream is made absurd, then, if a judgment that something "is absurd" is among the elements *included* in the dream thoughts—that is to say, if any one of the dreamer's unconscious trains of thought has criticism or ridicule as its motive. [p. 434, italics added]

Here Freud was talking about dreams in which elements of absurdity were evident in the manifest content, but not explicitly the idea of joking, whether manifest or concealed.

As mentioned above, I think that my own clinical material, like Mahon's, demonstrates surface variations on the same sort of psychoanalytic situation. Since the appearance of Freud's (1900) seminal work on dreams, there is no news in the observation that dreams express forbidden unconscious wishes in disguised forms. The many different forms these disguised expressions may take, including the use of jokes, conscious and unconscious, demonstrate the fascinating adaptability of mental life, and highlight the endlessly surprising challenge of doing analytic work.

Addendum

Freud was certainly aware that dreams have many layers of meaning, only some of which may be recoverable at any given analytic moment. This proved to be true of the dream of my patient as well. It was some years later, close to the end of his analysis, that we came to recognize that among his several fantasies of how analysis cures (see Abend, 1979), there was a version of the Pygmalion story, in which the analyst is the doctor who transforms him into someone new and wonderful. At the time the dream was presented, however, all that material was far from the working surface. What was then pertinent was the hidden joke that, for the first time, allowed us access to his aggression in the analysis itself.

References

Abend, S.M. (1979). Unconscious fantasy and theories of cure. *Journal of the American Psychoanalytic Association* 27:579–596.

Freud, S. (1900). The Interpretation of Dreams. *Standard Edition* 4/5.

——— (1905). Jokes and Their Relation to the Unconscious. *Standard Edition* 8.

Mahon, E. (2002). A joke in a dream: a note on the complex aesthetics of disguise. *Psychoanalytic Study of the Child* 57:452–457.

Part III:

Therapeutic Action and Change

CHAPTER 13

Factors Influencing Change in Patients in Psychoanalytic Treatment[1]

[Abend, S.M. (2002). *Journal of Clinical Psychoanalysis* 11(2):209–223]

General theories of therapeutic action are related to their respective underlying theories of the nature of pathology. Competing or overlapping theories emphasize one or another aspect of the analytic situation, with corresponding implications for technique. In addition to briefly summarizing a number of such theories and recommendations, the author points to another dimension of therapeutic response that reflects individual features of patients' psychopathology. Many, if not all, patients have conscious and unconscious views about being influenced to change that originate in their past relationships. Thus, it is important for analysts to attend to their analysands' fantasies about treatment, influence, and change in the hope that careful analysis of those elements may beneficially affect treatment outcome. Case vignettes illustrate this aspect of technique.

Every patient who comes for psychoanalytic treatment expects to be changed by the experience. When such painful symptoms as manifest depression or severe forms of anxiety or sexual dysfunction are what bring the person to treatment, the changes wished for center on

[1] Original version presented to the faculty of the New York Psychoanalytic Institute, November 10, 1999.

relief from those miseries. In other cases, where less circumscribed dissatisfaction with life, let us say in respect to career or relationships, is the stimulus for analysis, the patient will probably be less clear about what inner changes are needed in order to feel better. Either type of patient is likely to be uncertain about how treatment is supposed to bring about changes, but in my experience, he or she generally has some private theories on the subject. These are, in part, derived from impressions gained from what others have said about treatment, from formal or popular education, and from media exposure. However, their theories about treatment are also invariably shaped to some degree by unconscious fantasies peculiar to each individual.

Analytic therapists also have theories about how treatment will influence the patient to change. I have observed that many of our various theories of therapeutic action seem to be closely linked to a related theory of pathogenesis. It stands to reason that each of these sets of interconnected theories tends to be convincing to its adherents, if not to those colleagues who hold other views. Whenever treatment has a favorable outcome, there is little motive for analysts to question their preferred theories. Efforts to explain treatment failures are less satisfactory, but that is a difficulty common to all schools of thought.

All experienced therapists know that their patients' conscious wishes to change are only one aspect of a complex psychic situation; other components that will oppose the desire to change will surely be encountered in the course of treatment. Certainly, this balance of opposing intrapsychic forces, and how effectively it can be analyzed, must play a large part in determining outcome. Our theories of therapeutic action tend to ignore these individual complexities in favor of general formulations about the nature of psychic structure, development, and pathogenesis that are thought to apply to all cases. The clinician, on the other hand, whatever his or her school of thought, is primarily concerned with individual cases. Relative failures of treatment inevitably draw the clinician's attention to the specifics of the case, in an effort to account for the less than satisfactory outcome. Rothstein (1998) has observed that analysts sometimes invoke serious diagnostic labels in order to explain their failures, and that this tendency may represent a countertransference attitude aimed at assuaging our professional narcissism. The same might be said of retrospective assessments of the patient's severe developmental difficulties, or peculiarities of their psychic structure, as explanations for their inability to change in response to therapeutic influence. I have been impressed that there are some cases in which the uncovering of certain highly specific unconscious fantasies about treatment, and about influence and change, seems to be illuminating in the search for explanations of failure, and perhaps of success as well.

In this presentation, I shall review some of the ideas about what influences patients to change that are incorporated in certain theories of therapeutic action, although given the increasing theoretical pluralism that characterizes present-day psychoanalysis, I cannot promise to be comprehensive. Certain recurrent themes and pivotal issues nevertheless recur, and will be highlighted. I shall also suggest that it is often important to pay careful attention in analysis to the patient's fantasies and conflicts about the treatment process itself, since these may be significant contributing factors in determining the results in certain difficult cases.

Freud's protopsychoanalytic ideas, derived from hypnotherapy, centered upon the use of mechanisms of suggestion to overcome the sequestration of pathogenic memories. His first truly psychoanalytic theory of therapeutic action was a sophisticated derivative of his earlier ideas. The recovery of pathogenic memories remained a central feature of his theory, with emphasis being placed on the undoing of repression as the means by which infantile amnesia was to be lifted. He eschewed the mechanistic use of suggestion, and explicitly denied, presumably in response to hostile accusations, that the psychoanalyst could succeed in suggesting to patients what the actual contents of their crucial memories, or fantasies, might be. However, suggestion did not completely disappear from his therapeutic armamentarium, persisting in the subtle form of the unobjectionable positive transference, by means of which he thought the patient must be induced to do the painful work of overcoming his or her resistance. Along with the importance of repression, the role of transference was the other radical discovery incorporated into Freud's elaboration of what constitutes psychoanalytic treatment. However, consistent with the foregoing, he conceptualized it as a tool by which the buried past could be understood and brought back into the light of conscious recognition and control.

As is well known, the ink was barely dry on Freud's monumental series of papers on psychoanalytic technique of 1912 to 1917, before controversy about how analysis is supposed to influence patients to change erupted in the work of Ferenczi and Rank (1923). The innovations suggested by them hinged on the belief that the patient's immediate emotional experience in analysis is more important in determining outcome than Freud seemed to appreciate. They contrasted the conviction attained via the nature of the patient's experience of and with the analyst with insight that might be confined to intellectual understanding alone. This led Ferenczi (1950) to develop what he called "active technique," in which the analyst adopts specific forms of behavior designed to intensify the patient's emotional experience in ways especially suited to his or her therapeutic needs. I make much of these early theoretical differences because it is easy for current scholars to see in them the outlines of a controversy which has persisted to the present, in one form or another.

Even after Freud shifted to the structural hypothesis, the fundamental importance for patients of learning about their pasts, and about their buried infantile mental lives, in order to comprehend and thereby change what remained problematic in the present, persisted as a central tenet of therapy. To be sure, past mental states and fantasies, as well as actual events, came to be recognized as pathogenic influences. Clinical experience also taught that reconstruction of these unconscious contents, if accompanied by a sufficient degree of conviction on the part of the patient, could be mutative, even if actual memories did not resurface. The important but puzzling question then became one of how the necessary conviction is attained, and most clinicians have come to believe that transference experiences play a major, if perhaps not so precisely defined, role in this process. This constituted an area of overlap between the classical position and that of the dissident, experience-centered theorists, but there were important differences between them.

The innovations suggested by Alexander and French (1946) made these distinctions very clear. Following Ferenczi, he developed the concept of a therapeutically "corrective emotional experience," influenced by the analyst's adoption of specific behaviors designed to highlight the problems of the analysand. This departed sharply from Freud's recommended posture of a neutral observing and interpretive stance toward the patient. Freud believed it helped minimize or eliminate forms of interaction that might inadvertently gratify patients' unconscious transference wishes, the better to promote their expression in words rather than actions. Freud and his followers, in keeping with this emphasis, also discouraged analysts from consciously attempting to influence their patients to change, except through the medium of interpretation of what was observed of the patients' defenses, wishes, and fears. A moment's reflection will make it clear that all analytic treatment is a corrective emotional experience of one sort or another. However, the phrase became a shibboleth, thanks to Alexander, distinguishing the recommendation that the analyst try deliberately to influence patients' reactions and experiences in analysis through behaviors other than the classically approved forms of verbal clarification and interpretations.

In his formulation of how analysis works, Strachey (1934, 1937) laid emphasis on the impact on the analysand of learning, at certain moments of high intensity in the transference, that the analyst does not react to his or her wishes in the same way that significant objects in the past have done. Thus, a gradual change in patients' superego functioning can be facilitated, leading to alterations in unconscious conflict solutions. In Strachey's proposal, Kleinian and classical Freudian ideas are, for all practical purposes, melded together, despite other substantive differences in those evolving, divergent schools of analytic theory. Early Kleinians and their Freudian counterparts shared the view that the analyst is able to detect the architecture of the patient's unconscious, and then informs the patient about it via interpretation, and that this is best accomplished in an atmosphere of what later came to be called *technical neutrality.*

The difficulties of doing successful analytic work with sicker patients were probably the chief stimulus for the next major shift in theorizing about therapeutic influence. It is hard to attribute primacy to any individual, but certainly Winnicott (1955) was among the first and most influential of a number of analysts who concluded that technical modifications are necessary in order to bring about changes in patients' faulty psychic structure. Common to all these theoretical proposals is the view that deficiencies in the environment provided by the mother or other primary caretakers lead to failures of optimal psychic development during the period of very early childhood. It is suggested that the resulting deficits, or structural abnormalities, must be addressed from an analytic stance that differs from the traditional one of neutral, relatively abstinent observation and interpretation. In these versions of the increased focus on experience as mutative, the patient's relationship with the analyst provides an environment of acceptance, containment, nurturing, holding, and safety, which, it is hypothesized, can at least partially undo the developmental damage. According to some theorists, like Winnicott (1955), this preliminary work, if successful, constitutes preparation for subsequent, more conventional analysis of higher-level transferences and their imbricated oedipal phase fantasies and conflicts. In other variations of this theoretical posture, it is suggested that patients must, in essence, be taught that their thinking, reality testing, and judgment are faulty, and through experience, identification, and sometimes confrontation, be induced to change in order to be able to deal with the subsequent analytic tasks.

The innovations initiated by Kohut (1971), and embodied in self psychology, carried this thesis to a new level of specificity. Faulty early development is codified as failure to form a properly integrated self system, and a new therapeutic tactic for dealing with these problems was devised. Since failures of parental empathy are seen as the primary noxious agencies leading to problems in the development of the self system, a technically empathic stance on the part of the analyst is advocated. Analysis of the unavoidable transferential reactions of disappointment and rage at the inevitable periodic failures of the analyst's empathy is seen as crucial to the therapeutic endeavor.

Tolerance of the emergence of various aspects of pathological narcissistic transferences is also necessary; this requires careful monitoring of potentially damaging countertransference reactions, and an avoidance of interpretations of conflict that may be experienced as unmanageably critical, or unempathic. Such a technical stance is thought to provide what might be considered to be a variation of the safe, nurturing holding environment advocated by other theorists. It is presumed to promote a developmental correction that addresses the patient's essential psychopathology. It also calls for specific acknowledgment of the behavior of the analyst as contributing to the patient's pathological responses, thus bringing the analyst's contribution to the analytic milieu into a new kind of focus.

Among these increasingly divergent streams of analytic theory, we may take note of two interrelated evolving themes. One has to do with differing views of the nature of psychopathology, stimulated in large measure by clinical experiences of disappointment with the results of some analyses. Hypotheses about the underlying mental structure of the refractory patient, and by extension, in some theories at least, of all patients, have led to various recommendations for modification in the behavior of the analyst in conducting treatment. This second theme identifies a trend in our theorizing that we shall continue to follow in its more recent versions. Up to this point in our survey, we note that analysts have been encouraged to depart from the specific behaviors recommended by Freud for different reasons. First, it was in order to intensify or highlight certain transference experiences. Later, it was advised in order to beneficially influence certain deviations from optimum levels of psychic development that may limit patients' ability to participate in conventional Freudian- style psychoanalysis. Still later, it was to effectively address forms of psychopathology that require the analyst to acknowledge the role his or her own behavior plays in producing transference reactions, instead of restricting the discourse to the patient's internal reasons for how he or she reacts to the analyst and analysis itself.

We next turn our attention to an important trend in psychoanalytic theorizing that derives from a fundamental challenge to our previous notions of the psychoanalytic process. Influenced by recent thinking in the academic sphere, it characterizes psychoanalysis as a study of meaning, rather than, as previously, a form of medical treatment, rooted in biology, designed to relieve specific emotional ailments. Obviously, academic influence was only one source of this shift, since the extension of psychoanalytic treatment to forms of human distress such as the character neuroses has also led to an expansion and alteration, in some minds at least, of the nature of the psychoanalytic enterprise. It is beyond the scope of this paper to try to assess all the factors and forces involved in this proposed shift in the basic conceptualization of psychoanalysis, but some of its consequences are plain to see. One was to discard the earlier working assumption that the analyst is a competent, if not perfectly objective, observer and interpreter of the meaning of the patient's productions. A second was to abandon the archaeological analogy first proposed by Freud. Instead, it was stressed that neither the crucial formative events of the patient's past, nor, for that matter, the architecture of the patient's unconscious mind, can be definitively uncovered. Moreover, in some hands, other ways of conceptualizing the relationship between the present and the past were proposed. The death of positivism was declared by a certain segment of psychoanalytic thinkers, and subjectivity, in one version or another, arose to take its place in our analytic consciousness. The authority of the analyst as expert was, in some quarters at least, substantially redefined.

In the Lacanian universe, in which I include many European and Latin American analysts whose thought has been influenced by him, even if they do not regard themselves as Lacanians, the patient discovers something of the nature of his or her unconscious, essentially through the process of expressing in words what was previously inexpressible. This process clarifies, if it does not transform, the patient's dilemmas, from which more choice may emerge. In another version of this type of reformulation of the nature of psychoanalysis, patients are considered to have constructed a narrative history of their lives that serves multiple psychological purposes, some of which are unconscious. The treatment process may demonstrate the nature of this subjective construction to its author, including its constrictive consequences. It will also introduce the possibility of alternative narratives, and while, strictly speaking, this effect is not intended to induce the patient to change, it can be thought of as offering the patient greater freedom of choice in the conduct of life, as does the Lacanian conception. In these models, one can sense the emergence of a different way of thinking about the influence of the past from the former emphasis on more or less objective reconstruction provided to practitioners.

A case in point is the introduction of the term *après coup* in French analytic circles. It is difficult to present a concise explanation of its meaning and employment, as a symposium on intercultural psychoanalysis held in Paris (1998) clearly demonstrated that French analysts who utilize the term differ widely among themselves in that regard. Suffice it to say for our purposes that it is an attempt to explicate how traumatic experiences of the remote past can take on a different significance when reawakened at later stages of personal development, or in analysis.

Some other interpersonal or relational theories have come to focus more and more exclusively on the so-called here-and-now of the analytic encounter. In these versions, which emphasize the patient's experience as the center of the psychoanalytic process, what the patient gains as insight may have little or nothing to do with the reconstruction of the past. This stands in marked contrast to other models of psychoanalysis, even including those that utilize a more flexible view of how the past is to be apprehended and understood. Instead, an intense examination of the current patterns of interaction between analyst and patient serves to inform the analysand about his or her characteristic mode of psychic functioning, especially in the interpersonal sphere, as well as providing a milieu in which experiences of an ameliorative nature occur. In this approach, as in some others, the presumptive value of the analyst's abandoning the traditional stance recommended by Freud and his followers may be made explicit. In recognition of the inevitably subjective nature of the analyst's participation, and in the service of providing a more authentic, less authoritarian, climate of engagement between analyst and analysand, a continuing critical reassessment of the analyst's contribution is encouraged. Much more spontaneous self-revelation may be recommended, for example, and the expression of opinions, at least in certain circumstances, is seen as potentially helpful, rather than as a suspect attempt at influencing the patient.

Once again, in these theories, the analysand is seen as acquiring the opportunity to make changes through a combination of insight and experience. Insight, however, may be less a matter of having unconscious wishes and defenses revealed or interpreted than it is a question of being shown alternative ways of construing his or her experiences, past or present. Experience is understood partly as a means of obtaining conviction through here-and-now actuality, and partly as a matter of having a new kind of relationship with a significant figure, which is both healing and educational. It should also be noted that there are some current intersubjective approaches that combine aspects of the traditional interest in the formative past, and its unconscious conflictual elements, with the altered view of the nature of the analyst's interactive role. In the varied spectrum of approaches described, some may, but do not necessarily, incorporate the recommendation to rethink the optimal technical stance associated with classical analysis in favor of a more candidly personal alternative.

In a survey such as this one, it is hardly possible to do justice to the variety of theoretical models, in particular to the emerging, and still developing, set of possibilities collected under the rubric of intersubjectivity. I have tried to be accurate, if sketchy, and I hope I have at least presented a hint of the diversity that now confronts us as students of psychoanalytic theory. I have tried to indicate certain trends that, to my mind, represent recurrent themes and issues. I should like to summarize them once again.

Freud's therapeutic method, derived from his views of the nature of psychopathology, started by his codifying how he thought the psychoanalyst can most effectively influence the patient to change. He presented a set of recommendations for analytic behavior designed to provide suitable patients with the maximum opportunity to benefit from the procedure. Among its familiar elements are: (1) the admonition to eschew trying to influence the patient, except by informing him or her about unconscious aspects of that person's mental functioning; (2) maintaining a neutral posture toward the conflictual components that emerge in the treatment; and (3) suppressing the analyst's own personality and experience, in order to concentrate, as much as possible, on the patient's mental contents.

The technical posture that Freud developed, and to which his followers have adhered, was always a source of difficulty for patients and practitioners alike. Patients were inevitably frustrated at times, and designedly so, while analysts had to curtail their spontaneity and constrict their personal behavior. For some patients at least, this form of treatment just did not work very well, if at all, and for some analysts, it seemed personally intolerable and, in addition, a theoretically unjustified mode of functioning. Alternative theories arose from the earliest days of psychoanalysis. Some challenged the Freudian view of what is found in unconscious mental life, if not necessarily how he thought the analyst should behave in conducting analytic treatment. Other, different views, though, substantially and directly attacked the prescription for analytic conduct set forth by Freud.

As I have said, theories about the nature of psychopathology changed, inspired in part by experience with patients who did not respond well to standard analytic technique. Common to most of the newer theories was the dictum that the analyst's behavior should be altered in order to influence the patient by means that traditional analysis has regarded with skepticism. Among those recommendations have been: (1) adopting specific behaviors to underline and influence patients' problems; (2) providing a degree of nurturing acceptance designed to promote patients' development so as to undo deficits; (3) acknowledging patients' experiences of their analysts' behavior as plausible or valid, and thus giving the analyst's behavior and personality a place in the therapeutic milieu and dialogue that was previously ignored; (4) reducing the analyst's authority to make interpretations about the patient's unconscious that are based solely on the analyst's having been analyzed and trained, in favor of an increased mutuality in the assignment of meaning to patients' experiences, emotionality and productions; and (5) acknowledging the analyst's subjectivity, and on that basis, releasing him or her from restrictions against influencing the patient by expressions of opinion and personal revelations. It is interesting to me to note that as the nature of the analyst's authority in the analytic situation has been challenged, and his or her expertise redefined, the terms of engagement in the analytic situation have been set forth in a new way, liberating the analyst to attempt to influence patients to change by using his or her personality in ways that were proscribed in the days when analytic authority went unquestioned.

While it is fair to say that questions about the analyst's authority, motivation, and methods of influencing the patient to change have long plagued us as professionals, it is equally clear that these matters concern our patients as well. Whatever degree of accuracy we may be willing to grant our analysands' views of us on these counts, the analytic method surely demonstrates that patients invariably have conscious and unconscious views about being influenced to change, which originate in their past relationships. These inevitably color their transference experiences in analysis. In some instances at least, they seem to have a substantial impact on patients' experience of analysis, for better and for worse.

In 1979, I noted that it is sometimes possible to detect patients' fantasies about how psychoanalysis is supposed to help them to change, and I was able to illustrate that those fantasies of cure are related to and derived from unconscious fantasies originating in childhood mental life. One patient I had analyzed had unconsciously connected the analyst both with an idealized father, who would teach him about sex, and with a nursemaid of his childhood, whom he contrasted with his cold and frightening mother, and whom he had wished would initiate him into sexuality. The nursemaid and the analyst were seen to be ethnically different from the patient and his parents, and thus imagined to be "warmer" and more "earthy," and thus sexually permissive, rather than forbidding and forbidden. Just as he consciously hoped analysis, and the analyst, would provide a learning experience that would make him sexually competent and free, so he had once wished for sexual enlightenment from these figures of his childhood. There is some reason to believe he found these fantasies of cure powerful, since, in the course of his analysis, he met and married a woman whose background, he was convinced, was similar to that which he ascribed to his analyst.

It is fascinating that as he became increasingly enamored of the woman he eventually married, his image of the analyst shifted radically. First, he suddenly switched to identifying the analyst with his real mother, instead of her surrogate, and imagined opposition to his love affair based upon a wish to possess and dominate him, and keep him in sexless dependency. On the day he decided to marry, he also abruptly decided to stop his analysis; the material presented suggested that the analyst also had now come to represent the rivalrous, punitive version of his father, and the two forbidding transference images became a source of analytic resistance, instead of progress. The sudden breaking off of the analysis seemed to be a compromise formation that represented the parricidal fantasy, an attempt to escape from punishment, and a simultaneous enactment of the punishment in a milder form.

The patient was later able to return and resume analysis, and in the course of the subsequent work many of these transference fantasies were further clarified. As he went forward in building a life for himself and his wife, a deeper dimension of the paternal transference emerged, once again as a block toward further analytic change. Now the ethnically different analyst seemed to be equated with the envious and dangerous foreigners who had, according to family legend, stolen his father's assets. This fearful picture, part projection, part punishment for his increasing success, once more led the patient to flee the treatment, this time not to return. It is interesting to add that a chance meeting outside the office, some years later, was a warm and friendly encounter, with much apparent pleasure on the part of the former analysand, and no apparent memory of the hostile, suspicious atmosphere of the end of his treatment. It would also be interesting to learn how the current theories that regard the transference as a co-construction of patient and analyst would account for the sudden transformations that appear in patients' dominant transference convictions in cases such as this one.

In another case, that of a young man whose upbringing was profoundly influenced by the personality of his forceful, involved, and extremely domineering father, it seemed that his responses to analysis were very much a function of that relationship. In three attempts at analytic treatment, all with older male analysts, he consciously wanted to be taught, directed, and approved of in all things, including sexuality. His analytic experiences before he came to me had familiarized him with these wishes, and with the childhood homosexual longings and fears that expressed a core aspect of that relationship. What he apparently did not understand was how his rage and rebellion entered the picture in ways that affected his reactions to analysis, and to all of his analysts. He listened to interpretations and learned his analysts' formulations quite well, but was skilled at rendering them ineffective in various ways. He would turn analytic ideas into magical mantras, reduce them to absurd oversimplifications, treat them as banal repetitions, or find them intellectually compelling but emotionally unmoving. In all these ways and more, he symbolically reduced the powerful, consciously admired, loved, but hated father-analysts to impotence. He was convinced he was a failure at analysis, and at life, and he resisted being influenced to change while he longed for change. Through this masochistic compromise formation, he successfully disappointed and frustrated his father and his analysts, suffering punishment and inflicting it simultaneously. Despite the power of this array of fantasies in affecting his unconscious attitudes toward change, persistent analytic attention to these issues enabled slow, painstaking, but very real progress to be achieved.

In these illustrations, I have concentrated exclusively on some material directly pertinent to the question of what may influence the patient to change, or to resist change. It is, in consequence, intentionally narrowly focused and incomplete; many aspects of the analytic work with these patients have been omitted. I recognize that the material I have presented, while interesting and pertinent, does not constitute a complete explanation for how these analyses unfolded, and it can hardly be claimed that such fantasies are the definitive factors in determining outcome. Nevertheless, it does seem to me that analytic experiences of this type strongly support the idea that the patient's conscious and unconscious fantasies about analysis, change and influence, especially as they appear in the transference, do play an important contributory role.

We all subscribe to our preferred theories about how analytic treatment influences patients to change, and it is my opinion that none of these theories is to be regarded as proven. However, one can say that the ordinary work of analysis can make the patient's pertinent fantasies about how treatment influences him or her available for the analytic duo to explore. Historically, as I have noted, analysts' disappointment with the results of their work with patients who do not readily change has been a major factor contributing to the formulation of suggestions for modifying standard technique. We cannot suppose that diligent attention to the analysis of patients' fantasies about treatment will invariably produce good results, or that proposals to modify technique spring solely from a failure to attend sufficiently to patients' conflicts about change. However, it is reasonable to propose that systematic attention to the presence, nature, and power of such unconscious fantasies in our patients may help to enlighten both us and them about the difficulty of changing, and perhaps thereby to beneficially alter the balance of forces, at least in some cases. Whatever contribution to the outcome the existence of such fantasies may explain, it surely behooves the analyst to be alert to them, in the hope that analyzing that material can help the analytic treatment to achieve its rational aims.

References

Abend, S. (1979). Unconscious fantasies and theories of cure. *Journal of the American Psychoanalytic Association* 27:579–596.

Alexander, F., with French, T.M. (1946). The principle of corrective emotional experience. In: *Psychoanalytic Therapy: Principles and Application*. New York: Ronald Press, pp. 67–70.

Ferenczi, S. (1950). The further development of an active therapy in psychoanalysis. In: *Further Contributions to the Theory and Technique of Psychoanalysis*. London: Hogarth Press, pp. 198–217.

Ferenczi, S. and O. Rank. (1923). *The Development of Psychoanalysis*, tr. C. Newton. New York: Dover.

Kohut, H. (1971). *The Analysis of the Self*. New York: International Universities Press.

Rothstein, A. (1998). Fantasies of failure, name calling, and the limits of analytic knowledge. In: *Psychoanalytic Technique and the Creation of Analytic Patients*. Madison, CT: International Universities Press, pp. 77–89.

Strachey, J. (1934). The nature of the therapeutic action of psychoanalysis. *International Journo of Psycho-Analysis* 15:127–159.

Strachey, J. (1937). Symposium: Theory of the therapeutic results of psychoanalysis. *International Journo of Psycho-Analysis* 18:139–145.

Winnicott, D.W. (1955). Metapsychological and clinical aspects of regression within the psychoanalytical setup. *International Journol of Psycho-Analysis* 36:16–26.

CHAPTER 14

Analyzing Intrapsychic Conflict: Compromise Formation as an Organizing Principle

[Abend, S.M. (2005). *Psychoanalytic Quarterly* 74(1):5–25]

The author highlights the idea that analysts' recognition of intrapsychic conflict and compromise formation provides them with a most effective way to formulate their patients' problems. A clinical illustration is presented, with attention to the analyst's use of these concepts during the course of the patient's treatment. The author discusses ways in which his thinking about intrapsychic conflict, compromise formation, and unconscious fantasy informs his approach to clinical work. He emphasizes that viewing compromise formation as the organizing principle of much of mental life gives analysts an effective way to understand the underlying structure of the psychic phenomena in which they are interested.

Introduction

In order to describe what is involved in the analysis of intrapsychic conflict, it will be helpful first to set forth those fundamental ideas about mental functioning upon which the relevant technical precepts are based. The primary proposition central to the theory of the analytic significance of intrapsychic conflict is that a dynamic state of opposition exists between or among various important components of mental life, and that some of them lie outside the realm of consciousness, remaining unavailable to it by means of ordinary conscious introspection alone. Over the course of more than a century of psychoanalytic theorizing, the account of the constituents of conflict—of the motives for the state of opposition that characterizes them, of the range of possible consequences of the internal clash of the forces or elements involved, and of the role played by psychoanalytic intervention in altering the outcome of conflict—has undergone substantial refinement. To set the stage for a presentation of the technique of the analysis of conflict in contemporary terms, it will suffice to give a condensed outline of the historical development of the theory of intrapsychic conflict, and of the psychoanalytic techniques devised to address its vicissitudes.

Development of the Psychoanalytic Method

Almost from the very beginning of Freud's efforts to understand neurotic afflictions, he recognized that certain aspects of mental life are held in a state outside of consciousness precisely because they are, for one reason or another, unacceptable to the individual's conscious awareness. As he progressed from the earliest cathartic techniques to the development of the first truly psychoanalytic method, he soon realized that his analytic patients, without recognizing how or why they did so, silently struggled against permitting the unwelcome material to become conscious. Even more surprising and frustrating, he saw that they were often likely to again relegate it to the hidden realm, even after the threatening material had been identified and discussed in treatment. Freud termed this phenomenon *resistance*, since it made its appearance in the clinical situation as an obstacle to the analyst's efforts to help the patient understand the nature of disturbing unconscious contents. He reached the logical conclusion that the preexisting internal state of opposition, or conflict, between various components of the analysand's mental life became transformed in the analytic situation into a conflict with the analyst and his or her efforts to intervene in the patient's psychic economy.

Resistance emerged in spite of the patient's sincere, conscious desire to cooperate with the treatment in order to obtain relief from emotional suffering. This formulation of the paradoxical nature of the analytic situation has continued to intrigue and challenge theoreticians of psychoanalytic technique, even as our understanding of the complex nature of the relationship between analyst and analysand has grown in sophistication and subtlety over the course of time.

Intrapsychic Conflict

Years of clinical experience taught Freud that his initial focus on the identification and interpretation of unconscious libidinal wishes, whether in the transference or in the recaptured infantile past, was not sufficient to deal therapeutically with the range of emotional problems that psychoanalysis sought to alleviate. Clinical evidence documenting the frequent occurrence of self-destructive behavior forced him to abandon the view that self-preservation was his patients' sole motive for regarding the unconscious wishes as threatening, and he gradually developed a more comprehensive and accurate understanding of the nature of intrapsychic conflict. The importance of unacceptable unconscious aggressive wishes (in addition to libidinal ones), the complex variability of defensive aspects of mental functioning, the range of imagined dangers against which defenses are mobilized, and the elaborate part played in psychic life by self-punitive trends were all incorporated into his revised understanding of the true nature of intrapsychic conflict.

These revisions were comprehensively described in two seminal works, *The Ego and The Id* (1923) and *Inhibitions, Symptoms and Anxiety* (1926). However, it was not until a number of years after those publications appeared that psychoanalytic technique truly incorporated the implications of the new formulations, which we now collectively refer to as the structural theory. The emergence in the 1930s and '40s of what analysts called ego psychology, with its emphasis on the analysis of defenses and their role in conflict, was a further consequence of these theoretical developments.

Other subjects of interest, some of them originating outside the mainstream of Freudian psychoanalytic thought, came to influence the technique of the analysis of conflict, in some cases not without considerable questioning and debate. Without attempting to credit all the various sources of these additional factors (a task that would take us too far afield), I can mention that among the most significant were: (1) recognition of the role played by the therapeutic relationship in bringing about change; (2) utilization in psychoanalytic technique of countertransference data as a source of information about the patient's mental life; and (3) a vastly increased interest in certain quarters in preoedipal factors, whether as loci of conflict in themselves, or as developmental deficiencies that affect defensive and adaptive capabilities.

Perhaps equally important, analysts today are likely to have a far more extensive and subtle conception of what is included in the transference dimension of the analytic encounter than was the case when Freud concentrated more or less exclusively on the manifestations of unconscious libidinal wishes toward the analyst. It is also common nowadays to reflect on the interaction between analyst and patient as expressing a potentially informative blend of transference and countertransference elements, as well as to acknowledge the impact of the analyst's personality and behavior on the patient's experience in analysis.

These developments are certain to be familiar to analysts of every persuasion, and I do not propose to elaborate them here in further detail. Instead, I shall concentrate on the steps involved in the understanding and interpretation of instinctual conflict, and thereby on the effort to provide the analysand with helpful insight into its nature and origins, thus to mitigate its influence on his or her emotional difficulties. In order to do so, I shall place special emphasis on the theoretical and practical importance of the concepts of unconscious fantasy and compromise formation.

Unconscious Fantasy

The assumption of the importance of unconscious fantasies in normal and pathological mental life is hardly a new idea. Once Freud replaced his belief in the etiological ubiquity of experiences of childhood seduction with the recognition that imagined scenarios could also play a determinative role in producing adult neuroses, of necessity he assigned unconscious fantasy life a central place in psychoanalysis. His elaboration of childhood sexual theories and anatomical confusion in *Three Essays on the Theory of Sexuality* (1905) further underlined the lasting influence of unconscious fantasies in normal as well as in pathological development. His description of the part played by the growing child's conviction regarding a series of imagined danger situations (Freud, 1926) in determining the fate of infantile libidinal and aggressive wishes placed unconscious fantasies at the very crux of childhood instinctual conflict. Generations of analysts who followed in Freud's footsteps have employed the concept of unconscious fantasy to elaborate their way of understanding the meaning of patients' symptoms, beliefs, reactions, and behavior. It is clear that they attempt to detect the particular unconscious fantasies that lie beneath the surface of analytic material, and are likely to explicitly mention their conjectures about such entities in the course of doing analytic interpretive work.

While countless publications, panel discussions, and case presentations have documented the attention that analysts pay to unconscious fantasies in their clinical work, it is not always explicitly indicated that important instinctual conflicts are invariably involved in the formation of all such fantasies. Nevertheless, it does follow logically that analytic work on uncovering and clarifying the nature of important unconscious fantasies is necessarily, at the same time, an aspect of the technique of analyzing instinctual conflict. The relationship between unconscious instinctual conflict and the fantasies in which they are expressed has been further explicated as a result of the elaboration of the concept of compromise formation in the work of Brenner (1982) and those influenced by his ideas.

Quite early in his work (1896), Freud presented the notion that neurotic symptoms can be thought of as the product of a compromise between forbidden unconscious libidinal wishes and the defensive forces that impinge upon them to disguise their nature. This relatively simple conception of compromise formation persisted in the language of psychoanalysis, despite the growing understanding of complexity reflected in the introduction of such terms as *overdetermination* and the principle of multiple function (Waelder, 1936). Actually, Freud himself had long since provided a more complete and accurate outline of the nature and composition of instinctual conflicts, but he never troubled himself to incorporate this broader understanding into his conceptualization of compromise formation, nor did he apply his ideas about it beyond symptom formation into the realm of normal development.

Compromise Formation

Brenner (1982) revised our understanding of the meaning of compromise formation in order to bring it into harmony with the intervening evolution of psychoanalytic theory. He suggested that compromise formation should be understood to describe the result of the interactions among *all* the components of an instinctual conflict. Furthermore, he demonstrated that instinctual conflicts and their resultant compromise formations are not limited to the sphere of psychopathology, but also constitute the structural underpinning of much that is considered normal in mental life.

According to Brenner, compromise formations can always be shown to incorporate four categories of components. The first, of course, is some manifestation of the libidinal and aggressive drives, which on the manifest level appears in the form of wishes that involve a specific activity and its corresponding object. If the wish is a conflicted one, there is, by definition, also some form of moral injunction—the second category—in regard to it, as part of the compromise formation. This gives it the quality of being unacceptable to consciousness by virtue of its appearing to be forbidden and dangerous. The moral component of the compromise formation may well include some expression of the threatened punishment connected to it, such as the loss of parental love or castration, to mention familiar examples. A third component of the compromise formation must of necessity be some kind of unpleasure (whether or not it is clinically manifest): either one or another form of anxiety, depressive affect, or both. Finally, in the service of a more or less successful effort to disguise the forbidden wishful elements (and sometimes the punitive threats as well), compromise formations include some mental contents that function as defenses.[1]

While it is logically appealing to think of compromise formations as if they are functional mental entities or structures (and, in fact, any psychoanalytic dissection of a symptom, fantasy, or character trait will show that it consists of some version of the four categories of component elements described above), it is more accurate to think of compromise formation as an organizing principle of conflictual mental life. The importance of this distinction is that it can clarify what has sometimes been a source of confusion to some analysts—that is, the layered or hierarchical nature of compromise formations. Thus, for example, the defensive component of a given compromise formation may appear in the form of behavior that can itself be understood to be a compromise formation. A character trait such as extreme solicitousness toward weak and helpless individuals may well be more complex than is suggested by the familiar designation of it as a reaction formation against murderous wishes. This trait can, for example, include an unconscious identification with an admired and beloved figure from the individual's past, one whose kindliness the person wishes to emulate in order to gain the admired person's love and approval. The identification that lies at the heart of the solicitous trait is itself a complex unconscious fantasy—or, in other words, a compromise formation that in turn serves as a component of the compromise formation dealing with unacceptable sadistic wishes.

In my opinion, the most advantageous aspect of adopting the view that compromise formation is an organizing principle of conflictual mental life is that it provides the analyst with the most accurate and

---

[1] It should be noted that while defenses were originally thought of as a relatively simple set of mental mechanisms, such as displacement or reaction formation, it has long been recognized that, in fact, many aspects of mental activity, including quite complex ones, can be employed to serve defensive purposes in compromise formations.

comprehensive vantage point presently available from which to study and understand psychoanalytic material. Consequently, it constitutes a most useful guide for the conduct of clinical work, including the task of formulating interpretations. I do not mean to suggest that the analyst always holds the idea of compromise formation as the conscious central focus of his or her mind while assessing the patient's productions. However, if he or she has absorbed this conceptual framework as a meaningful description of the architecture of conflict as it affects the analysand's normal and pathological mental activity, it becomes an omnipresent template, often in the background, but sometimes ascending to the foreground, which will shape the listening analyst's grasp of the material. What is often subsumed under the heading of clinical intuition is given its structure, in fact, by this underlying theoretical framework, even though the theoretical considerations remain implicit.

Noting the evidence of dysphoric affect, for instance, may be taken as a sign of less than fully successful modulation of some of the patient's forbidden wishes. Nevertheless, in any given clinical moment, the analyst's attention is just as likely to be focused on the defensive aspect of the compromise formation under examination, or on the nature of the imagined punitive risk or condemnation attached to the wishes, as on the identification of the exact nature of the currently active unacceptable desires themselves. He or she may thus choose to interpret any aspect of the compromise formation, singly or in interactive combination (or may choose to say nothing at all), depending on his or her intuitive assessment of what the patient can absorb and utilize at the time. The same general technical posture would apply whether the analyst is considering a symptomatic act, a dream, an unconscious fantasy, a daydream, a form of interaction in the transference, or the patient's account of past or current experiences.

It goes without saying that in daily analytic work, the analyst's grasp of underlying compromise formations may be incomplete or inaccurate, and his or her judgment about what, if anything, to tell the patient will often be less than perfect. Those who remind us that such qualities and characteristics of our patients' mental lives as their innate intelligence, verbal and symbolic skills, special talents, biological variations of all sorts (including inherent limitations, damage, and the like) will be in evidence in the analytic material they produce are, to be sure, absolutely correct in that assertion. Those of us who subscribe to the view that the analysis of instinctual conflicts, and of the compromise formations to which they give rise, is the centerpiece of psychoanalytic therapy look on the infinite variability of our patients' individual mental qualities as most significant *insofar as they lend particular shape and color to the fate of their important instinctual conflicts.* Although we cannot fail to notice the effects of those qualities on our patients' lives, for better and for worse, we believe that the analytic task is to try to understand and modulate the disadvantageous outcome of conflicts.

We therefore concentrate our efforts on the problem of detecting the outline of those conflicts, together with the structure of the compromise formations to which they give rise, in the material our patients present to us. Using this schema to map our patients' mental lives, insofar as they become the subject of analytic attention, then leads us in the course of time to the interpretive offerings that we hope will expand their insight into the nature and origins of their emotional problems, providing the possibility of a modicum of relief of that dimension of their suffering.

At this juncture, I will present a sample of clinical work with which I hope to illustrate how this approach unfolds in the clinical situation.

Clinical Example

X, a successful attorney in his late thirties, came to treatment in large part because of his inability to form a lasting satisfactory attachment to a woman. His history, as it unfolded in the early months of his treatment, strongly suggested that conflict—derived in the main from the particulars of his childhood relationship with his mother—contributed to this problem.

One failed love affair that took place during the second year of his therapy gave some evidence of this linkage. The segment of his treatment on which I shall concentrate begins later, during the third year of therapy, when he fell in love with another woman, whom I shall call A, an attractive female colleague employed at a different law firm. It was not very long before his conflicts once again surfaced to disrupt the course of this affair, just as they had in the previous one. This woman was bright, cultivated, sexually seductive in a somewhat provocative fashion, and she came from an ethnocultural heritage quite different from my patient's. They were immediately attracted to one another, and after a passionate affair of only a few weeks' duration, they decided to marry, setting a date a few months away. My patient's fiancée disliked her job as an entry-level employee at a large law firm, feeling exploited, overworked, and underpaid. X, albeit with some hesitation, agreed to support her so that she could leave the position in order to look for a better situation. In the succeeding weeks, he said that she was devoting herself to planning their wedding, seeing friends, and going to exercise classes, but not, as far as he could see, to seeking a new job. He grew increasingly uneasy and resentful.

As I mentioned, at an earlier period in his treatment, X had fallen in love with another woman, who for the sake of clarity I shall call B. He had also rather quickly decided to marry her, only to become increasingly disenchanted as the wedding date approached. B, also of a distinctly different cultural background from X, was successful in another profession, and had achieved considerable financial independence. The problem was that she both lived and had established a business in a nearby city, and the negotiations over who should relocate and how it would be arranged became a source of mounting tension between them. I use the term *negotiation* deliberately, since my patient's descriptions of their acrimonious discussions took on the characteristics of a business deal, with demands and counterdemands, compromises, and conditions; this process became the focus of his increasing resentment. Though they remained very attracted to each other and still shared many interests, the relationship eventually foundered because of the mounting suspicion, anger—and, finally, contempt—that came to dominate his conscious thoughts about her.

It was notable that both X's former fiancée and his current one had described having had difficult emotional relationships with their respective mothers, each of whom was said to be grasping, selfish, and possessive, as well as antagonistic toward men, though neither of the mothers appeared to display the latter trait with respect to my patient, as far as I could determine. As I have indicated, the clinical material had long since documented the complexities of X's tie to his own mother, an unsuccessful artist who had constantly denigrated his passive, moderately successful, businessman father. Her attacks were sometimes about their different social and cultural backgrounds and preferences, but were much more often about money. According to my patient, his mother was a spendthrift, was perpetually dissatisfied, and manifestly contemptuous of his father's inability to provide a more luxurious lifestyle. She also favored my patient, who was her oldest son, in an openly admiring and somewhat seductive way, extolling his achievements and virtues, often at the expense of his siblings and his father.

His description of his family members and their interaction also included an acknowledgment of his intense childhood attachment to his mother. During adolescence, his possessive devotion had been replaced by a distinct, conscious ambivalence marked by an attitude of disdain. In the course of his up-and-down love affair with B, frequent spontaneous associations had linked his confused and contradictory feelings about her to thoughts about his mother, and, in particular, about his observations of his parents' contentious relationship. He had come to understand that his increasing uneasiness at the prospect of marrying B was to some extent influenced by his fears of getting caught in an intimate involvement that might somehow come to replicate what he had seen while growing up at home.

As he became more and more anxious about the prospect of marriage to A, X grew consciously suspicious of her, especially with respect to financial matters. He imagined that she never intended to work at all, and once or twice he quarreled with her about her expensive tastes, which clashed with his own frugal tendencies. His thoughts about her included disdain for what he regarded as the superficiality of her materialism. He concocted schemes in which he would educate her in fiscal responsibility, which he described to me without any apparent awareness of their dictatorial, not to say quite unrealistic, quality.

At this point, I will interrupt the clinical account in order to summarize certain aspects of X's relevant conflicts as I came to think of them during the course of the analysis, and to address the technical problems I encountered in attempting to analyze them. In the interest of brevity, I will confine my attention to those of his conflicts and fantasies pertinent to his trouble in forming and maintaining a committed relationship with a woman.

X had been a sickly boy, and felt that he had been utterly dependent on his mother's physical and emotional ministrations, which continued throughout his childhood. This intimacy colored their charged mutual admiration, which appeared to have dominated his psychological life until his adolescence. It seems entirely plausible that his teenage retreat into cold distance from her, and the development of a conscious attitude of ambivalence, were motivated by the need to defend against unconscious Oedipal wishes and their associated threats, which were reactivated and intensified as a consequence of his sexual maturation.

Although at this point it was still too early to say how work with the transference would eventually come to play a part in his treatment, X then maintained a determined focus on the reality-bound, doctor-patient aspect of our relationship, denying any awareness of an emotional tie to me. I am inclined to think of this as a transference defense against any kind of threatening emotional dependence on a caretaker that might constitute a repetition of his childhood attachment to his mother. There were also hints of a kind of skeptical, mildly contemptuous attitude toward analysis, suggested by his occasional use of derogatory terminology, which reminded me of his disdainful thoughts about his mother and both girlfriends, even though such hostility was never directed toward me personally. This was consistent with (although hardly proof of) my speculation that the main underlying transference paradigm was a maternal one. I do not mean to suggest that the transference was uniform or simple, and, in point of fact, it was at that point not possible to demonstrate any clear, unmistakable link to the objects of his past. Up until then, I had confined my interpretive comments about the transference to observing that X appeared to prefer to see our relationship as a mutually respectful, conventional, professional one, devoid of any emotional dimensions. I also suggested that he might be uncomfortable if he were to recognize that feelings of affection, need, irritation, disappointment, disparagement, or the like could also play a part. He acknowledged that much, but without indicating any willingness to explore what might be motivating this posture of his.

As my selective summary indicates, it is easy to conjecture that my patient's conflicts, stemming from his complex relationship with his mother, played a central role in the problems he had in sustaining an intimate, loving connection to a woman. As with the transference situation, the technical problems included that of assessing the evidence in support of my various specific conjectures about the nature of his conflicts and compromise formations, and about the unconscious fantasies in which they were embedded. It was also problematic to decide which questions, connections, or explanations were likely to be emotionally convincing, meaningful, and useful to him at any given moment in the course of his therapy.

For example, I believe that X's preference for women of an ethnic and cultural background different from his own combined an element of connection to his image of his mother, who stressed her cultural difference from his father, with a defensive denial of this oedipal link, since the obvious exogamy constituted a surface negation of the resemblance these women had to his picture of her. At that point in the analysis, we could talk only about how important it was to him that the woman he was drawn to should be demonstrably different from the stereotypic women of his own ethnocultural group, for whom he professed nothing but disrespect.

The other elements of the compromise formation whose existence I suspected were still too far removed from his consciousness to be usefully interpreted. He was certainly far away from any awareness that his childhood possessiveness toward his mother included an infantile wish for sexual possession of her. Consequently, he could not consciously recognize what I believed to be his fear that the imagined fulfillment of such a wish carried with it compelling fears of being devoured and destroyed by her, as well as crushing guilt in regard to his father. These and other conjectures about his conflicts were tentative hypotheses that rested in the background of my clinical thinking, but derivatives of them seemed to me to appear in the material.

For example, X was quite conscious of both pleasure and guilt connected to being favored over his siblings, but much less so with respect to his father. He could think about this circumstance in relation to a pattern he had long recognized in himself, that is, he needed to be assured that a woman he was to take seriously was unmistakably attracted to him, so that there was almost no chance of rejection. It was also the case that there could not be seen to be another man competing for her, because if there were an obvious rival, he would find a reason to retreat. He was not yet aware that guilt and fear of punishment might contribute to this pattern, in addition to the obvious need to preserve his fragile self-esteem. He had come to see that a certain element of playful struggle with the woman he was drawn to had to be present in order for him to be sexually excited by her, and that this had some as-yet undefined connection to the aggressive tensions he had observed in his parents' relationship. If the level of friction intensified beyond a certain point, however, his avoidant distaste overpowered the attraction. He had some degree of conviction that there were emotional links between past and present, but until recently, he had no appreciation of any specifics of the unconscious fantasies involved.

For purposes of illustration, I will return now to the case material and briefly summarize a representative segment of the work with my patient that highlights a particular aspect of his conflicts about marriage to A. For several sessions, with mounting anger, X had described his concern about her taste for luxury, expressing moralistic disapproval of her values. He voiced suspicion of her sincerity about intending to find a new job, and, with considerable anxiety, he expressed the fear that his substantial savings would be eroded, his future security threatened by her appetite for material pleasures. Although his angry tone and contempt were reminiscent of what had arisen during the end stages of his earlier failed relationship with B, the anxiety about depletion was a new symptom. I was inclined to attribute its appearance to a shift in his defensive armament, but I was not really clear about precisely what had changed.[2]

I drew the patient's attention to the anxiety, inviting his curiosity about the degree of threat he was experiencing and about his conscious fantasies of impoverishment and risk. He could readily agree that these seemed exaggerated and unrealistic, but he nevertheless remained anxious; he concocted various schemes for educating A in financial management and for restricting her expenditures after their marriage.

I conjectured that X was in the grip of an unconscious fantasy of being engulfed or devoured by a woman's uncontrollable appetites, and I proposed to him that such an idea might have originated in his early childhood in the form of a fearful characterization of his mother's possessive attachment to him. I did not add my suspicion that such a fantasy could well include disowned and condemned, projected elements of his own insatiable desires for his mother—since, even if accurate, such an idea was too far removed from his conscious views to be useful to him at that moment. Likewise, my guess that there might be fantasies of danger to his phallic identity made me think it was helpful to try to explore such an idea, even in order to determine more accurately whether it was relevant to his current distress.

At least intellectually, the patient could entertain the notion that his fears about A were magnified out of proportion by archaic images of his mother's appetites and attitudes. In one session in particular, immediately after talking about this linkage, his conscious preoccupations changed to incorporate a new element. He began to devise schemes of compromise, in which a certain amount of gratification of A's desires would be acceptable, but only if balanced by restraints that he would impose on her. I heard in this material echoes of the construction of possible compromises that had been a part of the end stages of his previous stormy engagement to B.

---

[2] In general, I am disposed to think that analytic progress leads to an increased tolerance for previously warded-off material, including permitting conscious recognition of unpleasure that had been blockaded. I must add that I have no evidence beyond my clinical impressions that would support such a belief.

I interpreted to X that his conscience now seemed to be playing a larger role in his thoughts about how to deal with A's desires. In response, he elaborated on his ideas that he always sought to be fair and equitable in the arrangements he was contemplating. I pointed out that his compelling concern with devising fair compromises was taking place entirely in his own imagination, much as had the antecedent fixation on condemning A's values and behavior and on the danger of impoverishment, none of which he had discussed with her. He reminded me that a few very tentative attempts to talk to A about finances had upset her very much; he had quickly retreated in the grip of frustration and guilt. He acknowledged that he was afraid of losing his temper and destroying the relationship.

At this juncture, the patient's thoughts returned to the theme of fairness, which now seemed clearly to be determined by his unconscious effort to deal with his guilt about hurting A. Just at this moment in the session I am describing, X suddenly recalled that, as a child, when he was witness to open battles between his parents about money and expenditures, he would silently but compulsively occupy his mind with devising plans of how to settle their arguments "fairly"! It seemed clear that this recovered memory served to increase his slowly growing conviction about the influence of the past on his present symptom picture.

Discussion

This brief case vignette, and the segment of material including the part of a session I have described, is presented in order to illustrate typical, rather than exceptional, work in the process of analyzing intrapsychic conflict. In my experience, analytic progress is rarely as concise, clear, or dramatic as some condensed case reports might lead one to think. Progress is incremental, and the steps are usually small ones, not infrequently repetitious. I have indicated that my patient gained some awareness that his childhood experiences continued to influence his current emotional life. The incident described, in part because a new connection occurred to him spontaneously, seemed to strengthen his acknowledgment of the ongoing power of the past, at least for this moment in his therapy.

I have also offered a sample of the kind of conjectures I entertain about what might be active in my patient's mind; these undoubtedly reflect my own theoretical preferences, in interaction with my individual clinical sensibility. They are also shaped by my attention to the long-established principles of context and contiguity in the patient's material as I hear it. My own interventions, as I have tried to show, are constrained by my best judgment about what my patient can make use of at the moment.

Inevitably, I make my way as best I can toward a sense of comprehension about my patients' mental lives, sometimes misunderstanding what is going on, sometimes misjudging what he or she can hear and find meaningful or interesting. My questions and interpretations sometimes lead to helpful clarification, but at other times are not so productive. Furthermore, at times I may be hesitant to go where other analysts would be bolder to venture, and I am sure I miss meanings others would detect. Such is the nature of the work that I do, although I take some comfort from the fact that many discussions have led me to conclude that my most trusted and respected colleagues have a similar sense of things in our demanding world.

I have tried to make it clear that I do not attempt to consciously formulate my patients' intrapsychic conflicts as a consistent feature of day-to-day work. As for the conjectures I consider, these can be fleeting or recurrent, vague and fuzzy, or quite sharp in my mind. They can emerge in my thoughts encased in doubt or compellingly insistent in my imagination. I am as likely to concentrate my attention on what I think are my patients' active unconscious fantasies, or to think in terms of compromise formations, or to wonder about affects expressed or concealed, as I am to think about the precise ideational content of their conflicts. I see these different clinical foci as parts of a single psychic tapestry, so it is not essential to examine all of it at the same time; in fact, it is not possible to do so.

There is no set system or progression that I follow—not even to give primacy to the transference, although I always think it is important to consider that aspect of the work. The same can be said of my interest in, and attention to, the defensive aspects of the material. While the concept of compromise formation is fundamental to my understanding of the architecture of the mind, I would probably never use that term in talking to patients, since I think such language is too abstract and intellectual. On the other hand, I would not hesitate to speak directly to a patient of his or her conflicts, or to label and discuss unconscious fantasies, whenever I think those terms might clarify for them what I believe is influencing their thoughts, feelings, and behavior.

I cannot do full justice here to the question of what constitutes evidence for my conjectures, although I have made passing reference to such familiar precepts as context and contiguity. However, this does seem to be the place to say something about how I utilize countertransference data in my technique. For me, the subject of countertransference is inextricably interwoven with the question of clinical intuition and with the problem of assessing evidence. I am certain that some conjectures about my patients' mental lives are more likely to occur to me, others less so, because of my own predominant intrapsychic makeup, as well as its day-to-day situational fluctuations. Given that view, monitoring my ideas about the patient—like attending to my affective state, fantasy life, and behavior in sessions—is a constant challenge.

In weighing the validity of my internal responses to the patient's material, I try to measure the force of their insistence and persistence in my mind as a general indicator that they deserve serious consideration. That said, I nevertheless always try to find as well some fit with the external data—that is, the shape and content of the patient's associations—in order to help me determine the reliability of my self-reflections. I do not doubt that what emanates from my patients has an impact on my mental life, just as I acknowledge that my personality and behavior have an impact on my patients. I must add that I never think in simple terms of projective identification or role responsiveness; this reluctance is a function of my inherent caution about possibly underestimating the influence of my own unconscious predilections on the moment-to-moment patterning of my responses. In short, as I have tried to indicate, I am aware of trying to do the best I can, while maintaining a healthy respect for the uncertainties of my analytic sensibility.

Conclusion

For me, then, the analysis of unconscious conflict, and of the compromise formations to which it gives rise, is the quintessential feature of my way of understanding the patient's mental life and the complexities of the clinical situation. I prefer it to other schemata because I remain convinced about the superiority of its explanatory power to that of other approaches, and I like to think that what I find of value in other theories can be assimilated into the framework of my accustomed theoretical stance. It is certainly true that I am comfortable with my approach because my psychoanalytic education was steeped in the teachings of Freud and his followers, and my further career development has been strongly influenced by the evolution of those ideas in the hands of modern conflict theorists. Consequently, I am most familiar with its many nuances and applications from years of clinical work and from many clinical interchanges with like-minded colleagues. Of course, I am also aware that colleagues whose work I respect hold exactly the same conviction about other theories and principles to which they adhere. I believe that engagement with alternative views stimulates all of us to try to find room in our preferred models for whatever we may find interesting and valuable in other approaches to our psychoanalytic task.

References

Brenner, C. (1982). *The Mind in Conflict*. New York: International Universities Press.

Freud, S. (1896). Further Remarks on the Neuropsychoses of Defense. *Standard Edition* 3.

——— (1905). Three Essays on the Theory of Sexuality. *Standard Edition* 7.

——— (1923). The Ego and the Id. *Standard Edition* 19.

——— (1926). Inhibitions, Symptoms and Anxiety. *Standard Edition* 20.

Waelder, R. (1936). Principles of multiple function. *Psychoanalytic Quarterly* 5:45–62.

CHAPTER 15

Therapeutic Action in Modern Conflict Theory

[Abend, S.M. (2007). *Psychoanalytic Quarterly* 76S(Supplement):1417–1442]

Recognizing that principles of psychoanalytic technique and conceptions of the analytic treatment process follow from the theory of therapeutic action to which they are linked, the author notes the difficulty of coming up with such a theory in relation to modern conflict theory. After reviewing Freud's initial descriptions of psychoanalytic theory and technique, as well as his later elaborations and modifications, the author summarizes the contributions of Freud's analytic contemporaries and traces the emergence of later theoretical variability in the field. He then presents an overview of recent developments in the theory of therapeutic action, discussing in particular the contributions of Arlow, Brenner, and Gray.

Introduction

To outline the theory of therapeutic action associated with modern conflict theory is surprisingly difficult to do. In fact, the theory of therapeutic action of any school of psychoanalytic thought is rarely stated in an explicit, unambiguous form in the literature of the field.

Instead, we usually find it necessary to derive it by implication from certain basic assumptions about what constitutes the structure of the problems in the analysand's psychology that analysis is supposed to address. In addition, therapeutic activity must be inferred from a study of the particular technical recommendations endorsed by a given approach to analytic practice.

To further complicate the problem, while modern conflict theory identifies itself as a direct evolutionary descendant of Freudian discoveries and postulates, in the current state of affairs there exist a number of somewhat different versions of what was at one point referred to simply as *mainstream* or *classical* psychoanalytic theory. All these variations of the mainstream share a conviction about the central importance of instinctual conflict in human psychology, and, despite the differences among them, all these related lines of thought continue to prefer to be designated as part of the classical tradition, rather than as dissident offspring of it.

Perhaps the clearest way to approach the problem is to outline the historical development of this affiliated collection of theories, indicating along the way where important shifts of emphasis and divisions have appeared. At the outset, I must point out that, in assessing Freud's theories of therapeutic action—as well as those of the analysts whose subsequent work elaborated, amended, or challenged some of his ideas—it will prove useful to keep in mind an astute observation offered by Abrams in 1990. In his introduction to a panel on the topic of therapeutic action, he commented as follows: "Therapeutic action remained linked to a general theory of the mind, to specific theories of pathogenesis, to technique, and to a view of the treatment process" (p. 774). Of the factors mentioned here, surely a particular, explicit or implicit theory of pathogenesis is directly and inextricably associated with every theory of therapeutic action. In their turn, the relevant ideas about pathogenesis are invariably related to an associated general theory of the structure of the mind. In each case, a specific set of principles of technique and conceptions of the treatment process follow from the theory of therapeutic action to which they are linked.

Freud and his Generation

We begin our historical survey, as usual, with Freud. Toward the end of his life, Freud (1937a) was still struggling to explain why analysis is not effective in certain conditions, but he seemed completely confident that he understood how and why it works in the usual, favorable situation:

> Instead of an enquiry into how a cure by analysis comes about (*a matter which I think has been sufficiently elucidated*) the question should be asked of [sic] what are the obstacles that stand in the way of such a cure. [p. 221, italics added]

His confidence in regard to his theory of therapeutic action is all the more remarkable in view of the fact that he changed this theory in important respects several times over the course of his career.

Freud's protopsychoanalytic theory rested on the later-discarded mechanism of catharsis. Therapeutic effect was supposed to be achieved through the recovery, by means of focused speech, of traumatic memories that had been stored in a so-called hypnoid state—although he soon replaced this concept of a locus for the unavailable material with that of the unconscious. This early theory evolved into a far more sophisticated derivative during the first two decades of the twentieth century, with the topographic model of the mind's forming the basis for Freud's ideas about mental structure and functioning. The emphasis on the recovery of sequestered unconscious material was retained, but the proposed mechanisms involved were now connected to Freud's newly acquired conviction that blocked or fixated libidinal wishes of childhood constitute the crux of that unconscious material. He concluded that repression, reinforced by other defenses, is the intrapsychic blockading element that resists the re-emergence of these wishes into consciousness. This obstructing force must be overcome in order to allow the analysand's more mature, adult judgment to beneficially alter the fate of the libidinal drives.

Freud had learned by then that the transference relationships he had noticed and come to understand as being displaced from the past provide a stage upon which the repressed wishes are displayed, thus permitting their nature to be ascertained. Furthermore, he conjectured, the transference constitutes an opportunity for the vivid, convincing, lively, and current reappearance of those important wishes, and thus facilitates the eventual reworking of them by means of the cumulative effect of the analyst's interpretations. The content of those interpretations was thought to provide the analysand with the necessary insight with which to effect changes.

The relationship to the analyst, in this schema, was assumed to supply two crucial ancillary functions. First, it makes up the background screen upon which transference distortions are displayed, and second, it provides a benign influence, the *unobjectionable positive transference* (Freud, 1912), which motivates the patient to do the uncomfortable work of counteracting his or her resistances. In short, analysis of the transference helps to overcome resistances, undo repressions, and thus relieve pathogenic fixations.

As is familiar to students of psychoanalytic history, experience eventually led Freud to change his theory of neurosogenesis yet again, and thus also of therapeutic action, in a substantial way. For our purposes, it will suffice to note that the revision of anxiety theory, and the development of the structural hypothesis as a new working model of intrapsychic life, irrevocably altered the nature of therapeutic emphasis. Although Freud kept the idea of tension between forbidden unconscious libidinal wishes and the forces that restrict their access to consciousness as the cornerstone of his theory of neurosogenesis, the complex nature of these conflicts was more fully delineated.

The motives for repression were now conceptualized as a succession of fears, quite convincing to the child, involving parental disapproval and punishment, which in the course of development became internalized and subsumed under the influence of the moral agency known as the *superego,* itself active in a largely unconscious mode. The *ego* then emerged as the primary locus of therapeutic attention. Its multiple roles as initiator of defenses, executor of actions, evaluator of conditions in the environment, and synthesizer of conflicting elements in mental life placed the ego at the center of the analyst's interest, so much so that the next phase of Freudian psychoanalytic theorizing became known as *ego psychology.* While divergent streams of psychoanalytic thought were already in evidence by the time this evolutionary trend made its appearance, and still other important currents would arise as time went on, our attention here will remain confined to tracing the further development of what came to be generally regarded as *mainstream* or *classical* Freudian psychoanalytic thought (Abend, 2002a).

In his later elaborations of the theory of cure, Freud always held to his concentration on conflict—that is to say, the opposition between the resources of the ego and the pressure of instinctual forces seeking expression and satisfaction. His therapeutic interest increasingly centered on the modification of the capacities of the ego and on the consequent taming of the instinctual drives that might thereby be achieved. By the time he wrote "Constructions in Analysis" (1937b), he had come to appreciate that it was not always necessary for neurosogenic, repressed traumatic experiences to reemerge into conscious awareness since, "if the analysis is carried out correctly, we produce in . . . [the patient] an assured conviction of the truth of the construction which achieves the same therapeutic result as a recaptured memory" (pp. 265–266).

Thus, the fate of the instinctual wishes that had been subjected to distorting censorship in the course of childhood development remained at the center of Freud's theory of neurosogenesis. The idea that constitutional as well as experiential factors contribute to pathogenic development was always part of his theoretical substructure. Later, he came to believe that variations in the ability of the ego to deal with these powerful forces also contribute to the form and degree of psychopathology. Thus, both sides of the conflicts at the heart of pathology claimed attention in his evolving view of therapeutic action.

Except for the aforementioned value of what he designated as the unobjectionable positive transference as a motive force in propelling the treatment process, for the most part Freud deemphasized the role of the analysand's relationship with the analyst, in favor of a focus on the crucial role of acquired insight in empowering beneficial analytic changes. He explicitly disagreed with the suggestion that the analyst should adopt a role tailored to the treatment of each analysand's specific neurosis, as was put forth by Ferenczi in his development of active technique. Freud also sought to counter the critical argument that the analyst's constructions and interpretations constitute no more than suggestions—which could quite possibly be altogether fallacious, yet could still influence patients to change.

However, it may be noted that Freud (1937a) was not entirely dismissive of the potential impact of the analyst's relationship to the patient in treatment, as witness his comment that "in certain analytic situations . . . [the analyst] can act as a model for his patient and in others as a teacher" (p. 248). Still, he did not elaborate these ideas about the function of the relationship, except perhaps insofar as he might have considered the analyst's formulation of constructions and presentation of interpretations as an educational activity. His emphasis became one of concentrating analytic efforts on modifying the analysand's ego so that it could better deal with instinctual demands. As he put it, "the business of the analysis is to secure the best possible psychological condition for the function of the ego; with that it has discharged its task" (Freud, 1937a, p. 250).

By and large, Freud's contemporary followers merely attempted to further develop and elaborate an analytic understanding of the means by which the therapeutic alteration of ego capacities could be achieved. Thus, Sterba (1934) dealt with one conundrum by conceiving of the ego as divisible into experiencing and self-observing segments. Meanwhile, Strachey (1934), in concordance with his Kleinian orientation, outlined the suggestion that the analysand introjects the analyst's more benign superego as a pathway to transforming the anti-instinctual part of his or her psychic structure.

In the papers presented at the 1936 Marienbad symposium on therapeutic action, all participants held an absolute adherence to Freud's central conception of pathogenesis arising as a consequence of the conflict between instinctual wishes and the ego-superego system. What each contributor offered was one or another minor variation on the theme of how therapeutic strengthening of the ego might be achieved

(Bergler, 1937; Bibring, 1937; Fenichel, 1937; Glover, 1937; Nunberg, 1937; Strachey, 1937).

During this period the publication of Anna Freud's book, *The Ego and the Mechanisms of Defense* (1937), and later of Otto Fenichel's *Problems of Psychoanalytic Technique* (1941), marked the evolution of ego psychology into a therapeutic approach that concentrates on the analysis of defenses. Fenichel's stress on analyzing from the surface was meant to support the shift of therapeutic technique away from the earlier tendency to interpret the presence of deep, unconscious, instinctual wishes that might be so far removed from conscious awareness, and so alien to patients' consciousness, as to be apprehended only intellectually, if at all. Thus, the theory of therapeutic action became crystallized as the systematic modification of the ego's capacity to deal with the persistent instinctual wishes of early childhood and to transform its function into one more appropriate to the circumstances of adult reality.

Despite the momentous introduction of the structural theory and its consequences for technique, analysts of the day and for many years thereafter continued at times to employ thinking derived from the topographic model, along with their adoption of the newer picture of how mental activity is organized. Even Anna Freud was said to have admitted as much during discussions held at the Hampstead Clinic years after the 1937 publication of her seminal volume on defenses (Spruiell, 1982). It was not until 1964, when Arlow and Brenner published *Psychoanalytic Concepts and the Structural Theory*, that an argument stating definitively that the two models of mental functioning are logically incompatible was framed and presented.

One form this adherence to the topographic model took was the continuing interest in conceptualizing clinical phenomena in terms of levels of consciousness (*e.g.*, Stein, 1965). Another was the persistence of Freud's interest in the idea of psychic energy and its postulated vicissitudes. Many analysts continued to be concerned with energetic concepts dating from Freud's earliest theorizing. Hartmann (1939) elaborated on a brief comment of Freud's (1923) about the ego's getting energy for its use from desexualized libido.

Hartmann suggested that drive energies can exist in a tamed, or *neutralized,* state that is somehow different from the form that charges the instinctual component of neurotic symptoms. It is this kind of energy that Hartmann imagined could provide the required force for the ego tasks concerned with adaptation. A related innovation was his introduction of the notion of a "conflict-free" sphere of the ego. This theoretical leap was part of Hartmann's effort to expand the purview of psychoanalysis into that of a general psychology, rather than confining it to the realm of psychopathology.

The Elaboration of Ego Psychology

Hartmann and his two frequent collaborators, Kris and Loewenstein, who, like him, had emigrated from Europe to the United States in the wake of World War II, contributed to the further development of ego psychology during the decades of the 1940s and '50s. As important as their influence was, the significance of their work for the theory of therapeutic action was far from radical, consisting mostly of small refinements. Kris (1956), for example, noted that other transference attitudes besides Freud's celebrated unobjectionable positive transference can serve as a motive for certain analysands' acquisition of insight, thus making analytic progress possible.

Most analysts of that period sought to preserve the Freudian legacy and did not change the fundamental assumptions about pathogenesis, and hence about therapeutic action, that they had inherited. To be sure, clinical experience by that time demanded that more explicit attention be paid to aggression and its role in conflict, and therefore to an expanded picture of what constitutes psychopathology and its alleviation. Other analysts who were interested in child development also broadened the frame of analytic conceptualization without at first changing the terms of a theory of treatment. They concentrated on specifying a fuller elaboration of preoedipal events and issues, both in terms of normal development and of pathogenic derailments and their consequences. This work affected the focus of analytic interest and hence the content of interpretations, but not necessarily the overview of therapeutic action. In the debates of the times, it was possible for one contributor, Gill (1954), to suggest a definition of psychoanalysis that included only the long-familiar elements of instinctual conflict that become clinically manifest in the transference neurosis, and that were to be cured through the resolution of the latter, "by means of interpretation [and hence of insight] . . . alone" (p. 775).

At mid-century, then, the Freudian psychoanalytic mainstream held to a certain set of shared beliefs. Among them were: (1) that neurotic symptoms are the consequence of the ego's conflictually determined, partially successful, warding off of the full and free expression of certain instinctual wishes of childhood origin; (2) that this symptom picture is embedded in an otherwise healthy personality (although uncertainty was already in evidence about how to understand and classify certain types of character development); (3) that, in analysis, these troublesome instinctual conflicts appear as a complex set of attitudes toward the analyst, known by the collective term *transference neurosis*; (4) that this formation can be observed and understood by the neutral, objective analyst; (5) that the analyst interprets to the analysand the constituent parts of the transference neurosis, as well as the reconstructed childhood antecedents that determine its shape; (6) that the analyst deliberately avoids trying to influence the patient to change in any other way besides offering clarifying interpretations; and, finally, (7) that in successful cases, the patient's transference neurosis is "resolved," and he or she is thereby restored to health. Other contending points of view, such as those of the interpersonal school and the Kleinian movement, were already well developed by that time, but the foregoing tenets constitute the core principles of Freudian ego psychology.

The Emergence of Theoretical Variability

It is probably fair to call this period the high-water mark of theoretical orthodoxy, because the winds of change were already in evidence and their effects would soon be discernible. Among the most important influences that would slowly move theory away from its faithful adherence to Freud's ideas, at least three took center stage during the 1960s. The first of these factors was the reconceptualization of the part played by countertransference in the psychoanalytic encounter. Introduced and elaborated by Kleinian analysts in the preceding decade, the suggested utilization of the analyst's self-observation of his or her own feeling states while with each patient, as an important tool for learning about the analysand's psychic activity in the analytic situation, was hotly contested for many years by mainstream Freudians. Although some of the latter held out for quite a long time, this particular theoretical resistance was to prove a losing battle.

A second major shift was the upsurge of interest in the nature of preoedipal development and its determinative influence on neurosogenesis and on character formation. This work, following the contributions of pioneers like Winnicott (1971) and Mahler (1965), among others, was gradually incorporated into the study of the limitations of ego capacities in certain analysands, especially those suffering from more serious forms of psychopathology.

Finally, other mainstream students of the complexities of the psychoanalytic situation, like Greenson (1967), Modell (1984), Stone (1961), and Zetzel (1970), developed the idea that realistic aspects of the relationship between the analysand and the analyst exist alongside, and are distinguishable from, the transference neurosis. This dimension of their relationship was presumed to constitute a form of alliance, called by various names, which was comparable to, but more complex than, Freud's idea of the unobjectionable positive transference. The alliance supposedly provides an essential substructure, which permits interpretive work on the transference distortions to be effectively performed. Especially with more difficult, disturbed analytic patients, some analysts suggested, the analyst must take steps to facilitate and strengthen the alliance as part of the therapeutic task of analyzing.

In the context of these developments, Loewald (1960) introduced an emendation to the theory of therapeutic action that was to prove crucial to the next generation of analytic theorists. He presented the idea that the analyst is much more than simply a detective, or an archeologist of the mind, whose work consists only of the discovery of the residues of a pathogenic buried past, followed by the disclosure of these fragments to the conscious awareness of the patient. Instead, Loewald compared the analyst's task to that of the mother of a developing child, emphasizing that a vital aspect of it is to articulate inchoate aspects of the analysand's unconscious mind, thus helping to shape and define his or her desires, capacities, and, ultimately, capabilities. In short, the analytic interaction does more than discover hidden meanings, according to Loewald; it actually helps to create new meanings in the mental life of the analysand.

The impact of this important new step in the evolution of the theory of therapeutic action was soon to be reinforced by certain derivatives of postmodern intellectual trends that a number of psychoanalytic thinkers found persuasive. The assault on positivism, as far as psychoanalysis is concerned, was used to mount a challenge to the comfortable assumption that the analyst is a scientific observer capable of arriving at reliable, objective judgments about the nature of reality and about the patient's psychic structure.

This attack on one of the foundation stones of what had been, up to then, prevailing psychoanalytic doctrine and practice soon became a focus of controversy. The development of a frankly relativist or subjectivist trend, characterized by the elaboration of the idea that all meaning is established only by the co-construction of the analyst and analysand working in tandem, would be taken up most enthusiastically by analysts who belonged to analytic schools of thought that were no longer part of mainstream Freudian conflict theory. However, it was becoming more and more difficult to determine which lines of thought constituted variations on the evolving Freudian mainstream, and which preferred to be regarded as separate, independent schools of psychoanalytic theory and practice.

Recent Developments in the Theory of Therapeutic Action

In psychoanalytic circles within the United States, it is certainly possible to distinguish several divergent versions of the theory of therapeutic action that emerged in the last quarter of the twentieth century, all of which would still be considered part of the mainstream directly derived from classical Freudian theory. The most fundamental aspect of the new complexity is probably the stress placed upon conceptualizing the role of the relationship between analyst and analysand as a prime determinant of therapeutic action. As I have indicated in tracing the history of this issue, balancing the effects of the relationship and the power of insight in bringing about therapeutic change had long been an active center of debate in psychoanalysis, especially between the strictest of Freudian loyalists and the proponents of other schools of analytic thought. However, over the course of time, many analysts who still regarded themselves as part of the traditional mainstream sought to incorporate some way of more thoroughly understanding how the relationship might play a role in analysis, in addition to the long-familiar idea that it constitutes a neutral platform upon which insight into the patient's conflicts can be formulated, communicated, and ultimately assimilated.

Before outlining these developing variants of the theory of therapeutic action, I would like to point out that there is still an important segment of the mainstream psychoanalytic community that believes the traditional Freudian emphasis on the detection and interpretation of the derivatives of conflict, which facilitates the analysand's cumulative acquisition of insight into his or her nature and history, remains the most important tool for bringing about therapeutic results. In the view of these analysts, this work is supported by the long-familiar precepts of studying emerging transference patterns, and, at least in some cases, by the recovery of important memories, as well as through the analytic reconstruction of the past. The sizeable number of analysts who adhere to this model of technique and therapeutic action, of whom I am one, respect the power of the relationship between analyst and analysand as contributing to therapeutic outcome, but harbor a certain degree of skepticism about some of the formulations concerning how this factor might have an effect on altering psychopathology.

In addition, for many of us, the current emphasis on the inevitably subjective limitations of the analyst is primarily useful as a caution to analysts about placing excessive confidence in the intuitive accuracy of their evaluations of patients' mental functioning and their understanding of the meaning of patients' productions. It implicitly serves as a reminder that careful attention to patients' responses, together with respectful consideration of their views of what transpires in analysis, is necessary in order to arrive at reliable interpretations of the analytic data.

However, in our view, acknowledging that the analyst unavoidably labors under the burden of certain personal constrictions, predilections, and imperfections does not completely abolish the analyst's decidedly advantageous position in the analytic situation. By virtue of training, personal analysis, and experience, analysts are able to perceive and understand things about their patients that the latter cannot see, and that—as has been appreciated since the time of Freud—analysands are motivated *not* to understand or accept as part of themselves. Therefore, the activity of interpretation, despite contemporary appreciation of the analyst's subjective limitations, nevertheless remains central to the performance of the analyst's task. Other differences among subsets of traditional analysts may become clearer in the descriptions to follow.

For example, derived from the contributions of such thinkers as Winnicott (1971) and Modell (1984), the idea gained in appeal among one large segment of analysts that the relationship that develops between the analyst and the analysand may have certain corrective features that can be incorporated into the psychic structure of patients who are burdened by faulty object relatedness, even if these changes are never explicitly discussed by the analytic pair. This subtle variant of the corrective emotional experience, in some hands at least, has also called for the analyst to behave in ways that are different from the classically prescribed technique of strict analytic neutrality. It was proposed that behaving in a less formally analytic fashion, and being more declaratively realistic and demonstrably reasonable, predictable, and caring in interactions with patients, particularly sicker ones, has a cumulative effect on their capacities for relatedness. While this change in the analyst's technique can be thought of as consistent with the Freudian analytic goal of beneficially altering ego capabilities, it represents a significant departure from the view that such changes should be brought about through interpretation and insight alone. A background assumption of those who have supported this prescription for strengthening the patient's ego has been that the difficulties they hoped to overcome were an experiential consequence of specific, preoedipal developmental problems. It is precisely this latter assumption about development and the nature of psychopathology that many other mainstream analysts have found less than convincing.

The student of mainstream analytic theory can observe a spectrum of opinion about the importance of the relationship as a therapeutic influence. Conservative voices, such as that of Stone (1961), emphasized the reality-based core of the therapeutic alliance as needed to support analytic work with all patients, but not necessarily as designed to modify faulty development. Other analysts, like Greenson (1967) and Zetzel (1970), were more openly in favor of modifying the analyst's behavior with patients—away from the restrictive model advocated by some followers of Freud, and into a way of relating aimed at helping patients respond to the demands of analysis. The crystallization of these approaches into one in which the relationship, as experienced by the analysand, slowly alters his or her developmental limitations, irrespective of interpretation, has gradually invaded mainstream thinking in many quarters, even though its most enthusiastic advocates have come from other schools of analytic thought.

More or less independent of this newly emergent stress on the role of the relationship in therapeutic action, there has been a growing interest in studying the vicissitudes of the relationship in the transference-countertransference matrix. The Kleinian focus on using the analyst's countertransference reactions as a tool with which to better understand the patient began to be incorporated into the work of a growing number of mainstream analysts who nevertheless did not subscribe to Kleinian metapsychology or its stress on projection-introjection mechanisms. Sandler's (1976) idea of role responsiveness, Jacobs' (1991) work on acute observation of the analyst's subtle nonverbal countertransference enactments, and Boesky's (1990) interest in understanding the co-creation of resistances are examples of this trend.

In all versions of this technical development, it has been recommended that the analyst attempt to examine closely the specific nature of certain of his or her interactions with analysands. Beginning by noting the manifest qualities of these interactions, analysts should then apply the usual effort to understand their subtle unconscious significance. Acknowledging that the analyst is an unwitting (*i.e.*, unconscious) participant in these interactions, these theorists insist that the analyst's at least intermittently mobilized ability to step back from, observe, and make analytic sense of the interactions constitutes an important step in the formulation of many interpretations to analysands.

While this change of focus affects the form of therapeutic technique, it is not necessarily true that it should be thought of as significantly modifying the theory of therapeutic action. Insight is still regarded as the essential element in bringing about change, and the study of the transference-countertransference relationship becomes an additional vehicle with which an understanding of the patient's mental activity—leading to interpretation, and thus to insight—is to be achieved.

Other evolutionary trendsetters in the mainstream current were far less enthusiastic about the tendency to promote the idea that the relationship might be an ameliorative influence in analytic treatment. Especially notable in this regard is the work of Arlow and Brenner (1964, 1990). Without holding to an illusion of the analyst's possessing perfect objectivity, they maintained their belief that usefully accurate assessments are possible, especially if scrupulous care is taken to examine the evidence provided by the appearance of prominent patterns and recurring sequences in the patient's verbal productions and behavior. They thus advocated maintaining analytic focus on the problem of detecting and interpreting signs of the components of patients' unconscious conflicts by a careful study of the analytic material, including, but not confined to, the transference.

Arlow (1969), in particular, emphasized looking for the presence and mode of expression of crucial unconscious fantasies that incorporate the elements of conflict. He also devoted attention to the nuances of constructing interpretations and to describing the nature of analytic evidence. Brenner (1979) challenged the idea of a therapeutic alliance as reliably distinguishable from transference, and he regarded variations of standard analytic behavior that were supposedly designed specifically to strengthen the alliance as actually liable to constitute invitations to subtle enactments, whose unconscious meaning might escape full analytic scrutiny.

Brenner also developed and promulgated the formulation that the outcome of instinctual conflicts can best be described as a set of compromise formations, although he used that term to designate a more comprehensive complexity than was implied in Freud's much earlier employment of it to describe symptom formation. According to Brenner (1976), compromise formations are composed of (1) specific libidinal and aggressive wishes, (2) an associated dysphoric affect, (3) moral concerns, couched in terms of potential punishments, and (4) a variety of ego functions arrayed defensively and seeking an acceptable, adaptive balance among these forces. Brenner has suggested that the familiar conception of the id, ego, and superego as agencies of the mind, the cornerstones of structural theory, is no longer an accurate or useful way of accounting for the mental activities that are of interest to psychoanalysts. He prefers to focus simply on the elements that constitute the varieties of intrapsychic conflict and their interaction in compromise formations as clinical phenomena, without reference to structural entities.

Brenner is one of the analysts who assert that the proof of any theory of therapeutic action cannot be demonstrated. Instead, it is only possible to observe and describe certain changes that accompany improved functioning in patients. In Brenner's preferred formulation, these changes consist of the substitution of new compromise formations, ones that permit more gratification and entail less dysphoria and/or self-punitive behavior, for the more pathological ones they replace. His understanding of how these changes are brought about remains centered on the patient's gradual acquisition of meaningful insight.

However, Brenner and many other proponents of modern conflict theory, myself included, acknowledge that the way in which analysands experience their relationships with their analysts is meaningful and influential in bringing about change. The analyst is, after all, a person who responds to the patient's transference demands and behavior differently from the way that all other figures of importance in the patient's life have, and this must carry a significant cumulative impact. In our opinion, though, how this influence is to be incorporated into a theory of therapeutic action remains a matter of speculation and is subject to debate. A sharp division exists between those analysts who are convinced that relational distortions resulting from early, even preverbal developmental difficulties can be correctively influenced by the very nature of the new relationship that forms between patient and analyst, and those who question this fundamental premise. As one of the latter group, I see this relational emphasis as consistent with the long-standing historical trend to de-emphasize the central importance to analysis of sexual and aggressive conflicts, in favor of increased attention to preoedipal developmental issues. To some analysts, including many in the expanded mainstream, this shift is an advantageous advance in analytic understanding, while others of us still hold to Freud's revolutionary focus on the complex consequences of the Oedipal period on both normal and pathological human psychological development.

Another, newer trend in the mainstream that presents still a different variation of therapeutic action derives from the work of Gray (1994) and those influenced by his ideas. He developed a unique technical stance known as *close process monitoring,* in which the analyst attends exclusively to the flow of verbal material produced by the patient during the analytic hour. This approach goes beyond the widely agreed upon technical principle of noting hesitations, breaks in continuity, and sudden shifts of focus in the patient's productions as of importance, since they indicate that defensive influence is at work on the flow of associations. Gray proposed that even if the patient presents dynamically interesting and significant material, such as dreams or accounts of meaningful past or current incidents, this should be examined as having possible defensive valence, depending on context. His view was that the analysand has conscious or unconscious anxiety at the prospect of verbally revealing certain charged mental contents in the presence of the analyst, and that this discomfort may initiate seductively interesting changes of subject matter, which the analyst who follows conventional technical wisdom might tend to regard as valuable to examine for its content alone.

Gray advocates, instead, a strict attention to the defensive function of such material, in addition to noting the more usual indicators of defense at work. This exclusive focus on defense analysis, with transference as the emphasis of concern for the analyst's possible judgmental reactions, becomes the centerpiece of analytic work with those patients who are capable of sustaining it.

Gray also formulates a subsidiary goal of educating the patient over the course of the analysis to be able to execute a similar kind of detailed scrutiny for him- or herself, without the aid—or, ultimately, even the presence—of the analyst. Therapeutic benefit from this procedure is assumed to be a function of the analysand's gradual acquisition of an enhanced freedom to admit to consciousness thoughts linked to desires or emotional attitudes that had previously been regarded as dangerously unacceptable. Other, more limited patients might require a technique in which the role of the analyst's suggestion, approval, or disapproval continues to contribute to therapeutic effectiveness, according to Gray.

Besides the factors outlined in all general theories of therapeutic action derived from specific sets of ideas about the structure of psychopathological formations and how they are revised, there may also be features of analysands' individual psychology, unique to each case, that can influence therapeutic outcome (Abend, 2002b). I have in mind the presence of unconscious fantasies about treatment, cure, change, and about being influenced by others, which are important aspects of the psychological makeup of certain analysands. While such fantasies invariably originate in earlier formative relationships, they can play a transferential role of great but subtle significance in determining how a particular analysand responds to analysis, either promoting change or, in other cases, resisting it. It is not necessary to incorporate such potential responsiveness into a general theory of therapeutic action, but it is important to recognize that this kind of influence may strongly affect therapeutic effectiveness, for better or for worse. From the standpoint of technique, it is necessary only that the analyst remain aware of this possibility, since dedication to the usual analytic task of sensing, understanding, and interpreting such transference fantasies and their infantile antecedents is all the analyst can do to modulate their potential influence.

Summary and Conclusions

Theories of therapeutic action are all connected to specific sets of beliefs about how the mind is structured, and, in particular, about the assumed composition of the psychopathological formations they are intended to relieve. In modern conflict theory, just as in Freud's conceptualization, the essence of the difficulties psychoanalysis seeks to address is intrapsychic conflict of childhood origin. This refers to the inherent tension between certain unconscious instinctual wishes that strive for gratification, and the developing child's anxiety-fueled, defensive need to conceal, modify, or modulate those wishes. These defensive efforts try to permit a degree of satisfaction, while also avoiding the anticipated dangers that the immature child is convinced are associated with the direct expression of such instinctual wishes.

Brenner's detailed description of these conflicts as leading to compromise formations seems to me a useful, accurate, and economical way of formulating these issues in psychoanalytic terms. It follows from this conceptualization that the therapeutic activity of psychoanalysis is, at bottom, an effort to alter the composition of certain compromise formations that account for symptoms or disadvantageous aspects of character, in favor of new compromise formations that afford more satisfaction of wishes and entail a lesser degree, if not a total relief, of the associated discomfort.

A great advantage of this way of thinking about the aims and actions of psychoanalysis is that it addresses one particular conceptual legacy of early Freudian theory that has outlived its usefulness. When

Freud began his career, his model for the neurotic disturbances he sought to alleviate was based on that of conventional medical diseases, like infectious illnesses. Accordingly, he sought to identify pathogenic agents, and to remove them in order to cure the patient's symptoms. When he learned that repressed traumatic memories did not account for all psychopathology, and replaced that idea with the concept that certain residual consequences of childhood instinctual conflicts lie at the heart of the problems psychoanalysis tries to address, he did not discard the fundamental assumption that these emotional pathogens must be removed in order to restore the patient to complete health.

Even much later in his career, when Freud had come to regard etiology in a more complex way, and to view outcome less categorically and less optimistically, he never troubled to revise the implications of his earlier formulation. Consequently, he and his followers carried over a more sophisticated version of his earlier disease template in the form of conceiving of the goal of the analysis as the "resolution" of the transference neurosis, with the implication that the full achievement of this aim is possible, long after accumulated clinical experience suggested that this was an inaccurate idealization.

Brenner's formulation requires analysts to acknowledge that instinctual conflict is never completely abolished; it remains a permanent and ubiquitous feature of human mental life. What is possible is to effect changes in the consequences of conflict, and hence in the manifestations that are the expressions of the compromise formations involved. To be sure, symptoms may be abolished, character traits altered in a profoundly beneficial way, object relationships improved, adaptations to reality significantly changed in the direction of consensual normality, and so on. Such important changes and other benefits of a successful analysis are in no way minimized by acknowledging that they result from changes in the way childhood instinctual conflicts are handled, and not by their complete elimination or resolution.

Among the several currents that may be considered part of present-day, mainstream, conflict-centered Freudian psychoanalysis, there is an evident consensus that therapeutic activity is attributable to two chief categories of agents of influence. The first of these, which dates back to Freud's original thesis, is that of *insight.* In short, psychoanalytic therapy is designed to result in an expansion of the analysand's conscious knowledge of certain crucial, previously unrecognized and unacknowledged aspects of his or her unconscious mental life. In essence, this increased self-understanding includes an appreciation of the continuing presence and importance of a variety of libidinal and aggressive desires, and a fuller understanding of the different ways that the person devised during childhood in order to deflect, alter, disguise, and also gratify those wishes. To make this self-knowledge more comprehensible, the analysand must also come to understand the real and imaginary dangers that he or she has associated with the expression, or even the revelation, of these wishes, as well as something of the real and imagined experiences of childhood that contributed to the development of the patient's particular set of compromise formations.

Insight may be generated by the analyst's interpretations, by the patient's self-discoveries, or both, but it is now widely agreed that this insight must be emotionally convincing to the patient, not merely intellectually apprehended. Experiences of the components of a patient's conflicts in the immediacy of the transference relationship are considered an essential part of the acquisition of truly meaningful insight. It should be noted that there are different assumptions about the precise content of the ideational components of these compromise formations within the mainstream psychoanalytic community, but these differences do not change the fundamental conception of conflict or the presumed therapeutic value of acquiring insight into its nature and origin.

The second broad category of therapeutic influence is subsumed under the general heading of the analysand's experience of his or her relationship with the analyst. No analyst today would deny that the lengthy, intense, emotionally charged involvement between the two participants in an analysis has a profound and lasting impact on the psychology of the analysand (and, to a lesser degree, on that of the analyst, for that matter). Likewise, none would disagree that this relationship is a unique experience for the analysand, since the analyst consistently strives to be helpful in a particular way and to respond to the patient's emotional needs, demands, and reactions in a fashion different from that of all others in the analysand's past and current emotional world. Furthermore, it is generally acknowledged that the analyst's emotional attunement to his or her own mental states and behavior during the conduct of the treatment can sometimes be a valuable source of data about the patient's mental activities. Beyond those generalizations, there lies a considerable difference of opinion among various subgroups of mainstream analysts about how to assess the therapeutic influence of the relationship.

Some rely much more than do others on the utilization of countertransference scrutiny as a tool for understanding the patient and formulating interpretations. Some even attribute so much importance to transference-countertransference interactions as to include this dimension of the analytic work in their basic formulation of the therapeutic process. Because I am one of those analysts who harbor significant reservations about what appears to me to be in some hands an overly optimistic attitude about the reliability of this kind of data, I personally lean quite heavily in the direction of caution about its employment. I also join those who call for making every effort to verify any formulation about the patient. This is most reliably done by carefully scrutinizing the patient's behavior patterns and the contents of the patient's verbal productions for evidence to support, modify, or invalidate formulations based on countertransference data.

As for the corrective influence that the relationship exerts on the psychological makeup of the analysand, the range of opinions among mainstream psychoanalysts is a substantial one. As I have indicated in the preceding historical survey, there are those who are convinced that the relationship has a beneficial effect on the analysand's capacity for object relations, all the more important in those cases where problems in that sphere are seen to be a major factor in the patient's psychopathology. Emphasis on the presumed pathogenic significance of preoedipal developmental disturbances is likely to be part of the rationale of those analysts who place great stress on the therapeutically important impact of the relationship, especially on its nonverbal (perhaps even nonverbalizable) components.

There are also a number of analysts who hold to the view that the realistic relationship between analyst and patient is a core feature of analytic work, constituting a kind of alliance between the participants that supports and sustains the analysand's ability to experience and effectively analyze transference distortions. A certain percentage of this subgroup of mainstream analysts also advocates that the analyst behaves in a fashion at variance with the restricted range of technical behavior recommended by Freud and many subsequent practitioners. These prescriptions vary from the adoption of specific attitudes and attributes designed to address particular problems to the less extreme suggestion that a more "natural" and "realistic" mode of conducting the relationship has the effect of strengthening the alliance. As noted, there are other analysts, of whom I am one (see Abend, 2002b), who regard such proposals as less valid and less analytically benign and useful than do their proponents.

Finally, it is potentially helpful to keep in mind that individual analysands may have significant unconscious fantasies, derivatives of which are active in the transference, that can have a positive or a negative impact on the patient's responsiveness to analytic influence. For example, certain cases where transference fantasies that determine a patient's reluctance to acknowledge the analyst's power to be helpful, or which support a resistance to accept change, are probably familiar to most practitioners. Transference fantasies that may serve to support accommodative growth and change may be less obvious, but are no less important to take into account.

In sum, there is much about the therapeutic action of psychoanalysis, and of the technical procedures that are best suited to achieve a favorable therapeutic result, that is uncertain and/or in dispute. The different configurations are connected to and derived from particular views of the mind, how it develops and functions, and of the structure of the disturbances analysis attempts to relieve. Modern conflict theory, like all other approaches, sets forth its ideas about therapeutic action in a fashion consistent with its assumptions about this greater context.

This cautionary note should not be taken to imply skepticism about analytic effectiveness. As we conduct our work, we are able to observe and describe undeniably beneficial changes in many analysands' mental functioning and in the way they carry out and experience their lives. In view of this, it seems entirely justified to attribute therapeutic action to our analytic endeavors. It is simply a fact that each of us is obliged to organize our observations and descriptions, and the theories of treatment to which they are connected, in the conceptual language of our particular preferred version of psychoanalytic theory. We continue to practice in accordance with our conviction that these endeavors provide a unique opportunity to help our patients attain the therapeutic gains that analysis can offer.

References

Abend, S. (2002a). In retrospect: reflections on a psychoanalytic career. *Psychoanalytic Inquiry* 22:43–54.

——— (2002b). Factors influencing change in patients in psychoanalytic treatment. *Journal of Clinical Psychoanalysis* 11:209–223.

Abrams, S. and Welsh, H. (1990). The nature of the therapeutic action of psychoanalysis: how analysis works. *Journal of the American Psychoanalytic Association* 38:773–788.

Arlow, J. (1969). Unconscious fantasy and disturbances of conscious experience. *Psychoanalytic Quarterly* 38:1–27.

——— and Brenner, C. (1964). *Psychoanalytic Concepts and the Structural Theory*. New York: International Universities Press.

——— (1990). The psychoanalytic process. *Psychoanalytic Quarterly* 59:678–692.

Bergler, E. (1937). Theory of the therapeutic results of psychoanalysis—symposium. *International Journal of Psycho-Analysis* 18:146–160.

Bibring, E. (1937). Theory of the therapeutic results of psychoanalysis—symposium. *International Journal of Psycho-Analysis* 18:170–189.

Boesky, D. (1990). The psychoanalytic process and its components. *Psychoanalytic Quarterly* 54:550–584.

Brenner, C. (1976). *Psychoanalytic Technique and Psychic Conflict*. New York: International Universities Press.

—— (1979). Working alliance, therapeutic alliance, and transference. *Journal of the American Psychoanalytic Association* 27(supplement):137–157.

Fenichel, O. (1937). Theory of the therapeutic results of psychoanalysis—symposium. *International Journal of Psycho-Analysis* 18:133–138.

—— (1941). *Problems of Psychoanalytic Technique.* New York: Psychoanalytic Quarterly.

Freud, A. (1937). *The Ego and the Mechanisms of Defense.* Madison, CT: International Universities Press

Freud, S. (1912). The Dynamics of Transference. *Standard Edition* 12.

—— (1923). The Ego and the Id. *Standard Edition* 19.

—— (1937a). Analysis Terminable and Interminable. *Standard Edition* 23.

—— (1937b). Constructions in Analysis. *Standard Edition* 23.

Gill, M. (1954). Psychoanalysis and exploratory psychotherapy. *Journal of the American Psychoanalytic Association* 2:771–797.

Glover, E. (1937). Theory of the therapeutic results of psychoanalysis—symposium. *International Journal of Psycho-Analysis* 18:125–132.

Gray, P. (1994). *The Ego and the Analysis of Defense.* Northvale, NJ: Aronson.

Greenson, R. (1967). *The Technique and Practice of Psychoanalysis.* New York: International Universities Press.

Hartmann, H. (1939). *Ego Psychology and the Problem of Adaptation.* New York: International Universities Press.

Jacobs, T. (1991). *The Use of the Self.* Madison, CT: International Universities Press.

Kris, E. (1956). On some vicissitudes of insight in psychoanalysis. *International Journal of Psycho-Analysis* 37:445–455.

Loewald, H. (1960). On the therapeutic action of psychoanalysis. *International Journal of Psycho-Analysis* 41:16–33.

Mahler, M. (1965). On the significance of the normal separation-individuation phase, with reference to research in symbiotic child psychosis. In: *Drives, Affects, Behavior, Vol. 2*, ed. M. Schur. New York: International Universities Press, 2:161–169.

Modell, A. (1984). *Psychoanalysis in a New Context.* New York: International Universities Press.

Nunberg, H. (1937). Theory of the therapeutic results of psychoanalysis—symposium. *International Journal of Psycho-Analysis* 18:161–169.

Sandler, J. (1976). Countertransference and role-responsiveness. *International Review of Psycho-Analysis* 3:43–48.

Spruiell, V. (1982). Personal communication.

Stein, M. (1965). States of consciousness in the analytic situation. In: *Drives, Affects, Behavior, Vol. 2*, ed. M. Schur. New York: International Universities Press.

Sterba, R. (1934). The fate of the ego in analytic therapy. *International Journal of Psycho-Analysis* 15:11126.

Stone, M. (1961). *The Psychoanalytic Situation: An Examination of Its Development and Essential Nature.* New York: International Universities Press.

Strachey, J. (1934). The nature of the therapeutic action of psychoanalysis. *International Journal of Psycho-Analysis* 15:127–159.

——— (1937). Theory of the therapeutic results of psychoanalysis—symposium. *International Journal of Psycho-Analysis* 18:139–145.

Winnicott, D.W. (1971). *Playing and Reality.* New York: Routledge.

Zetzel, E. (1970). *The Capacity for Emotional Growth.* New York: International Universities Press.

CHAPTER 16

Freud, Transference, and Therapeutic Action

[Abend, S.M. (2009). *Psychoanalytic Quarterly* 78(3):871–892]

The author traces the development of Freud's conception of the nature and significance of transference in the psychoanalytic process. He notes that from 1910 onward, Freud was convinced that the analysis of the transference is the sole factor involved in the therapeutic action of psychoanalytic treatment, despite the fact that, late in his career, he observed and described the power of reconstruction to be effective as well. The author agrees with those analysts who contend that, while the analysis of the transference is essential to proper analytic technique, it is not the only agent of therapeutic impact.[1]

Near the end of his life, in one of his last published works, *Analysis Terminable and Interminable*, Freud (1937a) wrote:

> Instead of an enquiry into how a cure by analysis comes about (a matter which I think has been sufficiently elucidated) the question should be asked of what are the obstacles that stand in the way of such a cure [p. 221].

---

[1] This paper was presented as the 56th Annual Freud Lecture at the New York Psychoanalytic Institute on May 13, 2008.

Although the paper is primarily devoted to Freud's ideas about the nature of those obstacles to cure, his parenthetical aside, which clearly expressed his confidence in his theory of the therapeutic action of analysis, deserves more attention than it receives, either there or elsewhere in his work. As evinced by the psychoanalytic literature of the past decade or more, few analysts today would profess a comparable degree of assurance about what constitutes the curative force or forces in psychoanalytic treatment. This is so even among those of us who remain convinced of the value and importance of Freud's revolutionary findings and theories. It is notable that Freud wrote as if he fully believed in his conception of the nature of the therapeutic process, despite the fact that his governing theories had evolved dramatically from the early days of catharsis, through the vicissitudes of libido and resistance, to defense analysis and ego psychology.

In this paper, I shall try to trace the development of his conviction that successful analysis of the transference is the sole key to the therapeutic efficacy of analysis. I also intend to raise questions about the nature and quality of the evidence supporting that belief.

It is true that psychoanalysts of every theoretical persuasion recognize the importance of transference phenomena and agree that these require attention from both analyst and patient. I believe that Freud's discovery, comprehension, and technical utilization of the transference in psychoanalysis is one of his most remarkable, creative, and useful discoveries. However, the idea that the analysis of transference is the *only* factor that is responsible for the therapeutic effect of the treatment has been the subject of considerable controversy.

I find myself in agreement with those analysts who assert that, important as it is, transference analysis is *not* the only agent involved in the therapeutic action of psychoanalytic treatment. As we shall see, late in his career, Freud himself noted some difficulty connected with his formulation of the exclusive role of the analysis of the transference in accounting for therapeutic efficacy (Freud 1937a). In light of his own observation, we can only wonder why he did not find it necessary to modify his position about transference analysis, as on occasion he did do in respect to other important elements of his theories.

I think it is always fascinating and rewarding to study the evolution of Freud's thinking on virtually any aspect of the psychoanalytic edifice. Despite his admirable gifts as a writer, students of his work often misunderstand or misinterpret him: this is all the more true of those with one or another motive to disparage or misrepresent him. In my view, the strength of his powers of clinical observation, and of his adherence to the primacy of those observations, should be tremendously impressive to all but the most biased reader. I think this is also true of his extraordinary capacity to construct and, as I have mentioned, to modify or abandon when necessary portions of the theoretical scaffolding with which he sought to connect and explain what he had noticed in his clinical work with patients.

I propose to follow precisely his steps in the discovery and elucidation of the phenomenon of transference, and of his assignment to it of the pivotal role in bringing about every truly psychoanalytic cure. I believe this is more than a mere academic exercise, since it is evident that even today this idea has practical implications for both theory and technique. Differences of opinion about the nature of therapeutic action, and about the exclusive focus on transference analysis, are evident in our professional conferences, our literature, and our varied psychoanalytic curricula in the increasingly pluralistic environment of our field today.

In the opinion of the editors of the *Standard Edition*, Freud's first mention of the term *transference* in the *Studies on Hysteria* (Breuer and Freud, 1895) and his discussion a little later in *The Interpretation of Dreams* (1900) both employed it in a rather imprecise, generalized context. It was only in the postscript to the Dora case (Freud 1905) that he presented a thorough description of the features of transference, along with an early explanation of its important role in the therapeutic process. He wrote there:

> What are transferences? They are new editions or facsimiles of the impulses and phantasies which are aroused and made conscious during the progress of the analysis, but they have this peculiarity, which is characteristic for their species, that they

> replace some earlier person by the person of the physician. . . . To put it another way: a whole series of psychological experiences are revived, not as belonging to the past, but as applying to the person of the physician at the present moment [p. 116].

He also hinted at the importance of positive transference as an aid to the patient's recovery, and said that the transference constitutes both an obstacle to, and at the same time an ally of, the treatment process. He stated unequivocally that the transference must be identified by the analyst and destroyed by explaining it to the patient.

In one of the *Five Lectures* (1910), Freud summarized his understanding of the issue up to that time, asserting that transference appears in every psychoanalytic treatment of a neurotic patient, and noting, without elaboration, that hostile transferences were often mingled with affectionate ones. He offered the generalization that

> . . .the part of the patient's emotional life which he can no longer recall to memory is re-experienced by him in his relation to the physician; and it is *only* this re-experiencing in the transference that convinces him of the existence and of the power of these unconscious sexual impulses [p. 51, italics added].

He added the astute observation that transferences are not unique to psychoanalytic therapy; they arise in all relationships, but are made use of in a unique way by psychoanalysis. In short, by 1910, Freud was evidently firm in his belief that transference experiences, when properly analyzed, are the only reliable means by which patients become convinced of the nature and significance of their unconscious impulses and beliefs. Thus, he thought that the analysis of the transference was not just the *most important*, but in fact the *only* method by which a genuine psychoanalytic cure could be achieved. As far as one can tell, this assertion was based entirely on his cumulative body of clinical experience, not on theoretical deduction. At any rate, as far as I can determine, he did not offer a specific theoretical rationale for reaching this conclusion, either there or elsewhere in his writings. Interestingly enough, neither did he provide detailed case reports illustrating systematic and thorough transference analysis!

The next steps in the elaboration of the subject were presented in the familiar series of papers on technique published between 1912 and 1917. It should be borne in mind that at that time, Freud still thought that neuroses were a consequence of libidinal regression that was caused by actual, current experiences of frustration; the regression, he believed, was then subsequently enforced by repression. It is also important to recall that at that stage in the evolution of his theories of mental functioning, what we have since come to call the *topographic model of the mind* was the foundation of his thinking about the nature of the mental apparatus. It seems safe to presume that Freud's evolving conception of the centrality of transference analysis was, in his mind, consistent with and supported by his views about the nature of libido and his emphasis on the distinction between the different levels of consciousness.

The Dynamics of Transference (1912a) spelled out his increasingly complex views of transference, neurosis, and therapy. He emphasized that libidinal cathexis, of which transference is a manifestation, is only partly directed toward reality, but is largely unconscious in nature and thus revives infantile imagoes of an unrealistic content (p. 102). He proposed that this pathological state sought to maintain itself, with the repressive forces functioning as resistances to the analytic technique of encouraging free association. Freud believed that it was the process of free association that constituted the essential tool for the recovery of crucial buried memories and the removal of the relevant repressions, and thus for achieving the relief of symptoms. The central mission of analytic therapy was then redefined as the identification and removal of repressions, thereby to liberate the libido from their pathogenic effects. Resistances were taken as evidence of the inner struggle going on between the patient's wish to recover and his unconscious need to try to maintain the neurotic *status quo.*

Transference then entered the picture, according to Freud, influenced both by the unconscious wishes and imagoes and the resistances against their expression. The most obvious evidence of this inner struggle with which analytic technique had to deal were stoppages in the flow of free association. These were caused, Freud said, by the patient's discomfort at the requirement to verbalize proscribed wishes and ideas about the person of the doctor. This was even more difficult for the patient because of the simultaneous presence of the affectionate transference, which contributed to the patient's wish to please the doctor. Here Freud set the stage for his emerging belief that the transference constitutes the arena in which every conflict must be fought out.

Freud saw that transference was divided into affectionate and hostile sectors, but still more important, he suggested that the affectionate ones were further subdivided. There were elements of it, derived to be sure from the libido, that he designated as "unobjectionable" forms that powered the recovery process. The other components of the affectionate transference were the frankly erotic ones that, in sharp contrast, constituted resistances. Freud summed up this formulation in this way:

> Transference to the doctor is suitable for resistance to the treatment only insofar as it is a negative transference or a positive transference of repressed erotic impulses. If we "remove" the transference by making it conscious, we are detaching only these two components of the emotional act from the person of the doctor; the other component, which is admissible to consciousness and unobjectionable, persists and is the vehicle of success in psychoanalysis exactly as it is in other methods of treatment [p. 105].

He then repeats the formulation that the transference, albeit a source of resistance, is also what makes the "hidden and forgotten erotic impulses immediate and manifest," and he concludes in his familiar and often quoted words: "For when all is said and done, it is impossible to destroy anyone *in absentia* or *in effigy*" (p. 108).

However long this ingenious proposal about the complex divisibility of the transference may have lasted, it has not survived, at least in this precise form, the convincing but subtle rebuttal of its tenets by Stein (1981). In a clinical *tour de force*, Stein demonstrated the concealed and powerful resistances he found to be embedded in the so-called unobjectionable positive transference. I qualify my notation of the demise of the term *unobjectionable positive transference* because the idea that there is a positive relationship to the analyst that provides essential support to the treatment hardly disappeared from the analytic scene. It was revived in the guise of a *realistic relationship* or as a *therapeutic alliance* or some such entity, which, according to proponents of these concepts, exists outside of or alongside the transference relationship. In many quarters, this way of thinking about the complexity of the relationship between patient and analyst persists today, although it, too, has been challenged by other analysts—among them Friedman (1969), Brenner (1979), and me (Abend, 2000). To pursue this familiar debate here would take us too far afield.

I must also mention, if only in passing, that a great many analysts, of many theoretical persuasions, have further developed the idea of a vital, supportive relationship that they contend arises between each patient and his or her analyst, elevating it to an even more significant degree of prominence. It is widely, if not quite universally, accepted that aspects of this relationship—or, more accurately, of the patient's experience of the relationship with the analyst—must play an important role in the therapeutic effect of analytic treatment. Furthermore, this therapeutic action is regarded as a powerful force for change, even though it may not ever be a subject for specific analytic interpretation and discussion; therefore, it may never be included in the domain of the patient's conscious insight.

Once again, to pursue this fascinating and controversial topic any further at this point would not be directly relevant to our designated task of following the path of Freud's developing theory. Suffice it to say, Freud apparently distinguished between the support and encouragement provided by the "unobjectionable" positive transference, and therapeutic action, which resulted exclusively from the proper analysis of the transference. This is a theoretical differentiation with which many contemporary analysts disagree. For those who are interested in this issue, there is certainly no shortage of analytic literature devoted to considering this subject.

To return, then, to Freud's explication of transference and therapeutic action, in *Recommendations to Physicians Practicing Psycho-Analysis* (1912b), among other nuggets of advice on technique, he strongly advised against self-revelation on the grounds that it might encourage resistance and was bound to complicate resolving the transference. In *On Beginning the Treatment*, subtitled *Further Recommendations on the Technique of Psycho-Analysis, I* (1913), he advised the use of the couch "to isolate the transference and allow it to come forward in due course sharply defined as a resistance" (p. 134).

A little further on, he added: "So long as the patient's communication and ideas run on without any obstruction, the theme of transference should be left untouched" (p. 139). He counseled waiting for the formation of a positive attachment before offering any interpretations at all, and waiting until the transference appeared as a resistance before addressing it with the patient.

Freud then tried to describe the mechanism of cure as different from simply bringing to consciousness past buried traumatic memories and forbidden wishes, as had been the point of view characteristic of his early technique. He had obviously learned that mere intellectual awareness of unconscious material on the patient's part could be transitory, as long as resistances were left intact. In fact, he asserted, it was the energy of the transference that was utilized to overcome the resistance. This reference to energy serves as a reminder of Freud's adherence to a biologically determined conception of the mental apparatus at work in neurosis and in efforts to treat it.

He continued to reveal his growing body of clinical experience and observation in ideas set forth in his next paper, *Remembering, Repeating and Working-Through* (1914a). There he gave a more elaborate description of how the forgetting of crucial elements of the patient's past is a motivated activity, and therefore the gaps could only be filled in by overcoming the repressions that enforced this motivated forgetting. He mentioned, just in passing, a vital addendum to his clinical understanding to which he would not return for more than two decades. While discussing problems of memory and forgetting, he commented that important unconscious fantasies are different from repressed memories, in that they may never have been conscious at all, yet conviction of their existence and importance might nevertheless be obtained (1914a, pp. 148–149).

Freud's most powerful new point in this most important paper, though, was the idea that significant repressed material may be "acted out," that is to say, repeated in behavior, rather than remembered. He introduced the phrase *the compulsion to repeat* in this context. Most important for technique and the theory of cure, he identified the transference as a particular and troublesome form of this tendency. He pointed out that this repeating action in the transference serves to replace the therapeutically effective and therefore desired activity of the patient's consciously remembering pathogenic events and fantasies (p. 150). He wrote: "Transference itself is only a piece of repetition, and . . . the repetition is a transference of the forgotten past not only on to the doctor but also on to all the other aspects of the current situation" (p. 151). He also thought that "the greater the resistance, the more extensively will acting out (repetition) replace remembering" (p. 151).

As far as technique is concerned, Freud asserted that the compulsion to repeat becomes channeled into the transference:

> We succeed in giving all the symptoms of the illness a new transference meaning and in replacing his ordinary neurosis by a "transference neurosis" of which he can be cured by the therapeuticwork. . . . It represents an artificial illness which is at every point accessible to our intervention [1914a, p.154].

He added that it takes time and patience to allow the patient to "work through" the resistances. This was essential to enabling the patient to then do the requisite analytic work, that is to say, to follow the fundamental rule of free association to the recovery of pathogenic memories. He believed that only by that method, in that sequence, could the patient acquire the necessary conviction about the existence and power of repressed instinctual impulses, which Freud thought provided the key to therapeutic effectiveness.

At that time, Freud also wrote an article about the management of the transference, *Observations on Transference-Love*, subtitled *Further Recommendations on the Technique of Psychoanalysis, III* (1914b). He described a typical case in which a female patient falls in love with her male analyst. His advice was to neither discourage these feelings nor to respond to them positively, even in little ways. He wrote, "We ought not to give up the neutrality towards the patient, which we have acquired through keeping the counter-transference in check" (p. 164). This reference to countertransference was an altogether new idea, and it was not elaborated in any detail at that time. He also added his since-famous dictum that the treatment "must be carried out in abstinence" (p. 161). In the same paper, he astutely dismissed the idea that transference love is not genuine, commenting that every state of being in love reproduces infantile prototypes.

In the *Introductory Lectures on Psycho-Analysis* (1916–1917)—in particular, those on transference and analytic therapy (27 and 28)—Freud summed up his then-current ideas about the mental apparatus, the nature of neurosis, its genesis, and its treatment by psychoanalysis. His explanations are full, explicit, and unusually clear, probably because he was writing for an educated but analytically unsophisticated audience, and not, as previously, for aspiring analysts. Rather than quote him *in extenso*, I will paraphrase and briefly outline his major points. We can reasonably think of this condensed explication as constituting the platform from which history tells us he was on the verge of ascending into new theoretical territory.

- Neurotic conflict is a struggle between libidinal impulses and ascetic repressive forces. Since the former are unconscious and the latter conscious, the task of psychoanalysis is to make the libidinal impulses conscious, so the decisions about them can be made on equal ground, that is to say, in consciousness.
- By lifting repressions, we remove the conditions that lead to the formation of symptoms. This is accomplished by discovering and showing the patient the resistances that maintain repression.

- Resistances are part of the ego, so when they are recognized, they can be given up. The adult ego is different from the weak ego of childhood, and hence can, with the doctor's help, find better solutions to conflicts.
- Freud described the phenomenon of libidinal transferences that appear, he said, in every analyzable case. He added that variations exist in which the frankly sexual dimension is concealed, and he also noted that negative, hostile transferences might be present as well.
- The analyst, he said, must pay attention to the transference only when it becomes a resistance. Interpreting it to the patient leads to transformation of the transference, which is in actuality a repetition in action of the past, into the opening of the pathway for the return to consciousness of the important memories that it replaced.
- The emergence of the transference leads to the creation of a new form of the patient's illness, the transference neurosis, which replaces the original presenting symptoms. The transference neurosis offers proof of the libidinal nature of repressed impulses.
- The work of overcoming resistances is the essential function of psychoanalytic treatment. The analyst aids this work by educative suggestion; incorrect suggestions will fall away, since they do not lead to uncovering the underlying obscurities.
- And, finally, therapeutic activity amounts to an alteration of the ego, aided by the doctor. The ego then becomes more conciliatory toward the libido and thus inclined to grant it more satisfaction. The key to this process is the attraction of a portion of the libido onto the doctor by means of the transference. At the end of a successful psychoanalytic treatment, the transference must have been cleared away.

Please note that this account holds to the centrality of the libido concept, which, as I mentioned earlier, was always conceived of as a biological entity's having psychological effects. Freud outlined its vicissitudes in neurotic illness and its treatment. Transference, or more precisely the transference neurosis, constituted the only vehicle of possible cure, since it expressed the libido in question in a form that could be directly observed and changed at the then-current moment. Perhaps the only hint of the tremendous modification of his theories that was shortly to emerge was provided by Freud's increasing emphasis on alterations of the ego as crucial to the mechanism of cure.

It is surely beyond the scope of our present inquiry to try to identify all the factors that led Freud to set aside the topographic model of the mind, and to offer in its place what has become known as structural theory, with its emphasis on the qualities of the ego, and the new subdivision of it that he named the superego. Among these factors must have been his observations about the importance of aggression, and particularly of self-directed aggression, which rendered his earlier view of the primacy of self-preservation as a core psychological motivation no longer tenable.

Furthermore, he must have come to recognize that his idea that all resistances were located in the domain of the conscious ego was also incorrect; many of them had the same quality of being unconscious that he had previously reserved for the instincts. He described this change in *Beyond the Pleasure Principle* (1920), offering instead the distinction between the ego and the repressed. Likewise, his accumulated observations must have led him to surrender his earlier belief that libido was somehow transformed into a toxic substitute, anxiety, by the process of repression. This notion had to be replaced by the recognition of anxiety as an integral component of psychic conflict, serving as a trigger for defensive efforts by the ego, rather than being a result of that activity.

It is fascinating to note that a careful reading of all Freud's published work that appeared during the years in which his theories were being so substantially modified does not indicate that he made any effort to revise his theories about the nature of transference and its role in therapeutic action. His two most extraordinary publications during this period, *The Ego and the Id* (1923) and *Inhibitions, Symptoms and Anxiety* (1926a), make no mention of these important issues. One can only wonder at this remarkable consistency—or perhaps one might say inconsistency—in view of the profound changes in Freud's understanding of the nature of psychic conflict, and the vastly increased attention he paid to the specifics of producing changes in the ego. Even though he clearly made the latter task the centerpiece of psychoanalytic technique, he was not moved to undertake a reexamination of his ideas about the transference, including either its technical handling, or the special, exclusive role he assigned to it in the psychoanalytic treatment of neurosis.

In fact, he repeated his formulations about those questions in familiar terms in *An Autobiographical Study* (1925), and again in *The Question of Lay Analysis: Conversations with an Impartial Person* (1926b). A brief quotation from the former paper will illustrate this:

> The transference is made conscious to the patient by the analyst, and it is resolved by convincing him that in his transference attitude he is *re-experiencing* emotional relations which had their origin in his earliest object-attachments during the repressed period of his childhood. [p. 43, italics in original]

Even though his last writings indicate that he held an unshaken belief in his ideas about therapeutic action, there are some rather notable, if subtle, differences. Most important, in my view, is a passage in *Constructions in Analysis* (1937b). After defining *constructions* as "conjectural versions of [the patient's] forgotten early history" (p. 261), Freud goes on to say:

> Quite often we do not succeed in bringing the patient to recollect what has been repressed. Instead of that, if the analysis has been carried out correctly, we produce in him an assured conviction of the truth of the construction which achieves the same therapeutic result as a recaptured memory [pp. 265–266].

He then adds the following interesting acknowledgment:

> The problem of what the circumstances are in which this occurs and of how it is possible that what appears to be an incomplete substitute should nevertheless produce a complete result—all of this is a matter for a later inquiry [p. 266].

This is the remarkable passage to which I alluded earlier in this paper. Is it merely a recognition that, because of his advancing age, others besides himself would have to try to solve this problem? Could there perhaps have been, on the other hand, just a shadow of doubt about his often-repeated assertion that only the analysis of the transference, and the consequent re-emergence of crucial memories, provides the key to the therapeutic effectiveness of analysis? On careful examination, I could find no hard evidence in his writings that would lend so much as a hint of confirmation to the latter speculation.

Certainly, there are definite shifts in emphasis about the curative elements of psychoanalytic treatment in Freud's last writings. In *Analysis Terminable and Interminable* (1937a), he says that decisive factors contributing to the success or failure of the treatment include the persistent influence of early trauma, variations in the constitutional strength of the instincts, and inherent alterations of the ego (p. 224). He was building on his increased focus on the qualities of the ego, both in terms of the malleability of its defenses and on a quantitative measure of its strength or weakness as compared to the power of their instincts. He summed up his late view of therapeutic action in the following words:

> The therapeutic effect depends on making conscious what is repressed, in the widest sense of the word, in the Id. We prepare the way for this making conscious by interpretations and constructions, but we have interpreted only for ourselves and not for the patient, so long as the ego holds on to its earlier defenses and does not give up its resistances [p. 238].

In his final paper, the posthumously published *An Outline of Psycho-Analysis* (1940), Freud says clearly that a relative or absolute weakening of the ego is a precondition for neurosis (p. 172), and its cure is a consequence of the analyst's helping the weakened ego, giving it back "its mastery over lost provinces of his mental life" (p. 175). Then, after summarizing once again the appearance and nature of the transference, he says forcefully: "A patient never forgets again what he has experienced in the form of his transference; it carries a greater force of conviction than anything he can acquire in other ways" (p. 177). I am afraid that many Freudian analysts of today would only wish that his certitude about the permanent impact of transference analysis fitted more consistently and precisely with their own clinical experience.

It seems to me that tracing the evolution of Freud's theories about therapeutic action amply demonstrates both significant changes in his ideas and an unyielding consistency. I suppose it is possible to regard the changes as no more than increasingly detailed elaborations or refinements of his basic concepts, which retain a persuasive fundamental constancy. However, I believe that one might reasonably arrive at a different conclusion. I propose to briefly review once again the steps in his relevant theoretical development, and along the way I shall try to indicate why I hold that opinion.

First, there was Freud the neurologist, treating neurasthenic and hysterical patients. He discovered that important traumatic memories were sequestered in a state outside the patient's conscious awareness. Treatment centered on bringing these memories back into the patient's conscious recognition. By the time of the publication of the Dora case (1905), he had observed and understood the fundamental nature of transference phenomena. He had also already become convinced that the pathogenic material of the neuroses, which was held out of consciousness by repression, consisted of childhood sexual wishes and fantasies.

Just a few years later, he stated definitively that it was *only* by means of re-experiencing the repressed emotional life in the transference that the patient could be convinced of the existence and power of these unconscious sexual impulses. He put forward the idea that explaining the transference to the patient, and thereby destroying it, was the key to therapeutic success in psychoanalytic treatment. I need hardly point out to modern analysts that Freud's concept of destroying the transference through interpretation has not stood the test of time.

Freud's theories were further developed and elaborated in the well-known series of papers on technique that appeared between 1912 and 1917. By then, libido theory had emerged, and the topographic model of the mind was Freud's controlling explanatory schema of the mental apparatus. Once again, I would like to remind the reader that libido was, in fact, a quasi-biological conceptualization, treated as if it were an actual substance, one with psychic energy attached to it. Consistent with the biological roots of libido theory, psychic energy was clearly conceived of rather concretely, not simply figuratively. Freud proposed that this energy could be split in different directions, with a portion of the libido held in a state of unconsciousness by countercathectic energies that enforced repression. These latter phenomena manifested themselves as resistances in the course of attempting psychoanalytic therapy. The task of proper psychoanalysis, then, was redefined as identifying and removing the repressions in question.

The transference in psychoanalysis was thought of as constituting a new pathway by which the pathogenic portion of the libido could rise to the surface of the patient's mind; it appeared in the form of action that was a repetition of the repressed impulses, rather than as conscious memories. This new version of the pathogenic libidinal impulses, which produced what Freud named the transference neurosis, could thus be directly engaged by the analyst, *mano a mano*, as it were. Genuine insight into the nature of the crucial repressed material could then be achieved by destroying the resistances. This was to be accomplished by interpreting them to the patient, which would then be followed by the patient's working through them in some unspecified fashion.

It is possible to recognize that this intricate theoretical evolution presents a very sophisticated derivative of Freud's earliest psychoanalytic theories of therapeutic action that emphasized catharsis. Surely, Freud had learned from clinical experience that mere intellectual recognition of the troublesome unconscious material was insufficient and therapeutically unreliable. For the patient, gaining emotional conviction about it was essential, and the transference neurosis, according to Freud, provided the stage on which the forces of resistance and repression could be observed in action. Thus, they could be identified and interpreted by the analyst in the present moment and thereby effectively destroyed, at least in therapeutically successful cases.

We cannot help but admire Freud's ability to grasp the implications of his ever-growing body of clinical experience. Even now, a century later, we can recognize in *our own* clinical work much that he was the first to see and understand. Still, the question must be asked, just what was the basis, so early in his theoretical development, for his insistence that *only* through the analysis of the transference could emotional conviction about the nature of the troublesome unconscious impulses be obtained?

He said that the transference neurosis was the sole locus in which the repressive forces could be appreciated and overcome. It seems to me that this assumption made sense to Freud precisely because it was a logical extension of his then still somewhat concrete view of the nature of libido, its dispositions and vicissitudes. How else are we to make sense of his dictum that the transference should only be interpreted when it became a resistance, as evinced by disruptions in the free flow of associations?

We do know for certain that as he gained even more clinical experience, Freud found his earliest basic assumptions less satisfactory. He substantially changed his opinions about the precise nature of the instinctual drives, he gained a more complex and accurate view of the unconscious portion of mental life, and he arrived at a better understanding of the constituents of intrapsychic conflict and their interrelatedness. Consequently, what became known as the "structural theory" replaced his earlier topographic model as an explanatory schema of the mental apparatus and its functioning.

As an accompaniment to these most important advances, he became much more interested in studying and understanding the operations of the newly christened ego and superego. Although he wrote less specifically about technique, it is abundantly clear that his emphasis became centered on how the ego could be helped to acquire a more mature, more advantageous way of dealing with instinctual demands.

The deepening grasp of mental functioning that was being acquired by Freud and his immediate followers resulted in the emergence of what became known as defense analysis, or, more broadly speaking, ego psychology. A series of technical papers presented at the Marienbad Conference in 1934 reflected this new overview of technique. The landmark book *The Ego and the Mechanisms of Defence* (1937) written by his daughter, Anna Freud, doubtless in consultation with her father, codified these principles of psychoanalytic theory and technique.

Freud's own specific, independent contribution to the new era appeared, as I have said, in *Constructions in Analysis* (1937b). As he reported there, he had observed that reconstructions of formative childhood situations offered by the analyst could become convincing enough to patients to have a full therapeutic effect, despite the fact that they did not fit the formula that he had for so long insisted was the only method by which such curative conviction could be reached. He acknowledged his puzzlement, but, as we have seen, he did not see fit to surrender or even modify his opinion about transference and therapeutic action.

It is certainly easy to see that the emergence of ego psychology was an outgrowth of Freud's long-held conviction that analysis had to identify and remove resistances in order to be therapeutically effective. His new emphasis on quantitative factors regarding the relative strengths of the ego and the instincts, and on what he called inherent alterations of the ego's also having an effect on outcome, seem to reflect his experience with less than fully satisfactory analytic results. Why, then, did Freud never find it necessary to extend his views of therapeutic action to include the possibility that factors other than, or in addition to, the analysis of transference might also play a role in producing beneficial analytic results? It is hard to say, but it does seem to me that his own work and that of his students should have led him to that conclusion.

To return now to my earlier assertion that the topic we have been pursuing is of more than simply academic interest, I had in mind the fact that the debate about the exact nature of the therapeutic action of psychoanalysis persists to this day. An important aspect of that ongoing controversy is precisely the troublesome question regarding the exclusive concentration on transference analysis. This approach, in one guise or another, is still advocated in some quarters, while others regard it as too restrictive a prescription for effective psychoanalytic technique. While I cannot hope to summarize in great detail this discussion as it has evolved through the post-Freudian years, I can call the reader's attention to a few representative highlights.

Strachey's well-known paper *The Nature of the Therapeutic Action of Psycho-Analysis* (1934) coined the phrase *mutative interpretation* to indicate the essential role of transference analysis in bringing about change; all other kinds of intervention were relegated to ancillary or preparatory status. His wording still echoes in psychoanalytic discourse. Shortly after the end of World War II, the British Kleinian school introduced the idea of utilizing the analyst's countertransference to learn more precisely about the specifics of the patient's transference. This change in technique—controversy about it aside—still maintained the principle of the analysis of transference at the center of analytic treatment. Although it is not easy to find literature that specifically addresses their theory of therapeutic action, exposure to the clinical work of the British Kleinians even today suggests that most, if not all, of that group concentrate their attention on the moment-to-moment analysis of the transference in a fashion reminiscent of Strachey's dictum.

Here in the United States, Gill long ago (1982) proposed an exclusive devotion to the analysis of transference as providing the most effective way to produce beneficial analytic results. Furthermore, there are large segments of the relational and intersubjective schools that also advocate focusing exclusively on the so-called here-and-now interactions in the analytic sessions, which amounts to another version of maintaining transference analysis as the sole pathway to useful therapeutic action.

That said, this technical approach, and the theory from which it is derived, has also been seriously questioned by many analysts over the years. Blum's paper *The Position and Value of Extra-Transference Interpretation* (Blum, 1983) provides an outstanding and thorough summary of the debate up to that time. He cites such prominent analytic scholars as Stone and Brenner, along with Fenichel, Anna Freud, Rangell, Arlow, and others who made the case against exclusively transference-centered analysis.

For example, Blum quotes Stone as follows:

> The extra-analytic life of the patient often provides indispensable data for the understanding of detailed complexities of his psychic functioning, because of the sheer variety of its references, some of which cannot be reproduced in the relationship to the analyst . . . extra-transference interpretations cannot be set aside or underestimated in importance [Stone 1967, p. 35].

And, further, Blum cites Brenner:

> [Transference] remains but one factor among many in any analytic situation. An analyst has always the task of deciding as best he can from the available evidence which factors are the most important at a particular time in the analysis. If his conjecture . . . is that something other than the transference is most important at the moment, he will interpret whatever that "something other" may be [Brenner 1976, p. 128].

In his own voice, Blum calls attention to the importance of reconstruction in illuminating the patient's past, and also points to the necessity of analyzing incidents of acting out in the patient's life outside the analysis: "Derivatives of unconscious conflict (and their interpretation) are not limited to transference" (1983, p. 586).

And, finally, lest it seem that this vital difference of opinion is by now anything like a settled matter, consider Blum's article entitled "Repression, Transference and Reconstruction," published in the *International Journal of Psychoanalysis* in 2003. It was written, he says, at the invitation of the editors of that journal, as a response to a

1999 guest editorial by Fonagy. Blum's summary of Fonagy's position includes the statement that, "while relying exclusively on the current transference, he [that is, Fonagy] proposes a new theory of therapeutic change through the experience of 'self-with-other,' rather than the primary analysis of unconscious intra-psychic conflict, trauma and their genetic determinants" (Blum 2003, p. 497). Blum quotes Fonagy as saying: "Therapies that focus on the recovery of memory pursue a false god. Psychoanalysts should carefully and consistently avoid the archeological metaphor" (Fonagy 1999, p. 220).

To mention but one passage from Blum's counterargument:

> Without the patient's life history, including education, family and culture, as well as character, the transference cannot be fully understood and vice versa. The repetitive reactions of childhood are important patterns, often vital to full comprehension of the adult analytic transference. Moreover, what is acted out, outside the analytic situation, may not directly appear in transference. The analysis of character is only loosely related to transference. The same character traits and attitudes are present everywhere, inside and outside the analytic process. We do not know our patients' character through transference alone, and the analyst is not the only transference object [2003, p. 498].

I said earlier that, given space constraints, it would not be realistic for me to attempt to present a truly comprehensive account of the continuing discussion about transference and therapeutic action. My intention has been simply to document my assertion that the argument did not disappear from the analytic world with Freud's passing from the scene. The multiplicity of contemporary ideas about the therapeutic action of psychoanalysis is widely recognized. A recent compendium on that subject published by *The Psychoanalytic Quarterly* (Volume 76, Supplement, 2007) clearly demonstrates the wide range of current opinions.

Winds of change were, in fact, already beginning to make their appearance in the 1930s (Greenberg, 2007). Different interpretations of exactly what constitutes paying analytic attention to the here-and-now interactions between analyst and patient further complicate how present-day analysts might think about the implications of Freud's emphasis on the specific value of the analysis of the transference neurosis.

For those of us who, following in Freud's original footsteps, are still convinced that understanding the patient's past is essential to an effective comprehension of his or her present circumstances and troubles, it should require no great stretch of the imagination to think that an analogous historical approach to understanding analytic theory is also valuable. That is the path I have elected to pursue and along which I have invited the reader to follow.

As far as I am concerned, the familiar saying that the past is prologue to the present describes part of the ineradicable legacy of Sigmund Freud. As to how that past is to be best understood and its consequences dealt with, that is another matter. I think we can still look with admiration at Freud's determined and inspired pursuit of those goals, without necessarily being obliged to adhere to his belief that it is *only* through the analysis of the transference that those ends can be achieved.

References

Abend. S.M. (2000). The problem of therapeutic alliance. In: *The Therapeutic Alliance: Monograph 9 of the Workshop Series of the American Psychoanalytical Association,* ed. S. Levy. New York: International Universities Press.

Blum, H.P. (1983). The position and value of extratransference interpretation. *Journal of the American Psychoanalytic Association* 31:581–617.

——— (2003). Repression, transference and reconstruction. *International Journal of Psycho-Analysis* 84:497–503.

Brenner, C. (1976). *Psychoanalytic Technique and Psychic Conflict.* New York: International Universities Press.

——— (1979). Working alliance, therapeutic alliance, and transference *Journal of the American Psychoanalytic Association* 27:137–157.

Breuer, J. and Freud. S. (1895). Studies on Hysteria. *Standard Edition* 2.

Fonagy, P. (1999). Memory and therapeutic action. *International Journal of Psycho-Analysis* 80:215–223.

Freud, A. (1937). *The Ego and the Mechanisms of Defence.* London: Hogarth/Institute of Psychoanalysis.

Freud, S. (1900). The Interpretation of Dreams. *Standard Edition* 4/5.

——— (1905). Fragment of an Analysis of a Case of Hysteria. *Standard Edition* 7.

——— (1910). Five Lectures on Psycho-Analysis. *Standard Edition* 11.

——— (1912a). The Dynamics of Transference. *Standard Edition* 12.

——— (1912b). Recommendations to Physicians Practising Psycho-Analysis. *Standard Edition* 12.

——— (1913). On Beginning the Treatment: Further Recommendations on the Technique of Psycho-Analysis, I. *Standard Edition* 12.

——— (1914a). Remembering, Repeating and Working-Through. *Standard Edition* 12.

——— (1914b). Observations on Transference-Love: Further Recommendations to Physicians Practising Psycho-Analysis, III. *Standard Edition* 12.

——— (1916–1917). Introductory Lectures on Psycho-Analysis. *Standard Edition* 15/16.

——— (1920). Beyond the Pleasure Principle. *Standard Edition* 18.

——— (1923). The Ego and the Id. *Standard Edition* 19.

——— (1925). An Autobiographical Study. *Standard Edition* 20.

——— (1926a). Inhibitions, Symptoms and Anxiety. *Standard Edition* 20.

——— (1926b). The Question of Lay Analysis: Conversations with an Impartial Person. *Standard Edition* 20.

——— (1937a). Analysis Terminable and Interminable. *Standard Edition* 23.

——— (1937b). Constructions in Analysis. *Standard Edition* 23.

——— (1940). An Outline of Psycho-Analysis. *Standard Edition* 23.

Friedman, L. (1969). The therapeutic alliance. The fate of the ego in analytic therapy. The fate of the ego in analytic therapy. *International Journal of Psycho-Analysis* 50:139–153.

Gill., M. (1982). *Analysis of Transference*, Vol. I. New York: International Universities Press.

Greenberg, J. (2007). Personal communication.

Stein, M. (1981). The unobjectionable part of the transference. *Journal of the American Psychoanalytic Association* 29:869–892.

Stone, L. (1967). The psychoanalytic situation and transference—a postscript to an earlier communication. *Journal of the American Psychoanalytic Association* 15:3–58.

Strachey, J. (1934). The nature of the therapeutic action of psychoanalysis. *International Journal of Psycho-Analysis* 15:127–159.

CHAPTER 17

An Analogue of Negation

[Abend, S.M. (1975). *Psychoanalytic Quarterly* 44:631–637]

It is a commonplace observation that people prefer to view their thoughts, feelings, and behavior as more or less rational responses to current external circumstances, rather than acknowledging the great influence of irrational, unconscious mental forces. Every patient in analysis reveals this tendency to some degree; in cases where it is particularly prominent, the analyst soon recognizes it as a defense which requires careful attention.

Patients who habitually introduce interpretive comments of their own or respond to those of the analyst with "Maybe," or some similar expression of doubtful assent, quickly alert the analyst to their unconscious resistance to psychological conviction and the technical problem this poses. Some patients, however, use a more subtle form of resistance which is less likely to be identified as defensive, particularly since these patients as a rule are quite unaware of the strength of their wish to disagree with interpretations. I have in mind those individuals who react not with doubt or disputation, but according to a formula that can be called the "Yes, but . . ." response, an analogue of negation. They appear to accept interpretations, especially those that are familiar because of previous analytic work. Characteristically, however, they add to their acceptance the belief—which they do not consciously regard as a contradiction—that certain factors in external reality have also played an important part in determining the behavior, thoughts, or feelings which are under analysis.

Although he had noted it in his clinical work at least as early as the Rat Man analysis (1909), Freud did not set down his understanding of the mechanism he called negation until he wrote a brief paper bearing that title in 1925. In it he said, "Thus the content of a repressed image or idea can make its way into consciousness, on condition that it is *negated*. Negation is a way of taking cognizance of what is repressed; indeed it is already a lifting of the repression, though not, of course, an acceptance of what is repressed. We can see how in this the intellectual function is separated from the affective process" (Freud, 1925, pp. 235–236). A patient may thus consciously say "No" to an idea, but his succeeding thoughts may indicate that unconsciously the idea is affirmed. Freud observed that this was a way in which some patients deal with unacceptable thoughts which emerge in free associations. The same process can occur as a defensive response to the analyst's interpretations.

As the findings of psychoanalysis began to be known to the general public, this aspect of mental functioning was one which was seized upon by critics and skeptics in order to deride the analytic method. In *Constructions in Analysis*, Freud (1937) attempted to answer the charge that analysts play false by discounting patients' negative replies, while accepting assent at face value. He pointed out that full reliance cannot be placed upon conscious agreement either. He stated: "A plain 'Yes' from a patient is by no means unambiguous. It can indeed signify that he recognizes the correctness of the construction that has been presented to him; but it can also be meaningless, or can even deserve to be described as 'hypocritical,' since it may be convenient for his resistance to make use of an assent in such circumstances in order to prolong the concealment of a truth that has not been discovered. The 'Yes' has no value unless it is followed by indirect confirmations . . ."(p. 262). In short, in order to be certain that a patient's conscious expression of agreement reflects true unconscious acceptance, the analyst must pay attention to the associations that follow. I believe that when patients use the "Yes, but . . ." response, the next associations are not in fact confirmatory in nature, and the agreement is to be regarded as intellectual at best.

In my experience, patients who are knowledgeable about analysis and who favor intellectual defenses are especially likely to use this particular type of resistance. They often appear to be quite reasonable: they present their combination of agreement and reality addenda in a most plausible fashion, devoid of stridency, stubbornness, or any other indicator of hidden contentiousness. Although I refer to this way of resisting interpretations as the "Yes, but . . ." response, neither the "Yes" nor the "but" need be an explicit part of the patient's remarks. What is present is some form of initial agreement with the interpretation, followed immediately by associations that purport to supplement the psychological explanation with a reference to some contributory role played by reality factors. As far as the patient is aware, he is elaborating upon his agreement, not attempting to contradict it.

Additions of this nature, however, seek to explain what is in question on a basis altogether different from that which has been offered by the analyst; therefore, they cannot be regarded as confirmatory in the sense used by Freud. The patient, in fact, unconsciously wishes to rebut the interpretation or at least to ward off its emotional impact by shifting attention to external factors. In the more familiar form of negation, the patient says "No" consciously and then "Yes" unconsciously, but here the reverse is true: his conscious "Yes" is followed by an unconscious "No."

An incident from an analysis still in progress has struck me as an apt illustration of this defense. The material has been condensed and edited in the interests of brevity and confidentiality.

A young, talented business executive had gradually come to understand through his analysis that his severe professional self-limitations, among other symptoms, resulted substantially from strong, unconscious self-punitive trends. These were centered primarily, at this point in the treatment, around a horrifying traffic accident that had left his older brother—the parents' favorite—a hopeless cripple. The patient had consciously loved and admired his brother; at the time of the accident he was entirely unaware of any feelings of hatred or envy toward him. As a result of the change in his brother's life prospects, the patient suddenly found that he had attained the leading role for which he had always unconsciously wished. This event, of course, also corresponded to the fulfillment of other hostile fantasies, involving rivalry not only with his brother but with his father as well. It is not necessary to discuss here all the ramifications of these wishes and the tremendous guilt they engendered, nor the complex set of defenses which prevented the patient's recognizing and understanding either the triumphant or self-punitive reactions. Instead I will confine myself to some of the material that illustrates the defensive operation under consideration.

For some months the patient had become increasingly discontented with his job; he was underpaid, exploited, and could entertain no reasonable hope of advancement. Analytic progress gradually permitted him to seriously consider improving his position. Finally, the imminent prospect of further increase in the demands placed upon him without any increase in pay mobilized him to seek a change of employment. Within a few days, he received an offer which promised much more pleasant and satisfying work and an improved future outlook as well. For several sessions he debated with himself about the change. He brought up many associations to his brother and the by now familiar elements of his conflict about advancing himself. At last he decided to accept the proffered position and gave notice to his employers.

His boss thereupon exerted pressure upon him to change his mind and stay on. He played upon his conscious guilt, emphasizing his responsibility to complete projects that were under way and implying that injury to the firm would result from difficulty in replacing him, *etc.* The patient immediately responded with hesitation and doubt about his decision to leave. Both dream material and other associations clearly pointed to an unconscious connection with the idea of gaining satisfaction at his brother's expense. His response was to agree with the interpretations of these irrational, unconscious sources of his guilt, but then he would invariably add that there was also some significant reality to the objections raised by his employer and to the way they made him feel. An example of the "Yes, but . . ." responses typical at this point might be put as follows: "*Yes*, I realize my reactions to my brother's accident have a great deal to do with why I feel guilty when I think of leaving the job, *but* you know it is true that I am not the sort of person who ever liked to leave work unfinished, and my boss is right. I can't possibly complete the so-and-so project by such-and-such date when I'm supposed to start at the new place." Finally after two or three days of this kind of "agreement," which did not increase his freedom to act, he seized upon an incident that underlined the insincerity of his employer as a justification for giving up his irresolution, and he committed himself to the move.

After he began his new job (his employer in fact had had no trouble in hiring a replacement), his immediate response was a paradoxical feeling of profound melancholy. He was puzzled by this reaction, because he was also consciously aware of underlying feelings of pleasure and satisfaction which were completely masked, however, by his unaccountable sadness. His verbal productions once more led to his brother and to memories of the period of shock and grief immediately following the injury. It was possible to say to the patient that at the time of the accident he would surely have felt obliged to conceal from others any hint of pleasure or satisfaction of which he might have been peripherally aware. This observation was in essence similar to many previous ones that had dealt with this material, including those of the earlier sessions which had been received with his version of a "Yes, but . . ." reaction. Now, however, it triggered a storm of angry protest and denial that lasted for the remainder of the hour. By the following day, the patient's anger had subsided, his melancholy had lifted, and further confirmatory material emerged regarding his rivalrous feelings toward his brother and their disturbing impact upon him.

We can see that when the patient's guilty hesitation about changing jobs was evoked by his boss's urgings, interpretations connecting this response to his unconscious conflicts—based upon current thoughts as well as upon data derived from earlier analytic work—were accepted in a superficial and intellectual fashion only. He "knew" it was so, but his insistence that reality also played a part in determining his reactions expressed his unconscious wish to thrust the analyst's explanation aside: to render it unimportant. It is not surprising that he required further justification before he could permit himself to act upon his desire to change jobs. His angry outburst when the same interpretation was repeated a few weeks later, following his associations to his paradoxical melancholy, clarified the usefulness of the defense. It confirmed the persistence of his wish to refute the interpretation, full acceptance of which would have made him acutely and uncomfortably conscious of his intense guilt toward his unfortunate brother. Furthermore, it spared him from acknowledging his anger at his analyst for telling him things that threatened to make him aware of feeling bad. Thus the defense served a double purpose: the warding off of uncomfortable affects which accompanied the content of the interpretation itself, and the avoidance of feelings which seemed to him likely to disturb his relationship to his analyst.

There could have been another, altogether different way of explaining the patient's repeated insistence that reality factors played a major role in determining his behavior. It might have represented an indirect expression of the unconscious idea that his childhood wish to supplant his brother in his parents' favor had in fact come true. Perhaps such an idea as "But *my* wishes are *really* likely to come true" served as an unconscious stimulus, the presence of which manifested itself in the conscious derivative of attributing importance to external reality.

Analytic material from this patient never convincingly supported such a hypothesis, however. What is more, two of my other patients, who also showed an inclination to use the "Yes, but . . ." response to interpretations, had had no such dramatic experiences which might have reinforced the tendency to believe that unacceptable wishes were very likely to come true. Finally, all persons, so far as we know from analytic experience, share to some degree the unconscious conviction that childhood wishes and fears can and do come true. To each individual, this belief is real enough, and a variety of external events may come to represent such fulfillment.

In sum, my observations support only the conclusion that the "Yes, but . . ." response is to be regarded as a defense. The patient's assent is, in the sense in which Freud used the word, hypocritical. The assertion that reality considerations also made a contribution, no matter how mildly and plausibly stated, should be taken as an unconscious rebuttal of the psychological explanation which has been offered. The patient remains emotionally unconvinced, and the analyst should be on notice that the critical part of his work remains to be done.

Summary

A particular way in which some patients respond to unwelcome interpretations is described: initial agreement is immediately followed by some reference to factors in external reality which the patient states also played a part in determining his reactions. The patient consciously believes himself in agreement with the interpretation, but the addenda emphasizing reality factors actually represent an unconscious denial of the correctness and importance of the analyst's explanation. This response is a kind of defense, the structure of which is analogous to negation.

A clinical illustration is presented showing this defense in operation. The purpose of the defense is to ward off uncomfortable affects associated with the content of the interpretation and also to avoid bad feelings toward the analyst for making the unwelcome observation. For convenience, this defense is called the "Yes, but . . ." response, although these words need not literally appear in the verbal content of the patient's remarks.

References

Freud, S. (1909). Notes upon a Case of Obsessional Neurosis, *Standard Edition* 10:155–249.

——— (1925). Negation. *Standard Edition* 14:235–239.

——— (1937). Constructions in Analysis. *Standard Edition* 23:257–269.

CHAPTER 18

Psychic Conflict and the Concept of Defense

[Abend, S.M. (1981). *Psychoanalytic Quarterly* 50:67–76]

Abstract

Anna Freud's classic work, *The Ego and the Mechanisms of Defence*, is reassessed from the perspective of our current understanding of its place in the history of psychoanalytic theory. The subsequent development of the concept of defense is then traced, with emphasis on its relationship to psychic conflict. The role of both defense and conflict in normal and pathological behavior is stressed.

The revolution in psychoanalytic theory introduced by the appearance of *The Ego and the Id* in 1923 and by *Inhibitions, Symptoms and Anxiety* in 1926 must have presented a most profound intellectual challenge to the analysts of that time. It is easy to imagine that the study groups, discussions, and meetings of the decade that passed between the publication of *Inhibitions, Symptoms and Anxiety* and the appearance of Anna Freud's *The Ego and the Mechanisms of Defence* (1936) were primarily concerned with understanding its implications for theory and technique. No longer was anxiety considered to be the result of repression and some mysterious psychobiological alteration in libido, but instead Freud had said it was produced by one of several danger situations related to instinctual expression, or by the anticipation of them. In fact, it was anxiety that initiated repression and other defenses, the latter term referring to a conceptualization he resurrected from his earliest, abandoned attempts at theory building to fit into the new formulations. Anna Freud's book might be thought of as a first attempt to present in an organized way the evolving understanding of these new ideas about the revised theory of psychic conflict, the role of psychic agencies in general, and of defenses in particular.

First of all, she presented the idea that defenses are unconscious mechanisms and that they need to be analyzed. No longer were the contents of the id to be thought of as the only gold for which analysts search and all else as dross—that is to say, as merely valueless interference, to be pushed aside by whatever means in the effort to bring to light unconscious instinctual derivatives. Now these defenses themselves deserved interested attention, even though the patients would not welcome it. The new technique required the analyst to stand, in Miss Freud's famous dictum, "equidistant[1] from the id, the ego and the superego." Symptoms were seen as compromise formations in which the part played by the ego was "the unvarying use of a special method of defence, when confronted with a particular instinctual demand . . ." (p. 36). She also observed that there are defenses against affects, of which the analyst could especially make use in analyzing children. She constructed a list of defense mechanisms that has surely been memorized by every student of dynamic psychiatry at one time or another, and she proposed that there must be a developmental hierarchy of defense mechanisms, while acknowledging that there were difficulties in elucidating it at that time.

She enumerated three sources of anxiety, hence motives for defense: 1) superego anxiety, 2) objective anxiety, that is, unpleasant consequences of relations with other people, principally the parents, and 3) fear of the strength of the instincts themselves, which she thought to

---

[1] Presented as part of a panel at the meetings of the American Psychoanalytic Association in December 1979: Classics Revisited—*The Ego and the Mechanisms of Defence* by Anna Freud; Jacob A. Arlow, Chairman.]

be the result of a fundamental antagonism between the ego and the instinctual drives that is independent of mental content. Interestingly enough, in reviews of the time, Jones (1938) felt she did not emphasize the latter strongly enough, but Fenichel (1938) expressed serious doubts about the existence of a basic fear of the instincts. He questioned why there should be any discomfort connected with the drives unless there is a problem in achieving satisfaction, and the obstacles to satisfaction, for all practical purposes, are problems involving relationships to others in some way, *i.e.*, of objective or of superego anxiety.

Miss Freud believed that dread of the instincts is especially important in explaining the clinical phenomenology of adolescence and of psychosis, among other things, and her views have gained wide acceptance, although, as far as I know, Fenichel's objections have never been satisfactorily answered. However, we all know how difficult it can be to modify or discard ideas in our field, even when subsequent developments and the accumulation of evidence suggest that they are inaccurate or obsolete.

Something of the sort can be observed in *The Ego and the Mechanisms of Defence* itself, in respect to some of the old, pre-1926 theories of psychoanalysis. It is as though the new ideas and their implications were amalgamated, in some respects, with those they superseded, instead of replacing them completely. For example, her explanation of the motives for defenses against affects is that affects are associated with the instincts and are in consequence to be warded off irrespective of their intrinsic nature, although she observed that painful affects are more likely than pleasurable ones to initiate defense. And then her elaboration of denial in fantasy, or by word or act, presents these mechanisms as methods of protection against painful external reality, *i.e.*, unwelcome perceptions. This is seen as parallel to, but not fundamentally the same as, the defenses against instinctual drives, since the latter originate within the mind. Certainly, the two may be interconnected, she thought, but neurotic structure was understood to be confined to the disposition of the instincts, while defenses against perceptions of the outside world are in some way different, normal only in childhood and malignant if they persist in mature individuals. A similar distinction was drawn between inhibition, which is directed against internally originating drive pressure, and ego restriction, a tendency to avoid external situations which produce pain.

It was not yet fully appreciated at the time that, from the standpoint of the mind, the external world interacts with the mental apparatus, of which drive organization, ego functions, and superego tendencies are continuously operating components, and that all behavior is inescapably influenced by the unconscious fantasies which are variously derived from these interactions, as Arlow has repeatedly emphasized (1961), (1966), (1969a), (1969b), (1972). Today, many analysts, although by no means all of them, treat this later view as a matter of course. Those who do are likely to understand a defensive fantasy, a misperception of reality, an avoidance of a situation, or a "normal" interest or activity as identical in underlying structure to a "symptom," that is, as a compromise between the ubiquitous wishes, fears, and the means of dealing with them, of which mental life is composed.

In tracing the evolution of these concepts I will include some highlights from a series of panels (1954), (1967a), (1967b), (1970) on aspects of defense theory. I shall present here only a highly condensed account of the major landmarks in the development of our understanding of defenses. Such an account, of course, cannot do full justice to the complexity of the thinking of various contributors, nor can it mention all of the important ideas which have emerged.

A panel report published in 1954 indicates that there was already some dissatisfaction with the concept of defenses as mechanisms. Miss Freud, in describing the complex defenses of identification with the aggressor and altruistic surrender, had thought of them as resulting from a combination of more basic defense mechanisms. Some participants in the panel thought that this description did not accurately portray the complexities involved, but Waelder wanted to hold to the original definition of defense mechanisms as involuntary, automatic, and unconscious. Furthermore, he insisted that successful analysis would lead to their elimination. Kris disagreed, emphasizing instead the emergent conception of autonomous ego functions and the idea of the modification of pathological defenses into appropriate, successful ego activities. It was noted that certain ego functions could be used as defenses against others. Greenson observed that instinctual gratifications may enter into the integral structure of certain defense processes. Brenner added that certain attitudes manifested in the analytic situation might, at the same time, represent both defense and instinctual gratification.

In 1966, to mark the thirtieth anniversary of the publication of *The Ego and the Mechanisms of Defence*, the American Psychoanalytic Association held two panels on aspects of defense. Arlow, who chaired the panel (1967a) on theory, observed that ego psychology had had twin lines of development, that of the defenses, initiated by Anna Freud, and that of adaptation, introduced by the work of Hartmann, the two having subsequently converged. Mahler presented a developmental or genetic point of view, characterized by an interest in precursors of ego mechanisms and in maturational sequences. She noted that adaptive and defensive functions are interwoven. Valenstein held that the adaptational view expanded the concept of defense from conflict and neurosis to normal development. The distinction rested on what he termed functional relevance: roughly, whether or not the defenses are phase-adequate and reality-appropriate.

Loewald made the point that the broad concept of defenses treats them as an effort to get rid of stimulation and hence makes of them the prototypic psychic process. Disagreeing with this, he suggested instead that organizing, internalizing processes are more fundamental, giving as an example so-called normal Oedipal outcomes. His suggestion, and particularly his example, gave rise to considerable debate. Zetzel offered the view that defenses operate against both anxiety and depressive affect, which are basic ego states. The former arises from danger, while the latter, she felt, following Bibring, stems from feelings of helplessness, *i.e.,* narcissistic injury.

Waelder, who chaired the panel (1967b) that focused on matters of technique, gave a historical survey in which he said that *Inhibitions, Symptoms and Anxiety* required analysts to ask what it is that the patient is afraid of. Anna Freud's book elaborated this question into the more complex form, "When the patient is afraid, how does he behave?" The technical shift, according to Waelder, elevated the defenses to a place of importance in clinical psychoanalysis. Eventually this gave rise to the understanding that the defenses and what is being defended against must often be interpreted together, while it also became clearer that defenses themselves "convey some indication of content as well" (Panel, 1967b, p. 152).

Greenson observed that every kind of psychic phenomenon may be used for defensive purposes. Brenner stated that conflict and defense may lead either to normal or to pathological results; and that the same psychic processes underlie all mental activity and its resultant behavior. Thus mechanisms of defense are part of normal psychological development and structure as well as of character distortion and symptom formation. This view represented not merely a convergence of the defense and adaptation lines of ego psychology, as Arlow suggested, but a true confluence. However, one gains the impression that not all analysts were so ready to agree with this unified concept. For some, at least, it remained an alluring belief that normality and pathology are, *au fond*, distinct from one another. They seemed to address themselves to aspects of development and adaptation as though a fundamental difference existed between them and conflict—or at least as if instinctual conflict and its outcome impinge upon development and adaptation only tangentially, or in a secondary fashion in favored individuals.

Not so thought Tartakoff, who presented data from the analyses of normal candidates which not only demonstrated that defenses can be seen to promote normal as well as pathological behavior, but furthermore that those defenses which were seen fail to validate certain theoretical assumptions regarding hierarchical layering. In other words, defenses usually presumed to appear earlier in development apparently were not correlated with clinical evidence of the presence of more severe psychopathology, as had been assumed to be the case.[2]

---

[2] This observation was recently reconfirmed by a study group of which I was a member, which conducted a detailed study of borderline patients in psychoanalysis (Kris Study Group, 1978).

Schafer (1968) elaborated the view that so-called mechanisms of defense are dynamic tendencies having mental content. He showed that they should be conceptualized as motives or wishes themselves. He suggested that there exists, in essence, a continuum of conflicted positions, in which one complex arrangement is set in opposition to another, even more threatening one.

A 1970 panel report on the fate of the defenses in the course of psychoanalysis presented interesting clinical material that attempted to illustrate the modification of defensive tendencies that takes place. Brenner reiterated his emphasis on the multiple determination of all behavior and mental functioning: hence, the contributory role of defensive considerations, as well as instinctual drives, superego pressure, and external reality, to all psychic activity. By the same token, he added, it is erroneous to consider a bit of behavior, thought, or fantasy solely as a defense, even though its defensive value may be what one chooses to interpret to a patient. More recently Brenner (1976) has proposed that to speak of modification of defense is, in fact, inaccurate as well. What is actually modified are the compromise formations which are the result of conflict, a shift that he felt better explains some of the observations about persistent defenses with which analysis had been concerned. In fact, Brenner went on to say, defenses are not specific mental phenomena, not "things," as it were, but postures—they are defined by their purposes or functions. Any and all ego functions may serve defensive purposes and promote gratification as well.

In a recent series of articles Brenner (1974), (1975), (1979) has also proposed that defenses are aimed at minimizing depressive affect as well as anxiety. He offered an explanation different from Zetzel's idea that depressive affect was attributable to a separate and distinct underlying condition, *i.e.*, feelings of helplessness and consequent narcissistic injury. He suggested instead that the typical dangers of childhood should be regarded as possible calamities. They are dangers if their occurrence is anticipated as likely to take place, in which case the associated affect is some form of anxiety. However, these calamities may also be regarded as having actually occurred already, and even if this belief is only a fantasy, it can produce some variety of depressive affect. Exactly as with anxiety, the mental apparatus attempts to eliminate or minimize the pain associated with depressive affect by means of defensive measures.

How can we summarize these progressive steps in the evolution of the concept of defense? Freud introduced it as a means of disposing of excitations; then it changed into a diffuse tendency to oppose the instincts, losing its name in the process, finally re-emerging in 1926 as a set of responses to danger. In *The Ego and the Mechanisms of Defence* these had crystallized into unconscious, automatic mechanisms which it was also necessary to analyze, just as it was necessary to analyze the contents they warded off. This analytic scrutiny soon made it clear that these simple mechanisms were neither simple nor mechanisms, but appeared instead more like complex structures which served other purposes besides defensive ones and were themselves the product of compromise formation. They were noted to defend against affects as well as instinctual drives, and to serve adaptation in addition to contributing to symptom formation. Gradually it became apparent that all behavior, normal as well as pathological, includes in its composition some aspects of defense. At last we understood that, as with other concretizations in psychoanalysis, it is inaccurate, not to say potentially misleading, to think of defenses as if they are specific mental entities or structures. We are likely to continue to speak and write about defenses and defense mechanisms, but this is only our psychoanalytic shorthand: a way of discussing those aspects of mental functioning whose aim—you can see how difficult it is to avoid the shorthand—it is to eliminate or minimize unpleasure. In attempting to do so, they may oppose the affect itself, the instinctual drive derivatives which lead to unpleasure, superego threats or punishments, perceptions or memories of the external world, or modify some other aspect of ego functioning, or any combination of these elements, even all of them at once. They may, and frequently do, defend against other complex mental contents (unconscious fantasies, for instance) which themselves fulfill defensive functions, the balance perhaps varying according to where the greater unpleasure is concentrated at any given point in the life of the individual, or in the course of his or her analysis.

Withal, the concept of defense is inseparable from that of psychic conflict, since defenses are by definition tendencies that oppose other elements, and conflict means nothing more than a situation in which forces or elements are in opposition to one another. In the case of psychic conflict we add the qualification that the struggle takes place largely if not altogether outside of conscious awareness. Unconscious instinctual conflict is the core discovery of psychoanalysis, in a sense the very ground from which it has sprung. We have learned that it exerts an influence on every aspect, normal as well as pathological, of the activities of the mental apparatus. Upon this finding rests the claim of psychoanalysis to be a depth psychology, and it is the basis for our conviction that psychoanalysis constitutes to date the most complete and satisfactory general psychology as well.

References

Arlow, J.A. (1961). Ego psychology and the study of mythology. *Journal of the American Psychoanalytic Association* 9:371–393.

——— (1966). Depersonalization and derealization in psychoanalysis: a general psychology. In: *Essays in Honor of Heinz Hartmann* ed. R. Loewenstein., et al. New York: International University Press, pp. 456–478.

——— (1969a). Unconscious fantasy and disturbances of conscious experience. *Psychoanalytic Quarterly* 38:1–27.

——— (1969b). Fantasy, memory, and reality testing. *Psychoanalytic Quarterly* 38:28–51.

——— (1972). The only child. *Psychoanalytic Quarterly* 41:507–536.

Brenner, C. (1974). On the nature and development of affects: a unified theory. *Psychoanalytic Quarterly* 43:532–556.

——— (1975). Affects and psychic conflict. *Psychoanalytic Quarterly* 44:5–28.

——— (1976). *Psychoanalytic Technique and Psychic Conflict.* New York: International University Press.

——— (1979). Depressive affect, anxiety, and psychic conflict in the phallicoedipal phase. *Psychoanalytic Quarterly* 48:177–197.

Fenichel, O. (1938). Review of The Ego and the Mechanisms of Defence by Anna Freud. *International Journal of Psycho-Analysis* 19:116–136.

Freud, A. (1936). *The Ego and the Mechanisms of Defence*. New York: International University Press, 1946.

Freud, S. (1923). The Ego and the Id. *Standard Edition* 19.

——— (1926). Inhibitions, Symptoms and Anxiety. *Standard Edition* 20.

Jones, E. (1938). Review of The Ego and the Mechanisms of Defence by Anna Freud. *International Journal of Psycho-Analysis* 19:115–116.

Kris Study Group (1978). *Psychoanalytic Considerations of Borderline States*. Unpublished.

Panel (1954). Defense mechanisms and psychoanalytic technique. E.R. Zetzel, reporter. *Journal of the American Psychoanalytic Association* 2:318–326.

Panel (1967a). Development and metapsychology of the defense organization of the ego. R.S. Wallerstein, reporter. *Journal of the American Psychoanalytic Association* 15:130–149.

Panel (1967b). Defense organization of the ego and psychoanalytic technique. E. Pumpian-Mindlin, reporter. *Journal of the American Psychoanalytic Association* 15:150–165 .

Panel (1970). The fate of the defenses in the psychoanalytic process. J. Krent, reporter. *Journal of the American Psychoanalytic Association* 18:177–194.

Schafer, R. (1968). The mechanisms of defence. *International Journal of Psycho-Analysis* 49:49–62.

Part IV:
Countertransference

CHAPTER 19

Serious Illness in the Analyst: Countertransference Considerations[1]

[Abend, S.M. (1982). *Journal of the American Psychoanalytic Association* 30:365–379]

Some years ago I had an illness that necessitated interruption of my practice for a number of weeks. There was a substantial interval between the establishment of the diagnosis and the actual institution of treatment, during which I was able to continue working, so there was ample opportunity for me to consult with colleagues about how best to handle the situation with my patients. As Dewald (1982) points out, the literature offers next to nothing of use on the subject, a fact which in itself requires explanation. I made notes on my patients' reactions to what I told them in anticipation of the break in our work together, and then again after its resumption. However, without much critical self-examination, I subsequently decided that what I had observed was not worth reporting. When the opportunity arose to discuss Dewald's excellent and courageous study, which focuses on his own as well as his patients' reactions, I was stimulated to reconsider my material and the reasons for having put it aside.

---

[1] Presented at the Fall Meeting of the American Psychoanalytic Association, New York, December, 1980.

It is my intention to raise certain questions about the technical management of these situations when they arise, and about the role of countertransference reactions in influencing technical decisions. I shall also attempt to demonstrate that some of those countertransference factors may play an underestimated role in contributing to analysts' evident difficulty in studying and reporting on the problem.

For the sake of clarity, it will be necessary for me to make a few comments on the subject of countertransference in general, and on the so-called reality relationship between analyst and patient. As important and interesting as both topics are, I have no intention to treat either extensively, nor even to attempt to present arguments for my views. I merely wish to avoid possible misunderstandings and to provide an accurate framework for the discussion of the specific issues related to illness in the analyst with which this paper is concerned.

The term "transference" should be understood to denote all the influences of unconscious mental forces—that is to say, the wishes, fears, and defenses of infantile origin, and the complex compromises to which they give rise—on the analysand's relationship to the analyst, as it is perceived, remembered, wished for, and enacted. These vary at different times, ranging from being silent and undetected to becoming so blatantly manifest as to totally dominate the clinical picture, and hence command the full attention of analyst and patient. Regardless of the apparent intensity, or clinical significance of the moment, transference forces are ubiquitous, since they are manifestations of a fundamental and omnipresent feature of human mental activity. Our term for them derives from Freud's initial grasp of the essential feature that they originate in the individual's childhood experiences and relationships.

My view of countertransference is that it is a full counterpart of this broad understanding of transference. It includes the impact of the analyst's unconscious mental life—all of the residua of childhood instinctual conflicts—on his or her analytic activity with each patient. Once again, this should be thought of as a ubiquitous factor that affects the analyst's work at all times. In optimal circumstances, its interference is minimal, negligible, or easily corrected with the aid of our habitual self-scrutiny. More limited definitions of countertransference as denoting only those unconscious reactions stimulated by the patients'[2] material are less useful, I think, since they suggest a fundamental distinction that is misleading. When they are of significance in the analytic situation, countertransference forces mobilized by events in the analyst's life have the same nature, composition, and effects as those stimulated by the patient. They are detectable, and hence correctable, only by the same means—self-analytic activity.

The reality relationship between analyst and analysand presumably refers to those features of their contact reflective of their mutual status as adults engaged in a specific activity—psychoanalysis—which has certain agreed-upon goals and features of conduct. Many aspects of their interactions with one another can of course be designated as derived from this adult dimension of their relationship, but analysts vary greatly in the way they think about this undeniable fact, and in how their views influence technique. My own position is that, for all practical purposes, the reality relationship is always experienced by the analysand (and the analyst, too, of course, though we hope to a lesser degree) as inextricably intertwined with its unconscious reverberations and meanings. It is to these latter that the analyst's attention should always be directed. Here I differ, in degree at least, with Dewald (1982) and many other colleagues as well. In my opinion, optimal analytic technique is more likely to suffer from an analyst's explicit focus, in conjunction with the analysand, on the reality relationship than it will from the analyst's insistence on attending to its unconscious meanings instead.

From the foregoing, it can readily be seen that I would seriously question the validity of certain distinctions. For example, it has been suggested that some emotional reactions stirred up in the analyst by major events, such as life-threatening illness, ought not to be regarded as countertransference, but as a sort of "normal" emotional turmoil. These are certainly normal in the sense of being usual, or unsurprising in the circumstances. However, the nature of the upheaval produced

---

[2] Presented at the Fall Meeting of the American Psychoanalytic Association, New York, December, 1980.

by such events will be specific for each individual, largely on the basis of its unconscious significance. In their composition and in their potential effect on analyzing capacity, these reactions are in no way distinguishable from other responses we unequivocally consider to be countertransference manifestations. In that sense, "normality" can only express a retrospective judgment that some reactions did not (in more-or-less ideal situations) adversely hamper analytic functioning.

Likewise, it is artificial to attempt to separate analysands' "realistic" perceptions, thoughts, worries, and judgments about the analyst and the analytic situation from unconsciously determined transference reactions. This is not to deny that there are real events which have an impact on the analytic situation, or that analysands, as well as analysts, possess the capacity to perceive and think about things realistically. I mean merely to emphasize that what is "real" for every patient is what that patient observes, feels, thinks, wishes, fears, wonders about, and decides by means of the operations of a mental apparatus of which the *unconscious* component[3] is invariably a significant part, just as is true for every analyst. While we surely attempt to keep reality factors in mind in our work, they should never be exempt from the general rule of paying attention to the unconscious component.

Dewald (1982) has summarized the very scanty literature applicable to the topic of the emotional consequences of the analyst's illness on analytic work. He has also documented quite convincingly the important role of denial and its potentially injurious effect on practice. His descriptions of the narcissistic concerns, the fears of vulnerability and of loss of capacities, the financial worries, and the guilt about enforced neglect of patients' needs when we are ill are all familiar to me and, I am certain, to others who have had similar experiences. I agree, too, with his observations about the effect of illness-induced regression on the relatively mature functions and capacities essential for the adequate performance of our workaday tasks as analysts.

---

[3] For a more complete exposition of this point of view see Brenner (176, especially pp. 29–33, 119–130. See also Stein (1981) for an excellent clinical demonstration of the value of this approach to analytic technique.

My own experience was more favorable than Dewald's in that I was able to handle personally all communications to my patients before and after my illness. However, my observations on analytic patients who had had other experiences with analysts who became ill or died has convinced me that, as Dewald has stated, a knowledge of what was actually told patients, by whom, and under what circumstances is helpful in understanding and analyzing their responses to such events.

The countertransference issues of the post-illness phase are especially important. I am aware of the desire to return to work in order to restore one's confidence and self-esteem through competent activity, and of the uncomfortable resonances patients' expressions of doubts and fears regarding the analyst's intactness may arouse. A subtle reluctance to surrender the "legitimized" gratifications of illness and convalescence, that is, enforced passivity, helplessness, and dependency, may influence an analyst to delay his return to work. More likely, however, reaction formations against these regressive gratifications may encourage taking on work burdens somewhat sooner than is medically or psychologically desirable. Finally, I agree that the technical handling of patients' responses after analysis has been resumed provides a field for the expression of the analyst's wishes to be reassured that he or she was missed, needed, and appreciated, and for the gratification of exhibitionistic and masochistic preoccupations as well.

My observations are also completely in accord with those of Dewald on an essential point with important implications for technique. He amply documents that the meaning of the interruption, of the analyst's illness, and of any observable alteration which persists is different for each patient. It is responded to by every analysand according to his unconscious disposition, which is another way of saying according to the state of the transference. As I have indicated, where I may differ with Dewald and others is with regard to the question of whether there are other factors in addition to the transference meanings that need to be taken into account by the analyst in handling the situation with patients. I fully agree with Dewald (1982) that, "The therapeutic problem lies in the need adequately to explore the full gamut of patients' responses, affects, and associations to the illness, and to do this in the face of countertransference temptations, either defensively to promote premature closure and evasion of more threatening affects, or to use the experience for exhibitionistic, masochistic, narcissistic or other neurotic satisfactions" (p. 361). As a general statement, this is a prescription with which few analysts would quibble, but precisely how is one best to pursue this worthwhile aim? Dewald has modestly refrained from recommendations; instead, he told what he did, which was to vary his approach to suit the needs of each of his patients, according to his best clinical judgment. The crux of the matter rests in how much factual information should be provided. It is my contention that the chief significance of the powerful countertransference elements mobilized by the analyst's experience of serious illness is their tendency to influence analytic technique. This means, among other things, that the very clinical judgment relied upon to assess the specific needs of patients (with respect to how well they can maintain analytic productivity in the absence of factual information) is exactly what is under pressure from the countertransference; at no other time is the analyst's judgment about this technical problem *less* likely to be objective and reliable. Countertransference reactions are liable to affect the analyst's perception, understanding, capacity for instinctual control, and judgment in subtle, or sometimes not so subtle ways, and therefore may well color his opinion of his patients' needs and capabilities.

In the years since my own experience with illness, I have discussed this technical problem with many able colleagues, some with formidable analytic experience and highly respected clinical and theoretical judgment. Each was interested in talking about the subject and had given it thought. Many acknowledged some uncertainty or dissatisfaction with their management of these situations. Almost to a man, they had arrived at something equivalent to Dewald's solution, *i.e.*, providing some factual information, varied in timing and dosage according to their assessment of each patient's needs. There apparently exists a sort of common-sense consensus as to management, yet the impression of malaise about it and the paucity of reported observations, not to mention thoughtful studies in the literature, support my view that countertransference issues which are particularly difficult to examine play a role greater than hitherto suspected in determining both the technical handling and the reluctance to write about such events.

The essential argument to be considered asserts that while too much factual information may inhibit the range of expression of patients' reactions, and thereby constitute an interference with analyzing fully, too little information may, for some patients at least, prove too burdensome, thus serving to limit the analysis of transference fantasies. It seems advisable to consider the potential countertransference motives for modifying the principle of abstinence in such situations. We are, in general, committed to the technical precept that it is the *patient's* thoughts, feelings, and fantasies that matter—nothing else; and our uniform clinical experience confirms that each patient reacts to the analyst's illness in unique and personal ways. What is the beneficial effect of revealing anything more informative than the fact of interruption and the scheduling of the resumption of sessions? What is the basis for deciding that specific information relieves unbearable anxiety? If we tell some patients something in advance (when possible) it must be on the grounds that prior assessments of their problems and capacities have dictated this approach. If, on the other hand, we succumb after the fact to their importuning for information, what marks these clinical situations as different from others in which our schedules, appearance, or general habits may have been changed for different reasons, in the wake of which we would be less inclined to provide analogous explanations?

It would be correct to assert that *not* to provide information, or answer questions about the interruption, or change in appearance, also has meaning to patients. However, we are accustomed to paying analytic attention to their reactions under those circumstances, and are therefore likely at least to attempt to understand the unconscious significance of not telling. On the other hand, the act of telling something has meaning and reverberations independent of the specific facts revealed. If we think of the communication as simply "realistic," made in response to the clinical assessment of the patient's needs, we may be less likely to pay attention to its unconscious meaning. Telling something can be a way to convey a covert message from the analyst, which may be more or less correctly received; it can also have significance for the analysand quite distinct from the covert communication, and that also would be very important to analyze.

Some of the hidden messages which might possibly be carried by means of giving factual information about the analyst's condition are relatively easy to indicate. For example, when we are ill, or recuperating, or in the aftermath of such disruptions, we do not consciously intend to dilute or deflect our patients' anger at us, but it may be harder than usual to bear when one is, or has been, seriously ill, and frightened or uncertain of one's strength and capacities. We would not intentionally ask our patients to be caring, sympathetic, and concerned about us, but telling them of our troubles may be a subtle way of doing just that. The regressive impact of pain, illness, injury, and danger can influence us unconsciously to invite such responses. Certainly we would not knowingly tell our patients they should or should not worry about our well-being or survival, nor ask them to reassure us. Yet are these not liable to be implicit messages contained in the giving of factual information about our condition, treatment, or prognosis?

Furthermore, the weight we assign to the psychic burden of vivid fantasies of death or mutilation must be affected by our own unconscious conflicts. These elements are enmeshed in the nuclear oedipal and preoedipal wishes and fears in all of us; they are bound to be stirred anew, in analysts as in others, by illness or injury. Under such circumstances, cool, reasoned, objective judgments are not favored. To admit this to ourselves constitutes a fundamental recognition of an analyst's humanity and limitations, which may have more important consequences for the conduct of analysis than does acknowledgment of specific reality events. At times it may actually be easier on the analyst to make patients privy to his or her personal plight than it would be to deal with patients' fully expressed fantasies and feelings; this choice is subject to rationalization on the grounds that the patients' interest is served by such sharing.

This list of possible complicating aspects of the transmission of factual information about the analyst's condition is merely a partial one. Many others will no doubt occur to practicing analysts upon reflection.

The above illustrations came readily to mind, based on my own experience and self-observations and on discussions with colleagues.

I had reached the decision before the interruption occasioned by my illness to provide no factual information about the reason for my enforced absence to analytic patients, and indeed was able to maintain this posture and to work productively with their individual transference elaborations of the anticipated break in schedule during that period. If anything, my own anxiety was allayed by my holding on to the familiar and far more comfortable role of physician, attentive to and concerned about the anxieties and illnesses of others, not my own. A couple of psychotherapy patients, both too ill to work with in a conventional analytic mode, and with whom transference interpretation was at all times more restricted, were told some of the facts. My impression was that this knowledge served to limit their freedom to express anger and concern for their own needs, but I cannot be certain that it would have been otherwise had I not given them the information.

I fully intended to continue my non-revelatory stance with my analysands upon the resumption of work; to my surprise, that proved all but impossible. Like Dewald, I returned bearing clearly visible signs of my recent experience, and I knew that my patients' reactions would be influenced by the change in my appearance. One of my patients was an adolescent whose father died during his childhood; he had repressed all awareness of the visual evidence of the progressive wasting illness that had killed him. I decided, before resuming work, the boy should be prepared for my altered appearance, and so said something about it to him when I telephoned to set the date for resuming sessions. The results were ambiguous at best. This youngster misinterpreted what he saw and what I said. Although some useful analytic work could be done with the reasons for this confusion and his reluctance to pay attention to the facts, the analysis on this point was not fully satisfactory. However, this does illustrate how imperative the need was to abandon the stance of restricting my interventions to interpretation, and how soon it influenced my clinical judgment.

Within three days after I began to see patients I had found equally compelling reasons to tell all but two of my analytic patients something factual about my illness. Several were in the field of medicine and had obviously noted the evidence of my having been ill. They either drew, or conspicuously avoided drawing, the conclusion that I might be irreparably damaged or even dying. Those I told what had actually occurred; others, I simply informed that I would recover fully.

Those patients to whom I did not tell anything factual did perfectly well. Of those I told, some disbelieved me, others distorted what they noted or what I had said, some complained of being told anything, others about not being told more; in short, each reacted to what I said or did not say in his own way. As I regained a more usual state of mind, I was profoundly impressed by the fact that it had proven impossible to do as I had intended with the majority of my analytic patients. In fact, I had ended by doing exactly as Dewald and many other colleagues had done: that is, I had attempted to assess each patient's needs on an individual basis. In retrospect, however, I believe that my assessments were neither accurate nor objective. I can only reach the conclusion that my own countertransferences, rather than a correct appraisal of what was best for each patient's analysis, decided me to provide factual information.

Consider, for example, one patient, a young psychiatrist, who had suffered very much in childhood as a result of prolonged separation from her father and repeated brief separations from her mother. Her reactions to my planned vacations and to occasional cancellations at relatively short notice had always expressed important transference material in the past. Much that was familiar, related to separations, had returned to prominence during the period just before the interruption. After we resumed, my appearance reminded her of the ill, malnourished look of her father upon his return to the family. She seemed very upset, but my telling her what had actually been wrong with me led to an unexpected outburst of anger. She interpreted my comments as a sign that I felt she could not tolerate not knowing the truth, as, she imagined, all my other stronger, more capable patients could. With some bitterness, she added that she had done well in my absence, as compared with previous times, and was feeling much worse since my return. This led to the uncovering of the fact that she alone, as she believed, of all her family, had not missed her father much, and had not been altogether pleased and relieved to have him return. She had subsequently felt extremely guilty because of these responses, which she had kept secret. Her guilt had been compounded by his evident illness.

Her initial angry reaction to my telling her what had actually happened to me turned out to be an attempt to defend herself against her unconscious reaction to this communication, which she had perceived as an accusation along the following lines: "I have been very ill, and you alone of all the children did not care enough to cry." That was what was behind her thought that she had been singled out to be told the facts.

A case could be made for the proposition that my telling her what had happened had a beneficial, if serendipitous, effect insofar as it served to bring to light important material. Perhaps the essential material would have emerged in any case, perhaps not; in analysis that question can never be answered with absolute certainty. It may also be true that I had misjudged her situation. I present this incident merely to illustrate how erroneous the basis for a judgment to reveal factual information can be. The assumption of a "realistic" processing of the interchange ignores the inevitable truth that it will be understood primarily in terms of its unconscious ramifications for the patient. In this case, the nature of her reactions led to useful analytic work, and no harm was done, so far as I am aware, to the subsequent course of the analysis. We have no assurance that this will invariably be the case, and no reliable way to predict when the results will be less than desirable.

The factor of visual evidence of the illness presents particular problems for both analyst and patient, but my experience suggests that these, like the meaning of the interruption itself, resist generalization. The meanings evoked, to each practitioner and analysand, are special and individual. While one would naturally expect narcissistic, exhibitionistic and scoptophilic concerns to be heightened by the phenomenon of altered appearance, their expression is extremely variable, and other related issues may be crucial. As I observed the reactions of my own patients, it was most impressive to me how even those with medical training misperceived and misinterpreted what they observed.

Attempting to analyze their distortions was both fascinating and instructive; in my opinion it is doubtful that providing correct information facilitates this task any more than factually correcting other kinds of transference misperceptions is advantageous to the analysis of their significance (Stein, 1966; Abend, 1982).

The analysis of patients' fears that the analyst can no longer function capably or may be at risk of imminent death poses one sort of problem when there is no substantive basis for them, as understood by the analyst, and another, very much more complex problem, when such fears correspond to the realities at hand. Eissler (1975) addressed this problem. He expressed as an ideal that analysts would possess both the capacity and the maturity to assess their own situation accurately and to place patients' welfare above personal comfort. Unfortunately, we all recognize (and perhaps have observed) that countertransference may all too often interfere with the attainment of this desirable standard. While consultation with trusted colleagues may be helpful in cases of doubt, the judgment required will be a severe test for the consultant, who is likely to be tied to the inquiring analyst by bonds of friendship. Should the situation be such that the proper advice is that the analyst's infirmity is such that he should retire from practice, one can easily imagine the difficulty in making such a recommendation—all the more so if the consultant is no longer young and vigorous. The best one can say is that these are extremely difficult situations, for which there is often no truly satisfactory solution (Brenner, 1981, personal communication).

My own experience inclines me to the view that it is better for the conduct of analysis not to reveal factual information about the analyst's illness. Many colleagues, probably the majority, seem to believe that it is more useful to give some information, at least to some patients. My observations do not support an unequivocal decision in favor of either course, but they do suggest the need for more investigation of this subject.

In discussions with colleagues, I explored the rationale for their various clinical interventions. Some of the reactions to the questions I posed about why and when information is provided included responses which are at least consistent with my view of the role of unrecognized countertransference. A sense of uneasiness with respect to specific clinical instances was by no means unusual. On occasion, my queries seemed to give rise to the misinterpretation that I was suggesting that to give factual information under any circumstances means one is a "bad" analyst, or practices "improper" technique. In clinical work, we are accustomed to similar attributions of condemnation when interpretations bring to light unconscious wishes which are accompanied by hitherto unsuspected shame and guilt. The parallel suggests that similar affects, connected to unconscious countertransference gratifications, are being warded off. Needless to add, we are convinced of the ultimate value of unearthing hidden discomforts in our patients, and in ourselves, because it leads to an improved likelihood of arriving at more satisfactory solutions to problems with which they, and we, must deal.

To state that what we do in analyzing patients provides us with gratifications, conscious and unconscious, is merely to express a truism about mental life. We do not refrain from making interventions, or decide to make them, because either course provides us with satisfactions; we only hope, insofar as possible, to understand those factors that exert influence on our judgment in each case. The burden of proof ought always to be on the side of justification of departures from standard technique, rather than on that of its maintenance.

I am certainly sympathetic to the dilemma of the analyst who must determine how to deal with his patients' reactions to his serious illness. What I wish to emphasize is that we sorely lack reliable data to guide us in making assessments and decisions in managing these situations. Furthermore, the inescapable influence of countertransference factors operates precisely against the very objectivity on which we are accustomed to rely in reaching clinical judgments.

Dewald's pioneering effort, and the discussions to which it gave rise, were received with much interest. The paucity of such studies cannot be explained by denial and narcissistic avoidance alone, although these surely contribute in a major way to the discomfort this subject seems to arouse. My own experience suggests that an additional element may be at work. The transmission of factual information about the analyst's illness subserves unconscious needs in the analyst which may not always be recognized and acknowledged. This is so even when the analyst is convinced it is technically correct to provide such information, and independent of whether the conviction is warranted, even if subsequent analytic work appears unimpeded or even enhanced by the analyst's divulsion.

Analysts are understandably reluctant to disclose to colleagues what has gratified them, even unconsciously. In part, perhaps this is because of guilt at transgressing an analytic ideal, and in part because of residual discomfort about personal exposure of deep, nominally hidden aspects of their own psychological makeup. If I am correct in my assumptions, this reluctance helps to account for the evident disinclination to study, describe, and report on the problem of the technical management of the analyst's illness. This is especially unfortunate, since such observations are needed in order to provide reliable and convincing answers to the questions I have attempted to highlight. Under what circumstances, if any, and for which patients, if any, is it advantageous to provide factual information about the analyst's illness? What are the advantages of doing so? What are the difficulties attendant therein, and what problems ensue if information is not provided? We do not have definitive answers to these questions as yet. A thorough and honest attempt to illuminate this topic is long overdue, and its investigation will be of benefit to many analysts and their patients.

References

Abend, S.M. (1982). Some observations on reality testing as a clinical concept. *Psychoanalytic Quarterly* 51:218–237.

Brenner, C. (1976). *Psychoanalytic Technique and Psychic Conflict.* New York: International Universities Press.

Dewald, P. (1982). Serious illness in the analyst: transference, countertransference, and reality responses. *Journal of the American Psychoanalytic Association* 30:347–363.

Eissler, K.R. (1993). On possible effects of aging on the practice of psychoanalysis: An essay. *Psychoanalytic Inquiry* 13(3):316–332.

Stein, M.H. (1966). Self observation, reality, and the superego. In: *Psychoanalysis—A General Psychology: Essays in Honor of Heinz Hartmann* ed. R.M. Loewenstein, et al. New York: International University Press, pp. 275–297.

——— (1981). The Unobjectionable Part of the Transference. *Journal of the American Psychoanalytic Association* 29:869–892.

CHAPTER 20

Countertransference, Empathy, and the Analytic Ideal: The Impact of Life Stresses on Analytic Capability[1]

[Abend, S.M. (1986). *Psychoanalytic Quarterly* 55:563–575]

Abstract

Analysts' emotional attitudes toward countertransference issues are influenced by unduly perfectionistic ideals that are partly derived from the early period of psychoanalytic theory. Analysts' unconscious receptivity, whether of the beneficially empathic kind or the disadvantageous countertransference variety, is a reflection of a dynamic internal state. This fundamental relationship between empathy and countertransference is illustrated with examples. Important events that occur in the life of the analyst, by virtue of their impact on his own central compromise formations, cannot but affect his analytic functioning. Minor disturbances in analytic capability are commonplace and do not significantly handicap effective work.

---

[1] An earlier version of this paper was presented as the introduction to a panel discussion, "Stresses in the Life Cycle of the Analyst," at the Regional Meeting of the Psychoanalytic Societies of the New York area and New Haven, Southbury, Connecticut, October 13–14, 1985.

My participation in a conference devoted to an examination of the nature of the stresses that various life events impose upon analysts' analytic functioning stimulated me to look for features which might be common to all such situations. I reached the conclusion, which will not surprise any experienced colleague, that fluctuation in the quality of the contribution of the analyst's own unconscious to his analytic tasks constitutes the critical factor; its vicissitudes will require more detailed and thorough study.

To state my thesis more precisely, a network of compromise formations, which reflect the analyst's own important unconscious conflicts, contributes vitally to his empathic capability and his interpretive skills, but it is anything but a fixed, autonomous, unvarying aspect of his psychological makeup. It is influenced by events and situations in the analyst's life, just as it is by the behaviors and productions of his patients. The relationship between analysts' countertransference potential and empathic variability needs to be clarified. I hope to illuminate some of these interrelationships in this presentation.

All analysts are familiar with the everyday exigencies of analytic practice. We are obliged to sharply curtail the instinctual gratifications permissible in our interactions with patients, to maintain a uniquely difficult kind of attention, delicately poised between the patient's productions and our own internal psychic activities, and to sustain a genuine neutrality toward whatever each analysand brings forth, regardless of our personal preferences, ethics, and values. Above all, we struggle to retain an attitude of patient confidence in the analytic method in the face of resistances, obscurity, repetition, ambiguity, and those familiar upsurges of doubt and despair which arise from our patients, and periodically from within ourselves as well. Finally, we somehow have to meld the authority that our arcane knowledge of the unconscious and our traditional role as healer confers upon us with an appropriate respect for the manifold capabilities as well as the limitations of each patient, as we attempt to forge with them the unique partnerships that compose successful analytic enterprises.

We are entitled to regard these formidable requirements as burdensome. Despite our conjoint familiarity with the problems mentioned, many of us also seem to bear yet another burden; that is the secret, irrational, but persistent conviction that each of us alone feels these burdens far more than is proper, and far more than do our colleagues. This is true, although we regularly reassure one another that, on the contrary, these feelings are shared by all of us. Why should that be so? Among the answers to that question is the fundamental issue which I propose to address in this paper.

Every one of the qualities I mentioned—instinctual restraint, evenly hovering attention, neutrality, patience, confidence, and narcissistic balance—places a *constant*, rather than intermittent, strain on analysts' psychic functioning. Our hard-earned ability to perform analytic work is subject to pressure during every hour we spend with patients. On the face of it, it is inconceivable that any one of us can sustain an optimum level of functioning in anything remotely like an absolutely unvarying state. Why, then, do we appear so prepared to expect it of ourselves, and believe it of our peers?

Part of the problem is the residual propensity we seem to have for unconscious narcissistic fantasies of perfection, with which we invest others and toward which we continue to aspire, since derivatives of them contribute to the formation of our personal analytic ideals and idealizations. Another aspect of the problem rests on an incompletely resolved dichotomy in our theoretical models, which reinforces the persistence of unrealistic and unrealizable analytic ideals.

The Freud of *Analysis Terminable and Interminable* (1937) speaks of the attainments of analysis and the mutability of instinctual conflict in a voice far different from that which expressed the categorical enthusiasm of the early years of discovery (see especially pp. 228-230). The conceptual language he used in the early papers, and for some years to follow, clearly implied that an absolute distinction could be drawn between pathology and normality. Repressions were to be lifted, fixations removed, transference neuroses resolved, libido enabled to find new channels for discharge, and pathological neurotic transferences differentiated from the useful benign ones.

Even after the introduction of the structural hypothesis and the revision of anxiety theory, which led to a new technical emphasis on defense analysis and eventually to the birth of what became known as ego psychology, there was at first no impact on the original, absolutist, medically derived model of health versus disease, or psychological normality versus psychopathology. Although clinical experience must have dictated the recognition that perfectionistic curative goals were all but impossible to attain, they continued nevertheless to influence both theory and aspirations.

All of which leads me to the conclusion that we may also have a tendency to believe, more than is justified by experience, that our personal analyses should somehow have managed to equip us to be freer than we actually are from the variability of functioning and from the persistence or reappearance of certain of the less desirable patterns of thought, emotionality, and behavior that are derived from our infantile conflicts. Analysts' attitudes toward the subject of countertransference are to some extent an expression of this tendency, and of the rigid division between normal and abnormal that characterized the opening phase of analytic theory.

Just as Freud first thought that patients' transferences could be divided into neurotic, pathological ones and benign, useful ones, analysts' emotional reactions to their patients have been divided along similar lines. Those responses determined by the analysts' own conflicts and leading to blind spots and distorted perceptions, to misunderstandings or even misbehaviors, have always been regarded as countertransferences. Other of the analysts' emotional responses are considered to be induced by the nature of the material presented by patients. These take several different forms. One variety consists of those responses unconsciously sought by the patient from the analyst, such as sympathy for suffering, erotic attraction and interest, or condemnation for guilty wishes. Another type consists of feeling states induced in the analyst because the patient behaves toward the analyst as some significant figure in the past behaved toward the patient, so that unconsciously the analysand wishes the analyst to feel as he or she once did in certain situations. Still other reactions would be classified simply as empathic responses to the patient's present or past feeling states, in keeping with the associational material. All of these latter types of emotional reactions of the analyst, if properly identified and understood, are of use in formulating interventions. They constitute a vital part of the analyst's armamentarium in performing the requisite tasks of conducting analyses.

There is a certain appealing rationale for continuing to distinguish analysts' emotional responses that more or less accurately reflect something going on in the patient, and thus aid in doing analytic work, from those that stem primarily from their own conflicts and therefore affect understanding and technique unfavorably. As a practical matter, we are often able to examine specific instances of analysts' responses and readily assign them either to the empathic group that is useful or to that which interferes with the progress of analyzing, the countertransferences.

I will not attempt to summarize the arguments that have been presented in favor of retaining a limited definition of countertransference and that appear in the substantial literature on the subject. However, it is interesting to note that even aspects of analysts' functioning which are usually seen as positive, such as attentive listening, can in certain instances be demonstrated to be countertransference manifestations, even in the strictest sense of that term, as Jacobs (1986) has recently demonstrated. His astute observation points to the very heart of the conceptual fallacy which complicates our view of the analyst's responsiveness.

I think we have failed to assimilate fully our current state of knowledge about the nature of mental activity into our views on empathy and countertransference. Analytic observations have demonstrated that the complex network of compromise formations, which are the resultants of infantile instinctual conflicts, form the basis of adult functioning which is classified as normal, as well as that which is pathological (Brenner, 1982). In order that I not be misunderstood, let me emphasize that this statement is not meant to dismiss physiological variability, inherent differences in capability, primary autonomies, or developmental experiences as vital contributors to outcome. All of those factors, however, are incorporated, just as are individual life circumstances and experiences, into the unique syntheses of the fundamental issues of childhood mental life which form the universal core of adult psychology.

More to the point, all of our self-knowledge dictates the admission that this synthesis is a *dynamic*, not a static one, in which aspects of psychic activity are in a constant state of flux. Not even the most successful personal analysis renders a person immune to recrudescences of those earlier compromise formations, in the form of symptoms, emotional states, patterns of discharge or inhibition, or distortions of memory, perception, or reality testing, which are closer to the infantile and the neurotic than are those forms which typify one's most mature and adaptive functioning. Larger variations of our state of integration, even of relatively short duration, are likely to catch our attention and perhaps be noticed by others as well. Variations of the same basic nature, which may be thought of as being of smaller amplitude, are part of the experience of everyday psychic life and contribute to its quality of infinite variety. The impact of daily events, inner as well as outer, plays upon our psychic integration and produces those fluctuations of mood, thought, and behavior which are part of our so-called normal personalities. Since our receptivity and reactivity to our analysands depends upon our own psychic balance, how can we imagine that this "analyzing instrument," as Isakower liked to call it, is unaffected by its constantly shifting dynamism?

Freud knew early on that analysts' capacity to understand patients rests upon our sharing with them an essentially similar unconscious mental life. He spoke, quite literally, of the analyst's unconscious tuning into that of the analysand.[2] Such experiences are a vivid part of our work. But if our own resistances to understanding our

---

[2] In "Recommendations to Physicians Practising Psycho-Analysis" (1912), he stated: "To put it in a formula: [the analyst] must turn his own unconscious like a receptive organ towards the transmitting unconscious of the patient. He must adjust himself to the patient as a telephone receiver is adjusted to the transmitting microphone. Just as the receiver converts back to sound-waves the electric oscillations in the telephone line which were set up by sound waves, so the doctor's unconscious is able, from the derivatives of the unconscious which are communicated to him, to reconstruct that unconscious, which has determined the patient's free associations" (pp. 115–116).

conflicts are not completely abolished by analysis, and if our propensity for regressive alterations of function does not disappear once and for all at the conclusion of the training analysis, this crucial receptive capacity is, of necessity, anything but a constant and unvarying function.

Perhaps what I have said appears to be belaboring the obvious, because it must be so familiar to every practicing analyst. Yet the conclusion to which it leads me is not necessarily regarded as obvious to all. It is that the identical psychological abilities and functions that provide an analyst with his essential empathic capability also constitute his potential for countertransference. Empathy and countertransference are distinguished by their *result*, that is to say, by the degree of accuracy of responsivity, and not by the nature of the forces in operation in the analyst's unconscious. In the analytic situation, to put it bluntly, countertransference is empathy when the analyst is wrong.

Of course, there is more to be said of both countertransference and empathy than what is encompassed by a study of their interrelationship. More is involved in an analyst's ability to understand and formulate his patients' emotional difficulties than his unconscious receptivity or his understanding of his own conflicts and compromise formations may provide. If that were not the case, there would be no need for psychoanalytic education; the training analysis alone would suffice. For our present purposes, I am confining my attention to the aspect of countertransference potential and of empathic capability that derives directly from the influence of the analyst's own unconscious mental life.

Perhaps it is easiest to illustrate the differences to which I refer by reflecting back to the early days of a psychoanalytic career, when the analyst is still a candidate immersed in his personal analysis. Surely everyone has had the experience of clarifying some aspect of his own difficulties and then immediately recognizing a related issue in the theretofore obscure analytic material being presented by a patient. On occasion, however, and I presume this is not so unusual either, I can recall the experience of believing that I had uncovered such thematic material as I had freshly encountered in myself in the associations of several of my patients simultaneously. The latter discovery invariably turned out to be a continuing manifestation of my own resistance. The belief, at the time of the occurrence, that it represented a broadening of my empathic capability, which was transiently quite as convincing to me as in other cases where that turned out to be valid, was in fact a bit of self-deception, *i.e.*, a countertransference distortion.

Specific illustrations of the favorable and unfavorable effects of the analyst's compromise formations on his analyzing capability are not easy to provide. I will draw upon a combination of personal experience and consultation with others to present roughly comparable instances which will, I hope, demonstrate the complexities involved.

A woman in her twenties was raised by a vague, passive, and ineffectual mother and a domineering, violent father who deteriorated into frank psychosis during her adolescence. Early in her analysis, many scenes of distressing interaction with her father were described with a relative absence of affective coloration. The analyst noted within himself responses of mounting dismay and anger at the patient's father while listening to this material. These served as cues to explore the woman's intense fear of her father and subsequently her rage at him as well; both affects had been largely repressed after his dramatic death, itself a product of his psychosis. The analyst's emotional responses were, in part at least, a manifestation of rescue fantasies derived from his own oedipal development. Although these compromise formations did not correspond exactly to the patient's situation as she described it, the unconscious links nevertheless provided important clues to warded-off aspects of the analysand's mental life.

In another clinical situation, a compelling need to rescue victims and condemn sadistic fathers, also derived from powerful unconscious forces within the analyst, promoted an identification with the patient that dictated selective interpretation of the victimized stance and effectively blinded the analyst for a long time to the provocative, masochistic elements in his analysand, despite advice from colleagues regarding the material.

To return to the first case: Later in the course of the young woman's analysis, the sadomasochistic erotic charge that had also accompanied the incidents with her disturbed father that had been reported earlier in the analysis, along with the patient's provocative contributions to some of them and her powerful, unsatisfied wish to have been rescued by her mother, all emerged clearly in the material. It seems most likely that this progression reflected the usual course of analysis, in which meanings deepen in accordance with the patient's growing ability to reveal and comprehend ever more complex and disturbing unconscious elements. However, the aspects of the incidents with her father that were dealt with later also corresponded more closely with elements of the analyst's related unconscious conflicts and compromise formations. It cannot be ruled out that the timing of the interpretive sequence was therefore also influenced to some degree by that correspondence. To the extent that that might have been the case, the analyst's unconscious contributions could be said to have affected both his empathic responses and his countertransference ones. It is not illogical to assume, given the nature of the unconscious forces involved, that some admixture, of varying dimensions, is often true of the operation of the analyzing instrument.

While all of this may be most readily observed when we look at the receptive side of analysts' interactions with patients, a moment's reflection indicates that the situation is the same on the expressive side of things as well. Both the analyst's accurate and productive interventions and the undesirable countertransference ones are in equal measure derived from and influenced by the analyst's unconscious. Of course, we use our best rational judgment to decide whether the evidence of the patients' associational material supports our intuitive responses and justifies the comment we intend to make. Our theoretical knowledge also contributes to how we time and phrase our remarks to patients; otherwise, we would be practitioners of wild analysis. However, neither theoretical convictions nor rational judgment are immune to influence from the shifting unconscious balance of forces of which the psychic activity of the analyst is composed, as I have noted in describing countertransference considerations when the analyst is, or has been, ill (Abend, 1982).

I will now attempt, in a schematic way, to illustrate the ubiquitous, necessarily unavoidable, nature of the potential for impingement on analytic functioning of events that may occur in the analyst's life. Such events as the illness and death of a parent, spouse, child, or close friend are more than merely worrisome and distracting to the analyst. Aspects of one's relationship to the individual in question are stirred up and are bound to affect one's sensitivity and responses in various ways. For instance, if one is grieving, it can be extraordinarily difficult to maintain an empathic, nonjudgmental stance toward an analysand who is caught up in expressing hostile, derogatory, or embittered feelings toward an analogous figure in his own life. It may be just as problematic to respond objectively to the analysand's expressions of love or longing toward such a person. Even if one is merely more restricted than usual in one's emotional responsivity, the transference is likely to be affected, thus complicating still further the analytic situation. In other cases, patients' wishes for sympathy, comfort, and care about whatever concerns them may also be responded to differently than usual, if the analyst is struggling with the upsurge of comparable needs as part of his reaction to such traumatic events as those indicated. Similar emotional scenarios could be drawn up around other important events which may occur in the life of the analyst, such as divorce, serious emotional problems in a relative, or more commonplace family crises, such as the departure from home or the marriage of children, unusual financial burdens, fulfilled or disappointed ambitious goals of one's own or one's family members, and so on.

It is not only such notable happenings which produce the inner effects that disturb our equilibrium, and perhaps the way we work analytically. It is not an exaggeration to say that some degree of alteration in our capacity to analyze is an everyday problem, albeit of only slight extent, since less notable and dramatic events than those mentioned above also have an impact. A quarrel with one's spouse, an unanticipated and perhaps worrisome demand on one's time or material resources, a minor illness, or even the aftermath of a night of excessive conviviality, all produce shifts in one's mood, and alteration, if only temporarily, in the matrix of compromise formations which forms our personality and determines in large measure the quality and sensitivity of the analyzing instrument. These cannot but affect the way we practice analysis, day to day, patient to patient; none of us can be fully immune to that minor, yet potentially significant, variability.

Since the analytic situation exposes us constantly to the instinctual conflicts of our patients and makes us the target of their primitive wishes and demands, we cannot afford to disregard the fluctuations in our inner lives in the way that those working in other professions apparently can without incurring comparable risk of impaired functioning. Our own conflicts are being impinged upon by the nature of our work, as well as by the events in our daily lives, and it is a continuous necessity for us to attend to, and struggle against, our own resistances, and those of our reactive patterns that complicate the proper conduct of analysis. That, I submit, is the true nature of the burden and stress of analytic practice, at all stages in the life cycle of the analyst.

In conclusion, it should be noted that to acknowledge the persistence of the variable quality of the integration of analysts' unconscious mentation need not lead us to pessimistic assessments of our effectiveness. It is certainly true that there are constant alterations in the nature of our compromise formations; and that life events play a role in those fluctuations. Our ability to perform our analytic tasks is, to be sure, affected to some degree by this variability in the analyzing instrument. However, unless the departure from a satisfactory level of functioning is very marked, or persists for an extended period, or both, analytic competence is maintained. I referred earlier to the important role that fantasies of perfection play in the formation of analytic ideals and standards. To expect of ourselves that we should become, and remain, free of all internal changeability as a condition for maintaining satisfactory professional self-esteem is, indeed, to make psychoanalysis into one of the "Impossible Professions."

The facts of observation indisputably demonstrate that our work is not impossible at all, merely difficult. The restrictions that result from analysts' psychological variability in sensitivity, comprehension, judgment, and control are, within rather generous limits, compatible with successful analytic activity. To be sure, progress even in the best of cases is unnervingly gradual and slow, with missteps and hard stretches to which we, as well as our patients, contribute. Every analyst, in the course of his psychoanalytic education and subsequent professional maturation, has to come to terms with those limitations on our wishes that both analysis and analysts could be more powerful, more perfect, and more ideal than is actually possible. Freud specifically addressed this question in considerable detail in *Analysis Terminable and Interminable* (1937, see especially Section VII, pp. 247–250). It may be appropriate to conclude this presentation with a brief quotation from that discussion: "Analysts are people who have learned to practise a particular art; alongside of this, they may be allowed to be human beings like anyone else" (p. 247).

References

Abend, S.M. (1982). Serious illness in the analyst: countertransference considerations. *Journal of the American Psychoanalytic Association* 30:365–379.

Brenner, C. (1982). *The Mind in Conflict.* New York: International Universities Press.

Freud, S. (1912). Recommendations to physicians practising psychoanalysis. *Standard Edition* 12.

——— (1937). Analysis terminable and interminable. *Standard Edition* 23.

Jacobs, T.J. (1986). On countertransference enactments *Journal of the American Psychoanalytic Association* 34:289–307.

CHAPTER 21

Countertransference and Psychoanalytic Technique

[Abend, S.M. (1989). *Psychoanalytic Quarterly* 58:374–395]

Abstract

This paper examines the evolution of the concept of countertransference, with particular emphasis on its relationship to psychoanalytic technique. Freud's original idea that countertransference means unconscious interference with an analyst's ability to understand patients has been broadened during the past forty years: current usage often includes all of the emotional reactions of the analyst at work. Some factors that have contributed to this shift are the introduction of the structural hypothesis, the impact of Kleinian and interpersonal schools on the theory of technique, the effect of analysts' experience in working with more severely ill patients, and the diffuse consequences of certain recent cultural and intellectual trends. The benefits, as well as some potential disadvantages, in this shift toward a more inclusive conceptualization are discussed.

The term countertransference, originally introduced by Freud in 1910 to designate interferences with the analyst's optimal functioning that are caused by residual pathological elements in his or her own psychological makeup, has in the last several decades gradually undergone a radical change of meaning. By way of illustration of the shift, countertransference has recently been quite plausibly, if somewhat tentatively defined by Slakter (1987) as a term that now denotes "all those reactions of the analyst to the patient that may help or hinder treatment" (p. 3). It will be my purpose to trace the steps in this evolution, indicating some of the controversy that has marked its progress. I shall also outline some factors that help to account for the change, and offer an assessment of its implications for psychoanalytic technique. My interest is less in definition than in identifying the factors that have shaped the present state of affairs, and in the complex issues that influence and are influenced by its emerging outline.

Freud wrote relatively little on the subject of countertransference. Here is an abbreviated version of his first remarks about it (1910):

> We have become aware of 'the counter-transference,' which arises in [the analyst] as a result of the patient's influence on his unconscious feelings, and we are almost inclined to insist that he shall recognize this counter-transference in himself and overcome it . . . we have noticed that no psycho-analyst goes further than his own complexes and internal resistances permit . . . (pp. 144–145).

Bear in mind that at this period in Freud's theoretical and technical development, his view of the analyst's role and activities was significantly less refined than what evolved later on as a result of his further experience. His initial remarks about countertransference are, however, fully consistent with the ideas expressed in his early papers on technique. In the first of these, published only two years later, Freud (1912) describes the importance of the physician's adopting an attitude of "evenly suspended attention," rather than conscious concentration, and, using the famous analogy of the telephone (pp. 115–116), he says that the analyst "must turn his own unconscious like a receptive organ towards the transmitting unconscious of the patient." It is reasonable to assume that he believed that the essential work of the analyst was first to recognize, and then to interpret to patients, those aspects of their unconscious mental lives that could be seen to contribute to their psychopathology.

Freud had already discovered the momentous significance of transference phenomena as a source of data, as resistance, and as a battleground for the therapeutic engagement. His clinical experience led him to advocate the value of the mirror-like stance and of the principle of abstinence. These technical precepts were designed to facilitate the clear expression of the patient's complexes—we would say conflicts—in the transference, so that the relevant unconscious material could most readily be identified by the analyst and interpreted to the patient. Analysts' familiarity with their own unconscious, and the implicit lowering of their own resistances that must accompany such self-awareness, were essential to their therapeutic effectiveness.

Thus, countertransferences were first conceptualized by Freud simply as those undesirable distorting influences that limited an analyst's ability to understand his or her patients' unconscious minds with accuracy and sensitivity. Freud cautioned would-be analysts against an excess of therapeutic zeal, as he did against attempting to exert either educational or moral influence on patients; but there is no indication in what he wrote at the time that he considered that analysts' possible failure to maintain the analytic posture he recommended might be a consequence of their countertransferences, although that is an assumption many of us today would take for granted. As far as I can tell, Freud thought of countertransferences exclusively as blockages to accurate listening to and understanding of the manifestations of the unconscious in patients' productions. Nothing he ever wrote on the subject later on suggests he substantially revised that formulation, although he did come to see that analysts would find it harder than he first imagined to maintain optimal self-awareness, and might need periodic re-analysis (1937) to assist them in doing so.

One factor that I believe should be regarded as an essential, albeit indirect, antecedent of the alteration of our view of countertransference is the introduction of the structural theory. Even though it took a decade or more for its revolutionary impact to be absorbed into the theory of technique (Fenichel, 1938; A. Freud, 1936), the ground was irreversibly changed with the publication of *The Ego and the Id* in 1923. That monograph and its sequel, *Inhibitions, Symptoms and Anxiety* (1926), laid the foundation for a more accurate understanding of what is really meant by technical neutrality, as well as for the subsequent development of the systematic analysis of unconscious elements of defense and of superego contributions to intrapsychic conflicts. The seeds were planted for the growth of ego psychology and its eventual advancement of our understanding of the complexities of unconscious mental functioning. Though it would take all of thirty years, or perhaps even longer, to be acknowledged, the intellectual nucleus was put in place for a revised, improved conceptual grasp of the relationship between normality and pathology, of character traits and symptom formation, of adaptation, sublimation, object relationships, and psychic development. The view that Freud held at the outset of his research that neurosis is a sequestered area of abnormality in an otherwise healthy personality, which held us in its appealing grip for so long, would eventually have to yield to the more realistic assessment of the complex and variable functioning of the psychic apparatus, in analyst and patient alike, that holds sway today. The explicit application of this fundamental reshaping of our views to our way of regarding countertransference, however, was a long time in coming.

A second factor that came to play a role in altering the meaning of countertransference was a consequence of the controversies that soon arose over Freud's theoretical position and technical principles. Ferenczi's (1921) advocacy of an active technique was merely the earliest of what seems like an endless series of challenges to Freud's opinion that the analyst should not seek to influence the patient's neurosis, except through the medium of interpretation. However, the only mention of countertransference in the book Ferenczi and Rank wrote together (1924), when the technical debate with Freud was already in full swing, referred to the possibility that analysts' narcissistic countertransferences might encourage patients to flatter them and/or to suppress criticisms of them. This is entirely consistent with the narrowly focused view of countertransference proffered by Freud. It would be left to subsequent challengers of Freudian theory and technique to explicitly modify the understanding of countertransference.

In Europe and later in South America, the followers of Melanie Klein, in particular, and others, like the British middle school, who were stimulated by her work, pressed for a broader, revised concept of countertransference. Meanwhile, in this country, Harry Stack Sullivan and his adherents, and subsequently all the schools of interpersonal and humanistic psychoanalysis, were also calling with increasing vigor for a new way of thinking about analysts' emotional reactions to their patients. A very few earlier papers, like one by the Balints in 1939, anticipate this emerging change, but most summaries of the countertransference debate pinpoint three papers, one by Winnicott which appeared in 1949, another by Paula Heimann, published in 1950, and the third by Margaret Little (1951), which came out a year later, as bringing the issue of countertransference to the forefront of theoretical attention. Heimann's is the most succinct statement of the new view, defining countertransference as "all the feelings which the analyst experiences towards his patient" (p. 81) and later stating, "My thesis is that the analyst's emotional response to his patient within the analytic situation represents one of the most important tools for his work. The analyst's countertransference is an instrument of research into the patient's unconscious" (p. 81). She goes on, "Our basic assumption is that the analyst's unconscious understands that of his patient. This rapport on the deep level comes to the surface in the form of feelings which the analyst notices in response to his patient, in his 'countertransference'" (p. 82). Finally, she expresses the idea that the analyst's countertransference is not only part and parcel of the analytic relationship, but it is "the patient's *creation*, it is a part of the patient's personality" (p. 83). It did not take very long for sides to be drawn up and theoretical passions to be unleashed.

Suddenly the journals were flooded with articles elaborating the contending positions. Since the push to expand and revise the definition of countertransference was powered by clinical theories that sought to revise the traditional Freudian view of analysis and its technique, one's attitude toward the proposed revisions was directly correlated with one's theoretical convictions. A. Reich (1951, 1960, 1966), in a series of papers, and Fliess (1953) articulately argued the classical position. Kleinians like Heimann (1950), Little (1951), (1957), and Racker (1953, 1957), and Americans in favor of revision, like Tower (1956) and Gitelson (1952), elaborated the new views. I will not summarize this intellectual conflict; those who are interested will find Slakter's chapter on the history of the countertransference concept (1987, pp. 7–39) an excellent introduction. It does bear notice that in the debate of the early fifties the classical position is no longer so narrowly defined as was Freud's original approach. Reich (1951), for example, says, "Countertransference thus comprises the effects of the analyst's own unconscious needs and conflicts on his understanding and technique" (p. 138). In other words, more than just certain blind spots and distortions could be regarded as countertransference; for example, the analyst's character structure might disadvantageously influence his or her attitude toward some or all patients, or even toward the work of analysis itself. However, Reich, Fliess, and those who agreed with them are all adamant in their insistence that countertransference effects spring from the analyst's unconscious reactions, and constitute interferences to proper analytic functioning. They vigorously dispute the redefinition of countertransference as comprising all of the analyst's affective responses to patients, as well as the entire technical emphasis derived from it.

Probably because of the centrality of the concepts of projective identification and introjection in their clinical theory, and the consequent emphasis they place on how one individual can be made to feel something by another, the Kleinians in particular developed the revised view of countertransference as a therapeutic tool. Racker (1953) goes so far as to propose that a countertransference neurosis comes into being in each analytic case. The Kleinians were not alone in their theoretical challenge; what Slakter (1987) labels the interactional approach broadly describes a shift in the interpretation of the basic nature of the psychoanalytic interchange that transcends narrow doctrinal differences. Many emergent trends can be grouped under the general rubric of "interactional," all the way from the various interpersonal schools, through what have lately become known as object relations theories, and perhaps self psychology and certain developmental approaches. One might well include in this category some shifts in analytic theory and technique that are still considered within the range of mainstream analysis, especially those that emphasize a more participatory, interactive style of analyzing, or the role of the analyst as a new object, one who actively promotes growth and development in his or her patients.

I shall take up these issues again further along, but first I should like to complete my enumeration of the major factors that I believe have played a role in the revision of the theoretical view of countertransference.

A third such factor was the effort to apply psychoanalytic technique to the treatment of borderline, severely narcissistic, and psychotic individuals. Winnicott's (1949) influential article on countertransference stressed the difficult emotional demands of working with very sick patients. Searles (1986), Savage (1985), Kernberg (1965), Kohut (1968, 1971), and others with much clinical experience with more disturbed patients all emphasize that the analyst must attend to his or her countertransference reactions as a prime feature of the treatment endeavor. Special problems of understanding these patients were thought likely to surface regularly in the form of characteristic varieties of countertransference reactions. To quote Kernberg (1965):

> When dealing with borderline or severely regressed patients, as contrasted to those presenting symptomatic neuroses and many character disorders, the therapist tends to experience rather soon in the treatment intensive emotional reactions having more to do with the patient's premature, intense and chaotic transference, and with the therapist's capacity to withstand psychological stress and anxiety, than with any particular, specific problem of the therapist's past (p. 43).

In suggesting one additional factor that I believe to have been influential in the modification of our understanding of countertransference, I will, with some trepidation, step outside the safe arena of the study of our professional literature. I claim no special qualifications for interpreting sociocultural or philosophical trends, and it seems to me that even those whose field of expertise it is are often overmatched by the task of objectively evaluating the trends of the times they live in. Nevertheless, I am struck by the fact that the active revisionary debate on the subject of countertransference emerged in the immediate post-World War II period, and its resolution in favor of modification has come about in the last two decades or so. Other historical calamities have doubtless often had an important impact on the subsequent attitudes and behavior of society. Perhaps precisely because I have lived through the period in question, I am personally impressed by the fact that in the forty-odd years since that particular world cataclysm ended, a profound sense of disillusionment and de-idealization of traditional authority and its motivations has characterized much of our social and intellectual climate. On the political, religious, societal, and scientific fronts, dissent, even derision, has led to questioning and modifying long-established aspects of many institutionalized cultural arrangements, and previously accepted authority structures have often gone from being automatically respected to being just as automatically suspected. It is not my purpose to comment either on the progressive or the regressive effects of the many changes that have taken place in areas outside of our own professional concerns, but I do propose that this cynical, skeptical, and actively revisionist atmosphere is an important part of the intellectual and emotional background against which what has evolved in psychoanalysis during this period has to be examined. Many analysts seem to regard the recently modified view of countertransference as less élitist and rigidly authoritarian in spirit than the classical interpretation it has supplanted, and they hail the revised conceptualization as seeming to be more democratic and humanistic. Slakter, if I read him correctly, takes this position, and in that respect he is representative of a sizable segment of our profession. I think it is possible that the broad and diffuse cultural shift I have described may have contributed to the readiness of so many analysts to accept the expansion of the countertransference concept.

Freud and his followers assumed the mantle of authority and expertise that was an unquestioned accompaniment of the physician's role in those days. If anything, their sense of having discovered a special new world of knowledge, hidden from even their most educated peers, must have strengthened their sense of conviction and authority. Furthermore, this assumption of special certitude appears to have been merely divided, rather than diluted, by the squabbling and theoretical schisms that soon emerged. Quite aside from the differences among them regarding theories of the mechanism of therapeutic action of psychoanalysis, or their views of analytic technique, the early psychoanalysts all thought of themselves as conducting analyses, as interpreters of the hidden unconscious meanings of patients' communications, and implicitly, if not explicitly, as the judges of what was realistic or unrealistic, normal or pathological. That version of an expert stance, long under assault from the interpersonal schools, has by now been all but battered into indefensible disrepute amongst even the most classical and conservative elements of psychoanalysis. But once again I am getting ahead of myself; I shall have to take up the relationship of expertise to authority a little later on, when I discuss the current state of affairs.

To return to the definitional turmoil about countertransference that flowered in the early fifties, it soon reached such a pitch that instead of revisionist versus traditional positions, a confused fragmentation of meanings took center stage. Orr (1954) wrote a thorough review article in which he summarized the situation neatly in the following statement:

> Discussion of the technical handling of countertransference inevitably varies with differences in definition of the concept itself. Is countertransference simply the analyst's response to the *patient's transference*, and does this mean his conscious response, his unconscious response or both? Or does it mean the *analyst's transference reactions* to the patient, whether to his transference, to other attributes of the patient or to the patient as a whole? Or does countertransference include all attitudes and

feelings of the analyst toward the patient whatever they are and whatever may give rise to them? (pp. 657–658).

While certain aspects of this confusing difference of opinion and interpretation persist to this day, I think one would be justified in making the following general statements about the present situation. One is that analysts of various persuasions have, as a result of this concentration of attention on countertransference, made many sharp and increasingly more sophisticated observations about different varieties of countertransference pitfalls. I shall try to illustrate some of these in a moment. Another is that our present understanding of the development of the mental apparatus, and how we view the way it functions, renders obsolete some of the distinctions that troubled analysts when Orr wrote his summation of the issues. Third, while the fact may not yet be accepted in all quarters, the definitional debate has for all practical purposes been settled by consensual usage, if not by logical persuasion. Countertransference is now spoken of by most analysts in something like the sense of Slakter's suggestion for a broad, revised meaning; those of us who still prefer to hold to some version of the original, more restricted definition of countertransference as unconscious interferences with analyzing capability are in an ever-shrinking minority.

The first of these statements is the easiest to document, as refinement of our understanding of how countertransference could influence technique was already in evidence even during the period of great controversy of the early fifties. One may recall that Reich (1951), while defending the classic view of countertransference as solely an interference with analyzing, broadens her interpretation of it to include its effects on the analyst's technique, as well as on his or her understanding. She describes and illustrates defensive countertransferences in which the analyst is unable to recognize intolerable material, much the way Freud originally used the term, but she also describes impulse-gratifying countertransferences, of which an extreme example would be when the analyst falls in love with the patient. Moreover, the absorption of ego psychology into theory and technique is reflected in her identification of countertransferences resulting from character problems of the analyst, such as a tendency to be overconciliatory as a way of dealing with guilt, or the frequent projection of one's own problems onto patients. Closely related are situations in which analysts' technique might be affected by a narcissistic need to be a great healer, or where a residual propensity toward intellectualization to deal with doubts might be reflected in an excessively discursive, explanatory, or educational style.

Racker (1953), whose idea of a countertransference neurosis was never widely adopted even by his Kleinian colleagues, nevertheless drew attention to the difference between countertransferences based on the analyst's resonances with some aspects of the patient, and those countertransferences when the analyst responds emotionally in accordance with the patient's treatment of the analyst as a projected internal object, that is to say, as an imago of one of the patient's past relationships. The latter variety he called "complementary countertransferences" and the former type, "concordant countertransferences." While the terminology and the metapsychological assumptions from which they are derived are less congenial to analysts of other theoretical persuasions, Racker's observation and depiction of different forms of countertransference demonstrate that increased clinical acuity characterized both sides of the theoretical debate.

Improvement of our understanding of various manifestations of countertransference has continued to the present day. A comprehensive survey of that continuing growth would require a long review article of its own. Mention of a few more recent contributions will suffice to indicate that lively interest in the subject continues. Arlow (1985) enumerates varieties of technical interferences that spring from analysts' fixed identifications with patients, from blind spots, and from enactments of unconscious responses to patients' fantasies or to aspects of the analytic situation itself. Blum (1986) calls attention to analysts' irrational reactions to the work of analysis itself, as well as to aspects of the patient, and to the impact that events in the analyst's life may have on countertransference potentials. I too have written about the latter topic (Abend, 1982, 1986). Sandler (1976) is representative of many analysts who have tried to look more closely at how analysts unconsciously respond to patients' needs for them to be and act a certain way, a phenomenon for which he suggests the term "role responsiveness." Porder's (1987) explication of projective identification in more traditional metapsychological language links it to a specific countertransference response in which the analyst is made by the patient to feel what the patient must have felt as a child at the hands of one or more of its caretakers. And Jacobs (1986) has demonstrated that even aspects of psychoanalytic technique thought to be of unquestioned merit, such as attentive listening, may be subtly drawn into the domain of countertransference enactments.

It would not be quite accurate to say that there is now complete agreement among analysts about the obsolescence of distinctions that were formerly drawn between analysts' reactions to the real personality and behavior of the patient, as opposed to the patient's transference, or about the corresponding distinctions between the patient's reactions to the real personality and behavior of the analyst and those reactions determined by the patient's past. However, it is widely recognized that Brenner's observations and theoretical contributions (1976, 1982, 1985), tracing the ubiquity and permanence of the influence of infantile instinctual conflict on psychic functioning, have come to provide a strong challenge to such previously unquestioned distinctions. Normal and abnormal, realistic and unrealistic, adaptation and defense, activity and acting out, conscious and unconscious, transference and real relationship, countertransference and analytic empathy are no longer seen in many quarters as denotations of easily and comfortably distinguishable classes of mental activity. To be sure, these distinctions do exist at the pragmatic level, and are sometimes of the greatest importance for analytic technique, not to say for the conduct of life itself. But Brenner and those influenced by his viewpoint make it clear that the polarities I have mentioned have boundaries that are fluid rather than fixed. The compromise formations that affect the clinical data that analysts need to categorize, as well as those that are involved in the analysts' exercise of judgment, are all subject to fluctuations. Therefore, the clinical distinctions analysts reach are inevitably subjective, individualistic, variable, and hence far from perfectly reliable. This is so even among colleagues of comparable training and theoretical convictions, and even in those practitioners, or perhaps one should say in those analyses, where the highest standards of quality work and satisfactory results are present.

As to Brenner's view of the countertransference issue, it may be summarized in this way: the choice of analysis as a profession, and one's mode of functioning in its practice, like all else in mental life, can best be viewed as the expression of one's compromise formations, some of which are regarded as normal, others as pathological. In analytic functioning, normal compromise formations are those which are advantageous to analyzing one's patients; pathological ones are those which are disadvantageous. Since each of us remains, to a considerable degree, vulnerable to the reappearance of less favorable compromise formations, because of the impact on us of the unique and variable quality of each analysand's material, as well as of circumstances in our personal lives, disadvantageous countertransferences are unavoidable. They are as omnipresent as the advantageous ones that make up our effective working armamentarium. Some of these problematic countertransferences are self-limited, others yield to self-analysis, while more severe and lasting ones might require the help of further analytic attention.

In light of this, many of us today believe that it is not so important as it once seemed to attempt to distinguish countertransference reactions to patients' transferences from those to other aspects of their behavior and character. It makes even less sense to suggest that analysts' emotional reactions to patients are ever simply realistic, or for that matter, merely accurate responses to the patient's material, wholly unaffected by the analysts' own past and particular psychic makeup. Arriving at practical and quantitative evaluations of the complex sources and nature of the analyst's emotional reactions are tasks integral to the work. How well one does that is a direct measure of one's professional skill, all other factors aside. However, it should be noted that while analysts may still hold different definitions of countertransference, absolutism about analysts' mental activities while engaged in analyzing patients is no longer tenable on intellectual grounds, regardless of one's theoretical preferences.

My third general statement, to the effect that the controversy about broadening the meaning of the term countertransference has been irreversibly settled, is a matter of opinion, but I offer in evidence the following observations. None of the many attempts at making a specific, delimited definition of countertransference seems to have achieved wide acceptance or, for that matter, to evoke much interest anymore. Even those who prefer to retain the idea of countertransference as signifying only unconscious interference with analytic functioning would certainly agree that attention to its forms and manifestations increases understanding of what patients bring to the analytic situation. Observing one's own countertransference reactions is so much an accepted part of analytic technique today that even our most articulate and forceful advocates of a classical analytic approach routinely include some reference to it in case reports, clinical papers, and discussions. One gifted analyst, who is also an unusually evocative writer, has even given us an entire volume in which a vivid and compelling picture of the interplay between his own psychic processes and the patient's material is the subject of his "self inquiry" (Gardner, 1983). Case reports that do not include some allusion to the analysts' countertransference seem almost old-fashioned. Countertransference can be said to have emerged from its former place in the dark, burdened by connotations of sin and shame, into the bright light of revelation. Acknowledgment of its impact has become a mark of one's analytic professionalism.

The passionate quarrels about definition and technique in respect to countertransference that I have recalled to your attention have subsided, but an assessment of the subsequent evolution and present status of our conceptualization of countertransference reveals ramifications that extend in several important directions, as I shall try to demonstrate.

Despite all the progress that has been made since Freud set forth his early theories about psychoanalysis and its technical implementation at the beginning of the century, we are still puzzled and intrigued by the mysterious processes by means of which analysts understand the unconscious meaning of their patient's productions, and are still hard pressed to give a good account of how we arrive at our judgments about what is accurate, useful, and objective in our formulations of it. Surely, every practicing analyst has had many experiences that remind him of Freud's telephone analogy, but we are not very comfortable with mystical explanations of unconscious communication. Fliess' (1942) early effort to explain the analyst's working processes in classical metapsychological terms is still frequently cited, usually by reference to his concept of "trial identifications." The recent burgeoning of a substantial literature on empathy, and on modes of analytic listening, testifies to our continuing search for better understanding, but it is evident that "empathic listening" has already evolved into yet another one of those conceptual thickets within which fierce doctrinal battles are being fought.

The attention that has been paid to varieties of countertransference responses, and to how these can be detected and utilized, has surely added immeasurably to our clinical sophistication, as even my brief summary of illustrative examples makes clear. Analysts' awareness of how we arrive at our clinical conjectures is also greater than it was before, but I do not think that any analyst, of whatever theoretical persuasion, would contend that his or her reformulation of countertransference and its employment provides us with a ready guide to distinguishing correct from incorrect readings of patients' data. Just how to transform countertransference into empathy and understanding, or how to distinguish the hindering from the helpful emotional reactions to patients continues to be the quintessential skill, even perhaps the ultimate test, of the gifted analytic clinician.

I do think we are justified in saying that it has been helpful to us in our work, and in our discussions, to make countertransference a respectable subject for study. An exclusive connotation of countertransference as error resulting from analysts' own difficulties emphasizes it as a source of shame and guilt, and encourages defensiveness and polemics. Insofar as any specific instance of countertransference involves the exposure of an analyst's infantile residua, the potential for discomfort still persists; but the creation of an institutionalized dedication to acknowledging the unavoidability of countertransference, and of routinely examining how it may be incorporated into one's working habits in a useful way, seems to have gradually had a beneficial effect, encouraging greater honesty, acceptance, and probably an improvement in clinical skills.

It has become fashionable to caricature the authoritative posture of early analysts as antiquated, unscientific, and prone to destructive misuse. No doubt, in the hands of authoritarian individuals, those prone to overestimation of their own correctness or those excessively gratified by the sense of being expert or superior to others, the analyst's role was open to distortion and misapplication. I believe that this is no less true today than in Freud's time; and that that kind of characterological problem makes for bad analysts and bad analyses, irrespective of the theories that inform such an individual's technique.

However, it would be entirely contrary to what analysis has taught us about the human psyche to think that authoritarianism is the sole pitfall of which analysts must be leery. It is hardly necessary to dwell on the familiar knowledge that an analyst's characterological need to be kind, or therapeutic, or understanding, empathic, and accepting, is not necessarily always or exclusively beneficial to his or her patients. All of those qualities may be part of advantageous compromise formations, and hence of qualifications to do analytic work, but like any compromise formation, they can assume disadvantageous forms as well. Countertransference potentials are as infinitely varied as the mind. There is no analysis in which issues concerning patients' attitudes and fantasies about authority, expertise, and equality, or assertions of and denials of real and imaginary differences, do not play an important role. Every analyst has to deal with those clinical problems, and if his or her theoretical preference or predominant character structure (the two may well be interrelated, but that is another matter, and not a simple one either) bias him or her in one direction or another, his or her analytic capability will be compromised accordingly.

The analyst is in a privileged position *vis-à-vis* his or her patient, precisely because he or she has training, experience, and greater, if not perfect objectivity. His or her status as a dedicated professional means precisely that he or she has special expertise to place at patients' disposal. If the old joke about analysis' being the only business where the customer is always wrong is out of date, is it any improvement on the climate it derides to substitute for it an atmosphere of false egalitarianism? Modesty, caution, and compassion are not incompatible with expertise, or with the exercise of appropriate authority in a professional setting. Any theoretical position that asserts otherwise is, from an analytic perspective, tendentiously naïve.

The question of what form or forms the helpful emotional reactions of the analyst may take also becomes involved in doctrinal, as well as technical, issues. The original Kleinian proposition that analysts' emotional reactions to patients can become an important source of increased understanding of patients' material has become accepted in all quarters. The conscious exercise of self-analytic activities is now universally utilized as means of gathering data about patients and of formulating interventions. We now also recognize that hindering countertransferences can operate in ways other than by producing blind spots or misunderstandings. Problems like characterological moralizing or excessive therapeutic zeal influence analyses in a fashion that goes beyond their effects on the way interventions are formulated and delivered. Some current theoretical positions suggest that there may also be helpful countertransference attitudes that have an effect in ways other than influencing one's ability to understand and interpret a patient's analytic communications. I have in mind, for example, the idea that analysts can provide a more intentionally supportive, or nurturing, or holding, emotional climate for some or all analysands.

Technical arguments about what kinds of activity are permissible in analysis have always been with us in some form or other. At the present time, there is an active focus of theoretical and technical dispute about certain unverbalized and unverbalizable aspects of the emotional interaction between analyst and patient. Are these integral parts of the analytic experience? Can they be formulated systematically for some classes of patient, or perhaps even for all patients? Should the analyst conceive of his or her therapeutic role as including these nonverbal dimensions or not? Where one stands on these questions necessarily involves this new, expanded view of countertransference, and directly influences one's judgment about what is helpful and what is hindering in the countertransference climate. What one analyst may regard as a benevolent countertransference attitude essential for the proper treatment of certain patients suffering from developmental defects that require something beyond interpretation, another will regard as a disadvantageous countertransference bias that substitutes surrogate parenting for legitimate analysis.

I can only add my personal assessment that the task of deciding exactly how an analyst arrives at judgments about what is (or what ought to be) transpiring between a patient and him or herself, about what unconscious content lies below the surface of the analytic material, and about what of significance is buried in the analysand's past is made no easier by placing special emphasis on the role of intuitive understanding of unverbalized interactions between analyst and patient. The further one departs from verbal material, the more one relies on one's emotional responses to nonverbal dimensions of the interaction with patients, the more difficult the challenge of verification seems to become.

I would like to conclude with a brief comment about trendiness. The revolution in attitude toward countertransference has apparently brought about a full swing of the pendulum, so that demonstrating one's awareness of it has become an almost obligatory aspect of presenting one's professional *bona fides*, regardless of one's theoretical preference. I have expressed my opinion of some positive consequences of this shift, and I have tried to show that the current attitude toward countertransference is also subject to less favorable applications, of which hidden value judgments, such as those about authority issues and other inequalities, are examples. Other forms of countertransference distortion, blind spots, and enactments may also spring from the newer view of countertransference, perhaps in somewhat unfamiliar guises. One may even wonder whether the pendulum of interest in countertransference has perhaps swung too far. As one analyst, less than enthusiastic about what seemed to him to be an excessive dwelling on countertransference reactions during a clinical discussion among colleagues, remarked in jest. "Countertransference has become analysts' rationalization for indulging themselves in their own self-absorption."

Progress generally has its price, and the change in the meaning of countertransference is no exception. Its real benefits include a better understanding of how we work and of patients' material, more realistic assessments of the multiplicity of factors that affect the analytic climate, and a greater sensitivity to certain subtle errors of technique. Improved standards are, in part, a consequence of this development in psychoanalysis. At the same time, the extended meaning and utilization of countertransference is no panacea, since it carries with it no sure new formula for distinguishing helpful from hindering reactions to patients. It certainly has not freed us from doctrinal disagreement. Nothing about the subject of countertransference has ever been easy, just as not much about psychoanalytic technique has ever been self-evident. The revision of our ideas about countertransference, while welcome and useful in many respects, has not changed those difficult fundamental truths.

References

Abend, S.M. (1982). Serious illness in the analyst: countertransference considerations. *Journal of the American Psychoanalytic Association* 30:365–379.

——— (1986). Countertransference, empathy, and the analytic ideal: the impact of life stresses on analytic capability. *Psychoanalytic Quarterly* 55:563–575.

Arlow, J.A. (1985). Some technical problems of countertransference. *Psychoanalytic Quarterly* 54:164–174.

Balint, M. and Balint, A. (1939). On transference and counter-transference. *Journal of the American Psychoanalytic Association* 20:223–230.

Blum, H.P. (1986). Countertransference: concepts and controversies in psychoanalysis. In: *The Science of Mental Conflict. Essays in Honor of Charles Brenner*, ed. A.D. Richards and M.S. Willick. Hillsdale, NJ: The Analytic Press, pp. 229–243.

Brenner, C. (1976). *Psychoanalytic Technique and Psychic Conflict.* New York: International Universities Press.

——— (1982). *The Mind in Conflict.* New York: International Universities Press.

——— (1985). Countertransference as compromise formation. *Psychoanalytic Quarterly* 54:155–163.

Fenichel, O. (1938). *Problems of Psychoanalytic Technique.* New York: Psychoanalytic Quarterly, Inc., 1941.

Ferenczi, S. (1921). The further development of an active therapy in psychoanalysis. In: *Further Contributions to the Theory and Technique of Psycho-Analysis.* London: Hogarth, 1950, pp. 198–217.

——— and Rank, O. (1924). *The Development of Psychoanalysis.* Madison, CT: International Universities Press, 1986.

Fliess, R. (1942). The metapsychology of the analyst. *Psychoanalytic Quarterly* 11:211–227.

——— (1953). Countertransference and counteridentification. *Journal of the American Psychoanalytic Association* 1:268–284.

Freud, A. (1936). *The Ego and the Mechanisms of Defence.* New York: International Universities Press, 1946.

Freud, S. (1910). The Future Prospects of Psycho-Analytic Therapy. *Standard Edition* 11.

——— (1912). Recommendations to Physicians Practising Psycho-Analysis. *Standard Edition* 12.

——— (1923). The Ego and the Id. *Standard Edition* 19.

——— (1926). Inhibitions, Symptoms and Anxiety. *Standard Edition* 20.

——— (1937). Analysis Terminable and Interminable. *Standard Edition* 23.

Gardner, M.R. (1983). *Self Inquiry.* Boston: Little, Brown.

Gitelson, M. (1952). The emotional position of the analyst in the psycho-analytic situation. *International Journal of Psycho-Analysis* 33:1–10.

Heimann, P. (1950). On counter-transference. *International Journal of Psycho-Analysis* 31:81–84.

Jacobs, T.J. (1986). On countertransference enactments. *Journal of the American Psychoanalytic Association* 34:289–307.

Kernberg, O. (1965). Notes on countertransference. *Journal of the American Psychoanalytic Association* 13:38–56.

Kohut, H. (1968). The psychoanalytic treatment of narcissistic personality disorders. Outline of a systematic approach. *Psychoanalytic Study of the Child* 23:86–113.

——— (1971). *The Analysis of the Self: A Systematic Approach to the Psychoanalytic Treatment of Narcissistic Personality Disorders.* New York: International Universities Press.

Little, M. (1951). Counter-transference and the patient's response to it. *International Journal of Psycho-Analysis* 32:32–40.

——— (1957). 'R'—the analyst's total response to his patient's needs. *International Journal of Psycho-Analysis* 38:240–254.

Orr, D.W. (1954). Transference and countertransference: a historical survey. *Journal of the American Psychoanalytic Association* 2:621–670.

Porder, M.S. (1987). Projective identification: an alternative hypothesis. *Psychoanalytic Quarterly* 56:431–451.

Racker, H. (1953). A contribution to the problem of counter-transference. *International Journal of Psycho-Analysis* 34:313–324.

——— (1957). The meanings and uses of countertransference. *Psychoanalytic Quarterly* 26:303–357.

Reich, A. (1951). On countertransference. In: *Annie Reich: Psychoanalytic Contributions.* New York: International Universities Press, 1973, pp. 136–154.

——— (1960). Further remarks on countertransference In *Annie Reich: Psychoanalytic Contributions.* New York: Int. Univ. Press, 1973, pp. 271–287.

——— (1966). Empathy and countertransference. In: *Annie Reich: Psychoanalytic Contributions.* New York: International Universities Press, 1973, pp. 344–360.

Sandler, J. (1976). Countertransference and role responsiveness. *International Journal of Psycho-Analysis* 3:43–48.

Savage, C. (1985). Countertransference in the therapy of schizophrenics. *Psychiatry* 24 53–60.

Searles, H.F. (1986). *My Work with Borderline Patients*. Northvale, NJ: Jason Aronson.

Slakter, E., Editor (1987). *Countertransference*. Northvale, NJ: Jason Aronson.

Tower, L.E. (1956). Countertransference. *Journal of the American Psychoanalytic Association* 4:224–255.

Winnicott, D.W. (1949). Hate in the counter-transference. *International Journal of Psycho-Analysis* 30:69–74.

CHAPTER 22

An Inquiry into the Fate of the Transference in Psychoanalysis[1]

[Abend, S.M. (1993). *Journal of the American Psychoanalytic Association* 41:627–651]

Despite universal agreement about the importance of transference, there is no single, comprehensive, generally accepted explanation for the place transference occupies in clinical psychoanalytic theory. In this presentation, I trace the origins of some major trends that introduced important issues into the evolving theory of transference are highlighted; this is followed by a brief outline of the ideas of a representative sample of current theorists. This comparison of the appearance of fundamental evolutionary modifications of transference theory with present-day differences in theoretical emphasis leads to the identification of four persistent themes: (1) the nature of the influence of the patient's relationship with the analyst in the analytic experience,

[1] Plenary address presented at the Fall Meeting of the American Psychoanalytic Association, New York, December 20, 1991. The author acknowledges his indebtedness to the following colleagues who graciously provided valuable assistance in the preparation of this lecture: Drs. Charles Brenner, Lawrence Friedman, Manuel Furer, Merton Gill, Arnold Goldberg, Ernest Kafka, Otto Kernberg, Carol Lindemann, Paul Ornstein, Michael Porder, Owen Renik, Arnold Rothstein, Morton Shane, Sherwood Waldron, Jr., Edward Weinshel, and Martin Willick. Accepted for publication February 13, 1992.

(2) how to account for the analyst's subjectivity and its role in the analytic process, (3) what weight to assign to the interpersonal dimension of the transference, and (4) differences among theoretical perspectives, as reflected in the precise content of transference interpretations. Difficulties in the path of comparative evaluation of differences in theoretical accounts of the transference and its handling are noted. A few reasons for my adherence to the theory I prefer are mentioned solely for the purpose of underlining areas of controversy that require serious attention and further clarification.

The clinical phenomena of transference and resistance are so fundamental to our work that Freud only began to refer to his treatment method by the name "psychoanalysis" after he had learned to appreciate their significance (1925, p. 30). At one point Freud even went so far as to say that any therapist who deals with transference and resistance is entitled to be called a psychoanalyst (1914a), although on other occasions he usually added that one must also recognize the importance of infantile sexuality in order to claim residence in the house he had founded. Under the circumstances, it would seem entirely reasonable to expect that all psychoanalysts would be in agreement about what constitutes transference, and would share a satisfactory understanding about its place in the theory of technique. Quite to the contrary, as every novice soon learns, we differ remarkably among ourselves both about the nature of transference and about how to conceptualize its role in treatment. Despite our universal agreement about the vital importance of transference, there is as yet no single, comprehensive, generally accepted explanation for the central place that transference occupies in our clinical theory.

For some years now, I have harbored the ambition to make a thorough study of the interesting questions involved in transference theory, only to become discouraged time and again by the magnitude of the problem. In our increasingly pluralistic theoretical field, the task of tracing the vicissitudes of the transference concept seems to take on Herculean proportions. I gave serious thought to attempting a more limited approach—that of trying to ascertain what is supposed to happen to patients' transferences over the course of their analyses, according to some of the clinical theorists who are most influential at present. This has proved surprisingly difficult, since clear descriptions of the fate of the transference are hard to come by from reading the literature; too much has been left to inference. While you may notice some residual of the abandoned alternative, it would be better to think of my title as implying a broad inquiry into the fate of the transference concept in psychoanalytic theory. On the grounds that we might learn something useful from history, I thought I would attempt to trace the origins of some of the major trends prominent in contemporary theoretical controversy to their antecedents, an appropriate enough model for a study of the subject of transference.

To begin with, then, I recall to your attention some of the seminal contributions of the early period of psychoanalysis, ones that introduced important issues into the evolving theory of transference. I shall outline the ideas of a representative sample of contemporary theorists, with the hope that identification of certain recurrent themes and preoccupations will help to focus attention on the key questions that continue to challenge us—questions that call for scientific resolution, difficult as that may be to achieve.

Freud left us a theory of the role of transference, stunning in its elegance, elements of which are still useful nearly 80 years after he set it down. In essence, Freud had observed that some patients transfer onto the person of the doctor emotions that originated in their pasts—emotions and, we might add, wishes and attitudes that are not accounted for by the actuality of the doctor's behavior or the treatment situation. He noticed that, while some aspects of this transference help to power the treatment from its beginning, later, as its intensity increases, other aspects of the transference instead tend to interfere with it. Thus, he made the inspired linkage of transference to resistance, and asserted that much of what is transferred constitutes a repetition of the same pathological disposition of libidinal investment that underlies the patient's symptomatology. Analytic work on the resistances affords an opportunity to undo the pathogenic repressions, thus enabling a new, less restricted distribution of the neurotic individual's previously hampered sexuality, and rendering unnecessary the neurotic symptoms that had heretofore substituted for it. Freud developed the idea of a transference neurosis that arises before the analyst's very eyes, and which, in favorable cases, can be resolved by the treatment.

I want to emphasize that Freud's idea of transference is, like his related ideas about object relations, inseparable from his developmental theory. For him, a full object relationship comes into being only as an expression of the Oedipus complex, and thus transference can only express oedipal wishes and fantasies, albeit often in regressively altered versions. According to Freud, the developmental stages prior to the phallic-oedipal period do not permit fully formed object cathexes, and consequently they play no clear part in his formulations about transference. Also, keep in mind that his elaboration of the roles of transference and resistance in psychoanalytic technique came at a transitional period (Friedman, 1991) in the evolution of his theories. In the account of the treatment process he set forth in his papers on technique, Freud (1912a, 1912b, 1913, 1914a, 19 14b, 1915, 1917a, 1917b) merely reshaped his earlier ideas concerning the noxious influence of sequestered memories and fantasies, and the importance of catharsis and abreaction, rather than relinquishing them and replacing them altogether. The transference neurosis emerged as a vehicle for the recovery of the repressed; memory, in place of repetition, remained the therapeutic goal. The transference experience was seen to provide a better route of access to the repressive forces, as well as to give clues to the nature of what was repressed. Undoing the sequestration of the unconscious pathogens was still the key to therapeutic success; only the tools had changed.

Prophetic rumblings began to be heard almost before the ink was dry on the metapsychological papers in which Freud's theory of transference was set forth. Ferenczi and Rank (1923), justifying their advocacy of a more active therapeutic stance, stressed that the experience of certain things in transference could be more important than the intellectual comprehension gained through reconstruction. They also noted that it is not necessarily the case that all the pathogens had ever been a part of conscious experience, capable of being verbalized, in the first place. At the same time, Freud himself, far from content with his new theories, continued his effort to account for data that seemed to him still not well enough explained. Before long he was moved to further revisions in his view of the working of the mental apparatus. An expanded awareness of the role of aggression in mental life; the recognition of anxiety as a reaction to imagined dangers, and thus the initiator, rather than the consequence of repression; and the introduction of the structural model—all these are the capstones of his final contributions. They have exerted a profound effect on our understanding of t transference, but the process of change has been a gradual one.

As Anna Freud took the baton from her father's hand, she presented (1936) an organized restatement of technical principles, which is noteworthy for its refined elaboration of the concept of defense, including the specific appreciation that defenses, as well as wishes, are expressed in transference. Meanwhile, Melanie Klein was bringing forward an entirely different metapsychological account of the transference phenomenon. Hers was not fully and clearly stated until many years later (1952), but its influence must have been absorbed by other analysts much earlier, because its stamp is very clear in Strachey's (1934) pivotal formulation of the nature of the therapeutic action of psychoanalysis. Strachey's focus was on the alteration of the aggressive quality of the archaic superego by means of mutative interpretations. Since his paper is still frequently referred to, and his term, mutative interpretation, lives on, although not necessarily with the precise meaning he gave it, we should briefly review his conceptualization.

According to Strachey, patients attribute aggression to the analyst in transference because of the universality of the projective and introjective processes Klein postulated in her metapsychological propositions. Whenever a patient becomes aware that such a transference attribution is incorrect—that is to say, is not a realistic perception of the analyst's nature and role—an opportunity exists for a mutative acknowledgment that this impression must arise instead from archaic inner sources. Only such transference interpretations have the power to institute convincing psychic changes, with all other types of interpretation being reduced to ancillary and/or preparatory roles. This is not to suggest that all Kleinians today would agree with Strachey's idea that only transference provides mutative opportunities, but one does still encounter versions of his conviction about its exclusive potential to bring about change in the work of theorists of otherwise quite different orientations.

By the decade of the thirties, then, we had a psychoanalytic technique in the process of fundamental change. Transference was seen to include defensive and superego elements, and aggressive as well as libidinal components; it was also probably affected by the mechanisms of projection, introjection, and identification. With the concurrent rise of the interpersonal schools in this country, it would soon take on other characteristics as well. In fact, as long ago as 1954, Orr could say in a comprehensive review of the subject, "From about 1930 onward, there are too many variations of the concept of transference for systematic summary" (p. 627).

His paper appeared in an issue of the *Journal of the American Psychoanalytic Association* in which a number of other significant contributions to the then current debate on transference were published. For instance, we find Fromm-Reichmann's (1954) opinion that classical and interpersonal adherents both accept that the dynamics of transference are the revival and repetition with contemporaries of all the characteristics of one's early modes of relating to the significant people of one's earlier life, but, "the difference lies in the conceptions of the content matter of transference material" (p. 714). What she meant was that her group did not accept the doctrine of the universality of the Oedipus complex.

The emergence of alternative schools of analytic thought was accompanied by the development of analytically based psychotherapies, and by efforts to adapt psychoanalytic thinking and methodology to the treatment of different classes of patients. An effort was underway to define just what constitutes psychoanalysis, and how it differs from other forms of psychotherapy. Gill's (1954) contribution to the discussion contains a definition of psychoanalytic technique that is often cited even today, although I am not certain that Gill himself would still be satisfied with it. At the time he said, "Psychoanalysis is that technique which, employed by a neutral analyst, results in the development of a regressive transference neurosis and the ultimate resolution of this neurosis by techniques of interpretation alone" (p. 775).

Also in that issue, Greenacre (1954) expressed a trend of thought shared by many when she described the transference bond as a matrix derived "from the original mother-infant quasi-union of the first months of life" (p. 672), and this concept of a basic, or, as some called it, primary transference, indicates the extent to which preoedipal development had come to command attention, and had affected the evolving views of transference.

In yet another paper in that issue, Alexander (1954) said that "transference involvement is predetermined by the patient's earlier experiences and *cannot be explained as reactions to the treatment situation itself*" (p. 685; italics added). However, only two years later, Winnicott (1956) published a short article on clinical varieties of transference, setting forth a pivotal modification of the viewpoint expressed in the latter part of that statement. The influence of Winnicott's ideas can readily be detected in the work of many contemporary theoreticians. Based on his experience with severely disturbed patients, he directed attention to what he regarded as transference sequelae of the earliest developmental stages, those characterized by incomplete self-object differentiation. According to Winnicott, in many quite disturbed patients, and even at times in the analyses of healthier ones, the degree of ego intactness necessary for true transference neurosis reactions is not present. He believed that the "setting," by which he meant the analyst's management of the analysis, becomes more important than the interpretations. As the patient perceives that the analyst provides a more consistently responsive emotional milieu than did crucial caretakers of the patient's infancy, a profound dependent transference attachment to the analyst develops. In working with this special variety of regressive transference, the analyst has to realize that the patient's angry responses are a recapitulation of early reactions to environmental failures.

Winnicott thought that such reactions are present in transference in response to mistakes of the analyst in the present, and that it would be incorrect to regard them as manifestations of resistance.

Only through constant self-awareness can the analyst hope to work with these patients, enabling them to deal with their characteristic responses to environmental failures differently enough to permit their ego integration to advance to the point where work on ego responses to higher-level instinctual conflict is possible. An alteration in the conceptualization of transference and in analysts' technical posture, which can truly be considered revolutionary, was thus quietly placed on the board.

Meanwhile, Klein (1952) had come around to describing her views on the nature and origins of transference in this way: "Transference originates in the same processes which in the earliest stages determine object relations. Therefore we have to go back again and again in analysis to the fluctuations between objects, loved and hated, external and internal, which dominate early infancy" (p. 436). She goes on to say that the analyst can represent ". . . a part of the self, of the superego, or any one of a wide range of internalized figures . . . [T]he picture of the parents in the patient's mind has . . . undergone distortion, through the infantile processes of projection and idealization, and has often retained much of its fantastic nature . . ." (pp. 436–437).

Let us stop to take stock of things for a moment, before moving on to consider our current debates. In the first forty years or so after Freud introduced the idea of transference as the expression of pathogenic Oedipal libidinal attachment to the person of the analyst, several increasingly divergent trends are clearly in evidence. One has to do with the importance of actual experience in the transference milieu, as opposed to achieving intellectual insight about the past, although no one would have argued against the view that a combination of both is what is most desirable. Another has to do with the recognition that defenses and superego attitudes, in addition to libidinal wishes, influence and are reflected in the transference. A third underlines the importance of aggression, as well as sexuality, in transference manifestations. Yet another sets aside libido theory in favor of a more generalized view that all aspects of the interpersonal relations of the past are repeated in the transference. Increased interest in the preoedipal period came to the foreground, partly as a consequence of analytic attention to children and severely disturbed patients, and we can see the appearance of theories about how preoedipal factors may be reflected in transference: from providing the basic matrix of helpful transference, to accounting for defective or otherwise distorted primitive ego organizations. And finally, the accustomed belief that transference is a distortion of the reality of the relationship to the analyst is complicated by the admonition that reactions to the present behavior of the analyst may be a kind of corrective transference reliving of past responses to actual environmental failures.

Only a few years later, analysts were confronted with evidence confirming something that had probably been a source of more disquiet than had been openly acknowledged up to that time. Pfeffer (1959) published the results of follow-up studies unmistakably documenting the reappearance of recognizable transference phenomena upon later interviews with patients who had satisfactorily completed their analyses. Analysts back to Freud himself had surely suspected that the resolution of the transference neurosis had to be looked at in relative rather than absolute terms, but nobody much liked saying so without qualification. Even so astute and experienced an analyst as Rangell (1954), for instance, felt obliged to say that psychoanalysis aims at the establishment of the transference neurosis, and ". . . the maintenance of optimum conditions for its *final complete resolution*" (p. 743; italics added). Clearly, complete resolution was considered the ideal, according to the template Freud left us, and analysts must have felt that anything less was the sign of an incomplete analysis, attributable to limitations either in the patient's capacity for change, or in the analyst's technical capability, or both. I wonder if the increasingly explicit focus we have seen since then on analysis as a renewal or resumption of development cannot be understood as a consequence of, among other factors, the necessity for analysts to come to terms with the recognition that analyzability is in fact a relative, rather than an absolute, quality and achievement.

Of course the transference theories of Freud, Klein, Alexander, Strachey, Winnicott, and others can all be seen as describing a kind of restored developmental process, but they thought of themselves,

Winnicott perhaps excepted, as treating specific emotional illnesses. The idea of psychoanalysis as aimed at restoring and promoting healthy development in adults is much more explicit among contemporary theoreticians than it ever was among those of the past.

Loewald (1960, 1971, 1979) has addressed the problem in a series of contributions spanning two decades. He suggests that the structural changes brought about by the patient's interaction with the analyst are tantamount to a resumption of ego development. Loewald's stress on the analyst as a new object is integral to "the patient's rediscovery of the early paths of the development of object relationships leading to a new way of relating to objects" (1960, p. 229). Again and again, he explicitly compares the nature of the analyst-patient relationship to that of the mother to the child. He emphasizes that instinctual life is organized by relatedness, *i.e.*, by interaction with the environment. As the patient successfully moves toward termination, the archaic transference neurosis is gradually transformed into an expression of a higher-level, better organized, more mature version of the influence of the unconscious sources of motivation; hence, it is less distorted than it was before. Thus the emergent new relationship with the analyst, constituting the real relationship between them, is not devoid of transference; it has a new, more mature and realistic quality instead. In his later thinking, Loewald places increasing emphasis on understanding the deficiencies and deformations of ego development, which he attributes to problems during the preoedipal years "prior to the relatively unblurred differentiation between self and object world" (1971, p. 308). Loewald also thinks that separation, the renunciation of instinctual claims, and individuation, all of which occur in the context of the transference experience, promote internalization, structural change, and a stable capacity for object relations.

Meanwhile, Kohut's work with a variety of difficult patients led him to adopt a tactical posture whose roots go back to Ferenczi, Alexander, and Winnicott. His focus on the analyst's empathic immersion in the patients' subjective experience, while it never led him to abandon an intrapsychic perspective in favor of an interpersonal one, did in time move Kohut to propose a radically new developmental metapsychology. Goldberg (1978) calls Kohut's delineation, description and elaboration of a new variety of transferences, the self-object transferences, his "most significant clinical contribution" (p. 5). Their chief subtypes, the mirroring and idealizing transferences, are expressions of the remobilization of the grandiose self and the idealized parental imago, cornerstones of Kohut's formulation of the early developmental stages of the self. Goldberg's summary points out that these "spontaneously unfolding transferences . . . will pinpoint [these patients'] structural deficiencies and thus permit the analyst to infer the nature of the parental failure in the course of their development" (p. 8). Analytic working through of these narcissistic transferences leads to insight and the expansion of the reality ego. The process consists of "the ego's repeated reactions to temporary losses of the narcissistically experienced self-object. It results in the acquisition of new psychic structures and functions through the transformation and reinternalizations of the mobilized structures—what Kohut has called transmutable internalizations" (p. 8). Endpoints of this restored developmental process are said to include the appearance of appropriate varieties of pride, ambition, ideals, and perhaps creativity as well. In his later work Kohut (1977) made it clear that he thought that the essential structural transformations did not take place primarily because of insight, that is, content interpretation, but instead by means of the transference experience. In his words: "in consequence of the gradual internalizations that are brought about by the fact that the old experiences are repeatedly relived by the more mature psyche" (p. 30). Finally he (1984) modified the idea that the successful analysis of self-object transferences inevitably leads to new structure formation, if that is understood to mean that patients acquire the capability to fully meet their self-object needs by themselves. Instead, in a more flexible vein, he suggested that analysands should have acquired the ability to find satisfaction of their self-object needs either from within or from acceptable environmental sources.

Originally, Kohut preserved a place for the more traditional formulations of transference alongside the modifications he at first proposed. Later, he took a more revolutionary view, one in which his theories of development, psychopathology, and the mechanism of therapeutic action of psychoanalysis completely supplanted what went before. By contrast, other thinkers have attempted to integrate their versions of the consequences of early preoedipal developmental problems with the familiar model of instinctual conflict, just as Winnicott had done years earlier. Modell (1984) is a good example of this trend. He maintains that narcissistic transferences are uniform in contour, because they represent the externalization of various portions of the self, or self-object. The analyst's constant, reliable presence, dedicated to the patient's good, his or her more benign judgment and empathic capability, in short what Winnicott subsumed under "the setting," are said to be symbolic to the patient of certain caretaking functions. Modell takes pains to note that no special caretaking behavior, support, or role playing by the analyst is either necessary or desirable in order for the patient to experience the analytic setting as a symbolic actualization of the holding environment. In those patients who have suffered sufficient developmental arrest, the analyst's technical handling of the narcissistic transference symbolically recreates an early phase of individuation. As a result, a new type of object relationship which is different from those in the patient's past promotes a symbolic working through of the patient's developmental problems. Only after this has been accomplished does analytic work on the individual features of the transference neurosis become meaningful.

Another integrative thinker is Kernberg, who has attempted to meld traditional Freudian concepts with certain elements of Kleinian and object-relations theories in his approach. He states (1982, p. 22), "The analysis of the transference is simultaneously the analysis of instinctual urges and defenses against them, and of a particular object relation within which these instinctual urges are played out." His view of severe psychopathology is that "early, primitive units of internalized object relations are manifest in the transference as conflicting drive derivatives reflected in contradictory ego states . . ." He goes on to assert that because of primitive defense mechanisms in such patients, "contradictory, primitive but conscious intrapsychic conflicts" are activated in the transference, which express highly fantastic, unrealistic precipitates of early object relations. Proper analytic activity, including interpretations of the primitive defenses, will in time enable the more realistic aspects of the developmental history to emerge.

Another very important trend that has gained prominence in recent years has to do with the importance that should be placed on the analyst's subjectivity. I believe this can be traced back to the same concerns that initiated the movement toward modifications in our views on countertransference, which I have summarized elsewhere (1989). Winnicott (1949), Racker (1957), and other contemporaries of like persuasion began to assign a different, far more extensive, and technically significant place to the analyst's emotional reactions in the clinical situation. The assumption that the analyst is in a position to objectively and accurately evaluate the patient's responses and perceptions, and that the analyst can, for purposes of interpretation, reliably distinguish the patient's distortions from reality, has become subject to question, and the analysis of transference is one area in which this altered posture has had a major impact.

From among a number of contemporary thinkers who have addressed this problem, let me take Gill as a most articulate example, even though his view of transference is uniquely his own. He is clearest in an essay written in response to a set of critiques of his ideas (Gill, 1984). "It is not merely that both patient and analyst contribute to the *relationship* but that both contribute to the *transference* [and] each participant also has a valid, albeit different, perspective on it." Transference, then, is *defined* as interpersonal. Every person both "construes interactions and constructs or shapes them in particular ways . . . since construal and construction are always operative and always based on past as well as present, all interpersonal experience is transferential." What Gill delineates as pathological transference "is characterized by the patient's ways of rigidly construing and compulsively constructing interpersonal experience" (p. 499). The logic of this position leads Gill to advocate a tactical stance that eschews passing judgment on the veridical quality of the patient's perceptions and reactions to the analytic situation, but he does nevertheless "agree that the basic goal of the analysis is to establish the patient's contribution to the transference"

(p. 518). I presume that he would expect a successful analytic treatment to reduce the magnitude and influence of the patient's pathological transferences.

Stolorow et al. (1987) take a developmental position that seems to combine features of Kohut's self psychology and the interpersonal dimension under the rubric of an intersubjective approach. According to Stolorow, "The concept of transference may be understood to refer to all the ways in which the patient's experience of the analytic relationship is shaped by his own psychological structures—by the distinctive, archaically rooted configurations of self and object that unconsciously organize his subjective environment" (p. 36). Later he states, "The patient seeks to establish with the analyst a nexus of archaic relatedness in which aborted structuralization processes can be resumed and arrested psychological growth can be completed" (p. 41). The therapeutic value of the transference experience is central, and pejorative associations to the term transference cure are challenged by the statement, "We hold that every mutative therapeutic moment, even when based on interpretation of resistance and conflict, includes a significant element of self-object transference cure" (p. 44).

Innovations in the theory of transference do not all come from such more-or-less revisionary perspectives as the foregoing ones. From a base in conflict-centered structural theory, Brenner (1976) offers the following view of transference: "The essence of the whole matter is that in analysis every patient's thoughts, wishes, feelings, and fantasies about his analyst recapitulate unconscious thoughts, feelings, wishes, and fantasies that originated in the instinctual life of childhood" (p. 111). In this respect, however, the transference relationship with the analyst is not different from any other object relationship; what does differentiate the analytic transference is "the analyst's attitude toward the transference and the use he makes of it" (p. 112). Brenner's idea about resistance is that "it is necessarily a consequence of the patient's conflict due to unpleasure associated with sexual and aggressive wishes toward his analyst, conflicts that mirror and repeat in the analytic situation ones that originated in the patient's childhood" (p. 119). His view of the omnipresent impact of conflict, and of the dynamic makeup of the compromise formations that express its outcomes, dictates that such long-familiar concepts as the transference neurosis, working alliance, erotized transference, and acting out be set aside. These imply either a tautological view of, or an artificial isolation or stratification of aspects of transference reactions that are logically and clinically inseparable. They should be treated by the analyst with the same consistently analytic attitude and comprehensive conceptual model applied to all other transference material. Brenner also states clearly that no transference is totally analyzable, since "One [should never expect] to understand everything about the dynamics and origin of any patient's psychic conflicts" (p. 124). In successful cases, however, new, more satisfactory compromise formations become possible, and thus different, more gratifying, less unsuccessful and painful modes of dealing with one's instinctual conflicts will be reflected in beneficially altered object relations, including the transference to the analyst.

It seems to me that we can readily detect certain main preoccupations in analysts' thought throughout the developmental history of the transference concept in psychoanalysis. I shall concentrate on four persistent, often interrelated themes: (1) the nature of the influence of the relationship with the analyst, (2) the analyst's subjectivity, (3) the interpersonal dimension of the transference, and (4) the precise content of transference material.

Freud's view of the influence of the relationship with the analyst was that an aspect of the positive transference provides the motive power, a form of suggestion he called it, that influences the analysand to do the uncomfortable work of overcoming resistances to remembering, the key to curing symptoms. Ferenczi introduced the twin themes of the importance of the patient's experiencing things in transference that may be outside the reach of recollection and intellectual reconstruction, and of the possibility that the analyst can behave in active ways to promote such beneficial experiencing. Winnicott made it an explicit part of his theory that the deleterious consequences for development of early environmental failures can be correctively relived in the transference relationship, an idea that has been elaborated in different ways by other contemporary thinkers, among them Kohut, Modell, and Stolorow. None of these latter theorists advocates a radical change in analysts' behavior, in my view. The emphasis on empathic immersion in the subjective experience of analysands is not in itself a behavioral prescription, since to some degree it is a recommendation common to all schools of analytic technique. The focus of Kohut and others is rather on what interpretive use the analyst makes of the products of this empathic immersion, and also on what the cumulative significance of that sort of emotional contact is for the patient who experiences it. There are, of course, other contemporary thinkers who, like Ferenczi and Alexander before them, do advocate taking a more interactive stance—one that goes beyond what is involved in merely trying to understand the patient and then communicating that understanding through interpretations. As we all know, this has led to ceaseless debate about what is to be considered truly analysis, as differentiated from analytically informed psychotherapy. It is my impression that this technical debate is diminishing somewhat in this country, but I believe the activist point of view is very much on the rise in Europe, and if the influence of third-party payment for intensive treatment takes on dimensions here that it already has in some other countries, we can anticipate that the pressure for reducing the time required for effective treatment will also bring such issues back into focus here. For the moment, however, our scientific attention can still be centered on other matters.

No experienced analyst doubts that patients take away from their experiences with their analysts far more than just the insight gained through content interpretations. Can we specify in terms that are generally applicable to all patients just what the analytic relationship, with its extraordinary combination of intimacy and restriction, actually contributes to the alteration of the analysand's psychic makeup? Or, if a single generalization is impossible, can it be described in a limited number of ways that are applicable to corresponding categories of patients? Or is it, as I suspect, necessary to try to ascertain what the unique meaning or meanings of the analytic relationship are to each individual patient, in terms of his or her past and predilections? This is a question that cannot at present be answered. Applicable data that are derived from extra-analytic sources, such as infant observation, require a high degree of extrapolation and inference. On the other hand, data obtained from analytic sources are apparently inescapably subject to the limitations of theoretical loyalties.

My own clinical experience has led me to become increasingly attentive to the idiosyncratic, at times quite subtle, ways in which patients construe the analytic situation in conformity with their own emotional needs. These often constitute ongoing experiences of transference gratification which may be very difficult for the analyst to detect, and even more difficult for the patient to surrender. There are some varieties of transference wish that are not as much subject to disappointment and frustration by the limits of the analytic situation as are others, *i.e.,* the wish to be taken seriously by an attentive listener. This poses a technical problem that deserves further study. I believe that it is advantageous to search for such hidden transferences on a case-by-case, individual basis, without employing any potentially restrictive formula derived from the analyst's preferred developmental schema. I also realize that it is probably impossible to follow this idealistic prescription.

So much for the nature of the influence of the relationship with the analyst, at least for the present. Now I shall turn to the topic of the analyst's subjectivity, and how to take it into account. I have related it to the question of our changing views of countertransference. I do not mean to suggest that there are no other factors, social and philosophical ones, for example, that play a part in this important contemporary trend; but the unmistakable tendency to broaden our definition, interpretation, and utilization of countertransference is a strictly psychoanalytic measure of the issue, which is why I shall stick to that factor. Freud began with the assumption that the analyst is in a position to recognize patients' transferences, defined as distortions derived from and shaped by the analysand's past, simply because the analyst had been analyzed. The reliability of the analyst's objectivity was soon enough called into question; the early years of analytic debate are studded with examples of analysts' accusing colleagues of being poorly or incompletely analyzed.

Countertransference started out as a label for the unconsciously determined limitations on analysts' objectivity. Gradually, the posture of the analyst as a good enough assessor of the patient's capacity to evaluate reality, and as the possessor of sufficient professional authority to make valid interpretations about it, came under assault. Alongside a greater appreciation of the complex variability of analysts' emotional reactions to patients, there grew an increasing mistrust of the analyst's privileged position as a judge of what was true in the patient's past, and of what is actually transpiring in the analytic encounter. For many of us—the majority, I think—acknowledging the human limitations on rationality, objectivity, and reality testing to which analysts are by no means immune does not dictate an untenable discomfort with the traditional notion that the analyst possesses special expertise about what takes place in the treatment situation. The analyst has neither absolute authority nor perfect objectivity, to be sure, but the analyst is nevertheless usually in a better position to evaluate the patient's mental activities, particularly his or her defensive aspects, than is the patient. After all, unconscious defensive activity is inherently and intentionally self-deceiving. Of course, the value of tact in dealing with differences in perception and perspective that arise between analyst and analysand is not in question; authoritarian, dismissive, or otherwise disrespectful attitudes toward patients are indefensible in any theoretical school. But the changes in posture toward analysts' subjectivity advocated by Gill, Stolorow, and others are said to go beyond tactical considerations. It is not immediately obvious to those of us who do not subscribe to them how many of these particular differences in conceptualizing the use of the transference in the theory of technique are a matter of style, and how many of substance.

As for the intrapsychic versus interpersonal reading of the transference, it has always seemed to me something of a displacement of emphasis from the true core of differences between theories. Even Freud's earliest intrapsychic focus had an interpersonal dimension, an associated theory of object relations, if you will. Certainly in the modern version of conflict theory, instinctual wishes are expressed as drive derivatives, meaning they are specific wishes involving specific forms of interaction with specific other persons. The organization of the drives and the complexity of how they are modulated and expressed by each individual are profoundly affected by accumulated experiences with the significant persons in one's childhood environment, and in later life as well. By the same token, any attempt to account for how interpersonal experience is apprehended and assimilated within the mind of an individual is, on the face of it, an intrapsychic theory. Integrative thinkers such as Kernberg, Loewald, and Modell, just like Winnicott and others before them, seem to have no problem in attending in transference both to the vicissitudes of instinctual wishes and to the consequences of early object relations. In my view, what is of far more significance in the differences among schools of thought has to do with the specific nature of the interpretation of the content of transference material, and with the differing assumptions that lie behind the observation of regressive modes of ego functioning, the two being by no means unrelated.

If the analyst is convinced, as I am, that quite severe manifestations of distorted ego capacities can be the consequence of compromise formations resulting from instinctual conflict, and that they are potentially reversible through analysis of their dynamic and historical determinants, then the content of his or her interpretive focus will reflect that point of view. If, on the other hand, the analyst regards the same manifest behavior as the reflection of altered ego states of a primitive nature, or as ego deviations, or as evidence of developmental arrest, or as a consequence of fragmentation or malformation of the self, then the content of his or her interpretive activity will just as surely be affected by those quite different assumptions. The history of psychoanalysis is full of such differences and their impact on the content of transference interpretations. Fromm-Reichmann put it as a question of belief in the universality of the Oedipus complex and its consequences. Klein introduced a heightened focus on oral-sadistic envy and associated guilt, in the formation of an archaic superego. Winnicott stressed beliefs about maldevelopment during the stage of incomplete or inconsistent self-object differentiation and its sequelae, and so on. Analysts of many schools of thought have paid attention to the way the preoedipal period may leave a detectable stamp on the patient's transference. Some see this as an added dimension of understanding, its influence lending shape, color, and consistency to the crucial fantasies of the oedipal period. Others more or less openly give preferential treatment to interpreting the preoedipal patterns of development, or individuation, or relatedness, instead of the sexual and aggressive issues that have claimed the attention of more traditional analysts since Freud's time. Some stress the impact of environmental failure more; others focus on how environmental experiences are integrated into the individual's ways of learning to deal with his or her own wishes. These are essentially questions of content, of selective or preferred emphasis. They are truly questions of substance. They exert profound effects on the way that transference is understood and utilized in psychoanalysis.

Lest anyone mistakenly think that what I intend to be a respectful comparative survey of our differences is to be interpreted as an ecumenical appeal, it is not. Some theories are better than others, and the one that best affords an explanation of what troubles our patients, and offers the best avenue to ameliorating those troubles, is to be preferred to the others. The problem lies in reaching a decision about which one is best. Assessing the essential concepts of unfamiliar theories just from reading about them often falls prey to reductionism, even if it does not lead to outright tendentious misrepresentation. I have regularly encountered interpretations of the conflict-centered structural theory that I employ that underestimate its subtlety, flexibility, and clinical utility. I have no great confidence that my own summaries of the views of others would escape similar criticism. There is really no satisfactory substitute for prolonged clinical immersion in its application to bring one to an appreciation of the advantages and limitations of a given theory.

Clinical research is expensive, time-consuming, and difficult to evaluate, and follow-up studies are so problematical to carry out that comparative ones are probably beyond our means, at least until we overcome basic methodological obstacles. Programs of debate between proponents of different theories are interesting exercises, but also suffer from inherent limitations. In light of these problems it is no easy task to address the many questions raised by our competing theories. One useful criterion that we should always employ in evaluating them is how comprehensively each one can account for clinical observations, especially those observations that the other theories call to our attention. Theoretical modifications that add something to our understanding of transference phenomena are always welcome; one must, however, be certain that they do not do so at the expense of our ability to explain other important aspects of what we observe.

I prefer the theory I employ for a variety of reasons, but I shall limit myself here to three points I consider important, just to further highlight the issues that confront us. First, aggression in transference can surely be triggered by the analyst's insensitivity or faulty comprehension, whether or not the patient has suffered from seriously deficient caretaking in the earliest phases of development. It can also be expressive of destructive wishes that stem from the ubiquitous tendencies to competition, envy, ambition, and distorted views of sexual functioning that are characteristic of childhood mental life. However much we would like to believe in the innocence of childhood, I think that psychoanalysis has taught us that aggression is an innate quality of mental life, not simply a reaction to frustration or mistreatment. Our theory of transference must be able to account for all aspects of aggression, not just some of them.

Second, many years of psychoanalytic experience have also amply documented the central importance of conscious and unconscious sexual wishes, theories, fears, and fantasies in our patients' early childhood development, and in their current lives. I do not believe that this is exclusively the result of childhood seductions and sexual abuse, any more than I think that all aggression results from environmental influence. These sexual interests have a profound effect on transference, unless generations of analysts have been completely misguided. Theories of transference that shunt these observations aside, or reduce them to the status of secondary or derivative data, are at best incomplete, in my opinion.

Finally, I continue to harbor more reservations than do many other analysts about theories of transference that are largely derived from work with severely disturbed patients, and that rest heavily on analysts' interpretations of nonverbal data. Such material requires us to place a high degree of confidence in speculative hypotheses about very early development, since sicker patients have so much trouble telling us clearly in words what they think and feel, including what they think and feel about us, what we do, and what we interpret to them.

These are among the reasons for my theoretical preference, and are offered here to focus on areas of dispute. I see no immediate escape from the fact that our search for comprehension of transference is an inquiry that can only be carried out from within, rather than from without, our various theoretical frameworks (Friedman, personal communication). To those who would say that the theory I favor reflects how I was analyzed, trained, and have always practiced, I can only reply that of course you are correct. We certainly ought to direct our best efforts to the problem of figuring out better methods to test, compare, and evaluate our theories, for scientific as well as educational purposes. For the present, I am afraid that we have no choice but to accept that the perfect resolution of the problem of the theory of transference remains, like the perfect resolution of the transference itself, an unattainable goal. We shall have to settle for partial achievements, while continuing to strive for better results.

References

Abend, S.M. (1989). Countertransference and psychoanalytic technique. *Psychoanalytic Quarterly* 58:374–395.

Alexander, F. (1954). Some quantitative aspects of psychoanalytic technique. *Journal of the American Psychoanalytic Association* 2:685–701.

Brenner, C. (1976). *Psychoanalytic Technique and Psychic Conflict.* New York: International Universities Press.

Ferenczi, S. and Rank, O. (1923). The Development of Psychoanalysis. Madison, CT: International Universities Press, 1986.

Freud, A. (1936). *The Ego and the Mechanisms of Defense, Writings 2.* New York: International Universities Press, 1966.

Freud, S. (1912a). The Dynamics of Transference. *Standard Edition* 12.

——— (1912b). Recommendations to Physicians Practicing Psycho-Analysis. *Standard Edition* 12.

——— (1913). On Beginning the Treatment. *Standard Edition* 12.

——— (1914a). On the History of the Psycho-Analytic Movement. *Standard Edition* 14.

——— (1914b). Remembering, Repeating and Working-Through. *Standard Edition* 12.

——— (1915). Observations on Transference Love. *Standard Edition* 12.

——— (1917a). Analytic Therapy. *Standard Edition* 16.

——— (1917b). Transference. *Standard Edition* 16.

——— (1925). An Autobiographical Study. *Standard Edition* 20.

Friedman, L. (1991). A reading of Freud's papers on technique. *Psychoanalytic Quarterly* 60:564–595.

Fromm-Reichmann, F. (1954). Psychoanalytic and general dynamic conceptions of theory and of therapy: differences and similarities. *Journal of the American Psychoanalytic Association* 2:711–721.

Gill, M.M. (1954). Psychoanalysis and exploratory psychotherapy. *Journal of the American Psychoanalytic Association* 2:771–797.

——— (1984). Transference: a change in conception or only in emphasis. *Psychoanalytic Inquiry* 4:489–523.

Goldberg, A., Ed. (1978). *The Psychology of the Self: A Casebook.* New York: International Universities Press.

Greenacre, P. (1954). The role of transference: practical considerations in relation to psychoanalytic therapy. *Journal of the American Psychoanalytic Association* 2:671–684.

Kernberg, O.F. (1982). The theory of psychoanalytic psychotherapy. In: *Curative Factors in Dynamic Psychotherapy*, ed. S. Slipp. New York: McGraw-Hill, pp. 21–43.

Klein, M. (1952). The origins of transference. *International Journal of Psycho-Analysis* 33:433–438.

Kohut, H. (1977). *The Restoration of the Self.* New York: International Universities Press.

——— (1984). *How Does Psychoanalysis Cure?* Chicago: University of Chicago Press.

Loewald, H.W. (1960). On the therapeutic action of psychoanalysis. In: *Hans W. Loewald: Papers on Psychoanalysis*. New Haven, CT: Yale University Press, 1980, pp. 221–256.

——— (1971). The transference neurosis: comments on the concept and the phenomenon. In: *Hans W. Loewald: Papers on Psychoanalysis*. New Haven, CT: Yale University Press, 1980, pp. 302–314.

——— (1979). Reflections on the psychoanalytic process and its therapeutic potential. In: *Hans W. Loewald: Papers on Psychoanalysis*. New Haven, CT: Yale University Press, 1980, pp. 372–383.

Modell, A.H. (1984). *Psychoanalysis in a New Context*. New York: International Universities Press.

Orr, D.W. (1954). Transference and countertransference: a historical survey. *Journal of the American Psychoanalytic Association* 2:621–670.

Pfeffer, A.Z. (1959). A procedure for evaluating the results of psychoanalysis. *Journal of the American Psychoanalytic Association* 7:418–444.

Racker, H. (1957). The meanings and uses of countertransference. *Psychoanalytic Quarterly* 26:303–357.

Rangell, L. (1954). Similarities and differences between psychoanalysis and dynamic psychotherapy. *Journal of the American Psychoanalytic Association* 2:734–744.

Stolorow, R.D., Brandchaft, B., and Atwood, G.E. (1987). *Psychoanalytic Treatment: An Intersubjective Approach*. Hillsdale, NJ: Analytic Press.

Strachey, J. (1934). On the nature of the therapeutic action of psychoanalysis. *International Journal of Psycho-Analysis* 15:127–158.

Winnicott, D.W. (1949). Hate in the countertransference. *International Journal of Psycho-Analysis* 30:69–74.

——— (1956). Clinical varieties of transference. In: *Collected Papers: Through Pediatrics to Psychoanalysis*. New York: Basic Books, pp. 295–299.

CHAPTER 23

Psychoanalytic Perspectives on the Treatment of Sicker Patients

[Abend, S. (1991). In: *The Moscow Lectures on Psychoanalysis*, ed. Arnold Rothstein, M.D.]

We will now discuss the application of psychoanalytic principles to the treatment of sicker patients. There is confusion about diagnostic criteria, and controversy about etiology, in respect to this group of patients. Theoretical differences among the schools of psychoanalysis, and between psychoanalytically oriented psychiatrists and those who are uninformed or unsympathetic to psychoanalysis complicate the study of these clinical problems still further. I want to be clear about one thing from the beginning; I do not feel that psychoanalysis in any form, or even psychoanalytically based psychotherapy, is the best way to treat schizophrenic patients, or those suffering from affective psychoses. Freud and the psychoanalysts who followed him have always been interested in what our methods and theories might be able to tell us about psychotic patients. Today, most efforts to apply psychoanalytic ideas to the treatment of sicker patients are limited to work with patients whose illnesses lie in the diagnostic borderland between the classical neurotics and the severely ill psychotics.

I will sketch some of the history of psychoanalytic thought about severe mental illness, including psychoses, because this will help to make clear where some of the etiological controversies and diagnostic confusion come from, and prepare us to see where and how the psychoanalytic approach can fit into the treatment options with some sicker patients. From the beginning there has been uncertainty about the roles played by constitutional factors, environmental biological influences, and psychological experiences of all kinds in the production of these syndromes. Aided by technological advances, research in neuroanatomy and neurophysiology is constantly changing our picture of mental functioning in health and disease. Even the great clinical psychiatrists who worked before the introduction of Freud's ideas were concerned about diagnostic issues. Kraepelin (1913) and Bleuler (1911) saw patients who were not hospitalized, and who suffered from milder forms of some of the symptoms associated with severe psychoses. Today, *The Diagnostic and Statistical Manual of Mental Disorders* (*DSM-III*) has a specific but limited category for what is called borderline personality disorder (American Psychiatric Association, 1986). It is based upon a purely descriptive definition that includes impulsive behavior, lack of control of anger and/or intense anger, impaired relations with others, volatile mood swings, disturbances in the sense of self and identity, and feelings of emptiness. A number of other diagnostic categories in *DSM-III* designate other varieties of severe personality disorders and some milder forms of psychosis, but those patients are not considered borderline in the strict diagnostic sense of *DSM-III*. Psychoanalytic diagnosis is less precise, and so psychoanalysts would call many patients borderline who would come under one of the other *DSM-III* diagnoses. In part, this is so because psychoanalytic diagnoses often go beyond the descriptive features of syndromes, and may include assumptions about the nature of the pathology that are based upon developmental ideas and theories, and sometimes upon theories about the specific qualities of ego functioning in the different categories of emotional illness.

Freud himself never used the term *borderline* in his published work. He retained the view that there were two distinct categories of mental illness, neuroses and psychoses. He based his distinction chiefly on the preservation or failure of these patients' relationship to reality. In the early part of his career, he also postulated that psychotic patients suffer from a more severe variety of repression than do neurotics, in that they withdraw emotional cathexis from aspects of reality. He thought that this produces some of the symptoms of schizophrenia, such as apathy and withdrawal, and that other symptoms, such as hallucinations and delusions, result from faulty efforts to make up for this problem. Freud always assumed that constitutional factors play a major role in determining who would develop one sort of illness and who another, but he also believed that the different forms of illness are probably based upon disturbances that appear at different stages of development. In his theory, and in the thinking of most psychoanalytically oriented psychiatrists and psychologists today, more severe forms of mental illness are the result of difficulties in the very earliest stages of development, while less severe problems result from developmental difficulties that occur later in childhood. As I will describe later in this chapter, there are those of us today, a small minority to be sure, who question the validity of this fundamental assumption about developmental level and the causes of adult onset of psychotic and neurotic syndromes. At this point, I will continue to follow the historical consequences of Freud's approach.

In his thinking, important pathogenic impacts on psychic development result in what he called fixation points at whatever stage of life either these psychological traumas, or other difficulties of a biological nature, have occurred. Subsequent appearances of pathology are set off by biological and/or psychological stresses in later life; these produce syndromes whose form is in part determined by partial regressions of psychological functioning back to the levels that characterized the stages at which fixations have taken place. The earlier in childhood the crucial fixations occur, the more severe the form of later illness will be. In this reasoning, he followed the medical tradition of seeking specific etiological causes for each disease entity. The current importance of Freud's theories about psychosis are not at all dependent upon the validity of his specific ideas about the mechanisms of psychotic symptom formation. It is related to the persistence of his idea that gradations in the severity of mental illnesses can be understood on the basis of difficulties that originally take place during certain specific phases of development, and on the fixations and regressions that are associated with those phase-specific difficulties, although theorists of today do not use the same conceptual language that Freud used to explain their versions of this fundamental idea.

Even in Freud's own subsequent work, absolute diagnostic distinctions that were based upon the theory of repression, and of the patient's relationship to reality, were gradually replaced by an increasing appreciation of the tremendous complexity of psychological life, and of the advantage, or perhaps I should say the necessity, of paying attention to the vast and variable range of the subtleties of the entire spectrum of ego functioning. For example, we now know that patients' relationship to reality cannot just simply be categorized as either normal or pathological. We see that this aspect of the way the ego functions is quite variable, rather than constant, in healthy as well as in sick people. A person can be more or less accurately in touch with reality in one area of life, but not in others, and this can change from one day to the next, and sometimes even from one minute to another.

While some of Freud's contemporaries and immediate successors tried to follow his lead and chart a precise correlation between stages and even substages of infantile development and later disease entities, as time went on, clinical observations made such simple connections appear less persuasive. As long ago as the 1930s some analysts and descriptive psychiatrists were recognizing a category of disturbances that was much more severe than the usual neuroses and milder character problems that are dealt with in outpatient psychoanalyses and psychotherapies. Yet, these sicker patients did not seem to progress inevitably toward psychotic decompensation of a schizophrenic or affective variety, even though they might have certain features that resembled those more serious syndromes. The concept of a borderline category that lies between the psychoses and the neuroses came into use, although even today there are differences of opinion as to whether this designates a true diagnostic entity, or only a vague description of a class of intermediately severe disorders of many different kinds, having few or no features in common. Even psychoanalytic clinicians who think that there are basic similarities in the pathology of all borderline patients recognize that there are many different types of such patients, with important differences in their manifest symptom pictures, and that these differences require explanation.

In the early days of psychoanalysis, case reports from the literature show that some of the patients being treated by the first generation of psychoanalysts were clearly psychotic. There were then, and still are, a few hospital centers that are interested in applying a psychoanalytic psychotherapeutic approach to treating even the most severely ill psychotic patients. In part this grew out of the discovery that if you pay careful attention to the communications of even quite psychotic individuals, you can learn to recognize and understand the meanings of some portion of the content of their speech and behavior, especially if you are familiar with the nature of the unconscious mind and the elements of psychic conflict. As I mentioned earlier, at first even Bleuler greeted the discoveries of Freud with enthusiasm, because of their power to explain what, up until that time, had been altogether mysterious features of the behavior of schizophrenic patients. There then arose a number of different theories about the causes of psychosis that hypothesized that severe psychological troubles in the very early period of infancy, perhaps without even any contribution at all from biological predispositions, are what lead to the development of psychoses and borderline conditions. Although the different schools of psychoanalysis that had by then come into being each had their own somewhat different theories about how that takes place, they all seem to have focused attention primarily on the effects of the early environment that was provided by the mother, or other caretaking persons, upon the development of the infant and small child's psychological capabilities and vulnerabilities.

In America, H.S. Sullivan, one of the pioneers of the interpersonal school of psychoanalytic psychiatry, based much of his work on the observation and treatment of psychotic patients. In Great Britain, and later in Europe and Latin America, the influence of Kleinian psychoanalysis, and afterward of the British school of object relations psychoanalysis led by D. Winnicott (1958), W.R. Fairbairn (1952), and W. Bion (1957), among others, also gave rise to theories and treatment approaches about psychotic and borderline patients. Among the mainstream of Freudian analysts, both in America and elsewhere, the further study of the psychology of the ego was advanced by the work of many individuals, including some who concentrated upon the development of more severe forms of pathology. Some notable names you will encounter in the literature that deals with these problems include Helene Deutsch (1965), Heinz Hartmann (1939), Edith Jacobson (1964), Phyllis Greenacre (1952), Robert Bake (1946), Harold Searles (1965), Margaret Mahler (Mahler et al., 1975), Arnold Modell (1976), Otto Kernberg (1975), and many others as well. In recent years, the school of self psychology, founded upon the work of Heinz Kohut, has called attention to other types of severe psychopathology, especially of narcissistic disorders, that some psychoanalysts attempt to treat. It is beyond the scope of this chapter to describe in detail all of these important contributions and point out the differences among the various theories and approaches to treatment.

Some of these theorists, and other contemporary workers whom I have not named, attach much importance to the part played by genetic disposition and other biological forces in the production of severe psychopathology, while others seem to think it is not so important as the psychological environment. Many think both are influential, but probably in varying degrees that are extremely hard to specify. In any case, all of these thinkers have more or less followed the assumption that in cases of severe mental illness, it is likely that very early in development, before the onset of the oedipal period, which usually begins sometime around the end of the child's third year of life, something has already gone wrong. They believe that elements of the psychic structure that are essential for the proper development of the fundamental capabilities that underlie the integration of perceptions, the modulation of affects, the assessment of reality, the control of impulses, and consequently the nature of relationships with others, and perhaps even the basic quality of thought processes, are damaged by something unfavorable in the child's caretaking environment. Some of these analysts speak of defects or deficits in the formation of psychic structure, others of pathological forms of early object relationships, while still others conceptualize the basic difficulty or difficulties in other terms. A very highly simplified and summarized version of these theories could be stated this way: Profound failures in development in the first few months of life will lead to the severe psychotic illnesses that appear in childhood. Problems occurring after the first few months, but still in the first year of life, will greatly handicap the ability to form stable differentiations between psychological representations of the self and of others, thus predisposing those individuals to develop some variety of schizophrenia. If the developmental disturbance happen a little later, from late in the first year of life through the second year of life, as the gradual differentiation of self and object images or representations is going on, several varieties of pathological outcome are possible: affective disorders of psychotic degree, or any one of a variety of borderline conditions, or severe disturbances of self-esteem regulation. If the major traumatic influences come into the picture only later in childhood, then neuroses and neurotic character disturbances of milder degree are the likely outcome. The majority of psychoanalysts would probably also suggest that affective psychoses reflect a traumatic origin at a slightly earlier stage of development than do the borderline conditions and the more severe types of character problems. Most treatment that is either called psychoanalytic, or is based upon psychoanalytic principles, will be based on some form of these fundamental assumptions.

At this point I will present some questions about the psychoanalytic ideas about sicker patients that I have just summarized. A few theorists, like Charles Brenner and Jacob Arlow, have long expressed doubts about the phase-specificity of the origins of mental illness. Clinical studies of psychoanalytic data in which I participated some years ago raised other objections to these various theories of etiology and treatment (Abend, Porder, and Willick, 1983). Recent work by colleagues who also participated in those studies, notably Porder (1987, 1990) and Willick (1983, 1990, 1991), will also be used to present to you some other ways to look at psychoanalytic contributions to the treatment of sicker patients. What I am about to discuss is not the viewpoint of the majority of psychoanalysts in the world today, but that of only a very small minority. Since I belong to that small group, and I believe these questions to be important subjects for future study, I will describe them now.

First of all, every psychiatrist is familiar with the fact that we have always had diagnostic problems when considering severely ill patients. Bleuler's (1911) early text referred to the group of schizophrenias, and generations of descriptive psychiatrists since then have argued about the definition of subtypes of schizophrenic psychoses. The same is true of the range of disorders classified as psychotic affective disturbances. Once the proposition that there are also a large class of borderline disturbances, distinct from the psychoses in some respects, was added to the diagnostic field, the possibilities for confusion were increased even more. As I have described, psychoanalytic diagnostic considerations are even more complicated than psychiatric ones, since they often go beyond the descriptive features of the syndromes, and add some of the assumptions about underlying psychic structure and even etiology to the picture. This has some value as a way of trying to differentiate between several possible sources of certain descriptive features that may look alike on the surface, but it also adds another element of uncertainty, because it makes the problem of verification more difficult, if not altogether impossible. One important consequence of these circumstances is that scientists have great difficulty in being sure that comparable patient populations are being studied and described by workers who report their findings and theories in the literature.

When the group of psychoanalysts with whom I worked some years ago examined the psychoanalytic literature on borderline conditions, we had great trouble in selecting the clinical criteria we should use for deciding which cases to include in our own study. We finally made up a list of general descriptive features of the borderline patients that excluded all propositions that are not clinically observable. We were interested in studying those borderline patients who could be treated with some success by psychoanalysis. The psychoanalytic treatment situation produces a different kind of data about patients' mental functioning than any other treatment situation can, in that it is far more detailed and comprehensive in respect to observations of some aspects of *how* the mind works, especially in regard to the effects of the unconscious layers of the mind on thought and behavior. However, it is only suitable to apply psychoanalytic treatment to a small percentage of the sicker patients, and only a small number of patients can be studied because of how much time is required to treat each case with that method. When we published our findings, many psychoanalysts argued that we had worked with a patient sample that came only from the extremely healthy end of the borderline spectrum, while some psychoanalysts use diagnostic criteria that would not even include our patients among the borderline group at all (Abend, Porder, and Willick, 1983). When you think that non-psychoanalytic psychiatrists may use still different criteria, and collect altogether different data, and that psychoanalysts of different theoretical beliefs all collect and interpret their data somewhat differently, it is not at all surprising that so much confusion still exists in our efforts to understand and evaluate sicker patients.

I will concentrate on some other problems in deciding about the validity of the various psychoanalytic theories about the sicker patient populations we study. There are many reasons to question the concept that specific developmental phases can be identified as crucial to the subsequent development of the different psychotic and borderline syndromes. For one thing, are we justified in accepting as reliable the assumption that the regressive symptoms and behaviors that are seen in adult psychotics and borderlines show us exactly how the mind of the child was working at the times of developmental disturbance and fixation? Today it seems more likely that at least some manifestations of the psychoses do not actually have a counterpart in normal early development. Studies of the withdrawal and deterioration evident in severe forms of schizophrenia, including childhood psychoses, cannot be regarded as providing precise reproductions of the mental states of infants in the first few months of life. Other manifestations of what are called regressive states may be the product of a primary biological disturbance instead. Furthermore, few psychiatrists or psychoanalysts have given sufficient weight to the possibility that some of the symptoms displayed by very sick patients could be psychological reactions to their awareness that they may be suffering from organic deficiencies.

Both regressive aspects of mental functioning and psychological reactions to physical trauma are commonly found in patients with a variety of organic brain dysfunctions, including head injury, stroke, drug toxicity, and Alzheimer's disease. In fact, some primitive modes of thinking, and some pathological manifestations of childhood conflicts, will be activated by any form of physical illness, acute or chronic, especially if the brain itself is affected. If childhood psychological trauma and fixation plays an etiological role in such cases, it is more likely to contribute to forming the specific contents of each individual patient's mental preoccupations than it is to produce the more general characteristics of the regressed mental state. Willick and others believe that, in the past, analysts may have been too ready to attribute psychotic patients' loss of distinction between their self images and their images of the outside world and other people to an underlying failure to develop this fundamental ability properly in early infancy. Neither current infant observation studies, nor reconstructions derived from life histories, nor those based on analytic data gathered from the treatment of sick adults, provide enough evidence to confirm the theory of early life developmental failures as primary etiologic agents in psychosis. The same caution should be applied to the theories about what causes the borderline syndromes, even though the evidence in support of the importance of possible constitutional and biological factors in those diagnostic categories is not so clear and convincing as it is in the case of the major psychoses.

Deciding the question of what causes the pathology is not a simple matter, either in the case of the psychoses or that of the borderline conditions. It has been argued that hereditary and other biological factors, even if proven to be present, may not be sufficient to explain the latter appearance of these emotional illnesses. Perhaps, at least in some cases, these merely constitute predispositions that act to produce the critical vulnerability only when combined with some of the psychological factors attributed to deficiencies in the environment provided by the mother early in the child's life. It is even possible that the biological factors, if they are involved, serve to interfere with early psychic development only if they are present at certain critical stages. We do not know the answers to these important and difficult questions at the present stage of psychological and physiological knowledge. It is hard to imagine that if such severe early developmental disturbances were present, they would not manifest themselves in some ways, even during childhood and early adolescence, in those patients whose severe illnesses seem to begin only later on in life. However, we are learning that some hereditary and acquired illnesses can require many years before their effects are visible as manifest symptoms, so perhaps that could also be true of these severe emotional illnesses. At this point, we simply do not have definitive answers.

What I have presented is not intended to discount the idea that seriously disadvantageous emotional environments have harmful effects on the development of children, and that they contribute to the onset of the severe, as well as the milder, forms of psychological illness later in life. In fact, it seems entirely logical that the more deficient the environment, and the earlier in the child's development these deficiencies occur, the more profound their effects will be. Whatever damage may be done to the infant's capacities, or to those of the very young child, will certainly have effects on the way these individuals experience and cope with the inner conflicts and external challenges of later childhood and adult life. In psychoanalytic terms, the way each child meets the problems of its oedipal stage of life will be influenced by what took place earlier in its life, and by whatever damage, physical and/or purely psychological in nature, has already taken place. It is also true that events of a traumatic nature which happen later in childhood, or during adolescence or adult life, can also have serious consequences.

The viewpoint we believe in is that some of the patients in what psychoanalysts generally classify as the borderline group, especially some of those who show the milder degrees of borderline disturbance, can be treated successfully with the psychoanalytic method, or with modifications of it. Other, perhaps slightly more difficult patients can be treated with forms of psychotherapy that are derived from psychoanalysis, based on the psychoanalytic perspective on psychological development and on the effects of conflict. Many psychoanalysts think that special forms of psychotherapy are necessary to treat borderline and narcissistic conditions and some forms of severe neurosis or neurotic character pathology. Their theories of treatment are at least to some extent based upon their etiological theories, especially if they think that early-stage-specific damage has produced the particular defects or deficiencies in psychological organization they believe are at the root of the pathology. Our doubts about the validity of these theories about the causes of these conditions lead us to take a more cautious position. We think that severely damaged individuals, apart from whatever biological influences there may be, have probably suffered more severe environmental trauma all through their devel9pment, and that this psychological damage has more than simply certain stage-specific effects. We doubt that their emotional problems can be understood and treated without also looking carefully into the consequences of infantile sexual and aggressive conflict, just as we study the effects of those problems in the psychoanalytic treatments of the less sick, neurotic individuals. In other words, in our way of thinking about the symptoms and treatment of borderline patients, we use the same basic organizing principles of compromise formation that we have been telling you about in previous lectures. We also realize that these sicker individuals have to be treated with a lot of patience and tact, if psychoanalysis or psychoanalytic therapy is applied. They are more sensitive than the usual patient in many ways, and have more difficulty in cooperating consistently in psychoanalytic forms of therapy. They cannot or will not talk as freely, they tend to demand more reactions and responses from their therapists, they are more fragile and labile in response to stresses in their lives, and in response to the stressful things that come up in their treatments. Their thinking may become more irrational, and their view of reality be distorted by defenses and by wishful thinking. They can be stubbornly blind to parts of themselves, and attribute to others, including the therapist, unacceptable or threatening aspects of their own minds. They can be very childish and inconsiderate, and even after making progress in treatment, they can quickly sink back again into illness. All this makes them very discouraging for even the most dedicated psychoanalyst or psychotherapist to treat.

Remembering and understanding the difficult experiences of childhood, and examining the ways in which these can be repeated in the analytic situation in relation to the analyst in transference, are hard enough for the most stable, mildly neurotic individual to endure. It is all the more difficult for these sicker borderline patients to go through such treatments, and to gain strength from them. Progress in even the most favorable cases will be slow.

Other, more difficult cases may not gain very much, even from extensive psychoanalytic treatments. Predictions for successful treatment are hard to make, and even experienced analysts are disappointed that some treatments they attempt do not turn out very well. On the other hand, we are also sometimes pleasantly surprised that patients who appear to be very disturbed emotionally can improve even more than we expect them to, with the help of good psychoanalytic treatment. In some cases, what might appear to be only very slight improvements in psychological functioning that are brought about by careful psychoanalytic treatment can make a great difference to the patient's life.

I have not discussed the possibilities for better treatment of the sicker patient that combinations of psychoanalysis, or psychoanalytic psychotherapy, with various programs of psychotropic medication may offer. Psychoanalysts are not unaware of the potential for enhancing their treatment methods that new discoveries in the area of psychopharmacology are bringing to the world. We are just at the beginning of exploring these combined approaches. Even Freud guessed that the future might provide psychoanalysts with new forms of chemical treatment that could make patients who seemed to be too sick for analysis to help become more accessible and responsive to psychoanalytic treatment. Many of us think that this part of his dream may also be about to be fulfilled. Still, there are and will be patients for whom psychoanalysis is not a good treatment, even with the concomitant use of medications. Other combined approaches may lie in the future, as will further advances in our understanding of the basic biology of all categories of mental illness. For the moment, I will leave the reader with the thought that psychoanalysis has contributed to our understanding of even the most serious forms of mental illness. It is best suited to exploring the psychological dimension, particularly that having to do with the effects of unconscious mental life.

Psychoanalysts have little to say about the effects of biological factors, hereditary or acquired, on illness, and as yet little to say about how other approaches to treatment, as alternatives or as adjuncts to psychoanalysis, will affect the outlook for sicker patients. We are eager to learn more from our colleagues who study these dimensions of the problems we face together, and we think we have something of importance to contribute to their effort to advance the treatment of the mentally ill.

I will conclude this discussion of the psychoanalytic perspective on the treatment of sicker patients with a very short clinical illustration. I have taken it from a case reported by my colleague and coworker, M. Willick (1990). I will describe one particular symptom that most psychoanalysts would agree is a typical borderline phenomenon. The patient, a thirty-year-old woman, began psychoanalytic psychotherapy because of severe depression following her divorce. Although she quickly became quite dependent upon her therapist, she could hardly speak to him at all in her therapy sessions, and she did not improve, so after a time she decided to try with a new therapist who might understand her better. With the new therapist, it was also very hard at first for her to speak to him about her thoughts and feelings. Again she immediately developed a very strong feeling of attachment to this new therapist, and she showed evidence of having very painful reactions to being separated from him on the days when no therapy sessions were scheduled. She told him that she was not even able to picture his face in her mind, or remember what he was like at those times. It was as if he no longer even existed for her. She sometimes would drive past his office as if to reassure herself that he had a real existence. Of course, she always remembered exactly where his office was located, so this thought that he no longer existed for her must have stood for some complicated unconscious fantasies, thoughts, and feelings.

A number of analysts think that this type of development of a quick, intense attachment, and such unusual experiences as her report that she lost the memory of the therapist when separated from him, or her feeling that he no longer existed, are phenomena encountered specifically in borderline patients. Those analysts assume these to be consequences of an early deficit in the ability to sustain and integrate the emotional perceptions and memories of the self and others in a stable and reliable fashion. In other words, they think of this as a deficit in psychic structure. Analysts who follow that theory often adopt special measures in treatment, including permitting those patients to telephone them when they feel anxious, giving them a photograph of the analyst to help them reassure themselves, and giving those patients information about where the therapist may be found and contacted whenever he or she is away on vacation or at a scientific meeting. They think such steps are necessary to help these borderline patients make up for their structural deficiencies in emotional memory, and to help control the anxiety that results from this problem.

We think differently about such symptoms. We think that there are underlying unconscious psychodynamic reasons for these problems with memory and emotions. We would say that this problem is a severe impairment of the patient's mental functioning that is caused by the severity of the patient's conflicts, and not by some failures in the early mothering environment. Understanding the patient's conflicts can relieve this symptom, just as it can any other symptom. That is precisely what happened in the case I am telling you about. At first the therapist understood and explained to her that one reason she could not remember him was to protect herself, because if she remembered him clearly she would feel even more lonely and sad that he was not with her. This made some impression on her, but did not relieve the symptom. A few months later he also could see and explain that her feeling that he did not exist for her when they were separated was a form of expressing her anger. It was as if she were symbolically getting rid of him by getting him out of her mind and life, both because she was angry at him and also to protect herself from feeling how angry she was, or how lonely she felt. Gradually the symptom improved. Still later, when she had recovered more completely from these feelings and reactions, she could talk about them with greater freedom, and the therapist came to understand that the patient was also feeling very jealous when he was away from her because she knew that he must be with someone else, either another patient or his family. Finally she could understand and admit her childish wish that he would exist only for her, all day and every day, whether she was with him or not. These selfish wishes also made her feel very ashamed and guilty.

Eventually, she came to understand that the feeling that her therapist did not exist had been a way of saying to herself unconsciously that she wished he did not exist, or, in other words, that she was sorry she had ever allowed him to become important to her. Since she always knew that she could never really have him entirely for herself, she thought it was almost better not to care for him at all, so she would never have to feel so jealous, angry, sad, and lonely. I propose that this example demonstrates that although it may take a long time to uncover the hidden factors, it is possible in cases like this one to understand the childish, unconscious conflicted thoughts and feelings that produce such symptoms, even ones whose surface appearance may lead other therapists to conclude that they are evidence of some fundamental deficits in the psychic structure of the patient. The great advantage of working with the symptoms of sicker borderline patients, as we have suggested, is that the therapist is much more likely to look and listen for the underlying explanations of the symptoms than would be true if his theory led him to assume that these symptoms are only manifestations of fundamental deficits in early development, instead of expressions of psychological conflicts.

CHAPTER 24

Unconscious Fantasies and Issues of Termination

[Abend, S. (1988). In: *Fantasy, Myth and Reality: Essays in Honor of Jacob A. Arlow, M.D.*, ed. H. Blum, Y. Kramer, A.D. Richards, and A.K. Richards. Madison, CT: International Universities Press, pp. 149–165.]

That the analysis of a patient's unconscious fantasies about the meaning of termination is a significant analytic task is an observation made frequently by analysts over the years. However, it is not often their principal topic; more often, it appears as a remark subsidiary to exposition of other termination issues (for a notable exception, see Boesky, Chapter 7).

Credit for first calling attention to the importance of analyzing unconscious fantasies about seemingly realistic termination issues might well be attributed to Hermann Nunberg (1926), whose paper *The Will to Recovery* elucidated the vital role played by unconscious fantasies about the meaning of cure in determining the course and outcome of analytic treatment. Many, though not all, types of fantasy about termination turn out to be variants of fantasies about how analysis works, and about the meaning of cure through analysis. Others express something about the relationship between analyst and analysand, or about the termination of that relationship and of the treatment itself.

My own interest in this question is an outgrowth of previous work (Abend, 1979) on the connection between unconscious fantasies and the theories of cure held by patients or analysts. In the present work I intend to examine some ways in which patients' unconscious fantasies about termination may affect the termination phase, and to consider how analysts' theories about the analytic process and its termination may influence their management of termination issues.

It is probably best to begin by examining the sorts of fantasies that condense and simplify complex analytic issues, in order to highlight the impact of the relevant fantasies and their practical consequences. Perhaps the most frequently occurring instance involves the emergence of a desire to terminate analysis prematurely, because of the upsurge of an unconscious fantasy, or set of fantasies.

Ms. A. entered analysis in her early twenties, primarily because of an unsatisfactory pattern of short-lived love relationships in which she invariably felt herself exploited, mistreated, or otherwise disappointed. Her masochistic character structure contributed to severe difficulties in the expression of aggression; the persistence of a resentfully submissive attitude toward parents, siblings, employers, and friends; inhibition of achievement; and a generalized diminution of conscious pleasure and satisfaction from activities and relationships. During the course of her analysis, steady improvement was made in all areas of functioning, although the influence of her character pathology on transference led her to experience the analysis as in general an unpleasant task that she carried out conscientiously, and the analyst as a powerful taskmaster to whom she had to submit. There was only intermittent recognition of the unconscious gratifications that accompanied these surface attitudes.

In the seventh year of analysis she became pregnant, having by then been satisfactorily married for about a year-and-a-half. She soon began to speak of a wish to interrupt her analysis for an indeterminate period after the birth of her baby. This was an intense wish, despite her opinion that there remained important problems requiring further analytic work.

Over a series of sessions, she elaborated the fantasies about interrupting treatment. At first she complained about the inconvenience of a fixed analytic schedule, even though she had selected her hours as optimal from the standpoint of her personal and professional commitments. Of course, she added, no other hours would be any more convenient. If only she did not have to come every day, but only when she chose—a multifaceted, overdetermined wish that had surfaced often earlier in the analysis. She worried that adequate care could not be arranged for her baby when she attended sessions, though she fully intended to keep on running her successful business. Finally she brought up the idea that she intended to breast-feed the child on demand, and worried what might happen if the baby became hungry while she was away. Thus, there emerged the unconscious fantasy of providing for her infantile wishes with respect to her mother, which represented in part a vicarious undoing of severe disappointments. She imagined becoming a reproachful example to her mother of what a real mother should be like. Complaints about her mother's self-absorption and lack of genuine devotion had been a major theme in her analysis. Although these were rooted in a consistent and presumably accurate depiction of her mother's character, the grievances also expressed an intense jealousy and envy of the attention and love her mother bestowed on others, especially Ms. A.'s younger sister. The analysis of many conflicts about this and many other rivals for her mother's affection had been an important part of the treatment all along.

The fantasy, or rather fantasies, of devotion also expressed an unconscious homosexual current in her emotional life; the analyst, standing for her baby's father, would be shunted aside while she gave her love exclusively to the child, who she said was certain to be a girl.

This material was apparently quite convincing to Ms. A., who soon commented on the impossible, even harmful, consequences that might follow if she actually attempted to institute so indulgent a relationship with her baby. Nevertheless, her wish to leave analysis in order to care for her baby persisted. Further associations indicated that this was an unconsciously determined attempt to deny any connection between the analyst and the baby. This was a defense against acknowledging yet another unconscious fantasy, one attributing the child's paternity to the powerful analyst-father. We then added to our understanding of her reactions the fact that unconsciously she thought of this baby as the fulfillment of a forbidden Oedipal triumph over her mother. The guilt attendant on this required that she sacrifice her relationship with the analyst, the gratifying aspects of which were usually expressed only in the concealed form of masochistic, obligatory submission. After this work, her idea about interrupting the analysis subsided, and the analysis moved on to other issues.

In summary then, her wish to terminate the analysis prematurely arose from a network of unconscious fantasies, the analysis of which averted its enactment and preserved the analysis, a technical matter of the greatest practical importance. In other cases, comparable fantasies prove resistant to analytic efforts, or fail to emerge with sufficient clarity, and termination under less than optimal circumstances cannot be prevented. When that is the outcome the analyst can hardly be certain that he or she is altogether aware of all the pertinent fantasies, but their presence can often be inferred.

One young man, in analysis for three and a half years for profound sexual inhibitions, had made sufficient progress to become passionately involved with an attractive and suitable woman. One day he arrived for his session, sat in a chair rather than going to the couch as usual, and announced that the previous evening he had proposed marriage to her and she had accepted. He had therefore reached the decision to terminate his analysis that very day. He had given no warning whatsoever that this sudden turn of events had been on his mind. He remained in the office just long enough to bring forth some associations to thoughts of his father's death, and some vaguely worded references to worries about what he imagined were the analyst's reactions to his decisions, but the analyst was unable to arouse in him sufficient interest in examining the meanings of these interconnected themes and concerns to prevent the abrupt and untimely foreclosure of the analysis. Though not always so dramatic, unsatisfactory premature terminations of a similar nature, and for comparable irrational reasons, occur more often than we might wish.

Here is an example of another type of termination issue, in relation to which the analysis of unconscious fantasies is of considerable practical significance. I have in mind the problem of evaluating the timeliness of the decision to terminate in cases in which analysis has gone on for many years, with evidence of steady and continuing improvement, but with much residual difficulty. In such cases the relationship with the analyst has often become an important source of gratification that the analysand, consciously or unconsciously, is reluctant to surrender. I do not intend to take up the general question of the appropriate criteria for termination, but instead to indicate how the analysis of relevant unconscious fantasies can contribute to clarifying the issues involved in arriving at a determination in certain difficult cases. In contrast to the previous illustration, in which the pertinent material emerged in the course of a week or so of analysis, in the next case the fantasies about termination or continuation emerged over the course of many weeks.

Ms. B., after the divorce of her parents when she was four years old, was shuttled back and forth between her well-to-do European mother, an unstable, jet-set type, and her expatriate American father. She had several years of productive analysis while in school in Switzerland as a youngster; this had helped her to attain a measure of emotional independence and stability, and to decide on the direction her life would take. She then moved to the United States, where her father had resumed living, and took up a professional career. After her marriage, however, internal conflict involving the prospect of motherhood versus the appeal of continuing her successful career led her to seek further analysis.

I will omit even a summary of the issues with which the analysis dealt in the several years of work before the question of termination arose, but it is accurate to say that slow, sustained progress in many areas of her life was evident, although it was equally clear that residual manifestations of her conflicts persisted in troublesome ways, both in the conduct of her life and in her behavior in sessions. She tentatively brought forward the question of whether we had accomplished as much as we were likely to achieve, if not all she had hoped for. As together we began to contemplate the implications of this question, including her reactions to the possibility of ending the analysis, an uncharacteristic amount of domestic friction arose in her life, and this claimed our attention during her hours. It soon became evident that this served to express her profound unwillingness to give up the analysis and the analyst.

Attention to her reluctance to consider termination seriously first made it clear that she unconsciously regarded the analyst as the benign, omnipotent, and attentive mother she had always wanted. She longed for a magical protector against the vicissitudes of fate, in contrast to her real mother, who had repeatedly failed to provide elementary care and concern even in circumstances when she might reasonably have done so. This aspect of the gratifying transference soon gave way to yet another, more subtle transference motive for continuing the analysis indefinitely. It turned out that the combination of serious application to the analytic work, marked by quite real productivity and dedicated cooperation, coupled with the apparently never-ending necessity for still more analytic work, perfectly expressed an aspect of this woman's lifelong relationship with her father. Separated from him by virtue of her parents' divorce when she was a child, she had nevertheless succeeded in establishing a unique bond with him that persisted into her adult years. Despite his two subsequent marriages, and the numerous other offspring that resulted, she had made herself special to him by choosing his profession as her own, by intellectual achievement, productivity, and an essentially cooperative attitude toward him and his preferences, all of which gave him great satisfaction, as she had always realized. She saw to it that their common interests served to cement their mutual attachment. His continuing special interest in her had seemed literally life-saving during her early years, when the environment provided by her mother was chaotic and unreliable. This very real need and attachment also served as the vehicle for more irrational, repressed Oedipal longings that had been brought to light by the analysis. Thus, the ongoing transference situation neatly replicated the consciously acceptable positive tie she had forged with her father; to bring the analytic work to a successful conclusion would mean surrendering once and for all the childhood romantic wishes and fantasies that were its unconscious accompaniments. To end analysis could in that sense hardly be regarded as satisfactory, but rather as the acceptance of painfully finite limits, of severe disappointment, of inferiority to successful rivals for the analyst-father's love, and of permanent unhappiness. So long as she continued to improve, however, her unconscious view was that she improved her chances of ultimate satisfaction of her Oedipal dreams. This unconscious conviction reinforced her reluctance to accept the disappointment associated with the realistic limitations of the treatment process.

The pragmatic issue of arriving at a mutually acceptable estimate of what analysis can be expected to achieve, never easy to resolve in cases such as this one, was complicated here by the fact that she was unconsciously motivated to maintain quite genuine analytic progress, while at the same time retaining unyielding islands of resistance that appeared to justify a continuation of the analysis. Once this aspect of the clinical situation was clarified, an extended period of work on the various unconscious meanings of termination ensued. In the course of months of analysis, a number of fantasies about termination emerged: termination as death of the analyst, as castration of the analyst and/or the patient, as surrender of her hopes for perfection and omnipotence, as irrevocable loss and loneliness, and as punishment for a variety of unconsciously desired transgressions.

I am not in a position to suggest that in all cases of prolonged analytic treatment one is likely to find unconscious fantasies like the ones described. In this case, attention to the possibility of termination brought them to light, and clarified both the course this analysis had taken and the patient's unconscious contribution to it. This increased understanding served to illuminate the practical decision with which the analyst and analysand were faced.

What constitutes the termination phase is a matter of dispute among authors holding different fundamental assumptions regarding the analytic process. Even so, most recent discussions are consistent with Firestein's proposal (1978) that the termination phase be considered to begin when the subject is introduced, whether by the analyst or by the analysand, and is regarded by both as a real possibility. A second stage of this phase commences when a definite decision to terminate has been reached, and a date has been selected. With some patients, fantasies about the meaning of termination make their appearance early in the course of analysis, but even in treatments where this is not a prominent feature, the serious introduction of the topic serves to mobilize fantasies, the analysis of which constitutes an important aspect of the analytic work of this period. Some fantasies, not previously mentioned, may come forth only after the actual setting of a date.

I believe it is always potentially disadvantageous for analysts to think in terms of typical fantasies or issues, as this may serve to inhibit the sort of open-minded receptivity to the uniqueness of each analytic un- folding that characterizes the optimal analytic attitude. The questions that arise in each analysand's termination phase are highly specific, not only in their minute details, but in their broad thematic organization as well. Arguing against the then-prevalent supposition that all analytic termination phases necessarily involve reactions of mourning-separation from the primary (maternal) caretaking figure, Arlow and Brenner (1966) presented data illustrating other varieties of termination fantasies. At the same time, Rangell (1966) independently proffered a warning against any stereotyped way of looking at the problems of this phase and noted that the overt separation "can represent any threat and can reawaken any form of anxiety" (p. 153).

The termination material presented in the literature suggests that while the fantasies that emerge may cluster about a recurrent set of manifest general themes and preoccupations, the unconscious meanings of these fantasies are not always easily to be inferred from their surface appearance. The reader is usually obliged to rely, with more or less confidence, on the writer's conclusions regarding the primary significance of the fantasies encountered. In Firestein's material, for example, in five of the eight cases described, important fantasies about a post-analytic relationship with the analyst, fantasies using an hypothesized; superficially plausible ongoing professional tie as a vehicle for maintaining the contact, were encountered. To what extent these served to deny irrevocable separation and loss, to what extent they represented rationalized derivatives of Oedipal wishes of some sort (whether in the form of insufficiently attenuated variants of identification with the analyst, or in other forms of unwillingness to surrender infantile wishes for fulfillment) these are determinations that cannot always be made from the presentations. The same might be said for fantasies on the theme of pregnancy, birth, or rebirth, another commonly encountered variety of termination fantasy. Birth and rebirth fantasies often express omnipotent wishes to undo the disappointments of childhood; they may arise in connection with patients' theories, conscious or unconscious, about how analysis will provide a cure for their emotional problems. However, birth and rebirth fantasies may also serve to undo or deny frightening ideas of separation and loss in preoedipal terms, as well as to convey elements of the wishful, conflicted material of the Oedipal phase.

Just as fantasies about mourning, separation, and loss can communicate unconscious ideas stemming from any level of aggressive or libidinal development, and are therefore capable of expressing *all* varieties of instinctual conflict, the same may be said of fantasies involving issues of omnipotence, limitations, and control. It is indisputably true that the ending of an analysis always means facing the inevitable loss of a significant relationship, and whatever unconscious significance that may have in a given individual's emotional life. It also necessarily has the meaning of surrendering, yet again, certain important infantile wishes, whatever these may be in a given case. Kramer (1986) refers to "the renunciation and grief following the recognition that we can never have what we always wanted" (p. 349). Wishes for omnipotence, for control over others and over events, are psychological issues related not merely to pre object relations or narcissistic development, but to all aspects of childhood mental life. Their significance as themes of termination fantasies are not limited to conflicts over separation anxiety in the earliest phase of development, as Miller (1965) has suggested, but can express aspects of central fantasies as well (see Loewald, 1962; Hurn, 1971).

It follows that the ultimate practical consequence of analyzing the unconscious fantasies mobilized by termination is furtherance of the analytic work. Whatever form these termination fantasies take, they express compromise formations derived from the central instinctual conflicts of each analysand's psychological makeup. Many authors (*e.g.*, Freud, 1918; Orens, 1955; Miller, 1965; Schmideberg, 1938; Hurn, 1971; Boesky, Chapter 7) have illustrated the fact that some important fantasies critical to the resolution of patients' neurotic difficulties may emerge only in the context of termination, and consequently are able to be fully clarified only in the course of analyzing the unconscious reverberations of the idea of termination. In some cases the termination phase may in fact assume a dramatic appearance that seems to justify regarding it as the culmination of the entire analytic experience. This is a somewhat deceptive way of looking at things, however. In all cases, whether or not demonstrably new or dramatic material is forthcoming during termination, analyzing the unconscious significance of whatever fantasies are called forth by the idea of termination cannot but advance the analyst's and the patient's understanding of crucial aspects of whatever led the patient to seek analysis in the first place.

If an analyst's theoretical preconceptions lead him to expect that certain issues will invariably arise during termination, or that certain themes and problems must always be faced and dealt with during termination, he may be predisposed to regard material that he encounters during the termination phase in accordance with those views. As I have stated, many fantasies of the termination phase have multiple meanings, and their most important unconscious significance is often far removed from their manifest appearance. It is a simple matter for analysts to agree in principle that all analytic data should be analyzed without prejudice, but theoretical convictions at times act as subtle funnels for channeling analysts' comprehension in the direction of their expectations.

Consciously held theoretical beliefs can influence analysts' handling of the termination phase disadvantageously, in ways other than a selective focusing on the aspects of conflict they expect to encounter. I will omit a consideration of individual countertransference difficulties, although it has long been recognized that potentially troublesome countertransferences can be mobilized by impending termination (for a succinct review, see Viorst, 1982).

I regard it as inescapable that the unconscious fantasies and predilections of analysts will to some degree influence their theoretical preferences and convictions. This fact does not of itself speak to the question of the validity of the theories held, though it may in some cases handicap the objective assessment of data. It is, however, only the careful accumulation of good clinical data that ultimately determines the validity of explanatory hypotheses in psychoanalysis. In examining the relation between analysts' theoretical beliefs and issues of termination, I shall concentrate on analysts' explicit or implicit conceptualizations of analysis, insofar as these may influence their understanding and management of termination.

We may as well begin with Freud (1918), whose decision arbitrarily to impose a time limit on the Wolf Man's analysis in order to overcome entrenched resistance was demonstrated to have been of more dubious benefit than he believed at the time. This technical device, however, has influenced subsequent generations of analysts faced with difficult or unusually protracted analyses. Freud's tactic was perfectly consistent with the opinion he held at the time that it was both necessary and desirable for the analyst to exercise his influence to persuade the analysand to overcome his resistances. Such is the compelling power of Freud's famous example that in clinical presentations one still encounters the rationale that only the imposition of a definite ending will mobilize certain crucial material. However, there is certainly nothing in our current theory of technique that supports the idea that powerful resistances should or will be curtailed by the exercise of the analyst's authority, or that analysands' attempts to retain transference gratifications can be arbitrarily prohibited without adversely affecting the analytic climate. The tactic of suggesting or imposing termination in order to bring out important issues should be discarded as anachronistic and technically unsound.

A selective survey of the literature will illustrate how analysts' different conceptualizations of the analytic process and its termination can, at least in part, determine what they are primed to attend to in the analytic material; what they think must be accomplished during the termination phase; what their criteria are for concluding that termination is timely and how that decision is implemented; and whether or not they manage the termination phase any differently from other aspects of the analysis.

Glover (1955) saw the termination phase in classical analysis as devoted primarily to transference weaning and ego readaptation, bringing to an end the state of regression that marks the transference neurosis. According to Glover, the analyst, not the patient, must decide when termination is indicated. Most analysts today would be more likely to hope that in the best cases the decision to terminate would be a mutual one, arrived at after appropriate discussion between the two participants. Goldberg and Marcus (1985) have gone so far as to describe a technical maneuver in which no mutually agreed upon date is ever set, the actual choice being left entirely in the hands of the analysand. Whether the adoption of such a self-consciously nonauthoritarian stance has any real advantage over what it was designed to correct is questionable.

Annie Reich (1950) believed that the gratifications inherent in the analytic situation can never be entirely resolved by interpretations alone, and that therefore, some pressure from the analyst for the analysand to accept termination will nearly always be required. Miller (1965) has suggested that only in the termination period can separation anxiety from the earliest phase of development be worked through; he regards this as a specific task of termination. Loewald (1962) has stated that "ideally, termination should culminate in or lead into a genuine relinquishment of the external object (the analyst) as an incestuous love object and in the transformation of the external relationship into an internal relationship within the ego-superego system" (p. 488).

Hurn (1971) has suggested that a termination phase "begins with the appearance of evidence that the patient has significantly accepted the impossibility of obtaining infantile gratifications from the analyst . . ." (p. 346). He thinks that although separation-mourning reactions derived in part from the realistic collaboration with the analyst as a real person are to be expected, they do not require special technical management. This latter question has at times been a subject of some controversy, as witness the American Psychoanalytic Association Panel discussion reported by Robbins (1975).

Karl Menninger (1966), in a succinct discussion of Rangell's excellent survey of termination issues (1966), makes the observation that analysts' models of psychoanalysis have a bearing on their concepts of termination. Among those he enumerates is the parent-child model, in which "the idea [is] . . . that the parent guides the child less and less and expects emancipation to occur in adolescence as a natural growth" (p. 169). Menninger himself prefers the model of visiting an art gallery, where the "law of diminishing returns" might serve as an indicator for termination.

Derivatives of what Menninger labeled the parent-child model of analysis are not hard to detect in the literature. Buxbaum (1950), writing on the technique of termination of analysis, states that technique should be adapted to fit the particular needs of each analysand. Which course of action is adopted by the analyst depends on an assessment of what will most likely promote the patient's independence and well-being; this cannot be accomplished, in her opinion, by interpretation alone. In a clinical example, she employs a tactic in the termination phase designed to demonstrate to the analysand that he could act independently, "and also [to demonstrate] . . . the analyst's faith in his ability to do so and her permission [for him] . . . to be independent" (p. 186). She does not appear to have considered that reaching these assessments and adopting tactics accordingly might themselves constitute maintaining a parental attitude, rather than an analytic one, toward the patient. It may be more accurate to say that Buxbaum regards it as proper for the analyst to have a parental attitude toward patients, as long as that attitude leads the analyst to behave like a better, more health-promoting parent than were the real parents. This conceptualization bears a certain correspondence to the wishes of many patients, as expressed in their theories of cure, especially those based on rebirth or adoption fantasies. For that reason, it may well become an issue for any analyst whose theoretical views or personal predilections incline him toward that model of the psychoanalytic relationship.

Novick (1982) has noted parallels between termination-phase processes in satisfactory analyses and normal adolescent maturational processes. He believes the imposition of a termination date may be necessary to provide the impetus for work essential to a proper termination, which should include (following the template of adolescent development) experiencing disappointment in the formerly idealized analyst, and mourning the loss of the real relationship with the analyst.

Shane and Shane (1984) are among those influenced by a developmental point of view, and thus their criteria for termination include an assessment, for which they present clinical guidelines, of the analysand's manifest capability for autonomous functioning. They also hold that it is essential to analytic work in the termination phase that the patient anticipate and mourn the impending separation from the analyst, as both transference object and real person.

In contrast to emphases on the transference or developmental criteria, consider the point of view expressed by Kramer (1986). According to him, the goal of analysis centers on the clarification of core conflicts and their registration on the analysand. Speaking of the analyst, Kramer says, "He can clarify for himself and interpret to the patient over and over again so that it becomes unambiguously clear and indelibly permanent what the patient's unacceptable wishes are and what his defenses against these are, and how they are connected with his symptomatology" (p. 348). Included in this conception is the idea that any resolution of conflict, and any change resulting therefrom, is entirely a function of the patient's inherent psychological capabilities and conscious choices. The task of the analyst is conceptualized as a purely technical one, and when it is achieved to the best of the analyst's ability, termination is in order. No special tasks are attributed to the termination phase except that of dealing analytically with whatever reactions to termination may arise.

It follows from Kramer's view of the analytic process that the analyst's technical stance, incorporating the familiar tenets of abstinence and neutrality, and confining interventions to the task of interpretation, will remain unchanged throughout the entire termination phase, right up to the very conclusion of each analysis. This view contrasts with that of such analysts as Glover, who view the termination phase as a period during which the regression that accompanies the transference neurosis is expected to be reversed. Some of these analysts have developed a rationale for adopting a modified technical posture toward their patients during the termination period. A relaxation of the principle of abstinence and its accompanying constraints, in favor of permitting some measure of interaction on a more personal level, along with accepting an increased focus on the realistic aspects of the relationship between analyst and analysand, and on the analysand's current and future realistic concerns, might well characterize their technique during the termination phase. At present very few analysts advocate a radical shift in technique to facilitate termination, but residues of older viewpoints are sometimes seen in the acceptance of a shift of emphasis onto aspects of the real relationship with the analyst, as distinguished from the transference relationship (Robbins, 1975).

Although the present generation of analysts no longer uses marked technical shifts to assist satisfactory termination, the various conceptualizations of analysis still contribute to significant differences among analysts with respect to other termination issues. The many discussions of criteria for termination to be found in the literature attest to the difficulty analysts encounter in arriving at this crucial practical judgment. This is all the *more* true in analyses like the one described earlier, in which productive work goes on for a number of years but important symptomatic and characterological problems persist. Arriving at a determination about ending such treatments is never easy for either analyst or patient. The analyst's own criteria must guide him, if not necessarily in the categorical fashion described by Glover (1955).

Shane and Shane (1984) have described the effort to identify signs of improved autonomous functioning in patients; Novick (1982) seeks evidence of a full-blown transference; Hum (1971) looks for signs that the analysand *sees* the impossibility of achieving satisfaction of infantile needs; Rangell (1966, 1982) would like to *see* that the analysand has succeeded in incorporating certain aspects of the analyst's analytic mode of thought into his own mental armamentarium; Miller(1965) seeks evidence of the confrontation with early separation anxiety; and Kramer (1986) emphasizes only the accomplishment of successfully understanding the crucial elements of the patient's conflicts and communicating them to him. In addition, these authors and others might differ in their expectations as to the nature of the material to be encountered during the termination phase.

In assessing the analytic material generated by their patients, analysts cannot but employ clinical yardsticks derived from their own conceptual preferences, and cannot help scanning the data in search of content that their particular expectations lead them to believe is important. A potential source of difficulty rests in the fact that most, if not all, analysands take on to some degree the clinical vocabulary employed by their analysts. When material is presented to the analyst in terms that approximate his own intellectual framework, he is perhaps a bit less likely to examine it critically, or to examine it for concealed transference expressions or subtle manifestations of resistance than might otherwise be the case (for a description of one variety of this complication of analysis, see Stein, 1981). The tendency to find confirmation of the analyst's own views with respect to the criteria for termination, as well as to expected reactions to the prospect of termination, is probably harder to overcome in such situations.

To the extent that any of this is true in an analytic situation, the ongoing analytic work of the termination phase is potentially compromised by the influence of the analyst's preferred theories, and any unconscious fantasies he may have that support those theories. Since thorough analysis of all the patient's unconscious fantasies about any aspect of termination is an important part of the analytic work, any constriction of the analyst's sensitivity to the unconscious meaning of analytic material is a definite handicap. Perhaps the best corrective available is to enjoin ourselves to maintain a certain degree of open-minded skepticism regarding our own theories, particularly when our patients seem to confirm them too explicitly.

Conclusions

I have cited a number of opinions (often quite contradictory) about how and when termination is to be induced, the nature of the termination phase, the kind of material one expects to encounter there, what is to be accomplished in it, and how it should be managed. My own experience suggests that deciding when to terminate an analysis is never cut and dried. In some cases it may seem relatively simple, but in many others it is extremely difficult. It may be the most problematic evaluation we face, especially in protracted or atypical cases. I believe that most analysts rely much more on their clinical judgment than checklists of specific criteria. This statement is not, and ought not to be, reassuring; we must in the end trust to our clinical judgment, while acknowledging that its very subjectivity renders it suspect. I recall one colleague who told me that five years was about as long as he would work with any patient. After that, he felt, he'd lost the ability to see things from a fresh perspective; since the patient had gotten all of worth that he was likely to get by that time, he would be better off with a new analyst. I admired my colleague's honesty, but not necessarily his clinical judgment. I respect the efforts of those who have tried to codify and objectify their bases for reaching clinical judgments about termination, but I think the subjective element here is unavoidable. Imperfect as individual clinical judgments may be, they are still the best tool we have available for this task.

I also believe that whenever the analyst comes to the conclusion that he must impose a termination decision on a reluctant patient, there is an implicit recognition that the analyst has encountered problems that are unanalyzable, at least in his hands. To be sure, an imposed termination decision may bring forth important new material that can be advantageously analyzed. Even so, the rationale that the analyst has taken the step of enforcing termination as the only way to bring forth hitherto undisclosed material and thereby carry the analytic work to a satisfactory conclusion is theoretically unfounded, and is potentially disadvantageous to the patient. This is not to say that everyone and everything can be successfully analyzed if one works long enough; obviously there are real limitations in even the best of analyses. I am quite certain that enforcing termination will bring forth patients' reactions to enforced termination. To think it can do anything else, it seems to me, is to invite patients to join in their analysts' rationalizations, and that is contrary to the intent of the analytic enterprise.

Another source of potential disadvantage to the patient arises from analysts' expectations of what termination entails. Any theory that leads analysts to believe that certain kinds of material must emerge during termination, or that certain issues and conflicts must be dealt with, can selectively narrow the analyst's field of view. As I have tried to indicate, commonly occurring themes reported during termination can have multiple meanings. An analyst who is convinced that mourning must take place, or devaluation of the analyst appear, or primitive separation anxiety be worked through, or cherished wishes be definitively surrendered, has unwittingly set a program for the termination phase. Some patients he sees will seem to fit it naturally and easily, but others will not. The consequences of his theoretical beliefs, insofar as they affect his technique, may not be beneficial for the latter group. The sole task of the termination phase is to analyze the analysand's reactions to termination, along with any other material that comes forward, in the most thorough fashion possible. Intentionally or unintentionally adopting selective foci, or other programs to be accomplished during termination, does not provide the optimum milieu for achieving that goal. Jacob Arlow was once asked by a neophyte about his technical management of the end of an analysis. He replied in words to this effect: "You analyze up to the very last minute of the very last hour." That recommendation, of course, is no less an outgrowth of Arlow's theory of analysis than is any alternative stance an outgrowth of some other theory. And since it happens to be the theory that I espouse, it also informs my technical management of the termination phase.

References

Abend, S. (1979). Unconscious fantasy and theories of cures. *Journal of the American Psychoanalytic Association* 27:579–596.

Arlow, J. and Brenner, C. (1966). The psychoanalytic situation. In: *Psychoanalysis in the Americas*, ed. R. Litman. New York: International Universities Press, pp. 23–43.

Boesky, D. (in press). *Termination as Orgasm.*

Buxbaum, E. (1950). Technique of terminating analysis. *International Journal of Psycho-Analysis* 31:184–190.

Firestein, S. (1978). *Termination in Psychoanalysis.* New York: International Universities Press.

Freud, S. (1918). From the history of an infantile neurosis. *Standard Edition* 17:7–122.

Glover, E. (1955). *The Technique of Psychoanalysis.* New York: International Universities Press.

Goldberg, A. and Marcus, D. (1985). "Natural termination": Some comments on ending analysis without setting a date. *Psychoanalytic Quarterly* 54:46–65.

Hurn, H. (1971). Toward a paradigm of the terminal phase: The current status of the terminal phase. *Journal of the American Psychoanalytic Association* 19:332–348.

Kramer, Y. (1986). Aspects of termination: theory and practice. In: *Psychoanalysis: The Science of Mental Content*, ed. A. Richards and M. Willick. Hillsdale, NJ: Analytic Press, pp. 321–351.

Loewald, H. (1962). Internalization, separation, mourning and the superego. *Psychoanalytic Quarterly* 31:483–504.

Menninger, K. (1966). Discussion of Rangell 's "An overview of the ending of an analysis." In: *Psychoanalysis in the Americas*, ed. R. Litman. New York: International Universities Press, pp. 168–170.

Miller, I. (1965). On the return of symptoms in the terminal phase of psychoanalysis. *International Journal of Psychoanalysis* 46:487–501.

Novick, J. (1982). Termination: Themes and issues. *Psychoanalytic Inquiry* 2:329–365.

Nunberg, H. (1926). The will to recovery. In: *Practice and Theory of Psychoanalysis*. Vol. 1. New York: International Universities Press, 1948, pp. 75–88.

Omens, M. (1955). Setting a termination date: an impetus to analysis. *Journal of the American Psychoanalytic Association* 3:651–665.

Rangell, L. (1966). An overview of the ending of an analysis. In: *Psychoanalysis in the Americas*, ed. R. Litman. New York: International Universities Press, pp. 141–165.

—— (1982). Some thoughts on termination. *Psychoanalytic Inquiry* 2:367–392.

Reich, A. (1950). On the termination of analysis. In: *Annie Reich: Psychoanalytic Contributions.* New York: International Universities Press, 1973, pp. 121–135.

Robbins, W. (1975). Panel report on termination: Problems and techniques. *Journal of the American Psychoanalytic Association* 23:166–176.

Schmideberg, M. (1938). After the analysis. *Psychoanalytic Quarterly* 7:122–142.

Shane, M. and Shane, E. (1984). The end phase of analysis: indicators, functions and tasks of termination. *Journal of the American Psychoanalytic Association* 32:739–772.

Stein, M. (1981). The unobjectionable part of the transference. *Journal of the American Psychoanalytic Association* 29:869–892.

Viorst, J. (1982). Experiences of loss at the end of analysis: the analyst's response to termination. *Psychoanalytic Inquiry* 2:399–418.

Part V:

Comparative Theory

CHAPTER 25

Intrapsychic Versus Interpersonal: The Wrong Dilemma

[Abend, S.M. (1988). *Psychoanalytic Inquiry* 8(4):497–504]

I do not want you to think that I plan to avoid the question this conference asks us to consider, but I must tell you at the outset that I think you have directed attention to the wrong dilemma. Freud was reputed to have said that history would remember him for discovering that children have sexual lives and dreams have meaning; however, both discoveries were already familiar to every nursemaid in Vienna. Although the implications of Freud's findings about dreams are not in question here today, the same cannot be said about his views of the consequences of children's sexual lives. The evolution of psychoanalytic thought is filled with divergences, labeled as advances by their proponents and as avoidances or mistakes by their critics. At the heart of the vast majority of those differences is one or another variation on the question of whether or not infantile sexuality is as important in the mental lives of human beings as Freud said it was. Is the dynamic unconscious as much a repository of fantasies embodying children's sexual wishes, worries, and theories as Freud believed, or do other desires, issues, and concerns occupy a more important place in development and adult character and behavior than Freud realized? Or, to reframe our question, are the interpersonal relations of children and adults influenced as much by derivatives of unconscious sexual fantasies as Freud thought, or are they instead manifestations of an entirely different set of developmental and social concerns?

I cannot present a brief position statement that sets forth the essentials of my theoretical stance without making clear certain preliminaries that provide background essential to an understanding of my point of view. For one thing, I believe there are significant limitations on our ability to understand what practitioners who espouse clinical theories different from our own really do in their treatment of analytic patients. Perhaps there is more overlap than sometimes seems the case, but there are nonetheless bound to be important differences among us; identifying what these are is complicated by the difficulties we have in comprehending what others' work is truly like. Most of my experience along these lines has come about in the course of discussions with colleagues who are self psychologists. In interchanges concerning clinical material, it is easy for me to see that their impressions of the classical position amount to caricatures of analysis as I understand and practice it. In fairness, I imagine the same must hold true for their assessments of my picture of what they do with patients. It is no criticism of the painstaking scholarship and attempted objectivity of Greenberg and Mitchell (1983) to add that I do not quite recognize my kind of analytic theory or its technical derivatives in their book, either. Perhaps the Biblical analogy so often mentioned in connection with our field of endeavor really holds, in that a study of the texts alone, without the benefit of learned discussions and of the commentaries of experts, is subject to too many different, often quite erroneous, emphases and interpretations. Perhaps even more important, the evolution of clinical theory is an active and complex process in which much that has gone before becomes amended or dropped, and gradual refinements that in time add up to radical changes may be hard to recognize, unless one is immersed in the mutative theoretical debates all along.

This leads me to my next preliminary point. There are many situations in which it is logically indefensible to accept only some elements of a theory and reject or disregard others, as suits one's personal preference. However, in other situations it is perfectly acceptable to be selective, so long as what is discarded does not materially affect the integrity and validity of what is retained. Distinguishing between those two kinds of selectivity is vitally important to[1] productive theoretical discourse. Freud was wrong about many things in the course of his theorizing, though usually astoundingly accurate in his clinical observations, and often amazingly astute in his ability to account for them as well. You will recall, for example, that as early as the psychotherapy character in *Studies in Hysteria* (1895) he had intuited that the same mental forces that must have isolated traumatic memories from unconsciousness in the first place were also what must account for patients' resistance to recalling them and recounting them to the doctor. My point is that we can retain such classical Freudian concepts as transference and resistance; as internal conflict between opposed interests, motives, or forces within the mind; as the importance of early childhood experiences in forming the patterns that account for adult psychopathology and normal mental functioning; as vitally active, influential strata of the mind existing outside of conscious awareness; and as the central importance in the emotional lives of children of sexual concerns that exert a powerful, often determinative influence on those aforementioned patterns of psychopathology and normality. I shall return to that last point later on, but for now I only wish to say that continuing acceptance of those foundation stones of Freudian psychology does not require that we also adhere to his views on the death instinct, or his hypotheses about preverbal infantile development, or psychic energy and its vicissitudes and transformations, or his explanations of the processes that underlie internalization, to cite a few examples.

Explanatory theories all change and evolve as the data of observation dictate; they are whatever best accounts for the data available in a field of study at a given time. Unfortunately, in our field it is uniquely difficult to observe and evaluate the data with reliable objectivity, and our theoretical differences with one another are in part a reflection of that human limitation. One of the most awkward discoveries of psychoanalysis is that in assessing our theories, the *ad hominem* argument

---

[1] Dr. Abend is Editor-in-Chief of the *Psychoanalytic Quarterly;* he is also a Training and Supervising Analyst at the New York Psychoanalytic Institute.

is always valid, rather than invalid. Fortunately for our self-esteem, it is far more comfortable, not to mention enjoyable, to apply it to the work of others rather than to our own.

And so I proceed to my final preliminary point, of which I have already given you a glimpse. I think that the title of this conference does pose the wrong dilemma altogether. With all due respect to Greenberg and Mitchell (1983), I do not think that intrapsychic and interpersonal are as incompatible as their assessment indicates. Freud's theorizing about the early development of mind is not an essential, indivisible aspect of contemporary classical clinical theory. Pondering about fundamental intrapsychic processes, however fascinating, always strikes me as something approaching a metaphysical debate, no matter who does the pondering. However, attempting to outline a schema of intrapsychic forces at work is another matter altogether, in my opinion. We all do it, or else we utilize someone else's schema, in our efforts to account for observable behavior. Those explanatory diagrams of forces, whether explicit or implicit, and regardless of the terms employed to designate the postulated components, are merely the inferential framework of our clinical theories—all of our theories, not only Freud's. Those intrapsychic skeletons are modifiable as our data improve, but they are logically indispensable. Even the behaviorists, who disregard the dynamic unconscious, seek for intrapsychic explanations, albeit largely in cognitive terms, to account for symptoms, therapeutic action, and change.

Freud's theory of development is as much an object relations theory as it is an intrapsychic one, and the same may be said of Sullivan's, or that of any other psychoanalytic theoretician of human psychology we can think of. Freud's account of development was the first to place such emphasis on the vital importance, for the understanding of adult emotional disturbances, of the interpersonal experiences and relationships of the period of early childhood. He began, after all, with the seduction hypothesis, as the current popular fascination with that hypothesis forcefully reminds us. He was obliged by accumulated data to modify it to emphasize the role of intrapsychic fantasy. Freud's shift amounted to a correction of his mistaken first assumption. He never relegated the actual behavior of caretakers, parents, and siblings to insignificance, but instead he expanded his theory to make room for the importance of what the small child understood, and misunderstood, of his or her interpersonal experiences. And he began to appreciate the importance of the child's own wishes in shaping the perception, organization, and memory of the child's formative interpersonal experiences. He also believed to the end of his days that one's biological constitution is a significant variable in determining developmental outcomes, and that such essential capabilities as cognitive potential, affect regulation, and the like are in part outgrowths of the biological givens, and in part the consequence of interpersonal experiences. These capabilities and potentials, along with actual events, contribute to the shape of emotional difficulties and of normal adaptation in all of us.

The same theoretical generalizations are incorporated in the thinking of those of us who are considered classical or traditional Freudian analysts today. For that matter, so long as the terms are kept broad enough, I believe they apply equally well to the theories advocated by practitioners of other schools of psychoanalysis, including those grouped under the rubric of object relations or interpersonal psychiatry. I maintain that the significant differences lie not in such global generalizations as intrapsychic versus interpersonal, but rather in the specifics of content or emphasis contained in the various explanatory frameworks utilized to account for what we encounter in our patients.

The bedrock of my interpretation of the so-called classical position of today is the belief that conflict and its consequences constitute the central concern of psychoanalysis. My use of the word *conflict* is a shorthand designation for the more accurate terminology: unconscious instinctual conflicts of childhood origin. I need not elaborate on why I specify unconscious conflicts or childhood origin, because if we are not in agreement about those qualifiers we can hardly begin to talk to one another at all. My use of the word *instinctual* requires further clarification: instinct—or drive, as it is more usually referred to these days—is a concept rooted in deference to man's biological nature, but it can function in psychoanalytic theory quite independently of that intellectual origin. Please note that advocates of traditional theory today rarely pay much explicit attention to the concept of psychic energy that so occupied our intellectual forebears. At the present time, only the critics of classical Freudian metapsychology and its elaborations are much concerned with psychic energy. In some measure, that is also the case with the question of the biological sources of the drives. I follow Brenner's clarification (1982) that the drive concept is a total abstraction. He pointed out that psychoanalysis, as an observational science, deals only with drive derivatives, which is merely another way of referring to the wishes that motivate children and adults. Though any given drive derivative is actually always a highly specific and complex wish, for heuristic purposes all the important wishes that enter into conflict can be roughly classified as either sexual or aggressive ones. In practice, neither variety ever appears in pure culture—there are always admixtures—but in the clinical situation we sometimes find it advantageous to speak of one or the other type of wish, hence the two corresponding drives. Brenner (1979, 1982) also suggests that the many possible outcomes or consequences of unconscious childhood instinctual conflicts can all be included under the general heading of compromise formation, a term that does require a word or two of explication, since it was used sometimes differently by Freud and his early followers. In accordance with Brenner's revised definition of the term, it should be understood to refer to the whole range of resultants of the counterpoised elements that make up conflicts. It is a broad, inclusive concept that applies to the entire spectrum of mental life, and is not limited to describing how neurotic symptoms are formed. Fantasies, identifications, complex defenses, normal interests and adaptations, modes of gratification, of affect regulation and discharge, normal and pathological character traits, and so forth, all can be described as compromise formations. This is not intended to suggest that inherited givens, neurologic sequences, and the influence of early infantile environmental patterning are insignificant, only that those elements are subtle contributors to the shapes the conflicts assume and the forms of the compromise formations that result. However, for our purposes, the real importance of this way of thinking is to emphasize that childhood sexual and aggressive wishes and their transformations and outcomes are conceived of as important determinants of all aspects of mental life that psychoanalysis is concerned with, and that can be studied in the psychoanalytic situation by the psychoanalytic method.

It follows from this statement that I regard the most crucial period of development to be the oedipal stage, during which these essential conflicts come to their efflorescence. That is when the outlines of relative resolution are laid down; I tend to formulate these clinically in terms of central unconscious fantasies, whose ongoing influence in later life shapes symptom formation, character traits, and preferred modes of gratification alike. Adequate verbal and symbolic capabilities are in place by the time of the oedipal phase, and progressive biological and social development have made that period of life into the arena for the initial unfolding of the enduring dramas of human psychology. Love, jealousy, possession, envy, rivalry, rejection, ecstasy, disappointment, betrayal, power, helplessness, self-esteem, procreation, sexual roles, identity, and function, triumph, defeat, guilt, revenge, restitution, and so on are the familiar themes that so preoccupy us for all the rest of our lives, as our art and literature, not to mention our clinical experience, bear witness.

Does this mean I think that preverbal, preoedipal development is to be disregarded, or that no important modifying impact on childhood compromise formations can come about later on? Not at all. Each child approaches the crises of oedipal development already somewhat shaped, armed, and limited by earlier experiences and influences. Events and experiences of later childhood, adolescence, and adulthood can be tremendously influential as well. Nevertheless, the importance of the formative impact of the issues confronted during oedipal development, and of the way they are dealt with by each youngster, cannot be overestimated, in my opinion, and it is on that ground that the real theoretical dichotomy, or dilemma if you will, emerges. For example, my clinical interest increases dramatically just where Stern's fascinating book (1985) on development leaves off. I am critical of self psychology and attachment theory, separation-individuation and object relations, interpersonal or humanistic psychology only when they are utilized as conceptual tools for shifting clinical emphasis away from what I regard as central, and toward a new center of interest. Of course that is not the way all theoreticians or all practitioners who are interested in these frames of reference employ them; some integrate these ideas into a complex and flexible way of understanding their patients. For many, though, it is demonstrably the case that, to a greater or lesser degree, they prefer to substitute preoedipal foci of interest for oedipal ones. The dichotomy then reflects the unresolved dilemma as I prefer to reformulate it: Does this shift advance our understanding of human nature and its most profound complexities to embrace issues ignored or minimized by Freud and his followers? Or does it, in the name of progress, focus instead on less critical, less difficult, less disturbing issues than those Freud regarded as most important, and that his intellectual descendants in the classical tradition still believe to be the bedrock problems that psychoanalysis must engage? I believe that the dilemma as I have outlined it is the true dilemma facing psychoanalysis today.

References

Brenner, C. (1979). The components of psychic conflict and its consequences in mental life. *Psychoanalytic Quarterly* 48: 547–567.

Brenner, C. (1982). *The Mind in Conflict.* New York: International Universities Press.

Freud, S. (1895). Studies in Hysteria. *Standard Edition* 2.

Greenberg, J. and Mitchell, J. (1983). *Object Relations in Psychoanalytic Theory*. Cambridge, MA: Harvard University Press.

Stern, D. (1985). *The Interpersonal World of the Infant.* New York: Basic Books.

CHAPTER 26

Relational Influences on Modern Conflict Theory

[Abend, S.M. (2003). *Contemporary Psychoanalysis* 39(3):367–377]

Despite the most untimely circumstance that occasioned this volume honoring Stephen Mitchell's contribution to our field, the subject matter itself is a very timely one. Never before in the history of psychoanalysis has it been as possible for practitioners from different theoretical orientations to engage in a respectful, mutually interesting and interested exchange of ideas as at the present moment. For my part, for the better part of the last decade I have been involved in a number of such clinical and theoretical interchanges, and I have also been attempting to gain a greater familiarity with the published work of colleagues whose training and point of view differ markedly from mine. Although I still strongly identify myself as a proponent of modern conflict theory (a direct derivative of traditional Freudian psychoanalysis), I also realize that I have been influenced by my immersion in a study of the thinking of others, including contemporary relational analysts. When one has embarked on such an intellectual journey, it is useful to pause from time to time, to check one's bearings and assess one's present position. I am grateful to the editors for the invitation to participate in this volume, which gives me reason to undertake such a review.

It seems to me that whenever I take a fresh look at my theoretical and clinical stance, I come to slightly different conclusions about where I stand, and how I have arrived there. Make no mistake, I shall not claim to have made any radical revision of my thinking, or of my psychoanalytic priorities. The fundamental landscape of my theoretical countryside is unchanged. However, just as the sets of Monet paintings that show the same scene in different conditions of light serve to highlight both the similarities and the differences, I find that the illumination provided by other points of view often show me my familiar surroundings in new and interesting ways.

I think it may prove useful to begin my review with a brief historical note. When I was trained in psychoanalysis at the New York Psychoanalytic Institute more than thirty years ago, psychoanalytic interchanges between adherents of different schools of thought were usually competitive, if not openly contentious. I have no reliable perspective on how much the edgy politics of our various professional associations followed from the theoretical differences among us, and how much it was the other way around, but common sense would suggest that both must have been true to some extent. In any case, the professional literature of the day usually emphasized our disagreements. For confirmation of this assessment one might reexamine, for example, the mid-twentieth-century series of debates about the definition and clinical usefulness of countertransference. When I was a candidate, I read the papers of thinkers who did not share our local orientation in the course of my preparation for seminars that were led by teachers who, by and large, were not sympathetic to other points of view. Consequently, they were usually more interested in demonstrating their flaws and limitations than in extracting anything of value from them. Some of my teachers, like Charles Brenner and Jacob Arlow, seemed very knowledgeable about the range of psychoanalytic thinking, and had been involved in many panels, meetings, and other discussions with colleagues from other schools; thus, they appeared to have come to their conclusions about the advantages of our particular orientation through much intellectual work, as well as their accumulated clinical experience. Other teachers, however, and most of the students they schooled, appeared merely to have adopted an uncritical, but passionate, parochial sense of superiority. I strongly suspect that similar statements could be made about the other psychoanalytic cultures of that time.

I also think it is pertinent to point out that, while all of my teachers had tremendous respect and admiration for Freud's ideas and achievements, some saw his work as a foundation on which an evolving psychoanalytic edifice was being constructed, and some others treated his legacy as a precious heritage that had to be preserved intact, without critical review or progressive modulation. I think it must be very difficult for scholars who are grounded in other psychoanalytic schools of thought to detect these crucial differences of perspective from a study of the literature alone. I am sure that would be especially true if one were to read only the seminal works, including samples of Freud's own writings, and to do so without a critical awareness of their time frame and interrelationship. In the same vein, outsiders, even knowledgeable ones, would have a hard time assessing the emerging controversies and changes that have shaped the relational field, or that of the Kleinians, the self psychologists, the Lacanians, or what-have-you. Consequently, even serious considerations of the value of other perspectives are often grounded on an incomplete, if not to say inaccurate, comprehension of the point of view and clinical work of the leading analysts who represent them. This is a genuine limitation on even the most thoughtful studies of comparative psychoanalysis. It can be argued, however, that one who stands outside of a particular school of psychoanalytic thought may benefit from having the advantage of a panoramic overview, free from the pressure of advocacy. Such a position could facilitate gaining a scholarly perspective not readily available from within the membership of the school itself. This is perhaps more easily attained for the express purpose of building a critique of pure theory rather than for the more subtle task of evaluating detailed and precise differences in clinical work. Only relatively recently has there been a proliferation of panels and meetings on diversity of views, in which clinical presentations are being featured and discussed, thus providing a better opportunity for the latter type of comparison to be made.

It would fly in the face of all that psychoanalysis has taught us to suppose that we can free ourselves completely from the shaping influence of our respective clinical traditions, or of our personal loyalties and their concomitant prejudices. This human limitation, I find, makes it rather difficult for me to attribute proper credit to external sources whose effects on my work and thought may be at once subtle and profound. My tendency, which I suspect others share, is to experience my own growth and change as an organic evolutionary process, and not as a series of major dynamic steps in response to enlightenment from without. In scholarly writing, we always strive to be scrupulous about crediting others' contributions accurately, but in considering the arc of one's own progression, such precision is more difficult. I offer this apologia in advance if I am unable to specify with crisp clarity just where to pay my respects to relational thinkers for what I have absorbed over the years.

Part of the problem is a function of the substantial common ground occupied by all schools of thought that deserve to be called psychoanalytic. Despite quite significant disagreements among us about emphasis, none of us would deny that humans are born with certain biological determinants of our future behavior. Nor would we deny that the development of the individual unfolds in increasingly complex layers, and that this developmental history plays an important part in shaping adult psychology and is therefore of great interest to psychoanalysts. Neither is there any dispute about the crucial importance of people's experiences with the environment as they develop; especially significant is the power of their patterns of interaction with others to influence the formation of character and psychic structure. Thus, these qualities of relationship can be seen to help determine both peoples' strengths and weaknesses, as well as their interests and resources. To be sure, these relational patterns and their vicissitudes also contribute in important ways to people's emotional problems throughout their lives. We analysts also share an awareness that all people are in considerable ignorance of much that matters about their own mental lives. Furthermore, and perhaps even more important, psychoanalysts, more than others, appreciate that people strongly prefer to remain in not-so-blissful ignorance of much that is central to their emotional functioning, despite the often high cost of maintaining this blindness.

While the commonality, or perhaps I should say the *overlap*, of theoretical fundamentals contributes to the difficulty of identifying the sources of certain clinical perspectives, it probably contributes to the tendency to characterize our differences in extreme ways, as well. For instance, I have the impression that some, though hardly all, relational analysts seem to imagine that a grounding in Freudian instinct theory means that an analyst of that persuasion thinks only about the patient's ways of modulating his or her sexual and aggressive urges, with the objects in his or her life significant simply in terms of their degree of convenience and suitability as targets of those urges. Similarly, it seems to me that some conservative Freudian mainstream analysts are of the opinion that relational analysts concern themselves exclusively with issues of separation and connectedness, self-esteem, affirmation, and aggressive reactions to disappointment and mistreatment, while ignoring fundamental human interest in sexuality, sadism, the complications of rivalry and envy, issues of bodily integrity or damage, and the like. Both views, I am certain, amount to caricatures, and fail to appreciate the textured complexity that all capable analysts, of whatever school, expect to find in the emotional lives of their analysands.

This is not by any means to suggest that all schools of thought understand the analytic enterprise in exactly the same way. Far from it. Differences of focus, of emphasis, and of technique are quite real, and of genuine significance. For example, even those analysts who acknowledge the multilayered content sensibility of other approaches would, in all likelihood, differ sharply about what material is of primary, or crucially determinative, significance, and what can be regarded as secondary derivatives of fundamental unconscious concerns. It is not my task in this essay, however, to assess those important differences, for to do justice to that endeavor would require a different paper altogether. Instead I confine myself to outlining how my own approach, rooted as it is in classical Freudian psychoanalytic principles, updated by the evolutionary contributions of his intellectual descendants, also reflects the impact of my exposure to the work of the relational school.

Nowadays, there are any number of analysts who contend that a focus on the internal dynamics of the analysand's mental functioning, the so-called one-person psychology approach, should be abandoned as a remnant of philosophically outmoded positivism. I disagree with this categorical challenge to the way I was originally taught to think about psychoanalysis, though I will not cite here the epistemological arguments in support of my stance. No doubt, we have all had our once confident assurance in the reliability of our interpretation of the analytic encounter permanently altered by the tectonic epistemological shift, and we now must embrace a modified view of what constitutes analytic authority and objectivity. By the same token, the challenge facing proponents of co-constructed meaning is to define more precisely the implications of the asymmetry of the two participants in the analytic situation, in a fashion that does not unwittingly bring back positivist authority, without acknowledgment and disguised by the rhetoric of mutuality. I suspect that the future of our science will see a softening of these distinctions, as accommodations are gradually assimilated. That said, it is very apparent to me that over the years I have increasingly incorporated specific attention to the interactive nature of the psychoanalytic situation into my thinking and technique. While there are multiple sources of this shifting perspective, surely the relational emphasis on the interpersonal matrix as a determinant both of the patient's psychological development and of his or her current reactions is the major one. In my work, the difference is mainly apparent to me in my handling of transference.

Years ago, I might have attended to the patient's notions about me and my behavior in the sessions, or about my personality and my life outside of analysis, strictly from the standpoint of their determinants in his or her past, as these have become embedded in his or her mental functioning. This was, of course, the original meaning of the term *transference*, and it was how I was taught to think about it. I am still just as convinced as I ever was that the analysand's past experiences, and the psychic structure to which they have contributed, go a long way toward shaping his or her transference attitudes, expectations, and responses, many of which are in place before the patient has ever met me. Furthermore, while as I suggested earlier I have come to recognize the validity of the subjectivist argument that undermines my former unquestioning faith in my ability to objectively discern these influences in my patients, I have not been persuaded that I therefore must abandon all confidence in my capacity to make usefully accurate judgments about what I observe in my patients' productions and behavior. I am aware that today I am far more likely than I would have been in the past to recognize and acknowledge elements in analysands' transference manifestations that reflect their perceptions and impressions of my character, attitudes, and behavior. I am still interested, as an analyst, in why they have noticed and incorporated whatever it may be that they have observed, and to what use it is being put in their psychic economy of the moment. In this latter respect I am no different, as far as I can determine, from my relational colleagues. As a consequence of this change in style, I think the analytic atmosphere in my consulting room is often somewhat different than might have been the case in the past. Here it is very hard for me to be specific, in part because I have to rely chiefly on my own impressions of what is going on, rather that on any reliable data from my patients. Certainly there is less formality and personal restraint on my part, and, accompanying that easing of my stance, I think there is a greater likelihood that I will put into words my understanding of my patients' viewpoints, thus directly inviting their responses to correct, modulate, or even perhaps agree with what I have noticed about them.

This shift does not extend to the kinds of radical self-revelation now endorsed by a certain segment of contemporary analysts. Almost without exception, I do not intentionally reveal the circumstances of my personal life nor the particulars of my feelings about my patients. I fail to see the advantages claimed for such a substantial alteration in technique, and I do see a number of potential complications, not to say disadvantages, not least of which is the possibility of seductively blurring the clear and consistent, and in my view essential, distinction between being the patient's analyst and being his or her personal, intimate friend. My altered repertoire of responses does, it seems to me, help to establish a less constricted, less artificial analytic atmosphere, one that is a bit less demanding for some patients (and sometimes for me, as well!), without sacrificing the opportunity to focus on what the patient brings to the transference. As far as I can tell, my patients these days are neither more nor less inclined to see me as approving or benevolent, or on the other hand, as authoritarian, withholding, critically judgmental, omnipotent, or what-have-you, than may have been the case earlier. Nor are they less likely to idealize, admire, resent, criticize, or attack me for those or other qualities they attribute to me than was true when I practiced in a fashion that took less account of the interpersonal dimension of our engagement. It seems to me that my current posture helps me to enlighten patients to the fascinating admixture of accuracy and subjective distortion that characterizes their views of me, and, in some cases more gradually than in others, helps me to engender in them a useful curiosity about their particular subjective tendencies. The implication that I also make an attempt to consider my own subjective limitations is more easily inferred from how I conduct myself with some patients than with others. I seriously doubt, however, that any direct revelations, assertions, or confessions on my part would do much to alter the hierarchical sensitivities of those patients who are more attached to their feelings about the differences in our respective roles in the analytic situation. I know there are many who would disagree with me on this score, but I believe that in the end, modulations of technique do not change the basic tasks of effective analysis. Neither do they eliminate the psychic phenomena that account for transference in the first place.

Although I know that my style of handling patients' transferences has been affected by my exposure to the work of colleagues from other psychoanalytic schools of thought, it is more difficult to identify other specific areas of theoretical or technical modification. For instance, I believe I have always been interested in understanding the relationships my patients had, and have, with other persons in their lives. To repeat a clarification offered by Brenner years ago, instincts are only observable in patients' psychology in the form of wishes, and wishes always involve some quite specific form of interaction(s) with other people. What those others are like, what they want, or appear to want, in respect to the patient, and how they respond to the patient's wishes, are of the greatest significance for their development, and are important determinants of their current satisfactions and dissatisfactions as well. In view of that truism, all psychoanalysts have always, perforce, been interested in their analysands' relationships. I do believe that, as the years have gone by, my focused appreciation of the apparent character of the significant individuals in my patients' determinative past, as well as that of those in their current lives, has become a more prominent feature of my clinical thinking. One analysand of mine gave persistent and consistent detailed accounts of his experience of his parents that seemed to document the extraordinary self-centeredness of his father and his mother's blatant favoritism of his older brother. My patient's sense of injury, disappointment, and consequent vengeful rage, along with accompanying confusion and guilt, had to be analyzed in the context of his often disorganized memories of his parents' limitations and peculiarities. His aggression and its complications needed to be understood in connection with his experiences of injury, as well as from other familiar and ubiquitous unconscious developmental sources. In some fashion that is hard to specify, much less quantify, I attribute this expanded palette of sensibility on my part to the impact of relational thinkers, and to that of Kleinians and self psychologists, and, I might well add, to the impact of discussions with many of my other colleagues who have themselves been more or less influenced by, and have in turn exerted their influence upon, the changing psychoanalytic scene.

Some years ago, when writing about the concept of identity, I compared it to the landscape of a beach that, from a broad perspective, gives the appearance of permanence and stability, but when examined in close detail can be seen as ever-changing in small but definite ways. I believe that analogy applies at least as well to my own psychoanalytic technique. To stay with the image of the beach for another moment, I could say that the shifts in its physical contour that result from the mutative forces of weather and sea are, in the comparative case of my psychoanalytic evolution, brought about by cumulative clinical experience, and by my continuing contact with the work and thought of respected colleagues. While I could hardly do justice to all those analysts from whom I have learned over the years, any list I compiled would include many names from the relational school, among them that of Steve Mitchell.

Perhaps a brief clinical vignette will serve to highlight what I have tried to describe. The material has been edited to some degree, for the usual reasons, but I believe it will serve to capture the essence of the exchanges which illustrate my comments.

Tom, a man of thirty-eight, has been in analysis with me for several years. I am his second analyst, so he is an experienced analysand. His parents divorced when he was very young, after which he saw his father only on rare occasions, and his mother subsequently abandoned the children when Tom, the youngest of his siblings, was still in his early teens. Other relatives provided essential support but, needless to say, sensitivity to loss and abandonment have been central features of his psychology all his life. Partly for this reason, in response to his inquiry, I told him how old I was during our consultation sessions, as he was manifestly worried about whether he could count on me to live and be around for as long as he might need me. This was particularly relevant at the time he started treatment with me because the relative who had been most consistently available to him was, at that point in time, at some risk of dying from heart disease, although, as events unfolded, the person did survive serious cardiac surgery.

The vignette I recount happened as his father, who had just recently made one of his scattered periodic reappearances in Tom's life, also faced life-threatening surgery. Tom was describing his concerns about his father, and commented that his father is the same age as I am, though he hastened to add that I appeared to be in much better physical condition. (In point of fact, this comparison was a parapraxis, since he misremembered my age, making me several years older than I am, apparently having distorted our interchange of some time before.) Tom then immediately mentioned that it made him nervous to talk about my age. I asked him why that was, and he replied, "It is like asking you a direct question."

"And what is the risk in that?" I inquired. He said he has always felt that to be the case, as he is sure I do not want to answer questions. "It comes from your technique of doing analysis. You only want my fantasies instead, but you would be forced to answer me anyway, and would resent it." I then asked him how he had reached that opinion of me. Had my behavior somehow given him to believe it? (Actually, from time to time I had answered his questions as we worked together, though I did not invariably do so. We had even discussed the issue, since Tom maintained that his first analyst never would answer any question, no matter how innocuous.) His answer was interesting. He neither said yes or no. Instead, he went on to say that he realizes such simple questions are harmless, but this emotional attitude of feeling forced to comply and consequently resentful, which he attributed to me, is actually exactly how he feels when others ask him for some favor or other that appears "simple" and "harmless." It is part of his lifelong pattern of needing to prevent people from leaving him by placating and pleasing them, while concealing his burning resentment at this form of emotional bondage. It will come as no great surprise to any analyst that, in subsequent sessions, he came to reveal how much he wanted to be able to bind me to him so that I cannot leave, whether I like it or not.

In the session at hand, however, I chose to correct his misrecollection about my age, by reminding him of what I had told him during our initial *vis-à-vis* meetings. At the moment, I had convinced myself that I was addressing Tom's concerns by doing so, but self-reflection after the hour made me realize that I had compelling countertransference reasons for correcting him, rather than adopting any other analytic course. Suffice it to say that I was at that very time serving on two committees that were struggling to address the problem of impairment among training analysts, including problems related to their age and infirmity! His response to my correction, regardless of my reasoning, or rationalization, was one of surprise and relief. He compared his reactions to the news to his feelings when his relative recovered from cardiac surgery. He went on to elaborate his fears, not spoken of to me before, that I might someday suddenly announce that I was retiring, before he was ready to terminate.

What I have reported is certainly different from how I would have handled Tom's situation at the beginning of my career. In all likelihood,

I would not have told him my age during our consultation sessions (although my countertransference concerns would probably have been related to my relative youth and inexperience in those days!), regardless of his personal situation. I would surely not have asked him what his experience of me had been like, in the process of exploring his fear of asking questions. In all likelihood, I would have stuck to pursuing his fantasies, much as he imagined I would do, and, in fact, we might very well have come out at the same place, in terms of understanding his feelings about being forced to comply. I doubt that it matters much in the long run if a patient expresses his or her resentment at being forced to comply with the analyst's view of proper technique in conducting analysis, or if he or she reveals it in some other context. What matters is that the analyst is able to hear and accept the patient's complaints and criticism without defensiveness or retaliation. It is very much to the point, however, for me to propose that analysis can come to the same material by various routes, so long as both participants are open to the possibilities. Some technical shibboleths, whether from the traditional perspective or the relational one, ought to be recognized as less consequential than their most impassioned advocates might think to be the case.

As for my decision to correct his parapraxis about my age, that is certainly different from how I was trained to carry out analytic treatment. In fact, calling it a decision is an overstatement, if *decision* is taken to mean a considered, conscious judgment. I may have had some vague sense that he was more anxious than he let on, and I imagined that I was intuitively responding to his needs, rather than to my own unconscious concerns. I was taught that it is not necessarily advantageous to analysis to correct the patient's reality testing, or memory, even if the analyst is quite certain that his or her view or memory is more accurate. Instead, the focus should be on exploring the patient's reasons for his or her view or memory. I long ago came to appreciate, however, that countertransference can influence analysts' technical judgments that are rationalized as being in the patients' best interest (Abend, 1982). Thus, I can say that I realized that countertransference sometimes helped to determine my behavior with patients long before

I was accustomed to systematic self-scrutiny. I still see no benefit's accruing from telling my patients about my self-reflections in most, if not all, situations. I certainly did not do so with Tom in the session described, nor those that followed it. In this case, the chief benefit of my internal review was that I achieved a heightened awareness about how I responded to his concerns about my health and availability. Interestingly enough, despite my increased sensitivity, when he later on asked me specifically whether I contemplated retirement, I still "reassured him" that I do not have any such plan, in more words than I think was necessary!

In closing, what conclusions can I draw from this vignette, and from my consideration of its lessons? Only that I hope it illustrates that one learns and changes as one goes along, not only in analysis, but in an analytic career as well. While it may not always be so clear what the exact sources of this learning are, surely our patients, our colleagues, and our dedication to being thoughtful about our experiences, all contribute. And, as I was pointedly reminded by this last interchange I mentioned, often enough we have to learn the same things over and over again. This latter observation, it seems to me, is central to an analytic perspective, whether that perspective is cast in traditional Freudian terms, in relational terms, or in any other truly psychoanalytic language.

Reference

Abend, S. (1982). Serious illness in the analyst: countertransference considerations. *Journal of the American Psychoanalytic Association* 30:365–379.

CPSIA information can be obtained
at www.ICGtesting.com
Printed in the USA
BVHW081015050819
555098BV00024B/1901/P

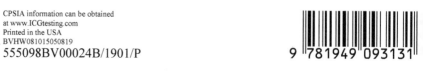

9 781949 093131